WITH GOD IN RUSSIA

With God in Russia

by

Walter J. Ciszek, S.J.

with

Daniel L. Flaherty, S.J.

IGNATIUS PRESS   SAN FRANCISCO

Cover art: Soviet propaganda poster
"Our Borders Are Inviolable!"

Cover design by Roxanne Mei Lum

Reprinted 1997 Ignatius Press, San Francisco
All rights reserved
ISBN 978-0-89870-574-4
Library of Congress catalogue number 96-76024
Printed in the United States of America ∞

CONTENTS

FOREWORD

In the pages that follow, you will read what might seem to be a strange and remarkable piece of fiction. But it is not fiction. Rather, it is a true story, recorded on one of the proudest pages of contemporary Jesuit history.

Somewhat in the role of an Evangelist, I have the privilege of telling you how that story ended. I was there, and it isn't often one gets the chance to be around when a man comes back from the dead. I can also tell something of how that story began. Then I must leave it to these pages themselves to unroll the complete record of the hidden years behind the Iron Curtain and to suggest, perhaps, that a new chapter has yet to be written.

The story began in 1939—a long, complicated, almost incredible tale that ran its course through an entire generation of the lives of the older ones among us.

While this tale was unfolding on the other side of the earth, millions died, a great war was fought, the hydrogen bomb was invented, men began orbiting the earth, babies were born and grew up and married, and four Popes sat on the chair of the Fisherman.

It was my great good fortune to know the central figure of this story some six or seven years before it all began. We were together in the chapel, along the corridors, on the paths that wound around the house where we both took our first vows as Jesuits, on a hilltop in the rolling Pennsylvania Dutch country just west of Reading, Pennsylvania.

I knew him in those far-off days as a trim young athlete, a promising linguist, unsparing in his work, quiet but outgoing in disposition, a young Jesuit unmistakably alight with the ideals of the Society. I remember, too, that he was always able to get things going again when they broke down.

Thirty-odd years ago, my friend went down that hill one June day, and I stayed behind. We never met again until . . .

My telephone rang about 3:45 on the afternoon of October 11, 1963.

The voice on the other end of the wire was that of an old teacher and friend, our former Provincial, Fr. John Mc-Mahon, calling from Auriesville, New York. Fr. McMahon had just heard from Fr. John Daley, the Provincial of Maryland, who was visiting Auriesville at the time, that at four o'clock that afternoon the State Department was going to release to the press an extraordinary piece of news.

In exchange for two Russian agents who had been apprehended in this country, the Soviet Union had decided to repatriate two American citizens held for some time in Soviet prisons. That very afternoon the two Americans were about to enplane in London for New York's Idlewild International Airport.

Fr. McMahon thoughtfully wanted *America* to get a "scoop" on this story of a generation.

And it really was the story of a generation. It was the story of that very same intrepid young Jesuit who had left our Wernersville novitiate in 1932 to continue—at Woodstock, then later in Rome—his studies for ordination to the priesthood in the Russian rite; who went into Poland as a parish priest in 1939; who was then engulfed in the great wave of World War II; and who—when the wave ebbed back eastward—was sucked into the *terra incognita* of the Soviet Union and heard from no more.

We thought of all this next morning, October 12, as we prepared to meet him at Idlewild.

We said our Masses for him at 4:30 that morning in the chapel at Campion House, home of the *America* staff. Afterward, I drove to the airport in the predawn twilight with Frs. Robert Graham and Eugene Culhane of our staff.

As we drove past the eerie shadows of the World Fair's strange new unfinished structures, someone recalled the last postal card that had come from Poland in 1940—followed by an interminable silence.

Another remembered that in 1947 it had been presumed he was dead, and we had offered the customary Masses of the Society for a deceased brother-in-arms when his name had been printed in the official roster of the Society's departed sons.

We drove on, as we relived again the day when, all of a sudden, and out of the nowhere of northern Siberia, a letter had come—the handwriting looked right enough—then another letter, and later still more.

There had been a request for a suit and for a heavy coat, for a pair of shoes. Another request had come for a set of books.

These letters had all been signed with our friend's name.

We were almost at Idlewild. We wondered: Would it really be he? Could it be someone else who had claimed his name or stolen his papers?

What would he be like, if it were he, when he came down the steps of the plane? What would the years in Siberia, where he had worked so long in the mines, have done to him?

Would he know us? Would he still speak English? Would he be sick in body or in mind?

BOAC flight no. 501 from London was on time. Right on

the dot of 6:55 A.M., the big plane trundled up to a stop on the asphalt apron. With the parents of the young man, Marvin Makinen, who was being released along with our friend, we stood there—eyes popping—as the steps were wheeled up to the plane and the plane's door opened.

The two returned prisoners were the first ones off. Down the steps they came in a rush—a tall, sunken-cheeked lad of twenty-four, an American Fulbright student arrested on a charge of espionage in the Soviet Union two years earlier; then a short, stocky, full-faced, gray-haired man in his later fifties. The older man wore a forest-green overcoat over a gray suit and a deep blue shirt. Onto his head, as he stepped off the plane, he put a big, floppy brimmed, purple-black Russian felt hat.

It all happened in two winks of your eye.

The two returnees stepped almost automatically into stride with the cordon of New York City policemen who immediately shaped up around them, and they began briskly marching off, like seasoned prisoners, to the Immigration Office.

I thought for a moment that the hefty Russian man must be—he looked for all the world as though he were!—a member of some visiting delegation of Soviet farmers or technicians.

Then we realized. He was marching past us in lock step with the police before it dawned on us. And he had marched off into the Customs Office before it really dawned on him that he was home again, that these were his sisters there to meet him along with a delegation of old Jesuit comrades of twenty-five or thirty years ago.

I refrain from saying anything of those indescribable first moments of meeting and recognition between him and his family. Even the eloquence of Gabe Pressman was not able to persuade State Department officials to allow photographers in to snap the scene.

Yet there are so many memories of that October morning: the hurly-burly in the newsroom, where five movie cameras and forty still photographers jostled our friend under the klieg lights.

Later, there was that long talk at the *America* residence, when he first began to tell his sisters and his fellow Jesuits about those years in Russia and ended by emptying out his pockets to show that he still had a few Russian rubles and seventy-four kopecks in change after buying tea in the Moscow airport.

After Mass, when we sat down to an American breakfast of bacon and eggs, he gave the blessing in Polish. He said the last time he had sat around a table with friends was four days before, when his beloved people of Abakan gave him a memorable Siberian going-away party.

I also recall his telling that he had never had a single day's illness in all those years.

. . . and how he had always somehow been able to continue his priestly work—sometimes celebrating Mass from memory over his suitcase in the barrack where he lived or, at other times, in the depths of the forest on the stump of a tree.

I recall he said he never doubted his powers and his duties as a priest. He never questioned the faith into which he had been baptized and ordained another Christ.

One doesn't, as I said, often have the opportunity to be there when a man comes back from the dead. We Jesuit companions of his were so privileged on the morning of October 12, when our old friend, like some new Columbus, flew in on BOAC flight no. 501 to rediscover America and to take up again the life of a free man.

Those of you who read this book will have that rare privilege, too—to share the experiences of a man returned from the valley of the shadow of death.

He has come back to us from the mines and prison camps of Siberia—his hair nearly white, his hands gnarled from labor as a miner and mechanic, but unbroken, not brainwashed, and with a heart filled with compassion for the people to whom his whole adult life as a priest has been consecrated. He will have our praise, assuredly, but he does not ask for our praise.

He asks only that we try to grasp the meaning of what, with God's grace, he has endured—the meaning of a life lived as a witness that the love of Christ knows no frontiers.

So his story ended. Or did it? Indeed, will it ever end? For it will be told and retold for generations along the long black lines of Jesuits. Somewhere, today—at Poughkeepsie or Wernersville or Woodstock in the halls he walked, in the Midwest or the South or the Far West, in Rome or Canada or England or India or Australia or Japan—there are fresh recruits awaiting the day when they will have their chance to write their chapter of the story that only begins with Fr. Walter Ciszek.

In reading what follows, give or take a word here or there. Go back in history nearly four hundred years. Change the word "Tyburn" to "Lubianka". For the addressee, "Elizabeth", substitute the current Russian premier. For "English students" substitute "men of the free world".

Then, as you read this story of Fr. Walter Ciszek, recall Blessed Edmund Campion and the conclusion of that eloquent document of faith called "Campion's Brag", written almost four hundred years ago to Her Majesty of England . . .

Many innocent hands are lifted up to heaven for you daily by those English students, whose posteritie shall never die, which beyond seas, gathering virtue and sufficient knowledge for the purpose, are determined never to give you over, but either to win you heaven, or to die upon your pikes.

And touching our Societie, be it known to you that we have made a league—all the Jesuits in the world whose succession and multitude must overreach all the practices of England—cheerfully to carry the cross you shall lay upon us, and never to despair your recovery while we have a man left to enjoy your Tyburn, or to be racked with your torments, or consumed with your prisons. The expense is reckoned; the enterprise is begun; it is of God, it cannot be withstood. So the faith was planted; so it must be restored.

THURSTON N. DAVIS, S.J.
editor-in-chief,
America magazine

ACKNOWLEDGMENTS

Only on my arrival in America did I become fully aware of the many people whose generous efforts went into effecting my return. In the first place, I find I owe a great debt of gratitude to Presidents Dwight D. Eisenhower and John F. Kennedy, and their White House staffs, as also to Attorney General Robert F. Kennedy, for the concern they showed over my case. I would also like to take this opportunity to thank the Honorable Thaddeus Machrowicz, former Congressman from Michigan, and Matthew S. Szymczak, former Governor of the Federal Reserve, for their efforts on my behalf.

Especial thanks, of course, are due to the Secretary of State, and particularly to Mr. Robert Murphy, Deputy Under Secretary of State, who started the proceedings toward my release, as well as to the Department of State Officers at the American Embassy in Moscow and in Washington who through all the eight years since my case first became known gave of their time and energy to bring about my release.

I owe another special debt of thanks to my fellow Jesuits Fr. Daniel E. Power, S.J., and Fr. Edward W. McCawley, S.J. It was Fr. Power who first brought information about my case to the attention of the State Department and Fr. McCawley who gave so generously and unsparingly of himself and his time to keep my case alive and help bring it to a successful outcome.

To my sister Helen Gearhart, I am sincerely and deeply grateful for all her untiring efforts in Washington on my behalf. She and my other sister, Sister Mary Evangeline, O.S.F., were a constant source of encouragement to me by the deep sisterly concern so evident in their many letters and their unfailing confidence during the long years of waiting and sometimes disappointment.

Finally, I want to thank all my other brothers and sisters, my fellow Jesuits and the many other priests, the Bernardine Sisters and many other nuns, the many friends and relatives and all those whose names I do not even yet know, especially the schoolchildren, whose prayers and offerings made possible my eventual return.

May the good effects of all those prayers continue still to "work together unto good" for the many people to whom I devoted so many years in Russia.

Walter J. Ciszek, S.J.

Chapter One

THE BEGINNINGS

An Unlikely Priest

Ever since my return to America in October 1963—after twenty-three years inside the Soviet Union, fifteen of them spent in Soviet prisons or the prison camps of Siberia—I have been asked two questions above all: "What was it like?" and "How did you manage to survive?" Because so many have asked, I have finally agreed to write this book.

But I am not much of a storyteller. Moreover, there were thousands of others who shared my hardships and survived; I have always refused to think of my experiences as something special. Out of respect for those others, I will try to set down honestly and plainly, hiding nothing and highlighting nothing, the story of those years. I will try to tell, quite simply, what it was like.

Still, I am not sure that story in itself will answer clearly the harder of those two questions, "How did you manage to survive?" To me, the answer is simple and I can say quite simply: Divine Providence. But how can I explain it?

I don't just mean that God took care of me. I mean that He called me to, prepared me for, then protected me during those years in Siberia. I am convinced of that; but then, it is my life, and I have experienced His hand at every turning. Yet I think for anyone really to understand how I managed to survive, it is necessary first of all to understand, in some small way at least, what sort of man I was and how I came to be in Russia in the first place.

I think, for instance, that you have to know I was born stubborn. Also, I was tough—not in the polite sense of the word, but in the sense our neighbors used the word those days in Shenandoah, Pennsylvania, when they shook their heads and called me "a tough". The fact is nothing to be proud of, but it shows as honestly as I know how to state it what sort of raw material God had to work with.

I was a bully, the leader of a gang, a street fighter—and most of the fights I picked on purpose, just for devilment. I had no use for school, except insofar as it had a playground where I could fight or wrestle or play sports—any sport. I refused to admit that there was anything along those lines I couldn't do as well as—or better than—anyone else. Otherwise, as far as school was concerned, I spent so much time playing hooky that I had to repeat one whole year at St. Casimir's parish school. Things were so bad, in fact, that while I was still in grammar school my father actually took me to the police station and insisted that they send me to reform school.

And yet my father, Martin, was the kindest of men. He was simply at his wit's end: talking to me did no good; thrashings only gave me an opportunity to show how tough I was. And with his inherited pride and Old World belief in the family and the family name, I know that it was shame much more than anger that made him take such a step.

Both he and my mother, Mary, were of peasant stock. They had come to America from Poland in the 1890s and settled in Shenandoah, where my father went to work in the mines. The family album shows pictures of him as a handsome young miner, but I remember him as a medium-sized man with thick, black hair and a glorious mustache, stocky, and, if not fat, at least not the trim young miner of those tintypes. By the time I was born, on November 4, 1904, the seventh child of thirteen, he had opened a saloon. He wasn't the world's best shopkeeper, though; he had too soft a spot in his heart for other newly arrived immigrants.

I don't think my father ever really understood me. We were both too stubborn ever to really get along. He wanted me to have the education he had never had a chance to have, and my attitude left him bewildered. On the other hand, although his humiliation and shame before the police that day —as they convinced him it would be more of a family disgrace to send me away to a reform school—made a deep impression on me, I would never have admitted it to him. I had inherited too much of his Polish streak of stubbornness.

Still, he was a wonderful father. I remember the day I went to a Boy Scout outing in another town and spent the money he had given me at an amusement park near the camping grounds. I had no money for the train fare home. Instead, I hitched a ride by hanging on to the outside of one of the cars. I was nearly killed against the wall of a tunnel we passed through, and I arrived back home in Shenandoah about 1 A.M., very cold, very tired, and very scared. My father, worried, was still waiting up for me. He lit a fire in the kitchen stove and then, without waking my mother, cooked a meal for me with his own hands and saw me safely into bed. Many years later, in the Siberian prison camps, it was that episode above all others that I remembered when I thought of my father.

If it was from my father that I inherited my toughness, it was from my mother that I received my religious training. She was a small, light-haired woman, very religious herself and strict with us children. She taught us our first prayers and trained us in the faith long before we entered the parish school. Two of my sisters entered the convent, but I could never be outwardly pious. Yet it must have been through my mother's prayers and example that I made up my mind in the eighth grade, out of a clear blue sky, that I would be a priest. My father refused to believe it. Priests, in his eyes, were holy men of God; I was anything but that. In the end, it was my mother who finally decided the issue, as mothers often do. She told me that if I wanted to be a priest, I had to be a good one. Since my father still had doubts, I was stubborn and insisted; that September I went off to Orchard Lake, Michigan, to SS. Cyril and Methodius Seminary, where many other young Poles from our parish had gone before me.

But I had to be different. Even though I was in a seminary, I took great pains not to be thought pious. I was openly scornful, in fact, of those who were. At night, when there was no one around, I used to sneak down to the chapel to pray— but nothing or no one could have forced me to admit it.

And I had to be tough. I'd get up at 4:30 in the morning to run five miles around the lake on the seminary grounds or go swimming in November when the lake was little better than frozen. I still couldn't stand to think that anyone could do something I couldn't do, so one year during Lent I ate nothing but bread and water for the full forty days—another year I ate no meat at all for the whole year—just to see if I could do it.

Yet contrary to everything we were constantly told and advised, I never asked anyone's permission to do all this, and I told no one. When our prefect finally noticed what I was doing and warned me I might hurt my health, I told him bluntly that I knew what I was doing. Of course I didn't; I just had a fixed idea that I would always do "the hardest thing".

Not just physically. One summer I stayed at school during summer vacation and worked in the fields, forcing myself to bear the loneliness and the separation from family and friends.

I loved baseball; I played it at school and then all summer long with the Shenandoah Indians, a home-town team that took on teams from other mining towns. I thought it would be very hard for me to give up playing the game—so, naturally, I gave it up. In my first year of college at Saints Cyril and Methodius, I just dropped off the team. We were supposed to play an important game in Ann Arbor, Michigan, and my decision caused something of a crisis. But I was as stubborn as ever. I refused to go.

It was while I was in the seminary that I first read a life of Saint Stanislaus Kostka. It impressed me tremendously. I wanted to smash most of the plaster statues that showed him with a sickly sweet look and eyes turned up to heaven; I could see plainly that Kostka was a tough young Pole who could— and did—walk from Warsaw to Rome through all sorts of weather and show no ill effects whatsoever. He was also a stubborn young Pole who stuck to his guns despite the arguments of his family and the persecution of his brother when he wanted to join the Society of Jesus. I liked that. I thought perhaps I ought to be a Jesuit. That same year, it was a Jesuit who gave us seminarians our annual retreat. I didn't talk to him, but I thought even more of becoming a Jesuit.

And yet I didn't want to be one. I was due to start theology in the fall; I'd be ordained in three years. If I joined the Jesuits, it would mean at least seven more years of study. I didn't like the idea of joining a religious order, and I especially didn't like what I'd read about the Jesuit hallmark of "perfect obedience". I tried to argue myself out of it all that summer. Characteristically, I asked no one's advice. I just prayed and fought with myself—and finally decided, since it was so hard, I would do it. God must have a special Providence for hard-headed people like me.

Then I had to do even that the hard way. I wrote a letter to the Polish Jesuits in Warsaw, telling them I wanted to enter the Society over there. Still, I hadn't told anyone at the seminary or at home. After a wait that seemed like an eternity, I got an answer from Warsaw. I went to my room and opened it with trembling fingers. The letter was most gracious, but the gist of it was that I would probably find life and conditions in Poland much different from in America, and it suggested that if I wanted to be a Jesuit, I might contact the Jesuit Provincial in New York at Fordham Road.

Was I relieved? No, I was stubborn. I had decided I was going to be a Jesuit, so one morning I caught the train to New York without telling anyone. Somehow, I found my way to 501 Fordham Road, the office of the Jesuit Provincial. The brother in charge of the door told me the Provincial wasn't in. I wouldn't tell him what I wanted; I just asked when the Provincial would be back. He said the Provincial would return that evening, and I asked if I could see him. The brother shrugged his shoulders, and I left.

I hadn't eaten anything, so I found a cafeteria, then spent the afternoon walking up and down Fordham Road, suffering from a delayed case of butterflies in my stomach. At six o'clock the Provincial still wasn't home; I went out and walked around the grounds of the Fordham University campus, feeling more nervous all the time.

At 7:30 I returned to the Provincial's residence and asked if he had returned. The brother told me to take a seat in the parlor. About eight o'clock, Fr. Kelly, the Provincial, came into the parlor and asked me what it was all about. I told him who I was and that I wanted to be a Jesuit. He looked at me for a moment, then sat down. He wanted to know about my parents. I told him I was twenty-four years of age and the decision was mine to make. Then I reminded him of Saint Stanislaus' walk from Warsaw to Rome to see the Jesuit Provincial there. Fr. Kelly just stared at me, so I rushed on, trying to explain why I wanted to be a Jesuit.

I really wasn't much help, I guess, because I simply kept insisting doggedly that I wanted to join the Society. About the only concrete facts he could get out of me were my marks at the seminary. After a while, he told me to wait, then left the room and sent another priest in to talk it over with me further. He was a wonderful old man whose name I've forgotten. He was quite deaf. He had some sort of hearing device, and with the aid of much shouting we managed to get through the story again. I remember I kept shouting that I was determined to be a Jesuit.

I also talked to another priest that night, and finally, about eleven o'clock, Fr. Kelly returned to tell me things would probably work out all right, but that I should go home and wait for his answer. It never occurred to me that when I heard from him the answer might be "no". I went home and began to pack, happy as I had ever been. It was more than joy—it was a deep and soul-satisfying peace. It was something more, too, than just the quiet and release from tension that follows the settling of any emotional problem—it was a positive and deep-seated happiness akin to the feeling of belonging or of having reached safe harbor, but deeper than that and a gift of God.

When Fr. Kelly's letter did come, it was a notice to report on September 7, 1928, to the Jesuit novitiate at St. Andrew-on-Hudson, Poughkeepsie, New York. Still, I waited to tell my father until the very morning I had to leave. He looked at Fr. Kelly's letter for a long time, as if he had trouble comprehending it, then said quite suddenly: "Nothing doing! You're going back to the seminary." "No, sir," I said, "I'm going to St. Andrew's."

We argued then like father and son, each as stubborn as the

other, until at last my father banged his fist on the table and said, "For the last time, you're not going!" With that, I banged my fist on the table and shouted, "I am going! I'm the one who's going, not you, and I am going to St. Andrews, even if I have to choose between God and you!" On that note, I took my bags and walked out of the house without a farewell or the traditional father's blessing.

Yet, after all my struggle to reach St. Andrew-on-Hudson, I was anything but an ideal novice. I disliked displays of piety, and I looked with disdain on those novices, most of them younger than I, who in their zeal and fervor for this new religious life moderated their external actions to conform with every little rule and regulation. I preferred to keep the corners a little rough. So it wasn't long before Fr. Weber, the master of novices, called me into his office one day and told me he thought I ought to leave the Society.

I was stunned. Then my Polish stubborn streak sparked up, and I almost shouted, "I will not!" Fr. Weber was startled in turn. He stood up abruptly and came around his desk toward me; I edged around the desk in the other direction. "What's going on here?" he said, almost incredulously. "Who do you think you're talking to?"

"I just won't leave, that's all," I said—and with that my stubbornness dissolved into tears. I had fought so hard to be here; I had done so much to get here; I had known such peace at last; and now it was all caving in around my ears.

Fr. Weber sat me down in a chair and waited for a certain amount of calm to descend upon us both. After that, we had a good long talk. Fr. Weber pulled no punches, but I could see that he respected me and liked me and, despite my failings, trusted me. He talked about my good qualities and talents and the necessity for channeling them properly if they were ever really to be put at God's disposal.

Early in 1929, at one of his daily talks to the novices, Fr. Weber brought in an important letter that had just come from Rome. It was from Pope Pius XI, "To all Seminarians, especially our Jesuit sons", calling for men to enter a new Russian center being started at Rome to prepare young clerics for possible future work in Russia.

The Pope went on to explain how the Soviets since 1917 had continually increased their persecution of religion; how all the Catholic bishops had been arrested in Russia and sent to concentration camps; how all the seminaries—Catholic and Orthodox—had been closed or confiscated; how hundreds of parishes were without pastors; how it was forbidden to teach religion to children. Above all, the Holy Father emphasized what a great need of well-trained and especially courageous priests there would be in that immense country. Even as Fr. Weber read the letter something within me stirred. I knew I had come to the end of a long search. I was convinced that God had at last sought me out and was telling me the answer to my long desire and the reason for all my struggles.

This conviction was so strong that I could hardly wait for the conference to finish. I became impatient and began to get restless. As soon as the conference ended, I went straight to the Master's room. He was startled to see me all flushed and excited, and he asked if anything was wrong.

"Nothing, Father," I said quickly, "but there is something I have to talk over with you." He told me to sit down, then listened to me attentively. "You know, Father," I blurted out, "when you read the Holy Father's letter in there just now it was almost like a direct call from God. I felt I had to volunteer for the Russian mission. I knew it from the beginning, and as you kept on reading that feeling grew until at the end I was fully convinced that Russia was my destination. I know, I firmly believe, that God wants me there and I will be there in the future."

Fr. Weber looked at me for a long time and then said slowly, "Well, Walter, you must pray over this. After all, you have just begun the novitiate. Things like this require time and God's grace. I wouldn't want to discourage you, so keep this in mind and pray over it. After you've taken your vows, perhaps we'll be able to see more clearly if this is God's will for you or not."

Then he sent me off, without a definite answer. Of course, I see now that my hurried declaration could easily have been the enthusiasm of a moment or an overeager and superficial desire for something new and extraordinary. But as I walked down the corridor from his office, I felt completely sure of myself. No doubt ever entered my mind, either then or at any time thereafter.

I could hardly wait for vow day, which was still almost a year and a half away, on September 8, 1930. Before that time, I was sent with the first class of novices to the new Jesuit novitiate of the Maryland-New York Province in Wernersville, Pennsylvania; we were the first group of novices ever to pronounce the vows of the Society in that house. It was a great day for all of us, but for me it meant the period of waiting to volunteer for Russia was over.

Immediately, I wrote to Very Reverend Father General, volunteering explicitly for the Russian mission. The time it took for the letter to reach Rome and for the reply to come back across the Atlantic seemed like forever. But when it finally came, the letter was simple and explicit, and my joy knew no bounds. The General said he was happy to receive my most generous offer to serve on the Russian mission, that he was even happier to be able to accept my offer and to inform me that from then on I would be considered as one designated for the Russian mission. For the time being, though, I was to continue the usual course of studies in the Society and to pray continually for the fulfillment of this dream; when the time came I would be summoned to Rome.

For two years, therefore, I remained at Wernersville for the period of studies in the humanities known in the Society as the Juniorate. After that, I went to Woodstock College in Woodstock, Maryland, to begin the course in philosophy. Before I left the Juniorate, though, I wrote again to Father General—just so he wouldn't forget me and hoping that he just might call me to Rome to study philosophy there.

The General's answer was brief but cordial. He assured me I hadn't been forgotten and mentioned that conditions in Russia were hard and that working there would not be easy. He therefore exhorted me again to pray constantly and prepare myself for a difficult period of study at the Russicum and the even more difficult work in Russia.

I needed no encouragement. I still kept up, almost religiously, my practice of forty-five minutes of calisthenics every day, a practice I had started as a young "tough". Although by this time I was finally learning to ask advice and guidance—and to do what I was told—I also continued my practice of going without certain things and of undertaking annoying jobs, just to condition myself to do the harder thing and to strengthen my will. And with this in mind, I wrote my thesis required for the degree in philosophy "On the Training of the Will".

Toward the end of my second year at Woodstock, I received the overwhelming news that I was to go to Rome that fall to begin the study of theology and to start my work at the Russian college. I sailed for Rome that summer of 1934, a very happy young man.

Like all the Jesuit students of theology in Rome, I lived at the old Collegio Santo Roberto Bellarmino on the Via del Seminario and studied theology at the Gregorian University just off the Piazza Pilotta. At the same time, I was studying the Russian language, liturgy, and history in the Collegio Russico, or Russicum, on the Via Carlo Cattaneo, not far from the basilica of St. Mary Major.

The years of theological study, for those of us at the Russicum, were pretty hectic. But, as a sort of sideline, I also studied French and German during those years and acquired enough mastery of the languages so that, when I was ordained three years later, I was able to hear confessions in the French and German parishes around Rome.

The greatest hardship for me, in fact, during those years of study was the Oriental liturgy. Those of us assigned to the Russicum had Mass every morning in the Oriental rite, and I couldn't stand it. But since I had made up my mind to work in Russia, I hung on grimly, trying to learn and appreciate it.

The man who did the most to help me come to love it was a big bear of a fellow named Nestrov. He was a native Russian with a fine bass voice, rich and deep, who loved and served the liturgy as only Russians can. We became close friends, not because of the liturgy, but because of our shared enthusiasm over the dream of going into Russia. Everyone in the newly founded Russian College, indeed, shared this dream of going into Russia to help the faithful who were now, in our Lord's metaphor, like sheep without a shepherd.

It was a very mixed and international group. There was a Belgian, Fr. Paul Mailleux, who became head of Fordham University's John XXIII Center for Ecumenical Studies, formerly called the Russian Center. There were three Englishmen, three Spaniards, two Italians, Nestrov the Russian, a Pole, and a Rumanian. I was the only American at that time, although there had been several before, and there were many who came after me.

Yet of them all, there was no one who could match my conviction or Nestrov's enthusiasm for going into Russia. The others, in fact, used to kid us about it; we were on fire with the idea. We studied everything we could about Russia—the customs of the people, their habits, the Russian character and culture, the nature of the land itself, and its history. We talked of it all the time—to the real or feigned dismay of our fellow theologians—hoping, scheming, planning, and dreaming about Russia.

Another almost constant companion was Fr. Makar, the Pole. "But my mother was a Georgian", Makar always added, and he was a mischief-maker by profession. A great schemer and practical joker, he could keep the whole crowd laughing for hours, and big, easy-going Nestrov was often the butt of his jokes. Yet the three of us got on so well together that we were nicknamed "The Three Musketeers".

After three happy but hectic years, I was ordained in Rome on June 24, 1937. Like almost all the men at the Russicum, I was ordained to say Mass in the Oriental rite, although we also had the privilege of saying Mass in the Latin rite whenever it was necessary. And so I said my first Mass as a priest in the Oriental rite, in the basilica of St. Paul, at the altar over his tomb.

My father and mother had died during my years of study, so they never had the consolation, after all they had suffered through with me, of attending the first Mass of their priest-son. None of my brothers or sisters was able to come to Rome either, but they wrote me letters of congratulation and joy at my ordination. In their stead, I was joined on the occasion of my first Mass by Fr. Vincent A. McCormick, S.J., the American Assistant in Rome to Father General, and by Mrs.

Nicholas Brady, the foundress of Wernersville. The three of us had breakfast after Mass, and, flushed with the joy of ordination, I chatted happily for hours of my dreams of going to Russia and my conviction that I would be there soon.

Frs. Nestrov and Makar were members of the Polish Province of the Society of Jesus, with headquarters in Warsaw. During their final year of theology after ordination, they were told that it was impossible for anyone to enter Russia at that time, so they would return to Poland to work among the Oriental-rite Catholics there. Nestrov was especially downcast at the news. Yet I was still convinced that I would go to Russia, and I had great hopes, somehow, of being sent there immediately.

Then one day I received word that Father General wanted to see me. I was startled; I knew that Father General Ledochowski had always taken a personal interest in the Russian mission ever since he had been asked by Pope Pius XI to assign young Jesuit volunteers to the work, but this was the first time I had a chance to talk to him personally.

Fr. Ledochowski, as I remember him that day, was a small, frail man with a thin, ascetic face, sunken cheeks, high forehead, and the most serene eyes I have ever seen. He was a man who radiated peace and quiet, impressive in his simplicity and dignity. He had a decisive, almost abrupt, way of speaking, yet he was most charming and easy to talk to. He welcomed me warmly and listened attentively while I spoke of my hopes and my ideals and my dream of working in Russia.

We talked together for over twenty minutes. He told me how much he appreciated my hopes and shared my dream, but for the time being it was impossible to send men into Russia. As he spoke, he got up from his chair and paced the room somewhat restlessly. "Conditions as we know them", he said, "would make it imprudent to try to send men into

Russia now. I know you must be disappointed, but the mission in Albertin, Poland, needs men right now, and the work there is very fruitful. The mission is flourishing and is a great source of vocations for the Oriental rite and the Russian College. I would like you to work there, if you would, for the time being. But I want you to keep your dream of going into Russia, and perhaps someday God may grant us both our wishes."

He could read the disappointment on my face, I guess, and he was very kind. At least, he asked me to keep him informed of my work on the mission at Albertin, spoke fondly once again of our joint hopes that the day would come when I might go to Russia, and gave me his blessing.

I agreed with his decision, of course; I had finally learned something of that spirit of obedience that makes the Jesuit. But to say I wasn't disappointed would be far from honest. I had dreamed so long of Russia, I had given up so much and trained so hard, that I couldn't avoid the emotional let-down when Father General told me that my entrance into Russia might be impossible for some time to come. Yet even then, in that moment of disappointment, I never for a moment doubted that I would one day be in Russia.

"To Russia in the Spring!"

My work in Albertin was two parts pastor and one part teacher. I taught ethics to the young Jesuits who studied at our Oriental-rite mission there and catechism to the children in the school. Most of the time, though, I was a horse-and-buggy priest who went around visiting the families of Albertin and the small villages nearby, advising them, chatting with the old grandmothers and the sick, doing the thousand

and one things a small-town pastor does anywhere. Since the community at Albertin was small—just three priests besides the Superior, Fr. Dombrowski—and since I was the newest member to arrive, I inherited all the chores that traditionally fall to the youngest curate.

Albertin itself wasn't much of a town. In fact, it wasn't a town at all. The real town was Slonim on the Shchara river, a manufacturing center on the main rail line from Moscow to Warsaw. From the bridge over the Shchara, you went east about three miles over a winding dirt road to the village of Albertin. The railroad also ran to Albertin, but the village was just what we would call a whistle stop on this line to Moscow. And about Albertin's only claim to historical fame was the fact that just beyond it, to the north, was a wide swath cut through the forest known as the *Napoleonski Tract*—the remains of the road built by Napoleon when he invaded Russia.

I had come to Albertin in November 1938, just after the Munich Conference, which dismembered Czechoslovakia and guaranteed "peace in our time", as Mr. Chamberlain put it. But soon after I arrived, Hitler began his campaign to get the Danzig Corridor. All during that winter the situation deteriorated; by early spring there were even rumors that German soldiers in disguise had infiltrated Danzig and were prepared to take the city in a sneak attack. The peasants of Albertin sowed their rye and other spring crops that year uncertain whether or not they would be able to harvest them. By late spring, the talk of war was everywhere.

On August 21, 1939, Ribbentrop and Molotov announced that Germany and Russia had signed a mutual nonaggression pact. Shortly afterward, I received a cable from the American Embassy in Warsaw advising me that war might soon be declared and that I should be prepared to leave Poland. I talked it over with Fr. Dombrowski and told him I didn't want to leave. I had come to Poland to work in the Oriental mission; moreover, I had never given up my hopes of someday going into Russia, and the war might give me an opportunity to do just that. I wrote back to the Embassy, telling them I was needed at the parish and I would stay where I was needed.

Within a few days, on September 1, 1939, Hitler invaded Poland. We listened constantly to the radio, and the news was all bad. In a matter of days, German troops had surrounded Warsaw, and the city was besieged and bombed. Remnants of the Polish Army began streaming eastward through Slonim and Albertin along the *Napoleonski Tract*. Warsaw Radio fell silent, and we knew that Poland's fate was sealed. What was worse, there were rumors that the Russians were massing on the eastern border and would soon enter Poland.

At last, Fr. Dombrowski decided to send the Jesuit novices home, at least until the situation had stabilized to a point where plans for the future could be made. He himself left to see the bishop at Vilna, to ask what should be done about the mission and the parish. Since I wasn't a Polish national but an American citizen, Fr. Dombrowski decided that I would be left in charge of the mission. Fr. Grybowski, who was in charge of the Latin-rite parish at the mission, and Fr. Litvinski, the other curate of the Oriental-rite parish, would remain with families in the village.

In those days we still presumed that the Germans—or the Russians, for that matter—would respect an American passport. If worse came to worst, though, the American Embassy would still know where I was and be able to help me. And so it was that I, the young American, was the only priest at the mission in Albertin on the day the Russians came.

The first Russian officer arrived one morning just after breakfast. I was in the courtyard when he rode up on horseback to look over our Jesuit mission. A man of medium height in a dust-stained khaki uniform with the red epaulets of the Russian Army, he greeted me pleasantly and was quite respectful. His eyes seemed tired under the peak of his uniform cap as he explained frankly, and a bit apologetically I thought, that it might be necessary to quarter some of his staff in our buildings for a few days. He seemed so polite, almost friendly, that I began to hope conditions in Albertin might not be too bad under Russian occupation. Unfortunately, that was the last I saw of that particular officer; I suspect he eventually decided Graf Puslovski's mansion would make a better headquarters for himself and his staff.

That afternoon the column of Russian troops arrived. The young captain in charge was neither pleasant nor offensive, just very matter-of-fact about the whole thing. He made it clear he had orders to take over the seminary for quartering his troops. He told me I'd be allowed to occupy my room on the first floor and to take what I wanted of the church goods, library books, or my personal belongings, but the rest of the building and its furnishings would be taken over.

He promised, however, that the church would not be bothered. To make sure, he had a pathway marked off through the courtyard so the people could attend services without having to pass through the army's quarters. He also gave orders that the entrance into the church from the seminary should be boarded up to prevent any military personnel from entering the church through that door.

The troops moved in to occupy the building. After long days on the march, they hit the seminary like old October revolutionaries storming the Winter Palace. Trucks were backed into the courtyard, and the men began to throw things helter-skelter out the library windows into them. Books flew in all directions. The soldiers on the ground, laughing and joking, yelled at those in the windows throwing books; the men in the library replied in kind. Eventually, the books were carted off to be turned into pulp.

While all this was going on, to my dismay one of the soldiers threw a rope around the Sacred Heart statue in the courtyard, hitched it to a truck, and toppled the whole thing over. It crashed in pieces, to a loud shout from the troops, then was loaded into the truck and carted away. Watching the scene, I couldn't tell whether that particular act was done on command or just at the whim of one of the soldiers.

That night was my worst in Albertin. With the troops moving around on the floor above me, I hardly slept at all. Next day, I was summoned for a "personal talk" with the *politruk*, the Communist Party or secret service agent who accompanied every unit of the Red Army. He wanted to know the whereabouts of the former Polish government officials of Albertin. I knew nothing and said so. In a technique I was to become familiar with later on, the *politruk* asked me the same question many times over in different forms. He was insistent, arguing that by helping him I would be helping the "people".

"My work", I replied, "isn't political, it's pastoral. As their pastor, I help the people spiritually and also materially when I can." I told him of cases where we had raised money to help the children of poor families continue their education through high school and beyond. He wasn't interested. He insisted I should help "the people" everywhere by revealing the names of their enemies and making public what information I had as a priest.

"Now you're going too far", I said. "There are confidences entrusted to me as a priest that I have no right to tell anyone. I can't betray the seal of confession. I'd only be harming myself and 'the people' as well by giving out that kind of information, which in any event has nothing to do with 'the people' or politics or anything else that concerns you!"

By that time, he was furious, and I was disgusted. I made a move to leave, but he stopped me. He told me to sit down. For the remainder of our "talk", though, he was once more smooth and courteous. After a short while, he led me to the door with the remark that he would send for me again in the near future.

Instead, it was the army captain who sent for me a few days later. Army regulations, he said, prohibited civilians from living in the same quarters with the troops. He "suggested" I move into the little house at the end of the mission garden, which had been the original home on the property. I moved that afternoon and was joined that evening by Frs. Grybowski and Litvinski. We were glad to be living together in community again, but after a short while the local Communist committee decided the four-room house was too big for just the three *bourgeois* priests, so they sent in other families to live with us. We priests were confined to one room, two families shared the big dining room, and a third family had a smaller room to itself; we all took turns using the kitchen.

Despite these inconveniences and harassments, however, we managed to keep the parishes functioning almost normally. We were able to celebrate Mass every morning, and on Sunday we had two Masses for the people, although some of the congregation stayed away for fear of Communist reprisals. The soldiers had taken over the seminary chapel next to the main church as a sort of duty room and classroom. At Mass in the morning, we could hear them moving about behind the door, and, often enough, as soon as we sang the responses to the litanies in the first part of the Oriental-rite Mass, they would whistle and chant in mimicry, "*Gospodi, Gospodi!*" (Lord, Lord!). Yet the door from that room into the church remained boarded up according to the captain's promise, and the soldiers did not physically interfere.

Then one Sunday, after the seven-o'clock Mass, I went out to give a short sermon to the people. As I started to speak, I noticed some soldiers lounging in the vestibule of the church. They were standing there laughing, caps on their heads and devilment in their eyes. I got mad. In my anger, I launched into a sermon on the classic text "The fool hath said in his heart there is no God." It was probably the most spontaneous sermon I ever preached; every word came right from the heart and flew straight at them. They were stunned momentarily, then bewildered, looking around sheepishly, shuffling their feet as they saw the eyes of the congregation turn to them. They started to go, then stood there, too proud to retreat but ashamed to react, until I had finished. It was a personal triumph of sorts for me, but it was bound to be costly, and even then I knew it.

To my surprise, however, the soldiers made no trouble during Mass the next few days. Though I knew they must have resented my words and their humiliation, I began to hope the incident might blow over. Then one morning when I came to the church to say Mass, I found the doors of the tabernacle swinging ajar, the altar cloths strewn about, the Blessed Sacrament gone. I was thunderstruck. When I noticed that the door from the sanctuary to the soldier's duty room was no longer nailed shut, I knew immediately what had happened, and why.

I tried to see the captain that afternoon to lodge a complaint, but it was no use. The Latin church was still functioning normally; its attendance, in fact, was greater than ever before. The soldiers seemed particularly to resent Oriental Catholics as members of a Church opposed to Russian Orthodoxy, but they hardly bothered the Latin Catholics, and many of our congregation preferred to attend Mass there. Reluctantly, therefore, I decided to close the Oriental-rite church. Before I did so, I went around on a last tour of inspection and found that the troops, unknown to anyone, had been using the attic as a latrine. From that time on, we said Mass only in the Latin church or in our room of the house down in the garden for the few people who came to attend.

Just about this time, I received another telegram from the American Embassy. This one came from Moscow, where the Embassy had gone after the fall of Warsaw. They advised me that I could either come to Moscow for aid in returning to the United States or go to the American Embassy in Rumania, if that were more convenient. I showed the telegram to the other fathers and discussed it with them. They thought I ought to go. The work of the Oriental mission seemed pretty well ruined at the moment; there was little I could do here that the others could not take care of. The NKVD[1] agent, through whose hands, of course, the telegram had to pass, also "suggested" that as an American citizen I should leave the country immediately. Despite such urgings, I felt that I had been left in charge of the parish and mission by Fr. Dombrowski, and until I heard from him I ought to remain. Accordingly, I wrote to the Embassy that same afternoon telling them of my decision to remain in the parish where I had been left in charge. I did not intend to leave my flock.

Not long afterward, I received another surprise. Frs. Nestrov and Makar arrived from the Jesuit theologate in Lvov with a message from Fr. Dombrowski to the effect that the bishop had decided, for the time being, to close the Oriental mission in Albertin. It was certainly a strange reunion for us "Three Musketeers" there in that little house at the foot of

[1] The secret police, afterward, according to changes in Kremlin policy, known as the NKGB, MGB, MVD, and KGB.

the garden, under the shadow of the Russian occupation troops.

Makar, the tall Georgian, was strangely elated. With his long, wavy hair, hook nose, and flashing black eyes, he seemed a born adventurer, and the trip from Lvov to Albertin had put him on his mettle. Nestrov was another adventurer of sorts, though he didn't look like one. He was heavy-set and practically bald, with a bulbous nose that made him look like a larger version of Tolstoy. But his dream of one day working in Russia drove him on, and that night he was alive with it.

He told me he felt the time had come to put our mutual dream into operation. The Russians had occupied Poland, so we were, in effect, already in Russia. Fr. Dombrowski had implicitly absolved me of staying in Albertin by closing the mission. Fr. Grybowski, I admitted, could take care of the parishioners in Albertin with the Latin church. Why shouldn't this be our chance to slip into the heart of Russia itself? Nestrov and Makar heaped up the arguments; my enthusiasm grew. At last, together, we decided to try it, if our superiors would approve.

As we talked into the early hours of the morning, our plans became more definite. Nestrov and Makar would return to Lvov, then Makar would come back for me. Since our superiors were in Lvov, everything would have to start from there. Meanwhile, I was to set things in order in Albertin as best I could without arousing suspicions that I might be leaving. I still remember my parting words to Nestrov as he left that night: "We'll be in Russia in the spring!"

In a week Makar was back, good as his word, and the two of us slipped out of the house at dusk on the road to Slonim. Trains were no longer running on schedule, and it was impossible to buy a ticket for those that did run, but that was hardly a challenge to my Georgian companion. We hung about the station in Slonim waiting for a train to Moscow and boarded it without tickets. We were already rolling before anyone bothered us; we passed through Albertin without even slowing down. I had only time for one brief, last look at the village.

When finally the conductor asked for our tickets, Makar began to berate him for the poor service and the disrupted train schedules. The conductor was somewhat taken aback at first, then insistent. Makar grew more indignant, the conductor more adamant. Baranovichi, he said, was the next stop. We would have to get off there and buy tickets, or he would have us thrown off the train—that was final. The poor conductor had no way of knowing that Baranovichi, the rail juncture with the line to Lvov, was our destination in any event.

Even at Baranovichi, however, there were no tickets to be had. There was a train to Lvov that night, but the coaches were jammed and the Pullman cars reserved for officers. That was good enough for Makar. We went along the siding to the Pullman cars and clambered aboard. An official approached to tell us the car was reserved for officers, but Makar, speaking rapidly in White Russian, succeeded in convincing him that we were members of a White Russian commission on our way to Lvov and that we definitely did not wish to be disturbed that night.

These incidents were typical of Makar. I remember another occasion, later in Lvov, when he and I were stopped at gunpoint by a member of the NKVD as we returned from a journey late at night. Makar was furious; if he was at all nervous, it was not apparent. He proceeded to tell a long, involved story and scolded the secret service man for accosting two "Party members" in the middle of the night with drawn gun. Finally, out of fright or perhaps bewilderment, the man let us go. The same thing happened now. The official found us a berth and promised we wouldn't be disturbed, and so we traveled to Lvov in style, arriving well rested after a good night's sleep.

Conditions at Lvov were not much better than at Albertin. The Jesuits were allowed to use only one section of our theologate building, for the Russians had begun to assign other families to the rest of the building. Again, they were out to make it clear that all buildings were the property of "the people"; they also hoped to impress the people by settling some of them in this residence formerly held by the Church. So Fr. Bienko, our Superior there, decided from the first that it would be better if Makar, Nestrov, and I could find a private room somewhere. We did find a place about six blocks from the theologate, in an apartment occupied mostly by refugees from Warsaw, many of them Jews.

Fr. Bienko was an ideal man for the job of Superior in such trying times. He was a tall, thin man in his late fifties, with a thin nose and light hair. But the first thing you noticed about him was his smile, for he smiled often. Under his pleasant exterior, however, he had a very shrewd and tough mind. An excellent theologian, considered by many of his fellow Jesuits one of the best minds in the Province, he proved to be an even better administrator and a sheer genius at adaptability.

Many of the young Jesuit theology students had already been forced to find jobs to help support the community, for the theologate's funds had been confiscated. Nestrov, Makar, and I also got jobs to support ourselves until we could leave for Russia. I drove a truck for one of the labor gangs that had been pressed into service to haul the furniture and household goods the Russians confiscated from places about the city and to deliver them to the railroad yards for shipment to Russia.

I soon found out there was a double game going on. Most of the men in my crew had relatives in the city, so many of the things we "confiscated" from these people were simply taken to relatives elsewhere in the city or to a hiding place in the country. Other people, too, paid us to deliver their goods, not to the Russians, but to relatives. It was risky, but there was so much stuff being confiscated and delivered to the boxcars that no one could check it accurately. The men on the truck, of course, took particular pleasure in outwitting the occupation forces.

No sooner had we settled in Lvov than Nestrov and I approached Fr. Bienko with our dream of going into Russia to help the communities deprived of their priests.

Makar, for the moment, couldn't be spared. But we urged that there might never be a better time to make the move than now, in the immediate aftermath of the occupation, when the roads and cities were crowded with refugees. Our plan was simple enough. The Russians were hiring large crowds from the occupied zones to work in the factories around the Urals. Stalin seemed to have no illusions about Hitler; Russian factories were working around the clock. We proposed to volunteer for work in the area of the Urals.

Since, as I have said, Fr. Bienko was a man of large spiritual vision and practical bent, he agreed to let us go. He told us, however, that we must first have the permission of Metropolitan Shepticki, Archbishop of Lvov for the Oriental rite.

Nestrov made the arrangements, and I met him a day or so later at the Archbishop's palace in the Platz Yuria, near St. George's cathedral. The Archbishop then was an old man but so revered by his people that the Communists could not attack him openly. He was so crippled he had to be carried in on a chair to meet us, but his eyes were bright and his mind as clear as a bell. He welcomed us warmly and heard us out before he said anything at all.

This shrewd and kindly patriarch knew Russia from personal experience. He began by telling us how much he appreciated our enthusiasm, but he also warned us of the difficulties we would face. Finally, when he saw how keen we were to go, he said: "I'll tell you what, suppose we try it for a year. I'll give you permission to try to enter Russia, but you must be very careful and take no chances. Your object must be simply to study the situation and see whether it is really possible to do much priestly work in Russia. Lord knows, the people need you."

Then he began to tell us in detail things we had heard from others in bits and snatches. He described how the Russians had been rounding up everyone who had served in the government or the police, teachers, lawyers, professional men, members of the nobility—or even those who were a little richer than the average—and had been sending them, according to reports, to work in the Urals. Certainly, he said, those people would accept us as priests if we could reach them. We could also explore further the possibilities of working among the Russians themselves.

"But remember," he said, "this is only an experiment, an exploratory expedition. I want you to return to me after a year or so and let me know your experiences." With that he gave us his blessing and told us to return for more detailed instructions when we had completed arrangements for the trip. Nestrov and I were so elated that we hardly heard the kindly old Metropolitan's warnings about the difficulties before us. "What did I tell you?" I said as we walked down the corridors of the Archbishop's palace. "Russia in the spring!"

Immediately we set to work on arrangements for the journey into Russia. We turned instinctively to our scheming

Georgian, Fr. Makar, who could arrange things if anyone could. Makar seemed to know everybody, to have contacts everywhere. Our first problem was to get some Polish identification papers. We wanted to be hired to work in the Urals, not be deported there. Obviously, we wouldn't be permitted to enter Russia as priests. Moreover, there was little chance the Russians would let me into the country on my American passport, and, though Nestrov was a Russian, the Communists would want to know why and how he had come to leave the country, what he was doing in Poland, and why he wanted to go back.

Identification papers, however, presented no problem to Makar. They would have to be false, but they didn't have to be forged. He knew just where to reach former government officials; from them he got two sets of official Polish identification papers and brought them home to us. Then Nestrov and I set about creating biographies for ourselves which would explain why we were two men traveling alone, without families, to work for the Russians in the Urals. I became "Wladimir Lypinski", a Pole and a widower, whose family had been killed in a German air raid. Nestrov became "Kuralski". When we were satisfied with our stories, Makar took the completed papers back to the former officials. They were stamped, sealed, and initialed according to form; our new identification was complete.

With those papers we presented ourselves at the office of Lespromhoz, a big lumber combine that was hiring men for work in the Ural regions. They were anxious to get workers, so few questions were asked; we were hired on the spot and given our working certificates. They asked us to report back in a week for further instructions, at which time also we would get train tickets and a 150-ruble (fifteen-dollar) advance on our salary to pay for food and expenses on the trip.

A week didn't leave us much time to get ready, but we were eager to go. We talked the situation over again for the last time with Fr. Bienko. We agreed to leave my American passport and Nestrov's Russian passport with the Jesuits at Lvov so we would have them on our return from Russia. Finally, Fr. Bienko appointed me the acting Jesuit Superior on the trip, so that if any decisions were to be made about the time of our return or what sort of work we would do, that responsibility would be mine.

Last of all, we returned to see the Archbishop. We informed him of our plans and preparation, showed him our identification cards and working permits. He was not happy with the names we had chosen. They sounded too Polish, he said; he thought we should have taken White Russian or Ukrainian names. "However," he said, "it's too late to change them now, so we will hope nothing comes of it." Then he went over with us again, very carefully, the limitations we were to set ourselves and the type of work we were to try to do.

As a final safeguard, the Archbishop tore a page from a book, tore it in half again, then gave us half the page and kept the other half himself. If we sent anyone to him with a message, he told us, or especially if we sent any candidates for the seminary to him from the Urals, we were to send along a piece of that page so it could be matched against the half sheet kept by the Archbishop to prove that the man or message had indeed come from us.

At the end of our long discussion, we knelt to receive the Archbishop's blessing. He looked at us for a long moment before he blessed us—but said nothing. Then, as a sort of anticlimax, a nun came in with a great wagon-wheel-sized loaf of white bread the Sisters had baked for our journey. They also promised us their prayers.

When we returned to the lumber company next day for our instructions, we were told to report to the Lvov station on the morning of March 15 and were simply handed a boxcar number in place of train tickets. Moreover, the money we had been expecting turned out to be not 150 rubles apiece, but 150 rubles for both of us. That had to last us until we reached our assignment in Chusovoy, a trip that might take anywhere from two weeks to a month.

The fifteenth of March, a week before the beginning of spring 1940—it seemed like a good omen. The last evening we went to confession to prepare ourselves for we knew not what, and received Fr. Bienko's blessing. The next morning we said Mass for the last time in a chapel, packed our Mass kit and suitcases, tucked the huge loaf of white bread and a pound of fatback under our arms, and set off for the railroad station and Russia, with the indomitable Makar to see us off.

Alias "Wladimir Lypinski"

Boxcar 89725 had two rows of rough plank bunks along the walls ("upper and lower berths", Makar called them), straw on the floor, and a ventilator at the top of the car. The only other furnishings were an old punctured oil drum, which served as a stove, and a slop bucket to serve as a toilet. There were no windows. The cracks in the side walls were big enough to see through, however, and equally drafty.

At the start of the trip, there were twenty-five of us in the car. The great majority of our fellow travelers were Jews who had fled before the Nazi advance into Poland. Franck was the first to introduce himself, a Warsaw Communist who had left the city just before it fell to the Germans. Homeless now, he had decided to take his family, his wife, his ten-year-old son, and his nephew, to live in that paradise he had read so much about in Communist literature.

Franck was not the only man with children on this trip. Whole families were on the train—grandfather, grandmother, father, mother, and children. Uprooted after generations, they were carrying everything they owned on their backs, like refugees everywhere, to a new life in an alien land. Yet there was a great spirit of friendliness among the group; everyone seemed to be trying to be as helpful and cheerful as possible under the circumstances.

The trip from Lvov to the Urals was long and rough. We went first to Vinnitsa and Kiev, then up through Bryansk and Kaluga to Gorki, east again to Kazan and Ufa, and finally north along the Urals and the Chusovaya River to the town of Chusovoy itself, about fifty miles from Perm, which was then called "Molotov". We moved in a series of fits and starts; every train on the tracks seemed to have priority over our work train. Sometimes we'd sit on a siding for two days before moving on again.

In a way, the frequent stops were a blessing. They gave us a chance to walk around a bit, to clean out the slop bucket used as a toilet. We also took turns fetching water for our constant thirst or trying to buy food. But there was little food to be had. The eating places in the towns along our route couldn't sell us anything. "What food we have", they would say, "is just enough for the workers in town here. We can't take care of refugees." It was something of a shock for Franck to discover that in his workers' paradise there might not be enough food, but he attributed it to the war.

Once a day we could each buy a small loaf of bread from the storecar on the train, sometimes a pound or so of little caramels. If we were really lucky, we might even buy an onion or a cabbage from a passing farmer. But for the most part our food consisted almost entirely of the little we had brought with us. Nestrov and I shared the pound of fatback we had brought along. We ate it raw, along with mouthfuls of the bread we bought and gulps of water.

Our one other great need in the raw damp air of March was fuel to heat the car. We all soon became adept at stealing from the coal piles at stations where we stopped or gleaning lumps of coal along the tracks. Sometimes we even snatched it from the engine while the train was standing on a siding.

People in the towns along the way were suspicious of refugees. One day, on a siding somewhere between Vinnitsa and Kiev, it was my turn to get the water. The closest place seemed to be a nearby collective farm. Franck's young son, Aaron, had become quite attached to me and trotted along beside me to the farm. No sooner had we reached the pump than a woman stepped out of one of the houses and began to yell at us like a shrew. She called us "Poles", "vagrants", and "dirty refugees", and said we had no business at the farm pump. Before she would let us "pollute" the water, she said, she would call out the dogs, so we had better get away from there in a hurry.

It had been a long ride that day; we were thirsty and bone tired. Her screeching was the last straw. I began to reply in kind. Words I hadn't used since I was a boy on the streets of Shenandoah somehow came pouring out. The lady with the fishwife's tongue was dumbfounded for a moment, then retreated safely indoors. Little Aaron said nothing, but he must have reported the whole story to his father because Franck sidled up to me in the boxcar afterward and said joshingly, "Well, I never would have thought you could get so mad. You really must have told that old lady off!" I was glad at that moment no one in the car knew Nestrov and I were priests.

I think it was that very night—although one day of that journey tends to blur in my memory into the next—that we crossed the old prewar border between Poland and Russia. I do remember that it was the feast of St. Joseph, March 19th. And I do remember, too, nudging Nestrov in the ribs and saying softly, as I had said at the Archbishop's palace in Lvov, "There you are—Russia in the spring!"

We looked at each other for a moment in silence. There was no way of knowing what the future would bring, but we were doing at last what we had dreamed so many years of doing. It didn't matter if no one else in that boxcar knew we were priests. We knew it. Crossing the border gave me a strange sense of exhilaration and, yet, of loneliness, of a beginning and an end to the life we had known. I couldn't help wondering whether, like so many priests before us, we would be asked to give our lives for the faith. I remember falling asleep that night repeating to the clicking rhythm of the train wheels, "I am ready. I am ready. I am ready."

The jolting, stop-and-go trip from Lvov to Chusovoy, well over fifteen hundred miles on our roundabout route, took better than two weeks. The scenery, unless we stopped at a siding or peeked out through the cracks, was the same four walls of the boxcar and a shifting shaft of sunlight from the ventilator in the roof. That was our world, and within it we existed as best we could. Conversation, as the hours lengthened day by day into weeks, became pretty much the same. The families talked among themselves of home and their new hopes. Together we talked about the opportunities that lay ahead in the Urals.

From time to time, at one of the sidings, more people would pile into the cars, other hopefuls on their way, for their own reasons, to work in the Urals. They met with a mixed reception. They took up precious space in the boxcars that had already begun to seem too small; they were other mouths to feed, and the food was almost gone. Even the storecar could no longer provide bread every day. But they also brought new topics of conversation and new stories, perhaps a snatch or two of news, to break up the monotony.

After two grinding weeks of tedium, we finally braked to a halt on a siding outside Chusovoy, the end of our pilgrimage. The town itself is strung out along the right bank of the Chusovaya River where it joins the Usva River in the foothills of the Urals, about seven hundred fifty miles northeast of Moscow. A great lumber center, where logs floating down the rivers were loaded on the railroad to Perm, Chusovoy now was a boom town, producing charcoal and pig iron for Russia's war effort in the Ural regions. There were great kilns all along the river bank to make charcoal for smelting ore, and the Russians were working hard to develop the rich iron-ore deposits discovered in the area.

We had arrived, but we were not to stay. At the railroad yards we were told we would be working, not in Chusovoy, but in the lumber yards of Teplaya-Gora, another boom town some fifty miles farther east. Then we were turned over to our conveyor—or supervisor—a tall, gaunt, shifty-eyed judge. He had us pile out of the boxcars, show our papers, and submit to a head count, lest any of the "volunteers" might have deserted on the way.

The judge seemed immediately suspicious of Nestrov and me, two men traveling together without families. I had to tell him the tragic story of how I lost my wife and children in one split-second during a German air raid. We had been crossing the street, I said, when the bomb exploded next to us. My wife and son and two daughters were killed outright; I was blown across the street. When I could crawl back to the crater, I found my wife lying across the body of our youngest daughter, both dead, and of the other children there was no sign. I felt my whole life had ended, so I decided to seek a new life in the lumber yards of the Urals, where the pay was rumored to be good and few questions would be asked.

The judge showed not a bit of sympathy. Aside from a few muttered remarks, however, and a couple of sidelong glances at us from time to time, he said nothing further. I decided, though, that I had better polish up my delivery to make the story more moving for the next inquisitor. After he made sure we were all accounted for, the judge proceeded to give us our instructions. He sounded as if we were prisoners before the bench.

Under no circumstances, he told us, were we to leave the cars without his permission until we arrived in Teplaya-Gora. Representatives from each car would be allowed to go into Chusovoy to purchase food: he supposed we might be hungry after our journey from Lvov. (That sarcastic comment was the closest we ever heard him come to a humane word.) We would be quartered, he continued, in barracks at Teplaya-Gora. We would be paid a minimum wage. Whether or not we earned enough to keep clothes on our backs and food on the table depended on how hard we worked and what bonuses we earned. We had volunteered to work and work we would; the Urals were not a summer camp. Then he added, almost as an afterthought, that deserters would be severely punished. Another crime that would not be tolerated was drunkenness. Parents would see to it that their children stayed out of trouble.

All in all, it was quite a reception to be given a volunteer labor brigade. Franck, with his dreams of a workers' paradise, was stunned. But at least there was food to be had—and we were famished. When the judge dismissed us, we climbed back into the cars, pooled our meager resources, and enjoyed our best meal in two weeks. It was a mistake, but we had no way of knowing we would sit on that siding for nearly three days before moving to Teplaya-Gora. During that time, we had little money left to buy food. In order to eat, some of the families even pawned the possessions they had guarded so preciously all the way from Lvov.

Three days later, nearly starving, we reached Teplaya-Gora in a pouring rain. The judge turned us over to another Party member and some Lespromhoz representatives, so we had to stand in the rain for another head count to make sure that everyone who had been at Chusovoy had reached Teplaya-Gora. When at last the formalities were over, we were told to load our belongings onto horse-drawn wagons for the trip to the lumber camp, well out into the slopes beyond the town.

We worked in the pouring rain, Nestrov and I helping the Francks and other families load their possessions into the wagons. The dirt roads were rivers of mud, and the horses had a tough time negotiating the mile or so to the camp. We were continually jumping out of the wagon to shove it over a bump in the road or out of a deep rut, standing ankle-deep in mud, splattered by the clods thrown from the horses' shoes.

At the lumber camp, the barracks were new and raw. Large sections in the walls, where the timbers had warped, were stuffed with mud and a plaster like stucco. The partitions between rooms were roughly done; through the ill-fitted boards you could see every move of people in the room next door. There was little enough privacy that way, but most of the families at least had a room to themselves. Nestrov and I, since we had no families, were assigned to a dormitory.

There were clean sheets on the beds—straw mattresses stretched over boards—and the floors were scrubbed. There were clean, rough-hewn tables and a stove in each section of the barrack for heating. Cooking was done on another stove at the end of the corridor that ran between the rooms, and everyone took turns at it during mealtimes. Most of the men in our barrack were old-timers who had been sent here during the collectivization of the 1930s. They greeted us warmly, if somewhat boisterously, assigned us beds, and gave us a run-down on the routine. For a day or two, though, we newcomers did no work. We spent our time getting acquainted with the camp and being interviewed for jobs.

Nestrov was assigned to office work. I was less lucky. All through that summer of 1940, until October, I worked as an unskilled laborer in a mixed brigade (men and women), hauling logs from the river and stacking them in long rows over six feet high and some thirty yards in length. It was rough work. The rows were higher than I was, so the last few logs had to be heaved into place above my head. I had no gloves and worked barehanded with the rough bark until my hands bled.

The pay scale depended upon how many cubic meters of logs you stacked in a day. For the first month or so, I earned very little. Often enough I was assigned to the position at the head of the line, where I worked half in, half out of the water to hand up logs to the rest of the crew. Sometimes I had to dive underwater for a sunken log, and trying to manhandle one of those water-soaked beams, six feet long and perhaps two feet thick, with my feet slipping in muck and slime, could be murderous.

Nestrov and I pooled our salaries for food, but since he was a newcomer to the office, he wasn't making much either. Sometimes we had only enough to buy a loaf of rye bread. There were nights we couldn't even afford that, since we also had to pay for our lodging in the barrack, and that was deducted before we even saw our paychecks. The second week we were there, our money was gone. I finally sold a fur coat I had brought along in order to get money for food.

The old-timers were friendly enough, but there were bo-nuses for extra work, and they saw nothing wrong in taking advantage of the newcomers—who soon got smart the hard way. If you weren't careful, the number of logs you stacked might be put down on someone else's tally at the end of the day. I learned to make sure I was on hand when the tally was made, and I double-checked to see that the work I'd done was reported as mine. Gradually, my hands grew tough, and I learned the ropes. Nestrov and I soon came to be accepted by the old-timers in the barrack.

Remembering Metropolitan Shepticki's instructions, how-ever, we were very cautious at first. We never discussed reli-gion with the men, but we kept our ears open trying to discover how they felt. There were enough professed atheists and Communists in the group who would bring up the sub-ject of religion from time to time, and we watched the various reactions all about us. The old-timers were mostly peasants who clung to religion as they did to other memories of their former life. In time of difficulty they would yell out "*Gospodi! Gospodi!*" interspersed with a few hair-curling oaths. They meant no more by the one than they did by the other, nor did they ever practice any religion openly, for this was a Commu-nist camp and religion was the "opium of the weak".

Sometimes, though, after one of the atheists had ridiculed religion, we'd sit down in a corner with a few others and try to sound them out. We were very careful in all this at first. We had been sent to find out whether it was possible to work as priests, not to be discovered as priests.

It was impossible to say Mass in the barrack, of course. From time to time, however, Nestrov and I would take a walk into the forest, when we were free from work, and say Mass there. We used a big stump as our altar, and while one of us offered the Holy Sacrifice the other stood guard on the road.

It was an experience I'll never forget. In the heavy silence of the thick forest, you could hear the chipmunks running and the birds gathering overhead. Suddenly, you seemed very close to nature and to God. Everything seemed beautiful and somehow mysterious, all dangers for a time remote.

At other times, if we had an hour alone but couldn't leave camp to say Mass, we would take turns reciting and memorizing the prayers of the Mass until we knew them all by heart. We were always aware that the Mass kit might be discovered, and we would lose our book and vestments, but we were determined that as long as we could get bread and wine we would try to say Mass.

Such high ideals and moments of closeness to God didn't blind us to reality. The living conditions in the barracks, the constant nagging fear of discovery, the propaganda speeches against religion by leaders at many workers' meetings, the seeming indifference of the men in the barracks—all this made our "mission", our dream, seem useless. It was easy to become discouraged and to brood on the hopelessness of really accomplishing anything.

Yet many of the people, we knew, were religious at heart. They, too, prayed in secret. Many at least said they wished there were a church where they could have their children baptized. (We told them how to baptize the children themselves.) In times of discouragement, Nestrov and I consoled ourselves with thoughts of God's Providence and His omnipotence. We placed ourselves and our future in His hands, and we went on.

In effect, our work had to be our prayer. We used to grin wryly sometimes as we reminded each other we were truly being "contemplatives in action", doing everything we did, as St. Ignatius says in his *Spiritual Exercises*, for the greater glory of God. We were working not only to get food to stay alive, or to be accepted by the men, but because for the time being work was our "vocation", our "ministry". We were workers.

The *Stakhanovite* in our brigade was a powerful young Russian about twenty-five years old who was always out to break his own record for the "glorious revolution". *Stakhanovite* derives from Alexis Stakhanov, a Donets Basin coal miner and hero of the early 1930s who reportedly bettered his assigned quota by 1400 percent in one shift in the mines. He is praised and immortalized in Soviet legend much as is Paul Bunyan in the lumber camps of the American Northwest or Joe Magarac in the steel mills around Pittsburgh. I decided that if he could do so much for the glory of Communism, I could do as much for the glory of God.

Of course, a little fellow like me couldn't really compete with that young Russian giant. But I gave him a run for his money. Week after week, he would set the camp record with 58, 59, 60 cubic meters of logs stacked in one shift, and Wladimir Lypinski's name would be right behind his on the list with 53, 54, or 55 cubic meters. The competition got to be a standing joke in the barrack, and the old-timers would egg me on to beat the strapping Russian.

My reputation as a worker, however, didn't allay the suspicions of our friend the judge. One night a barn caught fire about a mile away from the barracks. Even before the alarm reached us, the judge was there to see if Nestrov and I had been out that night. He was sure we had set the fire. It wasn't until he had questioned the men in our barrack and been told we hadn't so much as set foot out of the building that he finally got around to telling us about the fire and ordered us out to help fight it.

As the summer of 1940 turned to autumn, I applied for a job as a truck driver. By now I was a trusted worker (to just about everyone but the judge) who had merited a promotion, so I was sent to Chusovoy to take a driver's test and apply for a license. I passed the test with flying colors. I even made "Driver, First-class", the best rating possible. So back at Teplaya-Gora I was given a truck. It turned out to be a broken-down old pick-up that might have served Henry Ford as the inspiration for the Model T, and it was to give me some rather bad moments. Nestrov also won a promotion and moved up to the dispatcher's office. On the strength of our new jobs, we also got a private room, which we shared with two other drivers, a pair of Russians from the town of Magnitogorsk.

About this time, too, we also got Russian passports. In the evenings at the barracks, it was a regular thing for various Party members to lecture us on our work or politics, on Communism or atheism. One of them said one night that it would be an advantage for us volunteers to have Russian passports. With them, he said, we could move more freely about the country, whereas with only our working certificates we would have to stay where we were assigned. And a Russian passport, he claimed, would make it easier for us to get jobs wherever we went.

Nestrov and I talked it over. Russian papers might make it more difficult to leave the country. On the other hand, if they made it easier to travel about, they might make it easier to return to Lvov. When at length we decided to get them, there was no trouble at all. We simply handed in our identification cards and working permits, filled out a form, and in about half an hour had the passports.

We also wrote a report to Metropolitan Shepticki at this time as well as a letter to Makar. Makar wrote back almost at once, telling us he hoped to join us in the spring. By now, too, we were growing bolder in our attempts to talk about religion. I had made friends with many of the children in the

camp and used to ask them from time to time what they had
been taught in school about God. Still, we had to be discreet;
one time a *Komsomol* (Communist Youth) heard me talking
to the children about God and told them later to stay away
from me. They could get in trouble, he said, talking about
such things.

I found the teenagers, especially, interested in religion.
They had heard it discussed and ridiculed so much in school
they wanted to know more. Under the pretext of picking
mushrooms or huckleberries, we would arrange meetings in
the forest after work at night. There, behind a hillock or in
some sunken spot, we would talk for hours about God and
man's relation to God and his fellow man. They were full of
questions, eager to learn. Yet, at the end of such a session,
they would make me promise not to tell anyone what we had
talked about, and we would return to camp by different paths.

Winter comes early in the Urals, as it does to most of
Russia. Life in the lumber camp became harder than ever. It
was not uncommon for the thermometer to stand at 40° below zero (Fahrenheit), but the cold was bearable as long as
there was no wind. The work went on even in the snow.

One night shift, about 2 A.M., my truck stalled in the
woods with a clogged fuel line. I had the choice of trying to
repair it or perhaps freezing to death. It was pitch dark and I
had no tools, but I got the hood up and began to work just by
the feel of the motor. I located the fuel line and wrenched at
the coupling with my thumb and fingers until they were sore.
Finally, it began to work loose.

My hands by this time were numb from the biting wind
and cold metal. The snow was ankle deep, and I was wearing
just a pair of lowcut shoes. Before uncoupling the line, I
stamped about to restore some circulation to my feet, thrash-
ing my arms around to get the blood back into my hands. At

last I undid the coupling, pulled loose the gas line, and stuck my thumb into the opening to keep the gas from spilling to the ground. I tried to warm the fuel line in my hands before putting it between my lips to blow it clear. In sheer desperation I huffed and puffed until I finally felt the obstruction give way.

Now my hands were numb again. I couldn't seem to get the coupling threaded back on the gas tank valve. I'd try it for a few moments with the gas spilling down on my hands until they were white and frozen. Then I'd have to stick my thumb over the gas tank opening again while I put my other hand in my mouth to thaw my fingers enough to keep on working. It seemed like hours before I got the threads on the coupling to catch.

The feeling in my hands had disappeared completely. I began to think they might be truly frozen, but little by little they began to tingle, then throb with pain, as warmth returned. I stamped about and beat my arms across my body so I could finish before all the gas leaked out of the tank. Finally, I tightened the coupling with aching fingers, closed the hood, and crawled into the cab of the truck. The motor was flooded. There was nothing to do but wait for it to drain. It was dawn before I made it back to the garage.

I wasn't so fortunate the next time I had a breakdown. I couldn't fix it. I had to sit for forty-eight hours in the bitter cold, without food, until another truck came along. By that time, both my cheeks were frozen. The right side of my face thawed out, but the left side, which had faced the wind, remained inflamed from eye to jaw. Eventually, it scabbed over, and the sore spot shrunk to the size of a quarter, but it was only in my fourth year in prison that the cheek healed completely.

I began to think that perhaps my application to drive this

old tin lizzy was one of the biggest mistakes of my life. In other ways though, the truck was very helpful. I often drove supplies to work parties in the woods, many of them conscripts, and I'd have a chance to talk with the men while they unloaded the truck. I could also take occasion on these trips to drop in at the peasants' homes up on the hills beyond the camp. These were mostly the old exiles, White Russians and Ukrainians, who had been sent here in 1937 at the height of the farm collectivization drive. They lived in huts up in the hills and eked out a meager living by farming, or by working in the lumber camp or pig iron plant, when they could get work.

They were simple people, and it was easy to talk to them. Unlike the men in the camps or in the barracks, they would talk freely about God and prayers and how they wished there was a church or priest among them. Because I was still feeling my way, though, and very much aware of the Archbishop's cautions, I didn't tell them I was a priest.

About the only ones who did know I was a priest were those I visited from time to time in the hospital at Chusovoy. I thought it might console them more, give more meaning to my promised prayers for their recovery, if I told them I was a priest. I also hoped at first that I might be able to hear the confessions of those who were dying; hospital visits, however, were allowed only in the visiting room, which was always crowded. I never saw the seriously sick or dying, and I felt the risks were too great to attempt to administer the sacraments to the others.

Somehow, though, we must have aroused suspicions. In January 1941, Nestrov and I were suddenly ordered to Chusovoy. No reasons were given. With hardly time to pack, we were simply put on the train and sent to work at the lumber yards in Chusovoy. Perhaps our old friend the judge was behind the move, for otherwise it seemed strange that only Nestrov and I should have been singled out.

In the lumber camp at Chusovoy, Nestrov again worked in the office, but I was back in the work brigade, stacking lumber in the charcoal kilns. Still, there were advantages to the change. For one thing, we could buy our meals in town when we could afford it. For another, despite the suspicious circumstances of our transfer, we seemed to be a lot freer.

We shared a room in the barrack with a Jew named Valery and two Poles. One of the Poles, Fuchs, was a thin, emaciated man with black hair and tightly drawn lips. He wore a pince-nez on his narrow nose and seemed to be always squinting through them, like a caricature of a scholar. Actually, he was a former railway official from Vilna, who now worked as an accountant in the camp office with Nestrov.

Valery, the Jew, was a big, lively fellow, the center of every conversation and a great talker. He was still a young man, perhaps twenty-four years old, forever recalling his life as an actor and his days in the theater. He had fled from Warsaw when the Germans approached and had come to Chusovoy, but not to work. He and Janocz, the other Pole, were two of the cleverest "con" men in the camp. They would disappear for days at a time, living by their wits, bartering anything and everything, avoiding work at all costs. They returned to the barrack only when they got hungry or needed money. Janocz was a little man with chestnut hair, a former Warsaw businessman, he said, but he was always very vague about the business.

Valery and Janocz had also discovered how to get a drink in Chusovoy. If you ordered a full meal at a restaurant, the fare included three or four ounces of whiskey. If you got to the restaurant within a half hour after it opened, a full meal might consist of potatoes, a fruit cup, some beans, custard for dessert, and a piece of meat if you were lucky. If you got there later, a full meal meant a bowl of soup, some cabbage, and a dish of *kasha* (a grit or oatmeallike substance), with possibly a piece of caramel or custard for dessert. On Saturday night, after the restaurants had been open an hour or so, Valery and Janocz would pool their money and send me into town. I'd order a meal, eat the *kasha*, and pour the whiskey into a bottle. Then I'd go to another restaurant, order a meal, collect the whiskey, and repeat the process until my money ran out or the bottle was full. I rarely drank myself, so they felt their money and their whiskey was safer with me.

In return Valery and Janocz (if they were around) and Fuchs would stand in line each day at the commissary store to buy our daily ration of bread. While they were gone, Nestrov and I would say Mass in our room. He would stand outside the door while I said Mass, in case anyone might come, then I'd do the same for him.

At Chusovoy, we hid the Mass kit in the caretaker's room. She was in the building all day and could make sure the suitcase was not disturbed. We had become friends the day I told how I lost my wife and children in the air raid. She wept at the story, and I felt a little guilty about it, but it was too late to change my identity or my story. After that, when I came home in the evenings, weak from the alternating cold outside and heat inside the kilns, she would have hot water on the stove for me to wash up, and a cup of hot coffee or soup, and possibly some *kasha*, for me. In return, I used to teach her little boy to read and write.

At Chusovoy, too, the workers at the lumber camp were being inducted into the army. War between Germany and Russia, everyone said, was inevitable. We were required to report for training three or four nights a week after work. We had to learn the manual of arms, the usual drills, and how to defend a dug-in position, since we were due to serve on the

Leningrad front. We had no uniforms but just reported for training in our work clothes. The drills might last until 1:00 or 1:30 in the morning.

In early June, the first *rota*, or squad, was sent off from the camp at Chusovoy to Leningrad. Leningrad was one of the places that had to be held at all costs if the Germans came. I was informed that my *rota* would leave for Leningrad on the nineteenth of June.[2] For the first time, it became clear that Nestrov and I were going to be separated, since he had not yet been mobilized. We were not sure what to do. In the end, the decision was not ours to make.

Several nights later, at 3 A.M., the secret police surrounded the barracks. Nestrov and I, along with our roommates—Fuchs, Valery, and Janocz—were arrested as German spies. How many others in the camp were arrested that night I don't know, but there were a good many.

The young NKVD agent in charge held us at gunpoint while his men searched the room. They found two bottles of Mass wine in the room, a half-pound bag of tooth powder I had bought, a roll of cotton, and some papers on which the caretaker's little boy had been practicing the alphabet. These items were immediately identified as "bottles of nitroglycerin" (the wine was white), "gunpowder and packing for making bombs", and the secret ciphers of a "code". It still sounds ridiculous, but it wasn't funny that morning at 3 A.M., with the barrack in an uproar and the NKVD holding us at gunpoint. We were allowed to pack a few things, then we were marched off to jail in Chusovoy.

[2] Germany invaded Russia on June 21, 1941.

In the Hands of the NKVD

I was first held in the juvenile home at Chusovoy, an old, eight-room house that now served as a place of detention. There had been so many other arrests in the camp that night that the jails were crowded. My belongings were examined by the guard in charge, the contents carefully entered in a ledger. Then I was photographed—front and profile—and taken to a cell. Actually, the cell was simply one room of the old house, perhaps ten feet square, in which about twenty-five or thirty young men were already crammed, ranging in age from youngsters of about ten to adolescents of about seventeen.

It was stifling hot in the little room, and most of the boys wore nothing but a pair of shorts. I felt rather foolish being thrown in among them, but I had to make the best of it. *"Zdravstvuite!"* (Howdy!) I said, with a cautious smile in the face of their suspicious glances. Then I offered the older fellows in the room two packs of *makhorka* (smoking tobacco) I had in my pocket. They accepted with alacrity.

"What are you in for, Pops?" growled a short, stubby seventeen-year-old with smoldering eyes. "They say I'm a German spy", I said, and proceeded to tell them the story of the arrest. By the time they had finished laughing at the story of the "nitroglycerin" and the thought of making "bombs" with tooth powder and cotton, we had become friends. The little fellow with the black hair and smoldering eyes who had called me "Pops" seemed to be the leader of the group. His name was Vanya, and he seemed especially amused at the story of my arrest. He informed the crowd that anyone who bothered me would have to deal with him.

Actually, they were all friendly; they even put on a little show in my honor. Each of them told a story or a joke, most of them dirty, and they sang a number of bawdy songs. I took it as a sign on their part they had accepted me. At dinnertime, they gave me the first bowl of *kasha* before dividing the rest among themselves, and that night they gave me the best place to sleep.

Early the next morning, I was called out and sent by train, under heavy guard, to the *oblast* (district) prison at Perm. There I was photographed again, had my hair clipped close, was deloused, and finally led into a large cell, perhaps thirty by thirty feet. It held five people when I entered in the morning; by nightfall, it was crowded with more than a hundred.

Because of the German invasion, the Russians seemed to be arresting anyone of whom they had the slightest suspicion. As far as we could make out by comparing stories, they seemed to be working from lists drawn up long in advance. There were teachers, ordinary workers, minor officials in the government, lawyers, a few soldiers—just about anyone, it seemed, who might be considered a bad security risk or had fallen knowingly or unknowingly into enough disfavor to get his name into the NKVD dossiers. Martin, for instance, was a middle-aged man who held a very responsible position in one of the automobile plants in Perm. He had been a Trotsky sympathizer during the 1930s, however, and he was paying for it now.

As the day wore on and the crowd increased, the cell became a bedlam. The prisoners were understandably tense and edgy; fights started just because someone inadvertently stuck his elbow in his neighbor's rib. Late in the afternoon, a young redhead who proclaimed himself a Tartar was shoved into the cell carrying two loaves of bread. When he refused to share it, several people grabbed at the bread; he began to raise a row. To quiet him, someone threw a blanket over his head, and his neighbors beat him unmercifully until he stopped yelling. He got no sympathy from anyone. Those standing by told him he got what he deserved: in prison you have to share.

We got no food that first day because the arrests were coming so thick and fast no arrangements had been made to feed the prisoners. Afterward, we were fed three times a day. In the morning they gave us bread, six hundred grams (about one and a half pounds) apiece, some boiling water, and two small blocks of sugar. At noon we got a half-liter of soup; in the evening, two or three spoonfuls of *kasha*. At any rate that was the ration—but it wasn't always possible to get your share. The guards simply shoved the food into the room in buckets, and it was up to the prisoners to distribute it themselves.

I stayed in that cell almost two months. It was always crowded, but there was a constant turnover of prisoners. What happened to the ones who left we never knew, but the continual talk and terror of the prisoners was mass executions. Martin, the Trotskyite, shouldered his way to me through the crowd after he had been interrogated one afternoon and gave me a piece of bread he had hidden since breakfast. "This is for you," he said. "If you ever get out of here, try to find my wife. I know I'm going to be shot." That night he was called out. He never returned.

Of course, there was no such thing as privacy, even to perform the natural processes. Each evening we were led in groups to the prison toilet, but at all other times we had to use a covered barrel in the cell. The odor in the room was foul. Every afternoon, too, we were taken out in groups to walk in the courtyard for perhaps twenty minutes of exercise. Otherwise, we were confined like sardines, with not even enough room to stretch out and sleep. The only measure of privacy was to withdraw within yourself, as many did, or else to engage in conversation with one or two people nearest you and try to ignore what was happening in the rest of the room.

Every so often, the guard would call out a name, and someone would be led away. Sometimes he never came back; more often, he had only been summoned for questioning. Some would return crying, others angry, others dejected, some beaten black and blue. Those who had been in prison during earlier purges were quite willing to give advice on how to behave and what to say when you were interrogated. I soon found out, though, that the advice was of little help when you entered the interrogation room. You might well come away without having told them anything, but you never came back smug.

It was at Perm that I was first interrogated seriously and at any length. On the second day, I was called out by the guard and led down the corridor to a small office. Neither imposing nor terrifying, it was simply furnished with a desk for the interrogator, a chair or two, and an iron filing cabinet. The interrogator was a tall, black-haired, fine-featured man who might have been taken anywhere for a scholar. He was quiet and composed, precise in his speech, and had obviously done his homework. Yet he could swear with a venom to which I could never get accustomed; it made me flinch, no matter how often I heard it.

He invited me to sit down, then paused to read some papers. At last he looked up and asked softly, "Who are you?" I began to recite the story of Lypinski. He waved his hand as if he were wiping all pretense aside. "No, no, no," he said, "you are not Lypinski, you are not a Russian, and you are not a Pole. You are a priest and your name is Ciszek and you are a spy for the Germans. Now why don't you tell us all about it?" I was stunned. I wondered how long they had known all this, how long I had been under surveillance. They might have learned I was a priest from one of the Poles in the hospital at Chusovoy, but how had they learned my name? Was it possible that they had found some way to force Nestrov to talk? If so, how much did they know?

Having achieved precisely the effect he wanted, the interrogator smiled. "You see, we know all about you. So suppose you try telling me the truth." "Very well," I said, "the truth is I am not a German spy." Instead of answering, he stood up and walked to the filing cabinet. From the top drawer he took out the two bottles of wine, the bag of tooth powder, the roll of cotton, and the pages of writing found during the search of our barracks room at Chusovoy. He said nothing, but placed them dramatically on the desk, one by one.

If he had expected this to be a crushing blow, he was in for a disappointment. It was my turn to smile. "Do you deny that these belong to you?" he said at last. "No, they are mine." "Then how can you deny you are a German spy and saboteur?" I told him the whole story: how I had bought the tooth powder in Chusovoy to brush my teeth, how I had taught the young boy in the camp his alphabet and how to form the letters. If the interrogator wanted to think there was something mysterious about the combinations on the page, that was his business, but anyone could see they had been written by a child. "As for the nitroglycerin," I said, "go ahead and drink it. It's Mass wine."

Without a word, he pushed the bottles and the packages to one side of his desk and resumed the questioning. Who were my contacts? What sort of information had I sent the Germans? If I was not a spy, why was I traveling under another name? Who was Nestrov? (So they *did* know about him.) Were Fuchs and Valery and Janocz also members of the spy ring? Where had I gone when I drove the truck at Teplaya-Gora? How did I receive messages from Germany? What did I know about German invasion plans?

He must have gone over and over the same questions, like

a dog chasing its tail, for at least an hour. From time to time, he made a note on a piece of paper in front of him. Finally, I told him once and for all I wasn't a German spy and that if he didn't like my story, he could make up one of his own, since he had all the "facts". With that, he slammed his hand on the desk and shouted for the guard outside the door. I thought for one panicky second I might be shot, but he ordered me back to my cell. The interview was over. I had a lot to think about, though.

So began a series of interrogations that lasted through the period I was at Perm. Sometimes I'd be called out twice a day, sometimes not at all. The sessions might last anywhere from an hour to all day. The questions were always the same. Sometimes I'd have to sit bolt upright on the edge of the chair for hour after hour, and sometimes, if the interrogator didn't like an answer, he'd give me a blow in the face that would send me sprawling on the floor.

Two or three times in the months I was at Perm, the interrogator summoned a pair of guards and led me into an adjoining room with thick carpets on the floor and heavily padded walls. There I would be worked over with rubber clubs on the back of the head, and when I'd try to drop my head, I'd get a smashing blow to the face. The sessions were painful, but they never lasted more than a few minutes. The purpose seemed not so much to force me to talk—since no questions were asked during that time—but to soften me up so I would be more cooperative in answering the interrogator later, for fear of another beating.

Several times, too, instead of being brought back to the large cell, I was put in a small, black room like a box, so pitch dark I literally couldn't see my hand in front of my face, and stifling hot. I might be there an hour or overnight. I was told to think over the questions and my answers, and decide whether or not I might be able to remember a few more details of the "truth".

In the course of all these interrogations, it became evident they knew I was an American priest, a Jesuit from Lvov who had studied at Rome and crossed into Russia on a Polish passport. For some reason, the fact my Polish papers were false didn't seem to interest them. They rarely mentioned the fact. When it did come up, they brushed it aside. They kept insisting that I was a German spy—conceivably the Vatican might be mixed up in the business somehow—and they wanted the details of my espionage. Nothing else mattered, and nothing else would do.

Early one morning in August, the guard came into the cell and sang out my name. I shook my head, expecting another futile round of questioning, and answered, "Here!" "Come with me," he barked, "and bring all your things." That was a surprise. "All your things" was also something of a joke, because I had only a jacket, the clothes on my back, and a grubby little piece of bread I'd been saving since breakfast.

Immediately, the old-timers began to crowd around me. "That means you're getting out", they said. "You lucky devil!" Then they began to ask me to go to such-and-such an address, to try to get in touch with their wife or their family, or just to let people know where they were and that they were still alive. I promised to do the best I could and shuffled off to the door, dazed at this stroke of good luck and only half believing it could be happening to me.

The guard led me along the corridor and down into the basement, where he locked me into what we called a "box", a little detention cell used for processing prisoners in or out of the prison, with one small window at the top of the door. Before he shut the door, he asked the two routine questions of identification: "What's your name?" ("Lypinski, Wladimir

Martinovich") and "Your birthday?" ("November 4, 1910", the date I used for Lypinski). He closed the door but was back in a few moments to hand in a loaf of bread—a full loaf, about two and a half pounds—and six teaspoons of sugar rolled up in a paper cone. I was startled to find myself with so much bread all at once and went to work on it right away, without bothering to wonder what it was all about.

I ate almost half the loaf before the door opened again and three men came in—a young, black-haired lieutenant in the uniform of the NKGB (split from the NKVD in 1941, after the war began, a special department of "security") and two husky young guards in plain khaki dress. The lieutenant went through the routine again. "Your name?" "Lypinski, Wladimir Martinovich." "Birthday?" "November 4, 1910." "Charge against you?" "58:10:2"[3] "Come with us", he ordered. And so I walked out of the prison at Perm for the last time. The lieutenant led the way, the two burly guards walked behind me.

They took me to a waiting van in the prison courtyard. It was windowless, with a center aisle and metal-cage cabinets on each side just big enough for one man. There was barely enough room in the cage to stand, and it was impossible to sit. The motor started and we rattled off, the truck banging and lurching over the roads and bouncing me around in the cage from wall to wall like the little marble in a pinball machine. We drove for perhaps fifteen minutes, then came to a sudden stop, which slammed me against the front wall. I could hear the voices of the guards and the lieutenant reporting to someone.

At last the door opened, and the lieutenant went through the routine all over again—name, birthday, charge—checking

[3] The numbers denote the section and subsections of the criminal code under which the prisoner has been accused, convicted, or sentenced; "58:10:2" is "agitation with intent to subvert".

my answers this time against a set of papers. "All right," he said as he unlocked the door of the cage, "get out!" I walked out the little aisle behind him and jumped off the tailgate. The two guards immediately formed up behind me, and the lieutenant led the way onto the platform of the railway station at Perm. "Stay close behind me," he snapped, "and don't look around." We walked down to one end of the platform; I was surprised to see my suitcase standing there. We stopped. "Sit down on the luggage," said the lieutenant, "keep quiet," and again he added, "don't look around!"

I sat down on the suitcase, jealously holding my bread and sugar. When I heard someone walking our way quickly, I involuntarily looked around and caught a glimpse of a man who could have been Nestrov being pushed hurriedly by. Immediately the guard shouted, "Don't look around!" So I straightened up and looked back over the tracks. There were other people on the platform glancing curiously in my direction, but they rather obviously avoided catching my eye if I looked at them. At the lieutenant's orders, one of the guards went off to make whatever arrangements were necessary. I had no idea where I was going or why, and, to be honest, my whole concern at the moment was centered on that loaf of bread and those six teaspoons of sugar.

When the train pulled alongside our platform, I was hustled by my guards toward one door of the car, again with the injunction "not to look around". The car we boarded was a regular passenger car with individual compartments in the European fashion, and it was full, except for the last compartment. There were just two girls in it. "*Stoi!*" (Stop!) said the lieutenant as we approached their compartment; he walked in and ordered the girls to find a seat elsewhere. They grabbed their luggage and left hurriedly. No one in those days argued with the NKGB.

The lieutenant ordered me to sit in the corner by the window. One of the guards threw my suitcase up on the rack. I slumped over near the window, hugging my precious loaf of bread. One guard sat next to me; the other sat in the corner seat across the compartment; the lieutenant stayed outside in the corridor. Since nobody seemed to mind, I looked out the window. It was my first contact in a long while with the outside world, even if through a train window, and it had a certain unreal aspect about it, as if I were looking at a movie.

With two blasts of steam, the train began to move. I wasn't certain in what direction we were headed, for I had completely lost my bearings. I couldn't recognize the countryside, so I knew at least we weren't headed east toward Chusovoy. The names of the towns along the route—Krasnokamsk, Vereschagino, Kez, Balezino, Glasov, Yar—were vaguely familiar, but it wasn't until we pulled into Kirov next day that I knew for certain we were going west, in the direction of Moscow.

After a while, I propped my head against the window frame as if I were asleep and began to pray. This sort of mental prayer was what had kept me going until now; by means of it, I never lost courage. In the prison at Perm, as in the camps at Chusovoy and Teplaya-Gora, it had been my strength during the long night hours when sleep was sometimes impossible. I thought again of the lumber camps, of that other train ride into the Urals. It reminded me of my reasons for being here, of my resolve, no matter what the consequences, to do whatever I did only for God. He would sustain me. This thought —that no matter how lonely I was, I was never really alone— gave me courage again now.

The lieutenant spent most of his time in the corridor. When we pulled into towns along the route, he'd hop off the train to pace the platform, stopping now and then to buy a sandwich or a cup of coffee at the station kiosk. The guards also took turns bringing food to one another from the station platforms, but none was given to me. I began to realize that the loaf of bread and the sugar had been intended as my travel ration and were supposed to last me until we reached wherever we were going. By now, I regretted the fact I had eaten half the loaf in the detention box at Perm. I decided I'd better ration the rest as best I could.

At dusk, I ate a small bit of bread, then propped myself up against the window, this time hoping to sleep. The guards took turns sleeping in the compartment while the other remained on guard; the lieutenant found a place to sleep somewhere else on the train. Just before nightfall, we crossed a river, probably the Cheptsa, somewhere west of Kez. Then the landscape faded into blackness. I finally fell asleep to the rough rocking of the train and the steady rhythm of the wheels.

The next morning, one of the guards woke me and took me to the washroom before the rest of the passengers began to move about. I ate another piece of bread, then watched hungrily as the guards breakfasted on milk, bacon, and some white bread they had picked up at the last stop. We pulled into Kirov late that morning, and the two husky guards put away another whopping meal of fried fish, huckleberries, bread, and more milk. Again they gave me none, but no doubt they had their orders. Their constant snacks along the way, though, were making me even hungrier. I began to nibble from time to time on the bread despite the ration I had set myself.

That evening, in spite of my best intentions, I finished the loaf of bread: when I started to eat it, I just couldn't stop, because I was so famished. I also finished the last of my sugar and licked the paper cone to get the last few grains. The next morning I was starved. One of the guards brought in from the station a breakfast of rye bread, butter, cheese, and some cups of coffee. The aroma was overpowering, and the saliva began to run down my throat as if someone had turned on a faucet. I couldn't keep my eyes off that food all the time they were eating it, and I would have given anything to have a bite.

As we pulled into the station at Uren, one of the guards jumped up to get off the train. As he did so, he knocked a piece of bread and butter out of the lieutenant's hand. It fell to the floor half-eaten, the butter side up. The lieutenant swore at him briefly for a clumsy ox, kicked the half-eaten bread under the seat, and followed him out of the compartment.

The temptation was too much. For the rest of the afternoon, I kept fishing under the seat with my leg, trying to make my movements as inconspicuous as possible so the guard sitting opposite me wouldn't notice. Whenever he'd turn to look out the window or into the corridor, I'd swoop my leg around more violently until I began to get a cramp. That piece of bread now occupied all my thoughts; I spent the whole afternoon trying to retrieve it. I don't think I ever worked so hard for a meal in my life.

At last, I felt the bread with my toe and kicked it forward. Then, when the guard would look away, I'd bend down and try to pick it up. When he'd look back, I'd pretend to be scratching my ankle, pulling up my sock, or tying my shoe. Finally, he looked back quickly and saw me reaching for the bread. I caught his eye and, in desperation, said, "*Pozhalusta!*" (Please!). He didn't say anything one way or the other, just looked at me, so I snatched it up.

Just then, the lieutenant came into the compartment. I clutched that piece of bread and butter in one hand, tucked it under the elbow of the other arm, and tried to look nonchalant—at the same time wondering what the guard would say.

He said nothing. When the lieutenant went out again and the guard turned to watch him go, I jammed the whole half-piece of bread and butter into my mouth and finished it at a gulp. At last I had my meal.

That evening, we pulled into the station at Gorki. In accord with special wartime precautions, troops boarded the train here, all lights were extinguished, and we crawled through the night toward Moscow. At dawn, we were in the railroad yards around the city. As far as the eye could see, the tracks were covered with ammunition trains, troop and transport trains loaded with tanks, trucks, armored vehicles of all sorts, bulldozers, and equipment of every description.

As soon as we slid to a stop, I was led out—again with instructions not to look around—and immediately transferred to a waiting van. It was just a big, empty truck with benches, a screened-off section in back, and a place for the armed guard. We drove only a short while before the van came to a halt again. Nothing happened immediately, but I could hear the soldiers talking outside, then shouted commands. The van doors swung open and about thirty young people were shoved in with me. Though there was hardly room for us all, I was happy to see them just to have someone to talk to.

This crowd seemed to be boys and girls from the *kolkhozes* (collective farms), ranging in age from perhaps fifteen to the early twenties. We bounced around in the back as the van careened through the city, but still I managed to get acquainted with some of them. Five of the young boys told me they had been arrested for "killing a nanny goat". Others had been arrested for stealing chickens; some of the girls said they had been arrested for stealing wheat. There was such a crowd in the back of the truck we couldn't sit down, so we rattled around, sliding into one another, bumping elbows and knees, everyone talking at once.

All of a sudden, the van lurched to a stop. The doors opened and the guard began to call out names, one at a time. When all the young people had clambered out, I was still in the van. The guard slammed the door, and I heard the driver shout, "Come on, climb in, I'm leaving!" The gears ground and we raced off again. Once again, I sat down on the benches all alone. After a while, there was a sudden stop— then nothing. I heard the guards in conversation, then they seemed to walk away, and I could hear nothing but ordinary street sounds. Moscow in September can be very cold; the guards on the van were already wearing their big army great-coats. There was no heat at all in the van, and the metal was getting so cold it stung to the touch. At last I stood up in the truck and began to jump around, trying to keep warm in my thin clothing.

After perhaps an hour, I heard the exploding steam and screaming metal of a braking train. The doors opened and again a crowd of people were herded in with me. They were older people, in their thirties and forties, and again we ex-changed the customary greetings and the now-familiar ques-tion, "What are you in for?" They were peasants for the most part, arrested for robbery or draft dodging. Some, like me, had been picked up on political charges. Again we drove off, rattled along for a while, stopped, and backed up. Again the guard opened the door and called out the names; again, everyone was called but me. I was beginning to think they had forgotten about me.

The van returned to the railroad station. This time, I could hear the whistles and clanging train bells in the distance. It had been a long day, and I was cold and hungry, very hungry. I had had nothing to eat since that stolen bread and butter the day before. This time, when the doors opened, I could see that dusk had fallen outside. A small group of soldiers were shoved into the van, some in uniform, some in greatcoats. Most of them had been arrested for desertion, although they insisted they had simply gotten lost or had been separated from their outfits in transfer. One or two, however, admitted they had simply stayed behind when their unit moved off for the front.

We went off again, stopped again, backed up. Again the guard called every name but mine. The doors clanged shut, and I was left alone once more in that cold iron icebox of a truck. Then the doors swung open, and a guard called out to me, "What's your name?" "Lypinski, Wladimir Martinovich." "Birthday?" "November 4, 1910." "Charge?" "58:10:2." "*Vihoditie!*" (Get out!) he said. As I jumped down from the van, the stiffness in my legs betrayed me. I stumbled and almost fell. I felt the jolt of the impact stab through my cold ankles and feet. The guard led me down into a basement somewhere, though I had no idea where I was, and put me into a "box". Obviously, a prison. Only much later did I learn it was Lubianka.

Chapter Two

MOSCOW PRISON YEARS

Dreaded Lubianka

At least an hour passed before a guard came to unlock the door of the detention cell, ask me the three routine questions, and lead me away. My hair was clipped short again, I was photographed again, front and profile, then fingerprinted. Back to the box again. More time passed. I was called out, registered, locked in the box again. Still later, I was led out, ordered to strip, and went through the routine medical examination. This takes a little getting used to, since most of the doctors in the prisons, as elsewhere in Russia, are women. Their whole approach, however, was one of quiet efficiency and even boredom, so I soon learned to accept their probing and thumping and tapping like any other medical examination.

After the medical examination, my clothes were thrown into the disinfecting room and baked for an hour at such high temperature that they turned dark from the intense heat. Meanwhile, I was led to a shower, then led naked back to the box, where I waited for my clothes. What with the long intervals in the box between examinations and all the other routine operations, the whole night passed. It was nearly morning before I was led down a long corridor, up several flights of stairs, and into a cell.

I call it a "cell" because the building was a prison. Actually, it was more like a hotel room. Small, neat, and very clean, it had a shiny wooden floor and whitewashed walls and ceiling lit by a naked light bulb hanging from the center. A radiator behind a grill in one wall didn't seem to be throwing much heat. There was a bed in one corner with clean sheets, a blanket, and a pillow. The only other furnishing in the room was a *parasha* (a toilet bucket with a lid) in a corner near the door. The one window in the room was about normal size for a hotel room—and I found out later Lubianka had formerly been a hotel—but it was completely barred and covered over with a huge sheet of tin. The only thing I could see, if I stood up close to the window, was a little bit of sky through the "muzzle" at the top where the tin tilted away from the window frame. There was a round peephole in the door so the guard could see in, with a hinged cover on the outside to prevent the prisoner from seeing out.

After the first few minutes of inspection were finished, and I had gotten my bearings, a deep lethargy overtook me. I was sleepy, hungry, and cold, despite the weak heat from the radiator. I simply couldn't get warm. I began to walk up and back, up and back, in that little room six by ten feet, from the bed to the wall and back again. From time to time I could hear a clock chiming the hour; later I discovered it was the big clock in the Kremlin itself.

Then, as the clock chimed 7 A.M., I began to hear movements in the corridor. Suddenly, I heard the guard at the door. The guard was a woman, as were most of the guards in Lubianka, and she brought what seemed to me a feast fit for the gods—400 grams (¾ pound) of bread, a cube and a half of sugar, and a cup of *kipiatok* (boiling water). That was breakfast at Lubianka, and it never varied. By this time I had been without food for more than thirty-six hours. I sat down on the bed and tore into the bread, ripping it off in chunks and chewing it ravenously.

I learned later to be more miserly and more leisurely in savoring the delights of breakfast at Lubianka, but right now I was starved. Between bites of bread, I bit off pieces of sugar and drank them down with a mouthful of hot water; the mixture was sweet, and it felt warm going down. I also learned later that you could get more than one cup of *kipiatok* by banging the cup against the door and asking the guard for a refill. But that morning I finished the bread, the cube of sugar, and the hot water, and let it go at that. I was still hungry, but I felt warm and almost human for the first time in more than two days.

To be completely honest, however, I should admit that my first thoughts after eating breakfast were about dinner. I wondered how long I would have to wait. After the guard had come to collect the tin cup, I began to walk up and down again endlessly—partly to keep warm and partly to have something to do, to keep active. There was no sleeping allowed during the day. If you tried to lie down, the guard would spot you almost immediately and order you to get up. At Lubianka, there were only five or six cells on each corridor, and the guard was continually checking. I wondered over and over again why I was here, what they wanted of me. I was still tired and somewhat dazed, so I simply walked up and down, back and forth, going over the puzzle endlessly—and rather blankly—and listening to the clock chime the quarter hours.

No one bothered me until sometime after the clock struck noon. Then again I began to hear sounds in the corridor, the clatter of dishes, and my salivary reflexes started to work like those of Pavlov's dog. At length the guard opened my cell door and handed me a tin tureen of soup and an aluminum spoon. The soup was very thin, with a few grains of cereal in it we called *magara*, little pellets of grain that look something like birdseed. It smelled of fish, and there were a few bones in the bottom of the tureen. Since I had heard in the prison at Perm that bones are good for you and keep you strong, I ate the soup, bones and all. I simply ground them up between my teeth like powder and swallowed them with a mouthful of soup. No sooner had I licked the tureen dry than I began to think about supper.

Sometime that afternoon there was a twenty-minute exercise period when the guard led me down into the courtyard for a walk. The time for this exercise varied from day to day. It might be as early as eight o'clock in the morning or as late as six o'clock at night, depending on whether the guards began at the top or bottom of the prison. I didn't relish the trip to the courtyard, for I had just gotten warm, and the air in the prison yard was crisp and cold. Moreover, I was still wearing nothing but light pants and jacket, the clothes I had worn ever since Chusovoy.

Supper was at 6 P.M. Sometime after 5:30, I began to hear the clatter of dishes down the corridor, and I waited impatiently for the sound of footsteps, the rattle of the key in the lock, and the crash of the big bolt on the outside of the door. At last the guard handed in the same tin tureen, this time containing two or three tablespoons of *kasha*. The menu at Lubianka, in other words, was no different than it had been at Perm, and, indeed, Russian prison fare rarely varies. Two or three tablespoons made the evening portion. I learned to eat it slowly, savoring it almost grain by grain, then running my finger around the tureen and licking it clean until there was nothing left but the shiny wall of the bowl.

About an hour after dinner, the guard began to take the prisoners on her corridor to the toilet, one by one. Like the medical examination, this is another operation that takes some getting used to, because the prison guards watch you through a peephole even when you are in the toilet. The toilet itself consists of nothing but a hole in the floor, with two indentations for your feet on either side, and the wall to hold you up. Anyone who has ever traveled in Europe will recognize the description; there was nothing unusual about it except the feeling of being constantly watched. There were faucets in the room, so you could wash up, and a large slop sink in the corner in which to clean the *parasha*, which you brought along at this time. There was also a can of disinfectant to complete the job.

Everything had to be done quickly. If I was in the toilet for more than two minutes, the guard would rap on the door and tell me to hurry up. After that, it was back to the cell and the eternal walking up and down until bedtime at 10 P.M. The lights stayed on all night, unless the warden or the interrogator gave a man special permission to have the ceiling light turned off, with only the small blue emergency light over the door left on. That night, however, I had no difficulty getting to sleep, since I had been more than forty-eight hours without any. I eagerly undressed when the signal was given, crawled between the clean sheets, and threw the thin blanket over my shoulders. The mattress was thin, so thin in fact that I could feel the iron strips of the frame under my back or sticking into my ribs when I turned on my side to try and get comfortable.

I said my night prayers, then lay for a time flooded with thoughts. Above all, I wondered what was going to happen to me now. I couldn't believe I was so important that I had to be brought all the way to Moscow after the weary months of interrogation at Perm. I searched for a reason to explain this special handling of me; I couldn't find one. I went over and over those sessions at Perm. My head began to ache, but I was still puzzled. At last, I took refuge once more in the thought of God's Providence. I dwelt on the idea of His protection—and I fell asleep.

The next day began at 5:30 in the morning. The bell shrilled, and a few moments later the guard opened the door to shout "*Podiom!*" (Get up!). If she got no answering movement, she shouted again, then came over to double-check. In a short while, we were led in turn to the toilet, then returned to wait for breakfast. Seven o'clock came, but no breakfast. I learned by experience that breakfast, like the other meals or your turn at exercise, might be served anywhere from 7:00 to 8:30 in the morning, depending on from what end of the prison they began to serve the meal. I also learned by experience to hope that breakfast would be served as late as possible, so that the wait until dinnertime would be as short as possible.

A number of days passed without incident. As the days stretched out, I became more anxious to find out what I was doing here and what was going to happen to me. Since the guards were not supposed to talk to prisoners, there was no way to find out and nothing to do but wait, walking up and down, praying, or thinking endlessly over the same question, reviewing the interrogations at Perm for some hint or clue as to what might happen. In the end, for all my meditations and worrying, I knew precisely what I had known when I left Perm: I was a political prisoner, charged with subversive activity under Section 58:10:2.

After some days of such anxious waiting, I sprang up from a sound sleep one night at the sound of the bolt crashing in the door. This is all part of the psychological process, I suppose, because it immediately puts you on the defensive. Anyone who has ever been awakened suddenly at night will know the feeling. The guards wear special cloth shoes so you can't hear them approaching until they are almost on top of the door; when you're sleeping, the first thing you normally hear is the sound of the bolt springing back. You wake up completely tensed and confused.

That night the guard asked me again the three routine questions—name, birthday, charge—then said, "Get ready!" I dressed hastily, trying to clear my mind and prepare myself as best I could for whatever was about to happen. I was badly disoriented, however, and more than a little confused. The guard led me out of the room and, as is customary, immediately made me face the wall with hands behind my back while she locked the door. Then we went along the corridor through door after door, very quickly. At every door, again, I was made to stand with my face to the wall. If someone came down the corridor, I was hastily shoved against the wall or into a corner with a warning not to look around until they had passed.

After a long series of corridors and up several flights of stairs, we arrived at the interrogation section. Even though it was night, there were two or three secretaries working in the reception room. From time to time, NKGB men would wander by and glance idly at me. The guard led me into a large room beyond the reception room, medium-sized, rather pleasant, with a carpet in the center of the highly polished floor. There were two windows in the room, shuttered, and in the middle of the rug a large polished desk, behind which sat the interrogator. As I entered, he was looking over some papers. There were also a few stuffed chairs, a davenport along one wall, and over in the corner the usual three or four green filing cases.

The interrogator was a middle-aged man in the uniform of the NKGB, with a firm face, rather drawn at the moment and tired, and dark hair beginning to thin out around the temples. He greeted me noncommitally, as though it were all in the day's work, and asked me to sit down. I sat down, but I couldn't relax. At the beginning of any interrogation of this sort, the psychological tension is great. Your body is tense and the palms of your hands begin to sweat a little, as you brace yourself for the unknown questions. By the look of his face and the look of the room, I knew this interrogator would be a professional, an expert at the job.

All through our session, he was soft-spoken and quite matter-of-fact, like a personnel manager interviewing someone for a job. He began at the beginning—name, birthday, and charge—then went detail by detail through my whole story to date. He warned me perfunctorily before he began the detailed questioning that he already had all the details of my earlier interrogations as well as the results of several independent investigations. He told me frankly he already knew all there was to know about me, that this was a preliminary questioning, and that everything would go much more smoothly if I simply told the truth.

I began by telling him I was "Lypinski, Wladimir Martinovich, born November 4, 1910, and charged under Section 58:10:2." He looked up with a slight air of annoyance, like a man who had been distracted while thinking of something else. "Now look," he said flatly and without animosity, "you are Fr. Walter Ciszek, a Jesuit priest from Albertin, born in America on November 4, 1904. Let's just drop all the pretense and fill out your biography with as little fuss as possible, shall we?"

I began again to tell the story from the beginning. He interrupted so often, however, to ask questions about things I had never suspected they knew, that our session finally resolved itself into a question and answer period. He would ask the details one by one and I would say "yes" or "no", with as little explanation as possible.

The interrogator was not particularly insistent; he simply gave me the impression of a man who was doing his job and would appreciate a little cooperation. It was almost as if he had something else on his mind that night and was just going through an old routine. He wrote my story down, point by point, checking from time to time against some reports on his desk and asking about specific details. By the time we had completed the basic biography and his detailed questions, it was already morning; I could see the light filtering through the shutters on the window behind him. When he had finally finished, he told me to go back to my cell and think over what we had put down. He added that I would be called again soon and given an opportunity to fill in any forgotten details.

Back in my cell, after breakfast, I spent the morning puzzling over that session. The amount of background information they had on me was simply astounding. I couldn't understand how they knew so much. It was only much later that I found out. One of my subsequent interrogators told me that a good bit of the information had been gotten from Fr. Makar, who was arrested while crossing the Hungarian border into occupied Poland at the time Nestrov and I were working at Chusovoy. (That accounted for the fact that Makar had never joined us, as he promised; it also accounted, no doubt, for the continual surveillance we must have been under prior to our arrest.) To convince me, this later interrogator showed me the photos taken of Makar on his arrest. I hardly recognized the happy-go-lucky Georgian: his face was thin and drawn, and he looked as if he had lost a good deal of weight. But it was Makar; of that there could be no doubt.

All this, as I say, I learned much later on. But that morning, and in the days that followed, I was badly confused. I wondered whether perhaps Nestrov had talked, or whether we had been under surveillance ever since Albertin without suspecting it. I had no way of knowing. In the light of subsequent interrogations, things became a lot clearer to me, but that morning I was badly shaken.

I expected to be called out again that night, but nothing happened—nor the day after that, nor the day after that. The days began to stretch into weeks, and nobody called me. So I began to organize my days as if I were in a Jesuit house back home, and I made up a daily order for myself. Just as soon as I got up in the morning, I would say the Morning Offering; then, after the morning wash-up, I would put in a solid hour of meditation. The 5:30 rising hour and seven o'clock breakfast were much like the daily order in most of the Jesuit houses I'd been in, and the days began to fall into a pattern.

After breakfast, I would say Mass by heart—that is, I would say all the prayers, for of course I couldn't actually celebrate the Holy Sacrifice. I said the Angelus morning, noon, and night as the Kremlin clock chimed the hours. Before dinner, I would make my noon *examen* (examination of conscience); before going to bed at night I'd make the evening *examen* and points for the morning meditation, following St. Ignatius' *Spiritual Exercises*.

Every afternoon, I said three rosaries—one in Polish, one in Latin, and one in Russian—as a substitute for my breviary. After supper, I spent the evening reciting prayers and hymns from memory or even chanting them out loud: the *Anima Christi*, the *Veni Creator*, the *Salve Regina*, the *Veni, Sancte Spiritus*, especially the *Dies Irae* and the *Miserere*—all the things we had memorized in the novitiate as novices, the hymns we had sung during my years in the Society, the prayers I had learned as a boy back home.

Sometimes I'd spend hours trying to remember a line that had slipped my memory, sounding it over and over again until I had it right. During these times of prayer, I would also make up my own prayers, talking to God directly, asking for His help, but above all accepting His will for me, trusting completely to His Providence to see me through whatever might lie ahead.

After prayers in the morning, and during the long afternoons, I would also recite what poetry I could remember: Wordsworth's "We Are Seven" or Shelley's "Ode to the West Wind" or Burns' little poem to a field mouse, which I found amusingly appropriate in my present condition and which had always been a favorite of mine. Occasionally I'd make up an extemporaneous sermon or speech on some subject, just rambling along, talking out loud in order to keep myself sane.

I also enjoyed trying my hand at long, comic anecdotes of the type common in Russia then: e.g., Stalin's visit to a *kolkhoz*. I'd try to make up the silliest questions and answers imaginable, just to get myself laughing. I'd imagine the peasants asking for bread, or tractors, or milk, and telling Stalin how hungry they were. As "Uncle Joe", I would answer gruffly that it wasn't the first time they'd been hungry or tell them to work harder and at the end of five years everything would be all right, and the like. It was silly, but it helped to break any possible periods of depression.

Practically every night, during these weeks, the sirens would sound at dusk with that long, eerie wail peculiar to air-raid sirens everywhere, and the guards would run around putting out the lights and turning on the red or blue emergency lights over the doors. Still, we were not allowed to go to bed until the signal was given. After a while, I'd hear the nearby pom-pom-pom of the anti-aircraft guns, some of which must even have been on the roof of our building, for the walls would vibrate with the percussion of the guns.

In between shell bursts, I could hear the drone of the German planes overhead, then the louder explosions of bombs falling in the city. From time to time I could hear the thin, high-pitched whistle of a falling bomb, and the building would shake afterward with the loud boom of the explosion, which seemed just outside the window but was, undoubtedly, a good distance away.

It was not until almost the end of September that I was called out again for interrogation. I had just sat down in the chair, tense as always, when the sirens sounded. The interrogator jumped up without talking to me and grabbed the phone. Before he had even made his connection, the anti-aircraft batteries began to pound from the roof right above us; the whole room vibrated. My ears were deafened by the noise, and suddenly the lights went out. At that point the guard came in, shoved me out of the room, and led me quickly down along flights of stairs, through corridors crowded with shadowy figures in the ghostly red and blue lights, all the way down to what must have been, from the damp and musty smell of it, an underground shelter of sorts.

There I was put into one of those small dark "boxes", as we called the temporary cells for prisoners. I waited in the darkness, listening to the muffled thudding of the bombing. My next-door neighbor tapped on the wall, and I came to attention. I strained my ears and heard a loud whisper, "Who's there?" I answered almost by reflex, "Lypinski, Wladimir Martinovich", and we struck up a whispered conversation there in the blackness. From time to time, the guard would come over to tell us to keep quiet; at other times, the muffled thudding of the bombs would drown out phrases and sentences. I learned nothing, except that there were many of us here in boxes in the basement and that I was, in fact, in Lubianka. But in that blackness, with the bombs dropping around us, we felt trapped, and it was comforting to have company.

Suddenly, after what seemed hours, the bombs stopped. Far off in the distance I could hear the air-raid sirens die away with a haunting wail. Then absolute silence, thick and black, so quiet it almost seemed to press in on my eardrums in that pitch-black box. Shortly thereafter we were led, one by one, back to our cells and told to go to bed.

Every night, during the first week of October, we were taken downstairs to shelter. The bombing grew in intensity, and we knew the Germans must be making an all-out drive for Moscow. The bombing was almost constant now; even during the day there would be occasional raids. One afternoon, I was sitting on my bed during a raid when I heard the high-pitched whistle of a bomb very close and rapidly growing louder. Before I even had time to react, the bomb hit. The wall of my room shuddered so violently it bounced me around on the bed. I scrambled up and looked around anxiously, trying to see whether the wall had been cracked or the tin plate on the window blown off, but no such luck. Almost immediately, the door opened and the guard quickly took me downstairs.

Early in the morning of October 6, they began to evacuate us from the prison. There was a great deal of confusion and hustle and bustle in the corridors, with guards shouting at us not to look around or talk but to keep moving in a single file—and for God's sake to move quickly! We were all gathered together in what seemed to be a big basement room. Although we were strictly forbidden to talk, everyone was talking at once, and the guards were too busy with other things to enforce the rule.

From one of the prisoners there in the half light of the basement, I found out that the Germans were reported to be only 110 kilometers (less than seventy miles) from Moscow. All during the morning the bombing continued, and we talked happily and somewhat hopefully of liberation by the Germans. It was almost as if there were a party going on in the basement; everyone shared with his neighbor what information he had, along with whatever scraps of food he had managed to squirrel away in his pockets.

Down there that morning I met a Russian who had worked in the American Embassy in Moscow. I bumped into him quite by accident and discovered that he had been the one who sent me the telegram in Albertin. He told me how the Embassy had tried to keep tabs on my whereabouts and of the later telegrams they had sent to Albertin and Lvov, with no answer.

There were also a number of Russian Army officers in the basement, arrested for God knows what, who told us what they knew about the progress of the war. The German advance had been lightninglike; German spearheads now stood on a line running from Leningrad in the north, through Moscow, and down near Stalingrad in the south. The Ukraine had been taken, the Russian breadbasket; the Germans held Odessa and were driving into the Crimea; Rostov had fallen, and the whole Caucasus was threatened. There was a driver there from the German Embassy who added what details he knew, and there were former heads of Russian factories who told us of the all-out Russian war effort. Those were the black days of the Russian campaign, and the people in that room, talking excitedly, were torn between their loyalty to the motherland and their hopes of liberation.

Finally, we were all lined up in groups of about twenty and led up a flight of stairs, out of the basement, and into the streets. I had expected that we would be loaded into vans, but instead we were led on foot, so quickly that we sometimes even had to break into a trot, through the streets of Moscow down to the railroad station. We were guarded all the way by soldiers and trained dogs, an added precaution because the streets were scenes of mass confusion. The bombing was still going on, and from time to time the street would be almost blocked by a high tide of rubble blown across it. A few people were scurrying about the streets, probably seeking shelter, with no time to stare at us.

The noise was deafening, the pace was exhausting, and I was bitterly cold. I was still wearing only my light coat, and Moscow that October was already in the depths of winter. We didn't actually go into the station itself but took a short-cut, stumbling over the rubble, down into the railroad yards. There we were loaded into the regular *stolipinski*, or passenger cars—Russian versions of the European Pullman car, with small compartments about five by ten feet and a corridor down one side of the train.

Even in the midst of the bombing and the confusion (obviously the railroad yards were a prime target of the German planes), everything was done in order. We were loaded into compartments according to a list as our names were read out. About twenty or twenty-two people were packed into one of the five-by-ten-foot compartments; there was hardly room for us to stand, we were so crowded together, like a streetcar or subway during the rush hour. The first ones into the car took the seats, and some of the later arrivals scrambled up onto the upper bunks. In that way, we could at least breathe in the car without having our ribs crushed by our neighbors' elbows.

Since these were ordinary passenger trains, there were windows on both sides of the car through which we could observe the chaos and bombing as long as it was light. At night, we could see the flashes of the anti-aircraft shells and the distant lights of explosions in the heart of the city like the sudden shimmering glow of sheet lightning in the summer.

In my section, there were more than a half dozen high army officers, charged with treason or subversion or even desertion, a member of the Soviet upper house of parliament, a Russian who had worked in the Chinese Embassy, several directors of factories, a couple of chemists and lawyers, an engineer, two students, and a professor. All in all, it was a rather intellectual gathering, and most of them, except for a few of the army officers, were political prisoners in the strict sense. We spent the first hours getting acquainted, interrupted from time to time by the crash of a nearby bomb, which shook the cars—once we even thought we were going to tip over.

Then one of the senior army officers, an old general, decided it was time to organize the group and establish a daily order. He worked out an efficient system for rotating the seats and the bunks, allotting the older men a little extra time to sit or curl up, a little less time to the younger men. He also decided that, in order to pass the time, each of us in the car should give a lecture in our specialty each day; he himself began these "*stolipinski* courses" with a lecture on strategy. He explained in great detail how Hitler had mounted his offensive and how the lines were now drawn in a great arc from Leningrad down to Stalingrad, with Moscow at the pivot.

"But Hitler will lose," he said, "because he has spread himself too thin and his supply lines are overextended. During the winter he may hold the towns, but he is in constant danger of having his supply lines cut by partisan raids throughout the countryside. His real objective is not Moscow but the oil fields of the Caucasus down near Baku, and we know it. It's an elementary rule that you must have fuel for mechanized divisions, and, now that his *Panzers* are so deep into Russia, his only hope of supplying them is from the oil fields of Russia itself. Therefore, we shall drive from Stalingrad to Rostov and pinch off the Caucasus, exposing his flank to the north, isolating the oil fields, and with luck, capturing whole divisions behind the line of counterattack."

It was a fascinating lecture to listen to, there in that ice-cold Pullman car in the midst of the railroad yards of Moscow, with the German planes unloading death overhead. From October 6 to October 9, we stayed right where we were in the station. Perhaps the railway line was blocked, because from time to time our car would be shifted from one track to another, but we made no progress. We would move perhaps 150 yards, stop, back up, move over onto another track, go perhaps five hundred yards, stop, wait, then go through the whole process again an hour later.

Day and night for those three days, the Germans bombed Moscow, and the railroad yards were one of the principal targets. By some miracle or other we were never hit, nor was anything close by, yet it seemed impossible it could be so, because the bombs were raining all about us. Several bombs hit near enough so that we could see rubble and sections of track mushroom into the air, but nothing came in our direction—although we sometimes prayed fervently that it would! The idea seemed to be that if we were hit with a German bomb we would be free one way or another: either we would be dead and escape the Russians that way, or we might be lucky enough to pick our way out of the bombed train and get away.

About October 8, the train made an abortive move as far as Pieski, identified by an army officer in the car as a suburb of Moscow. There we sat through most of the night; the next

day we backed up into the Moscow yards again. The area
where the train had sat the previous day was a mass of rubble,
with boxcars stacked high atop another like the children's
game of pick-up sticks. Here and there a twisted rail stuck out
of the piles like a giant corkscrew.

Finally, on October 9, we began to move by slow stages.
During the day we would halt on a siding, for the Germans
were sure to aim a bomb at anything that moved. We traveled
only at night. While we sat on the sidings, we continued our
"*stolipinski* courses". The old general, who had served in the
army since the days of the czars, lectured us every morning
and evening on military strategy. One of the factory directors
gave us a long, technical lecture on how he had changed over
from making cigarettes to making bullets. Other factory directors and the engineer gave us a run-down on the progress
of the war effort, the scarcity of practically all the materials
needed for war, the demands for full production when there
was nothing to produce with. One of the directors, in fact,
said he had been arrested because he had failed to meet his
quota—and no explanations were accepted. Most of them
were pessimistic about Russian chances to match the German
onslaught in matériel, and they felt that the motherland's only
chance of winning the war lay in her manpower—and in the
United States.

For the first three days, while we were in the yards, we had
been given a ration of bread. Then the bread ran out. There
was not much anyone could do about it in the light of exist-
ing conditions; even the guards missed their regular rations.
Any system of supply would have been completely disrupted
by the continual bombing. After twenty-four hours without
food, for the next few days we received as a ration three or
four small herring, frozen solid. We would warm them in our
hands until they became soft, then simply eat them raw, be-

ginning at one end and working straight through to the other—tail, head, bones, fins, and all.

We ate them because we were absolutely famished. Yet we had no water ration either and, as a result, our thirst was simply intensified by eating the fish. After a day or so, we were almost wild with thirst. Some of the men in the car began to cry out violently, almost mad with the need of something to quench the burning in their mouth and throat. Things began to get completely out of hand, and there was even a rumor (which one of our officers heard from a young soldier on guard) that we might be shot to solve the whole problem.

The bombing was still intense, and the train could only creep along at night, showing no lights, hoping the track in front of it was still there. One night, after we had been running for a while, the train suddenly stopped in the middle of a forest. We thought the moment had come. In the dim half-light of the night, we could see the guards walking around the train, silhouetted against the snow with machine guns in their arms. The hours stretched out interminably, until the muscles in our empty stomachs were churning with the tension, and we were sweating despite the cold. The NKGB men marched back and forth with the dogs they had brought along on the train. It looked very much as if they might be going to herd us out into the forest. Yet dawn came and nothing happened.

The next morning, we pulled into Ryazan, where we got our first bread in two days and our first water. It was another two days before we saw bread again. Again we subsisted on herring, and again some of the prisoners began to get violent. At last we pulled into Tambov, one of the main rail junctions. The station yards were packed with troops and ammunition trains—every track was loaded. Still the bombing continued. For, while we had been moving all the time, we had actually been running almost parallel to the German lines along the

Moscow-Stalingrad front. At Tambov, we were shunted off onto a siding so that essential armaments could move through to the front.

Despite our own wretched condition, we watched with sympathy as the people of the town—some of whom had even pitched shanties along the edge of the railroad yards—begged for food from the passing troop trains. We sat there on the Tambov siding for two days, and at last we got some bread. We were told it would have to last until we reached Atkarsk, 150 kilometers away; at the rate we had been moving, there was no telling how long that would take. When we finally began to move, though, it took us only two days; of course, our bread had long since disappeared. As for the bread promised at Atkarsk, we sat on the siding and waited—nothing happened. After a while, the prisoners began to cry out, cursing the guards and demanding that we be fed.

We finally were. Big baskets of black bread were brought to the train, and we each received half a loaf. It was marvelous, homebaked country bread, fresh and chewy, with the unmistakable aroma of newly baked bread. Again, we were told it would have to last until we reached Saratov, but the smell was overpowering, and we ate it in huge gulps. I never tasted such delicious bread in my life as that thick, black rye bread in Atkarsk. At Atkarsk, too, we got as much water as we wanted, and with all that bread and water our stomachs swelled up until they were bloated and we could no longer feel the pangs of hunger.

We reached Saratov on the eighteenth of October. It had taken us almost thirteen days to make a trip normally made in a day and a half by passenger train. It was pouring rain when we arrived, but rain or no rain we had to stand in line while the officials ran a head count and checked our documents, name by name. We were worried, above all, about the little bits of bread we had squirreled away, trying to keep them from getting wet. Then we were crowded into prison vans and taken to the old governmental prison in Saratov.

Interlude at Saratov

When we reached the prison, we were checked off again in the pouring rain and at last led down into a basement with old stone walls, black with age. Once again we went through the usual routine: we were fingerprinted, photographed, barbered and shaved, examined by the doctors, and disinfected. While our clothes were taken to be steamed, we were herded into the showers. After almost two weeks in the cramped quarters of the railroad cars, we were glad to be clean again. The showers themselves at Saratov were filthy, for this section of the prison hadn't been used for a long time; the walls of the showers were damp, grimy, and covered with scum. But we did the best we could and felt better for it.

After all the processing, I was put back in the van along with others and taken across town to an old school building. The prison itself couldn't accommodate the crowds coming down from Lubianka, so the school was hastily pressed into service. The classrooms had been cleared, except for some platforms in the middle of the room on which we sat or slept—at least as many of us as could get a place on them. There were about 150 of us in a room that had probably accommodated fifty, or at most sixty, pupils in former days.

Our group was composed mainly of the political prisoners from Lubianka, a cultured and intellectual group on the whole, so we soon established a daily order similar to that which the old general had set up on the train. There in those classrooms, the professors would lecture, and some of the artists would perform—singing or dancing or working up impromptu monologues and skits—anything to pass the time. Between times, we engaged in the usual prison pastime of exploring each other's backgrounds, finding common interests on which we could while away the hours in lengthy conversations, comparing notes on our interrogations at Lubianka, etc. As always, you had to take many of these stories with a good dose of salt, because everyone would color the stories to protect himself. No one ever completely trusted anyone else. There was always the danger that someone in the group might be a spy or an NKGB informer.

One night while we were there, for instance, I woke with a start at the sound of loud talking and great commotion in the cell. By the time I was awake enough to get my bearings, the guards were already in the room, carrying out a bloody corpse. The officials came immediately, lined us up, and demanded to know who had killed the man. No one had done it, of course; everybody had been sound asleep. The inquiry went on for over an hour. The officials threatened that it would last all night if necessary and nobody would get any sleep, but they got nowhere and finally gave up. In the excited hubbub before we got back to sleep, I heard that the victim was an NKGB informer who had been discovered and dispatched. It may have been true, or it may have been just another prison story; perhaps the man was killed in a fight over tobacco or bread.

At the end of a month, the groups in the old school building were split up again, and I was sent once more to the main prison at Saratov. The cells there were small rooms about seven by twelve feet, with grimy stone walls and one little window high in the wall. The room was always dark. It was also very damp, with a dank, musty smell that permeated everything, so penetrating that I never got used to it. As many as seventeen people were sometimes packed into these rooms, but in our cell there were twelve.

Even at that, there wasn't much space to move around. At night, we all huddled together on the rough-hewn benches to sleep. If someone turned over in his sleep, he was liable to wake the whole crowd. On the other hand, the food was a little better than average. The bread, of which we got four hundred grams at breakfast with hot water, was delicious. We got the usual half liter of soup at noon, but instead of *kasha* in the evening we were handed three frozen fish, what we called *okun* (like little perch), and some warm water. We ate the fish, entrails and all, from head to tail, like sardines. Moreover, we had a gentleman's agreement—possible in such a small group—not to eat between meals. In this way we avoided the common prison experience of having our appetites whetted by watching someone else eat.

At this time, they began to call us out for interrogations again, one at a time, beginning sometime after breakfast. The first part of our daily business, therefore, was speculation about who might be called that day. Afterward, we observed the daily order that had become standard fare—lectures, monologues, and skits to pass the time—at least until someone returned from questioning. Then everything would stop, and we'd turn our complete attention to finding out how things had gone, what line the interrogators were working on this time, whether there was any news.

Here in the main prison at Saratov we also had another means of daily communication, the Morse code telegraph. The prison was built in the form of a hollow square, with a courtyard in the middle. On the second floor, where we were, there was a line of about thirty cells all around the four sides. Every day, while one man stood at the door to watch for the guard, the telegraph would go into operation. Prisoners would tap on the walls in Morse code, passing messages from cell to cell.

We would try to find out if there were any new arrivals and what news they brought, especially news from the front. Names were passed from cell to cell, in the hope of finding friends, and we would ask how many were in each room and who they were. The first messages of each day concerned those who had died during the night—mainly from dysentery—or those who were sick in other cells. Tobacco would be traded over the "telegraph" for extra food, or perhaps even for clothing, if the need was desperate. The telegraphers would rap out an appointed time and place (usually the toilet) for hiding the items to be picked up in exchange.

One morning, there was an excited rap at the wall. Word was passed around the corridor like wildfire that Steklov, a former editor of *Izvestia*, had hanged himself in one of the cells. He had been in Saratov almost a year, increasingly despondent, and the prison life and enforced confinement had finally driven him to this act of self-destruction. Because of his former position and reputation, this was a juicy tidbit for the prison telegraph and the subject of lengthy conversations all day.

About my second week in this cell, I was called for interrogation. As usual, I tensed up with that peculiar feeling of repugnance I always felt when starting one of these sessions. The whole business seemed so futile and frustrating. I knew I had done nothing wrong, yet their whole attitude seemed to be that I simply must be covering something up. To be sure, I had entered Russia on a false passport, for which the maximum penalty might be two or three years imprisonment, but that subject never received any serious consideration at all. They knew about it, but the fact itself never seemed to disturb them, except insofar as it tended to confirm their suspicions that I must have had some subversive purpose in entering the U.S.S.R.

That morning, I was led into a room before a whole group of interrogators. I sat down stiffly, and they began to fire questions from all sides about my life or my work as a "spy". "You priests", said one of them, "come into Russia as agitators under the pretext of religion, stirring up the people! Why don't you just come right out and admit it?" "I'm no more a spy than you are!" I flared back. He bridled immediately. "Who do you think you're talking to like that?" he said. "Just answer the question and don't get flip." "I'm not being flip", I said. "You know you're not a spy, don't you? Well, I know I'm not a spy, and that's what I'm trying to tell you."

All told, it was a very confusing session. It was difficult to stay calm or accurate in answering, because the questions came in rapid fire from various interrogators and not necessarily on the same subject. When I told my cellmates about it afterward, or at least as much of it as I could remember, we could come to no conclusion about what they had been driving at. Not that the cell was a particularly good board of estimate in these matters—or entirely without prejudice.

Three days later I was called out again, this time in the middle of the night. My interrogator was a tall young blond with a boyish face, and he was alone. It didn't take long for me to suspect he was a novice at the job; I had had experience with the professionals at Lubianka. He looked so young, and yet he tried to be so stern, that I couldn't help being amused. Instead of the detailed cross-examination I had learned to respect, and even dread, he would break in with exclamations such as "What! What are you trying to tell me? What did you say? What's that supposed to mean?" Once I smiled and said, "Well, what do you want? You tell me!" "Hey!" he said, "who do you think you're talking to!" He got up, trying unsuccessfully to look tough, and shook his fist in my face. "You see this fist? Well, watch it!" I lowered my eyes and tried to look respectful, but I could hardly keep from laughing.

All through the interrogation, he kept insisting that I sit up straight on the front edge of the chair. Yet he himself could barely keep his head up; he kept nodding off to sleep. By early morning, he was dozing at almost thirty-second intervals. He couldn't even write a complete sentence on the papers in front of him. Finally, he slammed the pen down on the desk, stood up briskly, and said, "Good! Now you go back to your cell and think that all over and tomorrow"—here again he tried to look stern—"you better decide to tell the whole truth!"

Late the next morning I was called out again. It was the same young fellow. I looked at him very seriously as I sat down, but I honestly couldn't take him seriously—he seemed such a beginner in the trade. He had obviously been brushing up on his techniques and decided to take a new tack. While we were still chasing around in circles on the usual preliminaries, a young girl came in with a tray of sandwiches, tea, bread, and butter, and put it on his desk. After she went out, he put one of the sandwiches and a cup of tea in front of me. "Eat it", he said. I shook my head. "No, it's all right," he said, "eat it." "I won't", I said. "Come on," he said, "I know you're hungry, eat up." "I don't want it", I said. Of course I wanted it, but the gambit was so transparent that I just refused to play the game. So the sandwich and the cup of tea sat there on the front of the desk throughout the interrogation. It seemed to bother him more than it did me, for he kept looking at it nervously, then glancing away again.

When he learned that I had been "Driver, First-class" at Teplaya-Gora, he started in on a lot of technical details about motors and machinery; "What's this screw for? Where is this valve located? Where does this wire go?" "I don't know", I'd say, or "I forget." "You call yourself a first-class driver? I thought Americans were supposed to be so technically inclined. Why, I wouldn't trust you to change a tire!"

For a while, we went around in circles on wires and screws and valves; then he became aware we were talking nonsense. "How many times do I have to tell you what you're here for?" he said. "You better start giving me some straight answers." Finally, the session ended without much of anything having been accomplished. "Now look," he said, "tomorrow will be your last chance to tell the truth. So think it over." But I wasn't called the next day, or for a long time after that.

Meanwhile, the conversations in our cell centered on the battle for Moscow. New men were coming into the prison daily, and the reports were spread over the Morse code telegraph. We even had a new member in our group, an officer from the garrison in Saratov, who told us that the Germans were not far off. A battle was expected in Saratov itself at any time, he said, and the town was full of soldiers.

There was little doubt the Germans were getting close. Almost daily, Saratov was bombed. During the attacks, we even began to root for the Germans vocally, hoping they'd drop one of those bombs right in the middle of our courtyard. Again, as on the train to Saratov, we spent a lot of time planning our escape if the Germans were kind enough to blow down the walls.

The nearness of the war had another more immediate effect. The food, which had been fairly good, was growing worse; some days there was none at all. There was little food in the town itself; there were too many prisoners now, and the prison kitchen was just not equipped to handle such a crisis. One evening, as our group was being led to the toilet, I noticed a big hambone in a corner of the corridor. When the guard wasn't looking, I snatched it up and hid it inside my coat. In the toilet I washed it off as best I could under the faucet and put it in my pocket. The rest of the day I sat in the cell, biting off pieces of it, grinding it to powder between my teeth and swallowing it. I broke it up and offered pieces to the others, but their teeth weren't strong enough to chew it.

One night in late January 1942, I was called out again for interrogation. Again, it was my boyish young blond interrogator, but he seemed strangely silent and dejected. He paced nervously up and down while he delivered a preliminary oration. This was my last chance to tell the truth, he said, so I had better think it over and tell it straight this time. He sat down, greatly preoccupied. He began to question me, but he kept shuffling things about on his desk nervously, and finally the conversation lapsed altogether.

We just sat there, until suddenly the phone rang. He scooped it up and listened a moment. His face changed immediately. He banged the receiver down, jumped up with a shout, and ran out of the room. I heard the other officials out in the anteroom, milling around and whooping it up. Suddenly the door opened and three other officials came in with my interrogator, chatting excitedly and slapping each other on the back. One of them finally noticed me. He called the guard and told him to take me back to the cell. I could hardly wait to get there and spread the news: from snatches of conversation, I gathered that the Russians had retaken Mozhaisk, the gateway to Moscow. The Germans were retreating. Moscow was out of danger.

The news caused a sensation in the cell. Everybody began discussing it simultaneously; the Morse code telegraph was soon rapping it out on the walls. We could hear murmurs up and down the corridor, and even the guards that night joined a bit in the general hubbub, confirming the news. Reactions to the Red Army victory among the prisoners were mixed. Most of them were Russians, many of them army veterans; their pride and patriotism keyed them up over this Russian success. But then they would reflect, or be reminded by someone, that with the German defeat our hopes for any immediate release from prison had also vanished, and they would be momentarily sobered. In the end, patriotism won out. All in all, it was another sleepless night.

On the morning of January 23, I was called out again for what I supposed must be that "last chance" interview with my tall blond amateur. Instead, I was led downstairs and put into a box. After a while, the guard brought my personal belongings from the cell and gave me a loaf of bread and three teaspoons of sugar in a paper cone. I knew I was going traveling again. At last, two guards took me out to the courtyard and a waiting prison van. They climbed in with me, and we bounced off to the station at Saratov. The crowds in the station were completely changed; there was happiness on every face. The whole atmosphere was optimistic, the people were elated. Even the soldiers thronging the station seemed to have a new lift to their shoulders and a new spring in their step.

My guards and I boarded a train heading north and sat down in one of the passenger compartments. This time it took us only fifty hours to reach Moscow again. I husbanded my bread and sugar carefully, though, because I had no way of knowing beforehand how long the trip would take or where I was eventually headed. All along the right-of-way I could see bomb craters and ruined houses in the wake of the high-water mark of the German invasion. But there was no bombing this time, the tracks seemed to be in fairly decent repair, and we ran through to Moscow without incident.

Sedov Gets a "Conviction"

Somewhere in the copious files of the MVD there must be a whole gallery of portraits of me—thin, thinner, and thinnest—because I again went through the whole weary process of admission to Lubianka. Photographed again, fingerprinted, barbered, the routine medical exam, then the bath and the wait while my clothes were disinfected. At the end, I was led to a little room in the basement that already contained five or six people, but I stayed there only a few days before I was moved upstairs again to a private cell. I was disappointed to be alone again. I was also beginning to wonder why I was so continually shifted around from place to place and why Moscow should be interested in me of all people. I didn't have long to wait to find out. Within two or three days, I was called out about 9 P.M. one night and entered upon what was to prove my most intensive period of interrogation, with almost daily sessions.

This interrogator had a suite of rooms. As I entered that first night, I noticed a pleasant-looking young fellow, black-haired and swarthy, seated at a desk in the first room, working on some documents. He stared at me rather curiously as I passed, but I couldn't place him at all. As I entered the second room, I glanced around quickly to give it the once-over. You soon get accustomed in prison to sizing things up and noticing quite a bit out of the corner of your eye.

It was a large, high-ceilinged room with two large windows on the outside wall and a floor of highly polished oak. There was a davenport along one wall, some large overstuffed chairs, and a whole row of green filing cabinets. A huge mahogany desk in the center, piled high with papers, added to the room's impressiveness, as did the drapes on the windows and the pictures on the walls. I figured immediately that I had reached the big leagues.

My new interrogator was a serious, calm, steady man of about thirty-five or so, well built, with chestnut hair combed to one side, which occasionally fell down into his eyes. His voice was quiet and well modulated; throughout our long series of interviews he was always a gentleman. He knew his business and went about it in a businesslike manner, with no animosity whatsoever, yet thoroughly professional. He told me to sit down, picked a sheet of paper out of the pile on his desk, and said, "Fr. Walter Ciszek, American, Jesuit, trained in Rome, born in America on November 4, 1904?" I nodded. There was a long pause, then he looked up from the paper and asked me quietly, "Now, are you going to cooperate and be quite open about this whole thing?" "Of course," I said, "I always am. Just tell me what you want to know. I have nothing to hide." "Good", he said, and stood up. "Before we begin, there is someone I'd like you to meet."

He went to the door and called in the dark young man who had been sitting at the desk in the other room. "This gentleman", he said, "is one of my staff. Have you ever seen him?" "I don't think so", I said. "Well," he said, "before you were arrested he was sent to Chusovoy to examine your case. He was preparing your dossier when the war broke out, and he was summoned back to Moscow. Do you understand?" Again I nodded. The other man said nothing, just stood looking at me, until the interrogator dismissed him.

As he closed the door and walked back to his desk, the interrogator said to me, "Now that you are properly forewarned, I expect no trouble—and I do expect the truth." He sat down, pulled his chair up to the desk, and said, "What language would you like to use?" Frankly, my Russian at that time was not the best. I used to mix in quite a few Polish expressions, especially for technical terms that I didn't know in Russian. In the Urals we had talked mostly Polish with the officials but Ukrainian among ourselves; I heard a good deal more Ukrainian there than I did Russian. In Moscow and Saratov, I could carry on a conversation with the Russians in the prison, especially the political prisoners, who spoke a cultured Russian, easy to understand. But my own expressions were limited, and for serious purposes my knowledge of Russian was badly inadequate.

"If you would like to speak Polish," said the interrogator in Polish, "feel free to do so. I understand it." That was not quite true. His active Polish vocabulary, I discovered, was not much better than my Russian. In any event, I began my biography in Polish. He kept copious notes, sometimes going over and over a section until he was satisfied he had all the details. This history lasted until almost five o'clock in the morning; I was beginning to grow very, very tired and felt as if I had been pumped dry.

After that I was interrogated every day. For the first week, we went over and over the details of my life in America. He was especially interested in establishing my relationships with the American government, which were, of course, nonexistent. From time to time, he'd make little comments like, "Don't you realize that we are now allies with America and England?" Presumably that was supposed to induce me to speak more freely about my nonexistent relationships with the American government.

At such times, I became close-lipped; I answered his questions, but I resisted the temptation to become cynical. I had no idea what he was driving at, and although I knew I had nothing to hide, I volunteered no information whatsoever, usually restricting myself to a simple "yes" or "no". He, in turn, was constantly complaining, in his gentlemanly fashion, that I was not cooperating with him to the fullest; he saw no reason why he should have to pump so hard to get so little information.

He was one of the few interrogators whose name I ever learned. One day, while he had gone over to the files to pull out another folder, I looked at his passport, which was lying on the desk: "Aleksandr Sedov".

After that first week we went on to details of my life in the seminary, my life in Albertin, my trip to the Urals, and my work in Teplaya-Gora and Chusovoy. He simply couldn't understand why I should have volunteered to go as a worker into the Urals. Or perhaps I should say, he was definitely not satisfied with my explanations. He'd listen to my attempts to explain the spiritual motives that prompted me to undertake such a vocation, very patiently, with a slightly quizzical and disbelieving lift to his eyebrows.

Probing and poking into all these details took almost a month. At the end of that time Sedov said, "I suppose I ought to congratulate you. You haven't told me a thing." I said, "I told you everything." "You didn't!" he said sharply, losing his gentle tone for the first time. "The trouble with you is", I said, "you think you know my life better than I do myself!" "Watch it!" he said, "Don't get out of line! I know better than to think you told me everything; I can put two and two together. I can tell from the documents you're hiding something. Your interrogation at Perm shows that much." "Don't you believe it", I said. "They can force you to say anything if they want to, but that doesn't necessarily mean that it's true."

"Force?" he said. "What do you mean force? We're not allowed to use American third-degree methods in the U.S.S.R." "Well," I said, "that may be the theory, but I got bounced around like a ball out there in Perm." "That's not true", he said. "It is true," I said, "and I was the one who went through it, not you!" He looked at me for a while but said no more. The interrogation ended at that point. It was obvious he didn't like my mentioning the subject; I didn't know what might be the result of my bringing it up, but, legality or no, the beating was true enough.

Back in my cell, that point began to bother me less than Sedov's closing remarks that he could tell I was hiding something. For the life of me, I couldn't figure out what he was driving at. As usual, he had given me no hint. Levelheaded as he seemed to be, there was obviously something in my background that puzzled him, and he seemed determined to get to the root of it. Perhaps it was because he simply couldn't appreciate religious motives. I spent the rest of the day trying to puzzle it out, but to no avail.

The next day, just before noon, I was called out again—a bit unusual, since our sessions were normally at night. When I walked into Sedov's office, who was sitting in one of the armchairs but my black-haired interrogator from Perm, looking very worried. I was stunned. Why was I so important that they should call him all the way from Perm on such short notice?

Sedov started right in: "Do you know who that is?" "Yes," I said, "of course." "Is he the one you said used force during your interrogations at Perm?" I nodded. The interrogator from Perm blanched. At that moment, I felt a twinge of sympathy for him. He was a man, probably a family man, doing the job assigned to him, perhaps cutting a few corners to get it done effectively in the least amount of time. I couldn't excuse him; on the other hand, I saw no reason to railroad him into his own prison. There were too many people in prison already.

"All right," said Sedov, "let's have the facts. Tell me the whole thing." "Well," I said, "this is the interrogator from

Perm who got the confession out of me, if you want to call it that. He was very abusive in his language and, as I told him at the time, completely out of character with his responsible position as a leader of the Soviet people. Nobody is going to respect or talk freely to a man who antagonizes you with abusive and profane language."

"Yes, yes, yes," said Sedov, "but you said he used force?" "Well," I said, "when he saw he wasn't getting what he wanted, he called in another man whose name I don't know, a stocky, well-built young fellow, who grabbed me by the neck and socked me in the face if my answer wasn't the one expected." "So!" said Sedov. He turned to face the interrogator from Perm and asked, "Who's that man?" "I don't know", he mumbled, paler than ever. "He does know", I said. "He must know, but I don't know." "Well," said the interrogator from Perm in self-defense, "it was done because he was hiding the facts from us, just as I wrote you in the report."

With that, Sedov motioned to him with his head, and they stepped outside the room. The man from Perm followed him, looking shaken. Again I felt a twinge of sympathy for him. In about five minutes, Sedov returned. He said nothing further about the incident, and I have no idea what happened to the interrogator from Perm, but in any event part of the riddle was now clear to me. The documents sent from Perm to Moscow had stated explicitly that I was keeping something back. That one remark was the cause of my summons to Moscow for more intensive and more experienced interrogation, as well as the reason for all the distrust I had met with in my Lubianka interrogators from the very first.

That session ended one complete month with Sedov. Theoretically, according to the penal statutes, a prisoner can be held for interrogation only for a limit of one month, then he must be either charged or released. (At least, that was how the system was explained to me by some of the old-timers in Lubianka and Saratov.) In extraordinary cases, however, the period of interrogation can be extended for another month. Mine was extended for two months.

During those next two months, Sedov dwelt especially on my relationships with Archbishop Shepticki and the mission I had received from him. Again, I tried my best to explain that my mission from the Metropolitan was the same as that of any other parish priest or missionary: to serve the people. I was their spiritual minister, pure and simple; no politics whatsoever were involved. Sedov couldn't see it, anymore than any other interrogator had been able to understand it. They had always insisted, as he insisted, that the priestly mission was simply a pretext for some political mission. He never said that in so many words, of course, but the implication was always there behind his questioning.

Sedov kept asking for details on how the Archbishop lived, who lived with him, who visited him, and who his "contacts" were. Time and again I repeated that I had only visited the Metropolitan at his residence twice, and then briefly. I simply had no information to give on the details of the Archbishop's life or his administration of the diocese. Somehow or other, I got the impression, though again this was never stated explicitly, that they were trying to link Archbishop Shepticki, and my own mission into the Urals, with some pro-German plot.

Again the eternal questioning about why I wanted to go to the Urals. And again I tried to explain that many of the Ukrainians and White Russians, who had been part of my flock at Albertin or the Archbishop's diocese in Lvov, had volunteered to work in the Urals, and, as a priest, I wanted to be with them and minister to them. At the root of Sedov's interest and insistence was the fact that the area around the

Urals was one of the major industrial centers for the Soviet war effort. My interrogators, therefore, were convinced that my choice of the Urals perhaps had something to do with sabotage. I denied it.

"Then why were you so anxious to go to Tula in particular?" said Sedov. "Tula?" I said. In the course of our subsequent sparring it developed there was a machine-gun factory in Tula, a town some sixty miles from Moscow and one of the defensive salients on which the German invasion had been broken. I had never heard anything about the machine-gun factory, but I had heard of Tula. It was one of the places Nestrov had always hoped we could reach, because of its closeness to Moscow. Mention of Tula, therefore, made me certain they had already interrogated Nestrov in great detail. The weary round of questioning continued; since there had never actually been any espionage or sabotage plot, they couldn't prove anything, but they kept doggedly insisting. Tired of the subject as I was, I was equally dogged in insisting that my only motives for entering Russia, or going anywhere in Russia—no matter where—had been purely spiritual ones, like those of priests anywhere.

The worst part of the whole three months came when Sedov went through my wallet and discovered the torn book page Metropolitan Shepticki had given me. Other interrogators had noticed it before but attached no importance to it. Sedov was a professional. It was something as yet unexplained, and it bothered him. I tried to explain to him that it was a means, something like signet rings of old, of assuring the Metropolitan that any message received from Nestrov or me was authentic. Sedov shook his head.

I tried again. "When we sent a letter to Shepticki," I said, "we were supposed to enclose a piece of that paper. He could match it up with the rest of the page, which he kept, and know that the letter did, indeed, come from us." "I see," he said, "some sort of code." I knew I wasn't getting through to him, but at moments like this my poor Russian and his poor command of Polish betrayed us. I couldn't get across to him in either language the distinction between a sign that was simply used to authenticate something, and a sign that was the key to a code, or a means of conveying some information other than itself.

One day, Sedov brought in an English interpreter. He was an older man, perhaps a native Russian, but he spoke perfect English—English in the British manner. He questioned me in English along the same lines as before. Again, I tried to make clear both the significance of that particular bit of paper and my motives for entering Russia to work among the people. He translated it all for Sedov, quite properly as far as I could tell, and also wrote it down in the transcript. For the first time, I felt I had made some progress in clarifying my position and getting them to understand it. At least it seemed so at the time. When I returned to the cell, I felt more confident and peaceful than I had in a long time.

This whole long process of close interrogation was beginning to get me down. It was my first experience with such prolonged and intense interrogation, and I simply couldn't get used to all the minute probing into the most intimate details. What bothered me most was the complete lack of respect for ecclesiastical persons and the realm of the spiritual. It was a whole dimension they simply couldn't understand and in which, in any event, they weren't interested. But their whole attitude was so much at odds with my own beliefs and background and training that the interrogations were becoming increasingly distasteful and repugnant to me. That night I prayed that this session in English had been as helpful as it seemed to be.

The English interrogation ended my three months with Sedov. For a short while after that nothing happened. I began to hope that we had made some progress, that perhaps he was beginning to believe me—or at least believe in my sincerity. Because that was the worst of the matter; Sedov had told me point blank one day he couldn't make up his mind whether I was hiding something or whether I was really sincere and just the dupe of higher-ups. That was the type of argument, of stone-walled prejudice, that really left me with a feeling of defeat and dejection when I returned to my cell.

Then one day I was called out by the guard and told to bring all my things. For a few moments the hope flickered that the English interrogation had really made a difference and that this time, certainly, I would be released. But it was not to be. I was simply taken to a different section of Lubianka and put into a larger room. Besides the bed, this room even contained a table, although there was no chair. It also had a much larger window, which of course made little difference since it still had the usual iron bars and the tin shield that allowed only a thin view of sky. But I was puzzled by the change and wondered what would happen now.

Soon after that, Sedov called me again. He informed me that my case was so exceptional that another three months had been officially granted for further interrogations. And so we began all over again the weary round of questions and answers. He warned me that this would be my last chance to "come out with the goods", because at the end of these three months I would surely be sentenced, and my sentence would depend on my answers and my cooperation.

"You know," he said, "I sometimes get the impression from your self-righteous answers that you think you're somehow better than we are. Forget it!" "No," I said wearily, "I don't consider myself better than anyone, and I appreciate the fact that you are simply doing your job, but all I can do is tell you the truth as I have been telling it to you from the beginning. I'm sorry if that sounds self-righteous. But the truth is the truth; what else can I say?"

Once again we went over the story, period by period and item by item. From time to time he'd bring in "specialists" in certain subjects to help in the cross-examination. This time around the insinuation was a little broader: they seemed to be hinting that the Vatican itself was behind my spy mission. The fact that I had been in Rome, that all through history Jesuits had been "notorious plotters" and the right arm of the Pope, was adduced as an argument for the Vatican's implication in my mission. They found it hard to believe that in all my years in Rome I had never come nearer to the Pope than seeing him in St. Peter's—or in his window at the Vatican while I was standing in St. Peter's Square—and that I had never in my life set foot inside the Secretariat of State or any other Vatican office.

As the interrogations dragged on, Sedov became very open and frank and, because we seemed to be making no progress, quite tense. One day, in fact, he completely lost his patience, threw down his pen into the pile of papers on his desk, and ordered me out of the room. It was the first time I had ever seen him lose control. I was afraid I might be put into the *karcer* (something like solitary confinement) I had heard about from other prisoners, but I was simply led back to my cell.

As the second three months of extraordinary interrogations drew to an end, it became increasingly obvious both to him and to me that we were getting nowhere. In spite of all my arguments and protestations of sincerity, he obviously couldn't believe I wasn't still hiding something. On the other hand, I had told him everything I knew to be true, and, no matter how tense the sessions sometimes became, I was simply not going to make up a story or agree to some of his insinuations, just to ease the tension.

At the very end, almost a week went by when I was not called for interrogations. Sedov must have been collecting all his data, because in our final few sessions he brought in a thick volume of bound pages, the results of all the interrogations, which we read through together. It was hard to read, because it was mostly handwritten and the results of notes he had made during our conversations. When we finished, he asked me to sign it. As far as I could tell, it was an accurate transcript of his accusations and insinuations, plus a fair representation of all my denials, so I saw no reason not to sign it.

After these last few sessions going over the transcript, Sedov told me the interrogations were over, and I might expect a verdict soon. I had no idea what it might be, but by this time I had given up almost all hope of anything miraculous. Still, it was a relief to know the interrogations were over. The verdict, however, was delayed.

For a week nothing happened. Then one day the guard brought another bed into the room, and a little later led in another prisoner. He was a young Polish officer from Anders' Army who had been arrested and recently transferred from Saratov to Lubianka. I had now been living alone more than five months, so I was delighted to have someone to talk to besides the interrogator. I welcomed him warmly, and we jabbered away in Polish. He told me all about his experiences, and then I told him my story, including the fact that I was a priest. As soon as I said that, his face changed.

He got up from the bed and began pacing nervously, then stood for a long while at the door listening for the guard. At last he came back and spoke to me very quietly. "I'll tell you the truth", he said. "I'm a Catholic and I feel terrible about this whole situation. I just have to tell you that I was put in here to have you tell me all about your activities in Russia. My parents and my wife and children are living in the Russian zone of Poland. If I find out what they want to know about you, then I can be reunited with my family. Otherwise—well, without putting it in so many words, they imply that I may never see my family alive again. Now, I've been honest with you. You've got to help me. Tell me what I'm going to tell them."

By this time he was so worked up that my first problem was to calm him down before we could even begin to discuss the situation. I tried to make him see that the NKGB couldn't expect more from him than they had been able to get from me. If we made up a story, no matter how much it might seem to the NKGB to confirm their suspicions of me, he'd still be held while they tried to verify the story. That was how they worked. And when they couldn't prove it, because it would be a lie, he would be in worse shape than he was now. On the other hand, if the Russians really intended to release him, he would stand no worse a chance if he proved no more successful in shaking my story than they themselves had been.

"Tell them the truth", I said. "Tell them my story just the way I told it to you when you first came in. It's the same story I've been telling them ever since I was arrested. If they press you for details I haven't mentioned, say that I'm as cautious as the next prisoner and don't talk much about myself—except for the story I first told you."

Nervous as he was, he could see the sense of that. He agreed to try it. We were together only four or five days, and he was called out several times. They didn't like the story, but they didn't blame him and just told him to keep trying. He felt much better, he told me, and his conscience didn't bother him because he was telling the truth. He also thought his chances of seeing his family were as good as they had been before; the interrogators hadn't mentioned that threat again, perhaps because they thought he was cooperating. After he was called out on the fifth day, the guard took his bed out of the room, and I never saw him again.

A few days later, about 2 A.M., the guard rapped on my door and walked in. She told me to get dressed in a hurry. I had been sleeping so soundly I couldn't get my bearings. I asked her what it was all about; she just answered, "Hurry up, hurry up!" I dressed slowly, trying to think, and she rapped on the door again. When I came to the door, she opened it, then led me down to Sedov's office. I remember it was quiet that morning; we could hear the people talking in the NKGB offices as we passed. It was Sunday morning, and not much was going on.

I was still sleepy when we reached Sedov's office; he looked tired himself. He apologized for calling me but said he was on duty that night and just wanted to go over things again to pass the time. He had on a shirt and tie, but no coat, and a pair of slacks. When I sat down, he picked up the phone and called one of the girls. "I suppose you're hungry?" he said to me. I didn't answer. "How do you feel?" he asked. "Tired." "Yes," he said, "I know what you mean."

When the girl came in, he said a few words to her in a low voice, and she went out again. Sedov leaned back in the chair with his hands behind his head. He seemed relaxed and began talking at random about his days in the Ukraine, when it was still part of Poland. He told me a little episode about a Polish teacher he had had who tried to influence him toward religion. "He didn't succeed," said Sedov, "because I had my own ideas. And yet, you know, when I was a boy, I did believe for a while."

The girl came back with a tray of sandwiches, a piece of cake, and two glasses of hot tea. She put it on the desk, made a passing joke, and went out again. Sedov offered me a sand-

wich. "A little treat", he said, "for breaking up your sleep." I
went over and got a sandwich and began to eat it. I really was
hungry. Sedov began to comment on the bologna and how
hard it was now to get meat with everything going to the
front. "Here, have some tea", he said. He pushed a glass toward me, dropped in a big lump of sugar and (I thought)
something else. Yet, I didn't suspect anything; he seemed so
relaxed and pleasant that night.

"Drink it while it's hot", he said, "and have some lemon."
I squeezed a little lemon into the tea and stirred it with a
small spoon. It was so hot I put the glass on a saucer and
began to sip it. I finished about half the glass along with the
sandwich. Sedov offered me another. I reached for the sandwich, touched it—then felt my jaws getting tight, my hand
falling to the desk. I couldn't swallow the bite of sandwich
still in my mouth. I slipped back into the chair.

I have a hazy memory of Sedov looking at me anxiously
just before I dozed off. The next time I woke, I was lying on
the davenport. Someone, a doctor I think, was sitting next to
me. There was someone alongside the doctor, and Sedov was
standing at the foot of the davenport. I opened my eyes wide.
"Here, take this!" said the doctor, and gave me a pill. I dozed
off again.

When I came to again, I was on my feet. Someone was
holding me, and there was a tight-fitting apparatus of some
sort, almost like a football helmet, on my head. I dimly remember a dull, fierce throbbing pressure in my head. Sedov
was holding my head and pulling at my eyelids, looking into
my eyes. He was staring intently, and his eyes blazed like evil
incarnate. That was my impression—of something almost
diabolic, certainly inhuman, for his eyes were staring, his hair
rumpled. I shook involuntarily, and I jumped. Then I blacked
out.

After that, I have a fuzzy impression of someone jerking at my neck with rubber cords, so that quick, sharp shocks ran down my back and stung my neck. Someone was also jerking at my wrists, and shocks were running up my arms.

Then I remember being at a table, propped up. Sedov was shouting at me loudly, shaking my face. "What's your game? What's your name?" I tried to say something. I couldn't. I kept trying, but no sound came. Sedov kept repeating, "Lypinski, Lypinski, Lypinski." He put a pen into my hand at one point and moved it. What I was doing with it, I don't know. Perhaps I was signing a paper on the desk, but I just can't remember.

I woke up again and was given more pills and a drink of water. When I finally came to, I felt all washed out. Sedov was there alone. He led me to the toilet, and I felt as if I had fallen down ten flights of stairs. Afterward, I remember sitting in a chair in his room. Other interrogators came up to me, shaking their heads and laughing. I just sat there, staring at one place, paying no attention to them. It was daylight in the room, but I couldn't focus.

Finally, I was taken to a box. I sat down and huddled into a corner. When I opened my eyes, everything seemed to be falling on me, the walls and ceiling pressing in. Everything was burning, fiery red. I wiped my eyes, but the fiery red persisted in the tumbling walls. I was terrified. I threw my arms across my head and yelled; I remember shouting and shouting. I felt menaced, attacked; I huddled deeper into the corner. Then I fell asleep.

When I woke up, everything was black. I felt a deep-seated feeling of resentment—almost hatred—for Sedov, a feeling of betrayal, mixed with unbelief, that I can feel stirring now as I recall the incidents. Never in my life had I had such a feeling for any man; it was more than a feeling, it was something almost physical.

Finally, a guard brought me back to my cell. There were two portions of bread and soup and kasha lined up on the table. I couldn't eat, but I knew then that I must have been out of the cell for at least forty-eight hours. I just sat in one place, staring at one place, with no thoughts and no feelings at all. I was simply washed out. The condition lasted for a couple of days, then I became active and hungry again. Toward Sedov, however, I always felt that burning feeling of betrayal, and from then on I was always on my guard.

I never again was fooled, never trusted any Soviet official, of whatever rank. After that, I prayed every morning and every evening, "Lord, deliver me from my enemies and their evil operations." It was a spontaneous reaction and a heartfelt prayer; only in God would I put my trust. From then on, I felt stronger and comforted. No matter what the danger, I always felt His help and a growing confidence in Him.

Several weeks went by. Then, one night, I was again awakened at 2 A.M. by the sound of the bolt crashing in the door. I sat up, tenser than ever before. The guard told me to get dressed and follow her. As we made our way along the darkened corridors, I prayed once more, and over and over, my prayer for deliverance and protection. I was taken downstairs this time, however, to a detention box. That really surprised me. I sat there for almost half an hour, trying to puzzle out what this meant. Was I going to be taken to another prison?—perhaps to court for sentencing?

Then I heard doors down the corridor being opened and closed again, the sounds of laughter and footsteps approaching my box. The door opened. A commissar came in with the chief of the prison, both of them slightly intoxicated, very talkative and flushed. The commissar handed me a paper to read. It was a simple document, not what they call a judicial verdict, but rather what is called an "administrative sentence". It stated quite simply that Walter J. Ciszek had been found guilty of the charges against him under Section 58:6 of the Soviet penal code. Section 58:6 deals with espionage. It was quite a change from the 58:10:2 charge under which I had been arrested—subversive activities.

"Do you understand it?" said the commissar. I nodded. "Are you content?" he said. The verdict as written out in the document was fifteen years at hard labor. I looked at him and smiled rather wryly. "I really don't have much choice, do I?" I said. They both found that uproariously funny. Then the commissar said, "You're getting off easy, you know." Since I had "no complaint", he told me to sign the document to indicate I was in agreement with the verdict. I signed; the commissar took back the paper. He and the chief of the prison then went off, laughing and exchanging a few comments I couldn't quite overhear as they walked down the corridor. According to the date on the "verdict" I had signed, it was July 26, 1942.

Lubianka "University"

Back in my cell after the verdict, I couldn't sleep. I spent a restless night thinking back over the past, wondering what might have happened if I had agreed to some of the charges they accused me of, or whether the verdict had been a foregone conclusion ever since I was arrested. I began to wonder what the prison camps would be like; I had heard stories from other prisoners and rumors of all sorts. At least, I thought, I'll see people again. Even if the work is hard, I'll be active and doing something, instead of being penned up here in a cell. Now that the verdict was passed, I was anxious to get going into whatever the future might hold. I knew God would take care of me. I certainly never thought that it would be almost four years before I saw Siberia.

Two days passed, and nothing happened. On the morning of the third day, a young woman came to my cell. She greeted me pleasantly and asked, "Would you like some books to read, *tovarisch*?" She was the prison librarian. "What?" I said. "Oh, of course, of course!" "Fine, you can take out one book at a time, and I'll come back every week to exchange it if you like. If you finish the book sooner than that, you just tell the guard to let me know, and I'll come and exchange the books. You don't have to wait a whole week."

So began the period of what I referred to as my "doctorate" in the "University of Lubianka". In the hopes of improving my Russian, I began to read Russian literature. I started with Tolstoy and read almost all his works. I established a new order of the day for myself; spiritual duties before noon, then read till dinnertime. Before dinner, I'd make my noonday examination of conscience and say the Angelus when the Kremlin clock chimed twelve. After the noon meal, I said my three sets of beads in Polish, Russian, and Latin, then went back to reading until it was time for the exercise period or the trip to the toilet. After supper, I'd say my evening prayers and hymns from memory, then back to the books again until it was time for bed.

That was my daily order, and nobody bothered me for more than a year. Except for the occasional visits from the chief of the prison and the weekly health inspection and examination for parasites, I saw no one but the guards. I became, in effect, a hermit, alone with my prayer and my books. I even found myself forgetting how to talk! Occasionally I was almost tongue-tied in talking to the doctor, or the warden on his infrequent visits.

Besides the daily twenty-minute exercise period, I tried to

keep myself active by polishing the floor twice a day. We were required to do this once a day at Lubianka in any event, but while many of the prisoners gave it the proverbial lick and a promise, I really worked at it, just for the sheer joy of being active. The floors at Lubianka were of good solid oak, which took a beautiful sheen. I'd dust the floor first with a soft rag, then rub in the wax, which came in big sticks, and afterward go over it with a heavy iron wrapped in cloth—and plenty of elbow grease—to polish it to a high shine.

With all the time on my hands now, I also set about mending the clothes I had been wearing ever since I was arrested at Chusovoy. By now they were in bad shape. Needles, knives, or anything of the sort were strictly forbidden in prison, but I occasionally salvaged some of the larger fishbones from the soup and sharpened them on the iron slats of the bed to make a serviceable needle. With that and my fingernails, I'd loosen one of the staples from the binding of the book I was reading, sharpen it on the bed, and use it to pierce a hole in the bone. Then I'd pull a thread out of my shirt or underwear or socks and proceed to practice the profession of seamstress. The needle, naturally, would be taken away when it was found, especially at the general inspection held every two weeks. It says a good deal for the efficiency of the inspections at Lubianka that I was seldom able to conceal anything so small as a fishbone needle either in the room itself or on my person.

So, during the four years of my "university education" at Lubianka, I stressed not only the spiritual side of life but the physical side as well. Every day I took at least forty-five minutes of calisthenics to keep my body as active as my mind was with the books. I kept myself and my clothes as neat and clean as I could, my room spotless. I was determined through all this long, enforced idleness to remain human and mentally alert and not to let the prison routine get me down. I was, as the saying went among the prisoners, "dumb but happy". With rare exceptions, I knew nothing of the outside world, but I kept track of the time and the days, remembering all the feast days of the Church as best I could, celebrating them with special prayers that I remembered or made up.

And I went at my course in Russian literature with a vengeance. Besides Tolstoy, I read Dostoievski, Turgenev, Gogol, Leskov, and many of the works of Jack London, Dickens, Shakespeare, Goethe, and Schiller—and even *Quo Vadis*—all in Russian. I also read quite a bit of Russian history and a brand new biography of Napoleon, by Tarle, an old Russian historian, who wrote the book while he himself was in prison. The most striking feature of his book, as I remember it, was that all the religious episodes in Napoleon's life—the coronation, the funeral service at his death, his marriages, and so forth—were not only omitted but were not even hinted at. I marveled a bit at the feat. I also began to understand more clearly what was meant by rewriting history for the proletariat and how it could be arranged that young people would hear nothing whatsoever of God.

One other book I read at this time made a similar impression on me. It was a large and lavish study of the Orthodox Church in Russia, published on the occasion of the election of a new patriarch "of Moscow and all Russia", Metropolitan Sergius, the first patriarch since 1925. Perhaps the idea was to combat German propaganda about the suppression of religion in the Soviet Union. The book was filled with color photographs of the churches, the rich ikons, and the famous art of Oriental liturgy.

At the end of the book, however, was an essay, purportedly written by a member of the Orthodox hierarchy, that was an outright attack on Fascism written in such a way as to arouse hate and revenge. The piece so shocked me when I read it that I was sure it couldn't be authentic. I simply couldn't reconcile the ideal of the priestly vocation and a priest's training in the central theme of Christianity—"Little children, love one another"—with the hatemongering in that essay. It was an awful blow to me.

As my grasp of Russian improved, I was devouring books at the rate of almost one a day. I read constantly, but, though I had no glasses, my eyes never bothered me in the slightest. At the librarian's suggestion, I also read the philosophical encyclopedia of Lenin. In it I found a striking, simple definition of Communism, which I memorized. One day later on, when the interrogator and I were sparring informally, between the tense periods of questions and answers, I quoted him Lenin's definition of the ideal Communist state. He looked at me blankly for a moment, then broke into a grin. "Ah," he said, "but when? Certainly not in my lifetime or yours, and probably not for a hundred years, if ever." And with an airy wave of his hand he dismissed the whole thing.

Aside from the weekly medical check-ups and routine inspections of the cell, I was not bothered at all during the period—except by hunger. Actually, after the verdict had been given, my rations were increased. I now got the standard prison-camp ration—six hundred grams of bread in the morning, a half liter of soup at noon, and a bowl of *kasha* at night—and sometimes even a piece of herring or potato. Technically, I was not a prisoner of Lubianka now; I was a prison-camp "detainee". As a result, I was getting more food than ever before, but for some reason or other I found myself thinking about food more than ever, too.

Sometimes, while I'd be walking up and down reading a book, I'd fall to thinking about dinner or supper. I'd become nervous, listening for the clock to chime, trying to figure how long it might be until mealtime. I simply couldn't shake the thought. The more I'd try to concentrate on the book or think of something else, the more it seemed to focus my attention on how hungry I was. The only solution was to do something active—in my case that usually meant polishing the floor—and to do it so vigorously and methodically I'd forget the passage of time and the thought of food.

Suddenly, after a year and two months, I was called out unexpectedly one morning and led to the interrogation section. I was disgusted. The thought of further interrogations, when I had thought they were all over, was completely repugnant. Moreover, I was growing used to my hermit's routine; I resented this invasion of my privacy.

This was a different interrogator, a mild-mannered man of about forty-five, with dark brown hair and square features, dressed in civilian clothes. He was pleasant enough, but intense; he always struck me as something of a driver. After the initial psychological tension and repugnance that I always felt at the start of such sessions, I was completely indifferent. I answered "yes" or "no" to his questions almost mechanically.

He became annoyed and said, "You can do better than that! Do I have to drag everything out of you?" "What's the use?" I said. "You know everything I have to say. It's all written down in the transcript I signed. The trial is over; I signed the verdict, so what's the use?" "Well," he said, "it's useful to us; this isn't an interrogation strictly speaking but simply an attempt to get some supplementary information." Still, he began all over again with the old story; it was quite obvious that "supplementary information" just meant they felt I was still hiding something.

Sometimes, he'd take a different tack and try to argue about religion, bringing out all the theistic arguments. I wasn't interested in arguing; I knew at bottom he wasn't really interested in the arguments either. I tried to cut him off one day by saying, "Look, we have the faith to guide us; what have you got? Nothing!" "Oh, but we have our ideals, too", he said. "We have a goal we're striving for and an ideal we believe in. Not the faith, but something else." It was useless to argue with him; I felt he was just goading me to talk, and I said so.

During the next three years, I was called out for these "supplementary information" sessions at irregular intervals. They proved as fruitless as always, and I resented them more each time. The atmosphere between myself and the interrogator was one of complete distrust, in any event. After Sedov, I trusted no one; on the other hand, the interrogator wouldn't believe me. In fact, he told me plainly on several occasions I must have an oath of some sort, a special vow to the Pope, or maybe even the "seal of confession", which prevented me from telling him everything. That much, he said, was obvious from my refusal to cooperate with him. "Ridiculous!" I said. "However, since I can't convince you of my honesty, go ahead and think whatever you want. If you can't take me at face value, I couldn't care less what you think!"

Sometimes he'd come in with a list of names: cardinals, bishops, and ecclesiastics. "What do you know about so-and-so?" he'd ask. "Nothing. It's the first time I ever heard of him." "Weren't you in Rome?" "Yes, but I never met him. Is he in Rome?" One day he gave me a book to read while I sat in his office; it was church history with a Communist vengeance, full of scandals about fifteenth-century cardinals. "That's what we want", he said. "Now, write out what you know about these people." With that he handed me the list of cardinals, bishops, and other churchmen. I took the list and wrote what little I knew about the names I recognized. When I had finished, he ripped it up. "What are you trying to do," he said, "make a fool of me?"

Another time he questioned me for hours about the Russicum and its people. Many of the names were new to me. Of the men I recognized, I told him what I knew: "He's a good religious. He's very zealous. He teaches a good course in Russian history. He has a fine voice." The interrogator would be furious. "You know that's not what we want to know!" "I'm sorry, but that's the only sort of thing I know." Several times he asked me about Metropolitan Shepticki; I tried to convince him of the truth, that I had only met the man twice. To all these questions, I answered very civilly what I knew. For the rest, though, I told him frankly I wasn't going to make up stories to suit him.

From time to time during these sessions, he'd come up with a "proposition". Wanda Vasilevski was forming an army to fight on the Eastern Front. A lot of Poles were enlisting in that army to fight against the Germans, he said, and they needed chaplains. He asked if I would like to join. I knew Wanda was a Communist; I didn't think the Communists would be too concerned about chaplains—unless there was some hitch. "Not interested", I said. "No thanks." "Well," he said, "you think it over; if you change your mind, remember the proposition still holds."

The next time he called me, though, he had a variation on the theme. Instead of joining Wanda's army, he suggested I might like to join Anders' Army in England, an army of Free Poles being formed to fight on the proposed second front. I shook my head. "No deal", I said.

"Deal?" he said. "Nobody said anything about a deal." "Now look," I said, "I didn't come into this prison yesterday. I'm under a fifteen-year sentence of hard labor, which you'd have to cancel to send me to England, or else you'd expect me to be somehow serving that term in Anders' Army. If you made a mistake with your verdict and are trying to get rid of me, just release me. Otherwise, I'm simply not going to play any games for you people."

After that, he was always coming up with different proposals. One time he offered me a Russian parish if I would break with the Pope, who, he said, was on the side of the Fascists, Mussolini and Hitler, and obviously playing politics. He wanted me to deliver a radio address to that effect on a certain date. "Ridiculous!" I said. "For two years", he said, "you've been trying to convince us you came to Russia only to minister to the people. Here's your opportunity." "Some opportunity," I said, "at that price!" "Well, I just don't understand you", he said. "Of course you don't understand me", I said. "That's obvious. You never have understood me. But I've been around here long enough to understand what you're driving at. I'm not interested in any deals. Let's just forget the whole thing."

He wouldn't give up. Another time he proposed that I go to Rome to arrange a concordat between the Pope and the Soviet Union. I laughed. "Who's going to authorize me?" I said. "Oh, we'll fix that up", he said. First of all, though, they wanted me to take courses in radio and telegraph. "What for?" I asked. "Why, to send us news from Rome!" he said. I laughed again and cut him short. He kept bringing up the subject again from time to time, but I told him I wouldn't even discuss it.

Only once during this whole period did I see Sedov again. I was taken to his room one morning and found him nervous and preoccupied. He told me to go back and take a bath, that I'd be given a clean shirt and trousers—I was to have a personal interview with Beria. I was stunned. Sedov was even more anxious about it, though, than I was. He himself didn't know what it was about. He warned me not to say anything that wasn't in the complete transcript I had signed.

So after I had washed and put on the clean clothes Sedov sent down, the guard led me back through the corridors, up a flight of stairs, and through a row of antechambers until finally we stood in a large, richly furnished room with heavy red drapes and a massive, polished mahogany desk. There was no one in the room when we arrived. I waited nervously and, in all honesty, quite anxiously for my meeting with the all-powerful head of the secret police. When the curtains parted, however, it was not Beria who entered. It was one of his assistants, a solidly built man in his fifties with gray hair and a solemn, impassive face, dressed in a trimly tailored uniform. He apologized for the fact that Beria himself had been called away suddenly to a meeting in the Kremlin.

It soon developed that our meeting had little to do with me personally. There was a Polish bishop in England, previously a chaplain to the Polish Army, who had come to Russia with some British commission to observe the conduct of the war and the condition of the people in the territories recaptured from the Germans. On his return to England, the bishop had written a book, or perhaps an article, in which he stated that one hundred thousand Poles had died in a camp somewhere in Russia, or maybe it was in the Russian occupation zone. The U.S.S.R. denied it and was worried about the effect this might have on the wartime alliance.

The situation was not particularly clear to me, nor was Beria's aide helpful in describing it. He was much more interested in finding out what I knew about the incident or any details I could supply—especially about the bishop. In the Kremlin's view, it must have been a serious situation to prompt this interrogation by the very top echelon of the NKGB, but I couldn't give him any information whatsoever. It was the first I had even heard of either the charge or the incident, and I had never met the bishop. When Beria's aide was at last convinced of that, he cut our meeting short. I was led back to my cell, startled and puzzled, but I never heard another word about it.

By the spring of 1943, the food in the prison began to get worse and worse because of the war. Occasionally the food situation came up in my conversations with the interrogator—in a most unpleasant way. He would remind me that thousands were being killed at the front and millions more were starving at home; then he'd conclude his little recital by adding, "We have been too lenient with you. Our people are suffering terribly and here you are, an enemy of the people, having it easy in prison, fed, clothed, and doing nothing to help us or to justify such treatment." When, at the very end, I was called in to sign a final document certifying the close of my interrogation, he said to me with an unbelieving shake of his head and a deep sigh, "I don't know how you are still alive."

In Residence at Butirka

In June 1944, I was transferred to Butirka, another Moscow prison. As always, the move was sudden, unexpected—and unexplained. One day, while I was reading in my cell, I heard a lot of movement in the prison corridors and out in the courtyard. I was curious, of course, but had long ago given up trying to figure out what went on at Lubianka. Suddenly the guard was at my door telling me to pack my things. Since I had recently signed a document officially closing my period of interrogation, the thought at once crossed my mind that I was leaving for the prison camps.

As the guard led me out the door, I saw a crowd of war prisoners in uniform clogging the corridors. The guard im-

mediately pushed me back inside the cell and told me to wait;
I wasn't supposed to see them. An hour or so later, the guard
returned. He led me down an altogether different set of corridors into the basement, then out to a waiting prison van.
The van was already crowded with other prisoners, and as
soon as I entered, we drove off.

I asked my companions where we were going, but no one
knew. We drove about half an hour before we stopped. We
could hear the guard talking to someone; the van moved forward perhaps 150 yards and stopped again. "Ah," said one of
the prisoners, "another prison. We stopped at a gate to show
our pass, and now we'll either get some company or be unloaded." The doors opened and we were ordered out. The
guards led us down into a basement corridor for the usual
prison processing. "Butirka, by God!" said one of the old-
timers.

Butirka, unlike Lubianka, is a prison in the old style, with
dark massive stones, always damp and unheated. After the
usual routine and processing, I was led up to a big room on
the second or third floor, crowded with prisoners. My most
vivid impression was the smell: urine and stale sweat, tobacco
smoke and the dank, musty odor of the black old stone walls,
all combined in a smell that was overpowering. The room was
so jammed there was no place for me to go, so I stood right
inside the door. One of the prisoners, the cell orderly, approached me and began to ask who I was, how long I had
been in prison, what the charge was, and so on. Finally he
said, "Well, welcome to Butirka! Make yourself at home.
Find some place to roost and get acquainted with the boys."

The cells at Butirka were large rooms about thirty by thirty
feet, with dark green or yellow plaster over the rough stone
walls, which were always damp. The air, too, was always moist
with condensed breath. There were two small windows high

up near the ceiling that afforded us a view of the sky but let in very little light; the huge cell remained in semi-darkness. From the door, a continuous shelf of rough planks, which served as bunks, ran all around the four walls. In the center of the room was a square platform, also of rough-hewn timbers, raised about two feet off the floor. This also served as bunk space. Between the central platform and the row of planks along the walls there was an aisle just big enough to walk through. But the room was so crowded—there were about 120 people in that room—that nobody did much walking.

Following the orderly's invitation, I began to work my way along the aisle to the left of the door. I had hardly gone three paces when one of the men on planks along the wall called out, "Hey, *tovarisch!* Where you from? Sit down!" With judicious use of his elbows and some softly muttered profanity, he got his neighbors to move over and cleared off a little place for me and my bundle. I hoisted myself up on the planks. After so long alone in Lubianka, it was a real treat for me to be among friends again.

My new-found *tovarisch* was a Pole. "And so are you", he said. "How do you know?" I said. "I could tell by the way you said *zdravstvuite*", he laughed. He was a young man, perhaps twenty-five years old, named Grisha, a lawyer who had studied in Moscow and passed his bar examination there, only to be arrested for alleged anti-Soviet activities. A quiet man of medium size with dark hair and black eyes, he had a tranquil face, big round nose, and thick lips. He told me of his studies and his arrest, and how his wife was now working to support their two children. The others in the group were squeezed in so tight they couldn't help but listen.

I was starved for conversation and for news. But I had just begun to trade questions and answers excitedly when the door banged open and we got a whiff of *bolanda* (prison slang for soup). Immediately all conversation stopped. Dishes clanged and spoons rattled as everyone lined up in order, sitting along the edge of the bunks and the central platform, all eyes fixed on the soup kettle. To avoid confusion—and to make sure that nobody got two bowls of soup—no one was allowed to move around except the orderly's helpers, who walked down the aisle distributing the soup. Another helper stood next to the orderly, watching carefully to see that nobody got two bowls. He was joined in this task by practically everybody in the room, for they wanted to make certain they got theirs.

Meanwhile, the orderly took the ladle and sank it deep into the soup. He stirred it slowly, then began to dish it out. His helpers started to take it around the narrow aisle to the right; there was an immediate protest: "No, no, no! We were first yesterday! You begin on the left today!" The helpers paused and started to the left. Those over there immediately protested that they didn't want it. Both sides began shouting; each was equally adamant that the other side should get the first bowls of soup.

Finally, several of them came to blows. The older prisoners jumped in to break it up and quiet things down. "Come on, come on," they said, "let's get this straight. We stick to the assigned order. The right side gets it first today." This Alphonse-and-Gaston act had nothing to do with charity. Despite stirring by the orderly, the heavier and thicker soup would always go to the bottom of the kettle, along with any particles of fish or grain. The soup on top was the thinnest and the least nourishing.

In fact, I became fascinated with the way various people in the room handled their soup. Some ate it very slowly, using a spoon and savoring every sip. Others drank it down almost at a gulp, then sat back watching eagerly to see if there was any left over in the bottom of the kettle, anxious to be there first. Everyone had learned the old prisoner's trick of running his finger around the inside of his tureen when the soup was gone, swabbing up the last precious drops and licking it dry. I noticed some who got out scraps of bread they had saved from breakfast and mixed it up with the soup, with perhaps a pinch of salt out of a dirty rag in their pocket. Others, after they had rolled the dry bread between their hands to form crumbs and dropped it into the soup, set the bowl aside and didn't touch it. That was new to me.

The distribution went on steadily. I got my tureen of soup, a thin watery liquid with some grains of cereal mixed into it. All my neighbors, as usual, looked at my bowl of soup to see how thick it was, and I dutifully checked theirs—all part of the game, to prevent the orderly from skimming off the top soup and saving the thick soup on the bottom for himself and his helpers, who drank last.

When the distribution was done, everybody stopped eating for a moment to watch the orderly and his four helpers. They put their bowls on the table, tilted the kettle, and scooped out two ladles apiece. At that there was a general murmur, "That's enough! That's enough for you!" "Pass the rest of it out!" Another fight of sorts developed over who should get the left-over soup. Again the older prisoners intervened, assigning portions to those who had got the first and thinnest soup. Then, with the distribution crisis over, everyone began to eat with gusto, completely engrossed in the pleasure of eating and lost to everything going on around them.

All at once the doors opened, and the guards took out the soup kettle and brought in another large kettle of *kipiatok*. Immediately, the orderly and his helpers began to ladle it out, a half liter of boiling water to everyone. This was also new to me; up to this time I'd never seen boiling water served except at breakfast.

Then I began to notice that those who had simply set their soup aside in the bowl were people who had managed by hook or crook to accumulate an extra tureen or an old tin can. They got their half liter of boiling water, then mixed it up with the soup they had set aside. In effect, they had two bowls of very thin soup. The others watched them with envy. Those who had already eaten their soup just drank the boiling water in slow sips, or perhaps at this time pulled out pieces of bread, rolled them into crumbs and dropped them into the hot water, mashing the whole concoction into a thin gruel. Others pulled out their rag full of salt and put several pinches into the hot water. If it didn't taste quite like soup, at least it didn't taste so much like water.

After the meal, things quieted down a bit. Some of the prisoners curled up on the planks for a nap; others returned to their interrupted conversations. The group near me started up again, anxious to hear my story. But at the first sign that food was coming down the corridor, the small groups of conversation around the cell erupted into the usual hustle and bustle: "Where's my spoon? Who took my bread? Shut up! Hand me that bowl!"

The guard opened the door and shoved in a big kettle of *kash*a. Two of the prisoners grabbed it eagerly, with a liveliness they never displayed at other times, and handled that heavy, steaming kettle as if it were light as a feather. Once again all the prisoners lined up on the edge of their bunks while the orderly prepared to ladle out the *kasha*. Again there was a general protest: "Tell the *viertuhai* (prison slang for guard) to bring in the *kipiatok*!" "No, no, no," said another group, "not yet, the *kasha* first!"

Those who wanted hot water with the meal were anxious

to mix it with the *kasha* and make soup; they carried the day. A half dozen men near the door began pounding on it with their canteens. The din was terrific, the door shuddered, the guard came running. He told them they would have to wait for the hot water, but the orderly's helpers slipped out into the corridor with him, bold as brass, and eventually came banging back, laughing, with a kettle of hot water.

We each got two hundred grams of *kasha* (about three tablespoons) and a half liter of boiling water. Some of the prisoners poured the water into the gruel, which was thin enough anyway, and ended up with a sort of oatmeal soup. Others again dipped into their little rags for salt and added a few pinches to the *kipiatok*, which they drank with the *kasha*. Everybody took tiny bits of *kasha* on the end of his spoon to make the pleasure of supper last as long as possible. Everyone, that is, except the thieves, the professional criminals, and the con men, who were always with us. They ate every meal as fast as they could, wiped out the bowls with their fingers, then began to look eagerly around for an opportunity to get a second helping.

The big feature after mealtimes at Butirka was smoking. Since the men here could occasionally get gift packages, tobacco was always available. There was never enough of it, of course, but there was always some. Everyone in the room knew who had received tobacco in gift packages or who had a package of carefully hoarded cigarettes or a pouch of *makhorka*, and after the meal was finished a crowd gathered around them, hoping for a puff. The man in the middle was always indignant, but in such surroundings there was no possibility of keeping anything so precious as a cigarette to yourself. If a few grains of tobacco spilled from the paper while a man was rolling a cigarette, there would be two or three dozen hands scrambling around on the floor to "rescue" the precious grains; the man who found them had a right, by that very fact, to a puff on the cigarette.

There was no such thing as matches or flint, but the prisoners had an ingenious system of their own for lighting the cigarettes. A fellow named Vasha was a past master at the technique. He was also jealous of his talent, because he exacted two puffs from every cigarette he lit. He'd take a piece of cotton, or stuffing from a pillow, or the lining of a quilted jacket, fluff it up and stretch it out very thin, then roll it up tight. Next, he would put the cotton between two boards and rub them together vigorously, faster and faster, sometimes for as long as fifteen minutes, while sweat poured down his face and a cheering section urged him on.

"That's it, that's it! Faster! Faster! You've got it, you've got it!" As soon as he smelled smoke, Vasha pulled out the rolled-up cotton, broke it at the point where it was smoldering, and very gently began to blow on it until it was completely aglow. Then, while he carefully shielded it in his hand, everyone who had a cigarette crowded eagerly around for a light. Vasha would take the first two puffs from every cigarette, drawing the smoke deep down into his lungs on each puff until it looked as if he were about to burst, hold the smoke as long as he could, and then exhale it—into someone else's mouth. Suddenly the room would be full of smoke, and a lull of satisfaction and deep contentment would descend upon the cell.

The next major operation was going to the toilet. With 120 men in the room, the *parasha* would be in continual operation after a meal. After an hour or so, the bucket would have to be emptied; the orderly would call the guard. Men were assigned to this job in turn, and the reward for doing it was an extra portion of soup the next day. Of course, if you were finicky enough not to want to take on such a dirty job, you could pass up your turn—but you also passed up an extra ration of soup. There were very few that finicky.

Our one recreation period in the day, as usual, was the daily twenty-minute exercise walk in the courtyard. There was no set time for it. When we were taken out would depend on what end of the building the guards started at and what the order of rotation was that day. When at last the guard opened the door, though, and announced that we were due for a walk, there was near chaos. With these prisoners, strict discipline was an impossibility, short of shooting them all. As soon as they got outside the door, they would begin looking around in the corridor for cigarette butts or for scraps of paper that could be used for rolling cigarettes. Some would make a break for the toilet, others talked through the doors to prisoners in other cells as we passed. All this was strictly forbidden, but it was done—and done every day.

Down in the courtyard, we'd walk around in single file, supposedly in silence. Again, strict discipline was out of the question; all kinds of devilment went on. Some of it had purpose and some of it was just for sheer devilry. The guards could hardly control it; as soon as they would stop to bawl out one prisoner, fifty others would be active—looking around for old pieces of tin or more paper, scratching messages into the stone wall with an old nail, leaving some prearranged bit of barter for a cigarette in a prearranged place.

Every day, when the guard signaled the end of the exercise period, a general protest would be raised: "No, no, no, we didn't get our full twenty minutes!" Every day the guard would try to explain, in the midst of the tumult, that the twenty minutes were counted from the time we left the cell until the time we returned—not the amount of time we were to spend in the courtyard. Yet the same argument would develop the next day, and the day after that, as if no one could ever quite get the rule straight.

That evening, I didn't get to bed very early. Frankly, I was uneasy in this new situation. Moreover, the scene around me was so fascinating I was determined not to miss anything. No doubt this interest in people, the ability to understand and sympathize, was one of the things that kept me going through the long years of imprisonment. I did try once or twice to lie down, but I was so wedged in between the other bodies, and the cell was so hot and sticky in that early summer, that I simply couldn't sleep. It was so crowded that we had to lie on the planks bumper to bumper, as it were, one man tight against the next.

The old man next to me had been in prison for many years and his teeth were decaying. His breath was so foul I simply couldn't ignore it. Normally I was so thoroughly washed out from lack of food and exercise that I'd be asleep almost as soon as I lay down. That night, however, I was keyed up by the new surroundings. After the years in Lubianka, I wasn't used to sleeping in a crowd. Try as I would, I couldn't ignore the stench or fall asleep.

At last, I got up very quietly so as not to disturb anyone, walked down to a corner of the cell, and just sat and looked around. The sea of humanity crowded together on the planks was unforgettable; the sounds indescribable. There was deep, rattling snoring and broken breathing that sounded almost like chortling in the darkness. I heard wheezes and whistles of every description, some quiet talking from the other corner of the cell. From time to time a man would cry out or yell loudly in his sleep.

Time passed. About one o'clock in the morning I heard someone get up and move in my direction. It was Grisha. He came over to me and whispered, "What's wrong, Valodga?"

"Nothing much," I said, "I just couldn't get to sleep." "I know what you mean", he answered. "The first night here is always hard, but you'll get used to it. And you better at least try to get some rest."

I followed him back to our spot on the planks along the wall and finally did succeed in dozing off. It seemed I was no sooner asleep than I heard the guard calling out, "*Podiom!* Get up! Get up!" Slowly the men began to uncoil themselves from the bunks, getting ready to go to the toilet for the morning wash-up, which we did in groups of twenty. After that, the same old conversations were struck up, the same old stories told, the daily jokes that had become part of the routine.

Then, suddenly, the smell of fresh-baked bread drifted down the corridor. We could hear the sound of the wicker baskets being dragged along. The door opened, the guard checked our ration against his tally sheet, and our four champions darted out to haul in the basket of bread. Immediately, all eyes focused on the basket. "Don't touch it! Don't touch the bread!" "Wait, wait, get the *kipiatok*!" "It's not ready yet!" "All right, all right, then keep your hands off the bread!"

Soon the guard was back for the empty basket and yelled at the orderly: "What are you holding things up for? We need the baskets!" So the orderly and some of the crowd cleared a place on the center bunks. Everyone watched intently as the *paika* (portions) were laid out on the platform. Some pieces of bread might not be exactly four hundred grams, so the kitchen would stick an extra piece to that ration with a toothpick. One hundred twenty pairs of sharp eyes would watch to see that the orderlies didn't knock those pieces off while they were pulling out the bread, leaving the pieces in the bottom of the basket for themselves.

When the basket was empty, the men crowded around, looking for any pieces at the bottom of the basket. If they found any, they'd raise the roof. And if they didn't find any, they would search the orderlies to see if a few pieces had been stuck up their sleeves while they were hauling out the loaves. "You lousy bloodsuckers," was the battle cry, "this is all we get to live on. You're stealing our blood!"

Finally the orderly shouted, "All right, all right, get back to your places! We're not going to start distributing this bread until everybody is in order!" Immediately everyone sat down on the edges of the bunks, right on the edge in straight lines, no zigzags. First of all, five pieces of *garbusha* (heel) were set aside for the orderly and his four helpers. Pieces of the heel were always much better than the middle section of the loaf; they gave you a lot more to chew on. Then the game of distribution began.

The orderlies tried to work it out so that their friends would get pieces of the *garbusha*. The crowd watched them like hawks. The loaves were distributed two at a time. When one of the helpers would see his friend was not next in line, but second, he'd come back and cross his hands in picking up the loaves so that the outside piece, the *garbusha*, would go to his friend. At that, the crowd would scream like spectators at a ball game, booing and cursing the distributor. The tension in the room would go up another notch.

When at last the bread was distributed, nobody touched it. Everybody waited until the guard returned with a big kettle of *kipiatok* and they had received the morning's ration of a half liter. Finally, they cut up the four hundred grams of bread into four pieces: one piece they ate now, one was saved for dinner, and another for supper, the extra piece to serve as an afternoon snack or, in many cases, as barter for a puff on a cigarette.

After breakfast, there was the morning ritual for striking a fire and the first cigarette of the day; then things would settle down for the morning round of stories and conversation. So I began to walk around and meet people, listening to their stories and picking up all the snatches of news I had missed during my years of solitary in Lubianka. A director of a freight station was telling of his arrest:

"Most of my work was to get things in order to ship to the front, and during the height of the German invasion it was hectic. One day a train pulled into the station with five cars of wheat in open bins, covered over with wicker tops. I immediately stationed guards around the cars, because it was my responsibility to see that the wheat got to the front. But the townspeople found out there was wheat to be had, and they poured down to the station in droves. I pleaded with the dispatcher to get it moving, but I never got an answer. The wheat was wet and beginning to spoil. Well, I just couldn't stand it any longer. I got my crew together and sold it off to the poor townspeople while it was still edible. As soon as I sold it, of course, the order came through to get it moving to the front. I was arrested with my whole crew and put in jail. I got twenty-five years."

A young private recalled how he had sat in the trenches, day after day, worrying about his wife. She had been very sick when he left home. He was so concerned about seeing her again that one day, when his unit was ordered on a dangerous mission from which chances were he might not return, he stuck his finger in front of the barrel of his gun and shot it off. He was taken to the hospital in great pain; while they were treating his wound, in his delirium he revealed that he had shot the finger off himself. After the wound healed he was taken off to prison: ten years. "Well," he shrugged, "at least I'll probably stay alive."

Then, just before noon, as we were beginning to count the minutes until dinnertime, the cell door opened with a bang.

There were loud voices in the corridor. Suddenly a young soldier marched in, saluted, and shouted out: "Howdy, *tova-rischchi!*" A young country boy of about seventeen, he looked as though he should still have been in grammar school. He wore a soldier's fur cap that was far too big for him and an army greatcoat that reached all the way to his ankles, with a collar five sizes too large and sleeves so long they covered his hands. And yet he was a happy-go-lucky lad whom nothing bothered, not even the following days of prison life.

I had a chat with him later on and found out he was from the countryside around Moscow. He was actually in the reserves and had never seen a battle. His whole platoon was arrested one day when they came to a village recently captured from the Germans and found the people raiding the supplies the Germans had left behind. "Well," he said, "I don't know what we were supposed to do, but we figured we might as well get in on a good thing, so we did. I couldn't get over how much better German rations were than ours, and I said so." Then he chuckled: "I got ten years for subversive talk."

The moments after the noon meal were always the best moments of the day. When everyone had finished smoking, a sort of quiet settled on the cell by mutual consent. Many of the prisoners took a nap. I used to sit there by the door, looking around the cell and watching the human scene. There was a row of sick over by the windows, for instance. We put them there hoping the windows would dissipate some of the stench, because the poor fellows were dying of dysentery. There was nothing left of some of them but skin and bones. The odor was so foul the other prisoners complained to the nurse who used to visit these poor wretches once a day. "I know, I know," she said, "but I can't do anything. There is simply no room left in the hospital."

All she could do was give them some sort of fluid every day, but most of them were too far gone for help. Sometimes, at night, I'd wake to hear a loud cry followed by that peculiar breathing called the death rattle; then the doctors would hurry in and take somebody out in the darkness. In the quiet period after lunch, I talked to the sick from time to time, trying to encourage them as much as I could. But there wasn't much anyone could do. I could—and did—give many of them absolution, and I'd sit close alongside them sometimes, whispering the prayers for the dying. I only hope it consoled them as much as it did me to be able to act as a priest again. It also served to remind me constantly to thank God for the marvelous health I had enjoyed all during these past years. I realized that without His protection, this sickness could strike me at any time, contagious as it was.

I spent seven months in that cell at Butirka. Then, one day in January 1945, I was called out and led up to a small room on the fifth floor. It was clean and neat, with dark green walls and a high upper window with the usual tin shield on it and—wonder of wonders!—two real beds in it. I didn't know why I had been singled out for such treatment. I remember thinking that perhaps, at last, I was about to be sent off to the labor camps. An hour later, the door opened and in walked Nestrov!

We couldn't believe our eyes! Together again at last, there in the fifth-floor room of Butirka, we simply didn't know what to think or say to one another. We stammered and stuttered in greeting, pounding one another on the back, half laughing, half shouting, almost crying. Then we just stood grinning at each other, not knowing where to start.

At last, we began to compare stories. Nestrov, too, had been interrogated by Sedov in Lubianka. He, too, had been sentenced to fifteen years at hard labor. We spent a while going over our interrogations point by point, comparing what he said and what I'd said, trying to figure out how it went. About the only real difference in our treatment was the fact that with him they had concentrated on the idea he was a Russian, playing on his patriotic spirit for the motherland in wartime to win his cooperation.

Our reunion was a wonderful experience in those years of hardship, and we made the most of it. Nestrov and I formed a little Jesuit community right in the heart of Moscow. First of all, after all these long years of being without the sacrament, we went to confession and made a manifestation of conscience. Then we made up a daily order for ourselves which was little different from that of any Jesuit community anywhere. We rose at 5:30—as did everyone else in the prison—made a morning meditation and said Mass (i.e., the prayers of the Mass) before breakfast. Then we'd talk or work until time for our examination of conscience and the Angelus at noon.

In the afternoon we said more prayers, including the rosary, in common. We'd say the Angelus again at six o'clock before supper, then after supper make our evening devotions, taking turns giving one another points for the morning meditation. Morning and afternoon, during the times between prayer, we kept busy. We spent some time reviewing our theology studies together; we preached extempore sermons or gave lectures, criticizing one another—then we'd fall to laughing over similar criticisms or incidents in our earlier training.

Occasionally we would turn to lighter diversions and impromptu skits. I was usually the comedian; Nestrov played the straight man. I'd be Stalin, for instance, and Nestrov would be a *kolkhoznik*, perhaps a "hero worker" from the collective farms whom "Uncle Joe" had called to Moscow to receive a medal. After the presentation, I'd take him through my office on a grand tour to impress him with the glories of Communism. All the poor *kolkhoznik* wanted, though, was a loaf of bread. Yet every time he'd start to ask about bread, "Uncle Joe" would launch into another panegyric about the glorious revolution and a patriotic plug for the war effort.

Finally, I'd send him back to the waiting group of his proud coworkers from the collective farm. As soon as my back was turned, the look of pride would disappear from his face and the faces of his coworkers, and they would crowd around him, asking him anxiously, "Well? Well?" Nestrov would shrug his shoulders and lift his hands in the peasants' expressive gesture: "Oi, what can you expect? The way it was before, that's the way it's going to be! The Kremlin, it is still the Kremlin."

If all this sounds silly, it was meant to be. There was nothing better than a joke to break the almost trancelike state of boredom that occasionally crept into the most active schedule in the midst of prison routine. Every group of prisoners I was with had certain standing jokes, or pet phrases, that almost never failed to evoke a smile, if not a laugh. Prison slang itself reflected this. Some of the phrases didn't necessarily mean anything; they grew out of a situation among a group of prisoners, such as a phrase somebody garbled in a moment of stress. Immediately, that would become a catchword, a rallying cry for other prisoners in times of temporary depression.

So too with Nestrov and me. We had been sentenced to hard labor, but there was no reason we had to be depressed. We were together again; we weren't being bothered for the time being. And so, we set out to make the best of it and have ourselves a good time. We did have a few problems; one was tobacco. Nestrov had begun to smoke in prison in order to relieve the tension, but there on the fifth floor of Butirka he had no tobacco, and no one was sending us gift packages. We

did have a whiskbroom, though, so we manufactured our
own tobacco.

The whiskbroom was used to clean the cell. The guard
would hand it to us daily, then come back later to collect it
and pass it on to the next cell. I had a small knife made out of
an old piece of tin I'd found in the courtyard and sharpened
on the stone walls. Every day I'd cut off about an eighth of an
inch of whiskbroom and chop it up into tiny pieces. Nestrov
would roll the ersatz tobacco into a piece of paper, and I'd try
the prisoners' technique of getting a light from a piece of
cotton. I couldn't get it to work the first few times I tried it,
but eventually I got the little piece of cotton to glow enough
to light Nestrov's "cigarette". I felt like the first man in prere-
corded times who had "invented" fire.

Smoke from our whiskbroom "special blend" was terribly
acrid. It even made me cough, and I wasn't smoking it.
Nestrov puffed away at it, though, as if it were the finest Ha-
vana leaf. One day our turn to use the whiskbroom came late
in the afternoon, just before a changeover of guards. When
the new guard came to collect the whiskbroom, we told him
the other guard had already collected it. He never did find it.
And there we were, tobacco millionaires with a six-inch piece
of whiskbroom. When that ran out, we started in on the
straw mattress.

Another problem was food. It was getting worse and worse
all the time because of the war. But one day about this time
we got an unexpected treat—soup made of powdered eggs.
When the guards brought the soup ration into the building,
we could smell the pungent odor of sulphur all the way up to
the fifth floor. Nestrov and I caught a whiff of it and wondered what on earth it was. When the soup came, and the
smell came overpoweringly with it, we decided it must be egg
soup. Hunger in prison doesn't stand on ceremony; despite

the sulphurous fumes, we both said, "What a treat! And a full bowl, more than ever before!"

The odor was really nauseous. To give up a big bowl of soup, however, would have been a crime under the circumstances. So to it we went, eating and smiling, sipping it out of a spoon first, then drinking it right from the bowl. After about half the bowl, my stomach began to feel queasy. I wondered whether I ought to finish the bowl or not. But hunger overcame caution and—down the hatch! Before the last gulp reached the bottom, the first gulp came back up with such force that it shot out of my mouth and splattered all over the wall. Nestrov was not far behind me. Eventually, the whole bowl came up, and the cell stank to high heaven.

We salted that experience away in our treasury of prison lore: sometimes it's better to be hungry than to be sick. A man has to be careful what he eats, hunger or no. We found out later the egg-powder had spoiled in shipment, but the cook had decided to boil it in the hopes it would somehow be decontaminated. We also found out later the reason we got such big portions: the older hands on the floor below wouldn't take the soup.

During these weeks with Nestrov, I decided to write another petition to Stalin. (I had written two others in Lubianka during my "university days".) Nestrov laughed at the idea, but I felt I had nothing to lose. The procedure itself was simple enough; I just told the guard I wanted to write a petition. "To whom?" he'd say. "To Stalin", I'd answer. Then he would tell me to wait while he found out from the commandant whether I could write such a petition. I was never refused. The guard would come back with pen, paper, and ink, then stay there outside the door while I wrote the petition. That was all there was to it.

What I wrote was also simple enough. I told the Premier I

was Walter Ciszek, a priest and an American, and asked him
to inform the American Embassy, so they might in turn be
able to inform my relatives in America that I was all right.
That was all. I asked for no favors and I made no charges; just
a request for an act of diplomatic courtesy. What happened to
the petitions after I turned them over to the guard I never
knew. After a while, when I got no answer, I just stopped
writing.

Nestrov and I were together for two pleasant months.
Then, one evening as we waited for supper, the guard told us
to get ready with all our things. We knew that meant a move
of some sort. In the few minutes before the guard came back,
we made one last confession. We blessed each other, then
shook hands. There were no words we could think of better
than "God be with you."

Nestrov was led out first into the dim corridor, and I
waited. When the guard came back for me, I looked around
in the corridor but couldn't see Nestrov anywhere. Downstairs, I was put into one of the small, dark detention boxes.
After only a short wait, the guard opened the door, asked the
usual three questions, and led me out to the courtyard and a
waiting prison van. It was the type with closed individual
compartments or cages, hardly room enough to stand.

As soon as I was locked in, the van drove off; I presumed I
was the only one in it. As we bounced out of the prison
courtyard, though, I heard someone call out in a loud whisper, "Lypinski!" It was Nestrov! "I'm here", I answered. We
tried to talk above the noise of the motor and the rattling of
the van, but I couldn't understand much. There really wasn't
much to say, anyway, except to wonder where we were going.

After about half an hour, we stopped and the doors
opened. One by one, the guard called off the names of the
prisoners; I was surprised to find that the van I had thought

empty was really full of men. Nestrov was called before I was. Finally, my turn came. I jumped down out of the van with my hands behind my back in the approved fashion. We were back at my old alma mater, Lubianka.

Last Days in Lubianka

Processing procedures at Lubianka were always strictly observed, so it was 3 or 4 A.M. before I had finished with all the questions, the medical exam, the bath and haircut, the disinfecting, and another session with the photographer. Then the guard led me up the old familiar corridors with their green dado and whitewashed walls and the smell I would recognize anywhere. Frankly, it felt so familiar it was almost like a homecoming.

I followed the guard down the corridors, looking around surreptitiously. I figured I must be on the fourth floor, but it was a section of Lubianka I had never seen. When at last we reached the cell, I saw it was a large one—eight beds. There were seven people in it already. As I entered, they looked at me immediately as one man, that eternal question in their eyes. "*Zdravstvuite!*" I said, and smiled. They welcomed me warmly, showed me my bunk, my cup, and wooden spoon; in this section of the prison, we were allowed to keep utensils in our room.

The first one to introduce himself was Nikita, a young construction worker from the island of Sakhalin, but a native Russian. He was a small, bandy-legged little fellow, thin and swarthy, with a big nose and darting eyes, friendly and extremely talkative. The next was Porphyry, a lanky, fair-skinned Russian, with a small head and finely chiseled features. An atheist and a Party man, he had actually studied theology with a view to writing atheistic propaganda for the Party. The other five were just young soldiers from the front, concerned only with getting enough to eat and surviving in order to return to their families.

Since it was almost four o'clock in the morning, after a few brief interchanges we agreed to get some sleep. Next day, though, I found them a lively group; they wanted to hear all about me. When breakfast came, of course, all conversation stopped. Breakfast in this section of the prison was better than average. We got our ration of bread plus a kettle of boiling water that held about four quarts, so we could each have as much as we wanted.

After breakfast, I noticed the table in the cell was covered with books, checkers, dominoes, and a chess set. "Well," I said, "how did you get that stuff?" "Oh," one of the soldiers said, "we're not in here for very long. Our charges are already over, and they'll be sending us back to the front soon." Nikita, too, had been told he would soon be sent to Warsaw to supervise the reconstruction of bridges and buildings; Porphyry said there was a chance he was going to get his job back with the Party. In this section, everyone seemed to be just waiting for notice to move on. Perhaps I'd soon be leaving for the labor camps.

When they asked about me, I told them I had been sentenced to fifteen years of hard labor in July 1942. "So far," I said, "it's been almost three years and nothing has happened, except that they keep shuffling me around from prison to prison and calling me in for supplemental interrogations." Nikita got a big kick out of that. He launched into a long satirical tirade on the system in general and the bureaucracy of prisons in particular and soon had us all laughing until the tears came. When Nikita got warmed up, he was a marvelous comic, more entertaining than any book or movie.

After a while, though, we settled down a bit. The soldiers began to play checkers or dominoes, while the others stood around kibitzing. Nikita took on one young soldier at chess, and since I had played a little of the game, I drifted over to watch. Nikita had him mated in no time. He did the same with another soldier, then laughed and called out, "Next!" I thought the soldiers must be rank amateurs, so I sat down. By the time I had made five moves, it was mate. Nikita laughed.

In three minutes, I lost two other games, to Nikita's delight, and I told him he was a real master at the game. "No, no, no, *tovarisch*," he said, "you're just all bad players. None of you knows the theory of the game. So gather around here, brothers, and I'll show you how it's done." With that he proceeded to lecture us on the theory of chess. If I remember him correctly, he said there were sixty-four basic moves you had to know by heart. With those moves, you would never lose a game against most normal players.

"Now, have you got that?" he said. "I'll tell you what. All of you get here around the desk and figure out your moves; I'll take on the whole seven of you at once. Take all the time you want to decide your moves. I'll go over on the bed and read a book. When you're ready, just call out the position of the pieces and I'll give you a countermove."

Nikita took a book and went over on the bed while we brain trusters held our consultations. When we would call out a move, he'd look up from the book and almost immediately call out a countermove. We were doing fine until about the fifteenth or sixteenth move. Then, when Nikita called out his countermove, we could see we were in trouble, so we changed his move without telling him. On his next move he called, "Check!"

"What do you mean?" we said. "Nothing of the kind!"
"It's got to be check," he answered with a grin, "and the next

move is mate; there's nothing you can do about it!" Still on the bed, he described where every piece should be on the board. "No," we said, "that isn't where your bishop is. There's no check." "Oh, well, then there's something funny here", he said and, still without getting up, proceeded to play the game from memory, move by move and piece by piece.

For all the pleasant associations, though, I found it much harder to pray in this cell or to perform the other spiritual duties I had set for myself. In order to make a meditation, for instance, I'd take a book and sit down on the bed, pretending to read turning the pages from time to time, but actually praying. Then, in the afternoon, I'd pace around the cell saying my rosaries with my hands in my pockets, counting off the beads on my fingers.

One afternoon, our atheist, Porphyry, asked me to talk with him for a while about God. He knew I was a Catholic but not that I was a priest. That conversation practically developed into a seminar, with regular afternoon sessions. Porphyry would quote from memory all the seeming contradictions in the Bible he had learned in his courses for atheistic propaganda. I'd try patiently to explain them, pointing out the background and context of the Bible passages, plus all the details of the argument I could remember from my own courses in theology.

In a way, it was stimulating and challenging, almost a review of biblical theology, but it was not very satisfying. I think Porphyry was out to convert me, or perhaps he was just brushing up on his technique. In any event, whenever I'd answer one objection or be just on the verge of getting him to admit a particular point, he would immediately jump to a new objection. He had the knack of meeting an answer to his objection by skipping to a completely different problem. "Well," he'd say, "that may be so, but what about this . . . ?"

Then, one afternoon in April 1945, I was told to pack up and be ready to move. I thought perhaps the time had come when I'd be leaving for the prison camps. My hopes, however, were short-lived. I was simply transferred to a different section of Lubianka. Here, on what I estimated was the first floor, I was all alone. I began again my daily order of prayer and reading, trying as best I could to adjust once more to the life of a hermit. It was hard to be alone again. I kept busy, but I knew I was just killing time. I hadn't been interrogated in over a year. Why hadn't I long ago been packed off to the labor camps?

Here again I had little contact with anyone. I wasn't called out for interrogation; the guards were not supposed to talk to prisoners. I began to experience once more that feeling of timelessness—and, what was worse, of purposelessness—as the days went on and on, always with the same routine. And yet, I never lost sight of God's Providence. I knew that nothing was too small or insignificant in life when looked on from the standpoint of His will. At least, I tried to keep sight of that. Lubianka was a hard school but a good one. I learned there the lesson that would keep me going in the years to come: religion, prayer, and love of God do not change reality, but they give it a new meaning. In Lubianka I grew firmer in my conviction that *whatever* happened in my life was nothing else than a reflection of God's will for me. And He would protect me.

One evening in May, about 8:30, while I was in the midst of my evening prayers, I was startled to hear the cheering of a crowd. I hurried over to the window. I could see only the blackness of the sky, but I strained to pick out voices in the crowd. Suddenly, from somewhere quite close, came the sound of cannons firing. There was the roar of planes sweeping low overhead and then, to my amazement, fireworks! I could see reflections of the various colors in my little patch of sky. I stood there entranced. I was also amazed that the guard hadn't looked in or said something to me about staying at the window so long. I wondered if there had been a great victory somewhere.

All at once, there was silence. The echoes of the crowd, still reverberating in the courtyard of the prison, slowly died away. Then I could make out a loud voice echoing in the night with the peculiar metallic ring of a loudspeaker, addressing the people in an elevated and thankful tone. But the words banged out so loudly they were garbled in their own echo; I couldn't make anything out clearly. Yet I knew the noise must be coming from *Krasnoya Ploschad* (Red Square), and I grew increasingly excited and curious. For a long time after silence finally fell in the darkness, I lay in bed distracted, wondering, unable to get to sleep.

About midnight, I heard the guards change in the corridor. Shortly afterward, a young girl who was new to our floor came into my cell and asked if anything was wrong. "I've been watching you," she said, "you're restless. Do you want a doctor?" "No, I'm not sick," I said, "just curious about the crowds outside. I've been lying here trying to figure out what's going on." "Don't you know?" she asked excitedly. I shook my head. "*Tovarisch!* The war is over! The Germans have surrendered! It was announced tonight!"

Then she went on to tell me that she had been outside, watching the parade in Red Square, before she came on duty. She described the victory celebration in detail. I knew our conversation was against the rules, and I was grateful to her. It was the first time any of the guards had shown me a soft and friendly side—they had never been cruel, just businesslike—and it was also the last.

Now that the war was over, I wondered what would happen. I never dared to hope that I would be released. I knew I had ultimately been convicted of spying for the Vatican, not the Germans; that verdict, and my sentence, would no doubt still stand. But there was a chance, I thought, that the atmosphere of the prison might change for the better. Yet no change took place; the days passed. May gave way to summer, then to fall. The cold settled into the prison walls again.

It was October before anything happened. One afternoon, just before supper, the guard told me to pack my things. I was led from the first floor to an upper floor, then to a cell midway down the corridor. There were two people already in the room—one of them was Nestrov! This time I walked in on him, as he had done to me at Butirka. Again, we were overjoyed.

After a moment of emotion, Nestrov introduced me to his cellmate. He was a Frenchman named Champon, a gifted writer and a candidate for the French Academy, who impressed me immediately with his gentlemanly bearing and aristocratic manners. A man of medium height, slightly taller than I, he had a long thin nose, firmly chiseled jaw, and thin, crisp lips. His long blond hair, streaked with red, was just balding back from a widow's peak. He had the French aristocrat's elegant hands, with long tapering fingers, and tiny feet.

Champon was a great talker. He had been in prison for about a year, and his story was a strange one. Like me, he had been accused of spying. Actually, he said, he'd been in China and other countries in the East to photograph backgrounds for a movie he was producing based on the story of one of his own novels. He told us he'd been offered a half-million dollars for the movie rights, of which the NKGB had "confiscated" $400,000 when he was arrested. He had been returning to France through Russia in order to avoid the long trip around Africa.

It was a great story, but I thought it didn't quite ring true. Champon said he'd had only a two-week travel visa to journey through the U.S.S.R., yet he spoke Russian extremely well. That made me a bit suspicious of his story, but I never asked him the obvious question. You never ask such questions in prison.

In this cell, we received an extra bread ration of 150 grams. We also got two blocks of sugar in the morning with our boiled water, and twice a week there might be three little raw fish with the evening meal. The extra food was certainly welcome. I began to feel somewhat stronger and a good bit more chipper. In this part of the prison, too, the heating conditions were much better; the cell remained reasonably warm all during that winter of 1945–1946.

To pass the time, we began discussions. Champon lectured on etymology—he knew several languages besides French and Russian—on painting, and on film production. Nestrov lectured on philosophy, Oriental liturgy, and the Slavonic languages. I concentrated on English and, after my course at Lubianka "University", on Russian literature. One language Champon didn't know was English, so he and I began to instruct one another. I taught him English, and he improved my French; every day we learned twenty new words. Since it was all done without pencil and paper, our memories got a good workout as our vocabularies increased.

All during this time, too, we were careful to attend to our regular spiritual duties—weekly confessions, morning and night prayers, a sermon every Sunday. Champon was a good Catholic, and he entered wholeheartedly into what he laughingly referred to as our "Jesuit community". "I've heard and read a great many things about Jesuits," he said, "and here I am living the Jesuit life for a while."

In these pleasant associations, winter turned into spring.

Then, at the end of May, Champon was called out one afternoon for interrogation. When he returned, he was strangely noncommittal; he wouldn't say anything definite about his session. I suspected immediately he had been questioned about us. That same evening, Nestrov was called out. He returned looking depressed. "What happened?" I said. He glanced at Champon, shook his head, and didn't want to talk about it.

A day or so passed, then Nestrov was called out again. He returned from this session even more depressed. He told me in passing that they were really putting the pressure on him, proposing various deals and trying to play on his patriotic sentiment as a Russian. With Champon there, he refused to say any more. I felt something strange was going on. The atmosphere in the cell had changed completely; Champon was uncommunicative and Nestrov began to brood. And when Nestrov, the Russian, fell into one of these black moods of depression, you needed a bulldozer to dig him out. I tried to encourage him in a general way, but since I had no idea of the specific propositions he was facing, I couldn't offer any advice.

The very next day, just before noon, I was called out. I distinctly recall the peculiar feeling that came over me after having been so long away from this sort of thing—a mixture of tension and extreme repugnance. The interrogator was a stern man, in his late forties, with gold-rimmed glasses and flecks of gray in his hair. I had never seen him before, but he opened the session by saying, "Well, now this is your last chance. Have you changed your mind?" He was obviously familiar with the Ciszek dossier. "What I have told you is the truth", I answered. "What is there to change?"

Without another word, the interrogator picked up the phone, called the guard, and put the receiver slowly back on the hook, as if it were a gesture of finality. When the guard entered, he simply said, "Take him away." I was led, not back to the cell, but down to a detention box. What now?

I was wearing only a pair of heavy socks, and the cement floor in the basement was cold. The guard came back with my suitcase and another small bag. All at once, I knew this wasn't a shift from one cell to another; I was being transferred again, at least to another prison. So I told the guard I hadn't had any dinner and pointed out that I had no shoes. The ones I had been wearing ever since Chusovoy were at last being repaired in Lubianka. "All right", he said and went out. He came back shortly with a bowl of soup, then went to find my shoes. He returned to tell me that they were not in the repair shop and not in my cell. He couldn't find them, and he had done all he could.

While I sat there waiting, wondering what was ahead, I hurriedly ate the soup so I would finish it before I was led away. But my thoughts kept turning constantly to Nestrov. Quite frankly, I was worried about him; I had never seen him quite so depressed. I said a prayer there in the detention box that he would be all right. I never saw him again. After a short while the door opened, the guard asked the routine three questions, and ordered me to follow him. So, bag in hand and wearing only my heavy socks, I walked out of Lubianka for the last time.

Chapter Three

IN THE PRISON CAMPS OF NORILSK

En Route to Siberia

I walked behind the guard to a waiting prison van. It was one o'clock in the afternoon and hot for June in Moscow. For the time being at least, my lack of shoes created no problem. There were already people sitting in the van when I climbed in. Despite the guard's admonitions, we began talking at once. Then three young women climbed into the van with babies in their arms and conversation stopped. We immediately stood up to give them a seat, and everyone crowded around for a peek at the babies.

The women didn't seem at all disturbed. They were eager to talk. The babies, they said, were only a few months old and had actually been born in prison. We didn't go into the details. The babies, though, didn't like the crowds and the commotion. They protested quite vocally, crying until their little faces were red with the effort. Their mothers produced bottles of milk prepared by the prison doctors, and we all watched in a sort of happy and crowded conspiracy while the youngsters settled down in contentment.

By this time, the van had been standing a long while in the courtyard, with the sun beating down on the roof and no air to speak of in the crowded compartment. The atmosphere was stifling. We were sweating profusely, and some of the prisoners began to get dizzy, weak as they were after a long stretch in prison. We started banging on the doors, calling for the guards to open up and let in some air or bring some water. They did neither, but in a few minutes the van lurched off.

We drove to Moscow station and stopped next to a long line of railroad cars. I didn't get a good look ahead, but I counted at least ten cars behind the one I boarded. These were jail cars, with compartments like European passenger cars, but they had no windows, and the compartment doors to the corridor were simply iron grills. Guards, mostly young army fellows, were stationed at the ends of each car.

I was put into a compartment that already had more than twenty people in it. As I walked in the door, my suitcase and bag were snatched from my hand; I was told to sit in the corner. It happened so fast I hardly had time to react. I looked around and immediately recognized my traveling companions for what they were: young thieves and criminals with a law and order all their own, who figured that everyone else was fair game. When I sat down in the corner, though, I found my bag and bundle had been put there, too.

For the most part, the thieves and common criminals I was to meet stood out quite markedly from the political prisoners, whom they despised. They had long ago learned how to make the best of situations in which they found themselves. They showed little respect for anyone, especially the guards, whom they constantly badgered and from whom they took very little abuse without retaliating in kind. Among themselves, though, they took orders from anyone strong enough to lead them.

The leader of this particular gang was a short, dark little fellow with shifty eyes black as coal. He was wearing only an undershirt and trousers, with some sort of hempen sandals on his feet. His arms and hands, even his chest where it was visible through the undershirt, were completely tattooed. Afraid of no one, he delighted in baiting the guards. At every station, he'd bang on the grill and ask for water or a smoke or something to eat. He would even outline the menu he preferred. If the guards ignored him, he'd keep it up until at last he had provoked some sort of reply.

I sat quietly in my corner, trying to guard my luggage. The thieves kept eyeing me, and eventually two of the leader's cronies crossed over to sit next to me. Then they told me to sit someplace else because there wasn't room for all of us. I was the only political prisoner in this den of thieves, so I moved. Immediately, they opened my suitcase, looked over everything, and put certain articles aside. They picked out a sweater, a few shirts, some new underwear—with a few passing remarks to amuse the crowd. Finally, they closed the suitcase and told me to go back and sit down.

They took the spoils over to the leader, who winked at them, got up, and banged at the door. When the guard came, the leader leaned out and whispered to him. The guard shook his head. I couldn't hear much over the noise of the train and the whistling and shouting among the thieves, but I gathered the leader wanted to make some sort of deal—my clothes for food. "A nice clean job in broad daylight", I thought to myself. Yet there was no use complaining to the guard; I'd be in this compartment for a while at least, and there was no telling what revenge the thieves might take.

At length, the guard walked away, seemingly unconvinced. A little later, though, two other guards came to the door, and the leader handed them the bundle of my clothes. After our next stop, he began to lean out the door anxiously, sticking his head through the bars and straining around, looking up and down the corridor for the two guards with whom he'd made the deal. At last they came down the corridor with their arms full of bread, bologna, fish, tobacco, a few packages of cigarettes, and some butter.

Immediately, clean jackets and shirts appeared miraculously from nowhere. They were spread on the bench to keep the food from getting dirty. The leader sat down, took out a knife (strictly forbidden), and began to cut the bread up into assigned portions, with a little bologna or fish and some butter for each. He himself got the lion's share, naturally. Nobody looked in my direction; there was no sign that I so much as existed.

After they had devoured everything in sight, they began to yell for a bucket of water. A guard brought it. The leader himself took the tin cup that came with the bucket, then handed the bucket around so the rest could drink from it. Afterward, some of the men took out cards and began to play, settling down into little groups. The leader, as he lit a cigarette, happened to look at me over the flame. Then, as if performing a great act of mercy, he picked up a piece of stale bread and sent it to me by messenger with the remark, "Give that to that dirty Fascist!" By this time I was so mad I would have liked to refuse, but I was also famished. I took the bread and ate it, greedily enough. They all laughed, then ignored me completely.

It was gradually getting dark now, and I sat in the corner staring into the dim light, partly fascinated by the novelty of it all, yet uneasy among this gang of thieves. Torn by the twin emotions of anxiety and curiosity, wondering what would come next, I began to pray. Again, I put my trust entirely in God. I finally dozed off, tired and hungry after a day of strange experiences, with the thieves still swearing loudly at one another over their card games.

Early the next morning, the train halted somewhere in a railroad yard. We sat listening to the clanging and banging of trains, the sharp hisses of steam and air-brakes, the constant hustle and bustle of the yards. Suddenly, we heard the sharp slap, slap, slap of soldiers marching in the German goose-step style. Immediately, the thieves knew where we were. "Here they come," they said, "the guards of Vologda!"

The troops came along at a smart pace, in snappy khaki uniforms with special decorations, high leather boots, and round kepis with blue tops and red rims. Within moments, they were on the train, and an officer spoke in stern, commanding tones: "Prepare to detrain, keep order and absolutely no talking! You will be transferred under guard, and any violation of these orders while under transfer will be severely punished!"

We were marched off the train in single file through the station, until we came to another cordon of Vologda guards standing, with rifles and machine guns at the ready, in the station courtyard. As we were being formed up, a prisoner from one of the other cars noticed that I had no shoes. He slipped me a pair of hemp slippers, whispering, "Here, put these on!" While I was tying them up with the string, the order was given to march. The road itself was rough, especially near the railroad station, and I was grateful for the slippers. We were marched off almost at a trot, and the guards, some of them with dogs on leashes, held us to that tempo all the way to the famous Vologda transit prison, an old building in a city that itself is a very ancient town.

The check-in procedures at Vologda were different from those in Moscow prisons. The guards of Vologda were completely sure of themselves. Once they took a group of prisoners, they never bothered to count them again; they just handed over the group and the documents to the prison authorities. According to prison lore, these guards had never lost a prisoner. Many had tried to escape and were either hauled down by the dogs or shot. The guards at Vologda, therefore, were a byword among the prisoners for their efficiency and professional methods. They weren't cruel, but they were jealous of their reputation and meant to see that it was maintained.

The transit prison at Vologda is made up of big cells down in the basement, damp and dark, with walls as thick and slimy as the dungeons in old Hollywood movies. When we reached the basement, we were checked in against the documents the guards handed over to the prison authorities. We were asked our name, surname, the year we were arrested and where, the charge against us, how many years we had received in sentence and who gave the verdict, whether the verdict was rendered in court or was merely administrative. Then we were asked if we had any complaints—about the trial, about the sentence, about the treatment we had received, and so forth. Finally, we were asked if we wanted a physical. Here at Vologda the medical examination was given only if requested; your name was taken and you'd be called out later for the exam.

After we were checked in individually, we were sent off to another room and collected into groups. As soon as twenty men had been collected, we were taken to our cells. These were large rooms, perhaps a hundred feet long by thirty feet wide, with six windows, fitted with the usual iron bars and shields, high up on a long wall opposite the door. There was only one door in the room. It had a barred opening halfway up, but this had also been covered with a tin shield. The cell was a dismal-looking place, with a floor of loose wooden planks that creaked and gave way under foot.

Four big wooden beams ran down the center of the room, supporting the crossbeams of a very high ceiling. The walls were plastered and completely covered with carved and written scrawls as high as a man could reach. There were written the names and dates of those who had been here before, when they came, when they left. There were also pathetic little notes: "If you see so-and-so, tell him you saw this name"; "If you get to such-and-such a place, look up so-and-so, and tell him his son was here." To this latter note was added in another hand "and his daughter, too." The walls, in effect, were the prisoners' perennial bulletin board. Just about everyone, sooner or later, spent some time in Vologda en route to his fate. Therefore, the messages included notes like "so-and-so died in Lubianka", so that his friends or relatives might somehow be informed.

When our group reached the cell, there were already more than 150 people in it, sitting or lying on the floor, for there were no benches. At Vologda, there were all sorts of people waiting to be shipped elsewhere. In our cell, they were mostly political prisoners, but there were also forty or fifty of the thieves or criminals, bunched up together as usual in one end of the room. In fact, the large cell was really a series of little ghettos. Each nationality huddled together in one section, and the newcomers moved around until they found a congenial welcome—the Lithuanians with Lithuanians, Russians with Russians, the Caucasians and the Poles and the Lats each in their own little group.

Here at Vologda, the guards paid little attention to us. We were transients waiting for transfer elsewhere, so the discipline wasn't too strict. Groups might stay here anywhere from a day to six months, depending on when they arrived. For it was here at Vologda that the *étappes*, or work brigades, were formed for the various camps and various regions. Sometimes, if an *étappe* was something special, it might take a long time to form. On the other hand, it might be formed within a day of a group's arrival.

Such conditions of constant turnover and lax discipline were tailor-made for the thieves, who had an organization all their own into which they were welcomed everywhere. Half an hour after we arrived, five tattooed thugs from the far end of the cell made a tour of the place. "What have you got there? Let's see!" they said, as they inspected the newcomers and made us open our luggage, almost as if they were customs clerks. If anyone was wearing good clothes, he would be told to take them off and exchange them for old clothes. But if a newcomer was wearing old clothes, the thieves would insist on seeing his bag.

It was hot in the prison, and everyone was standing around in shorts or trousers, stripped to the waist, trying to avoid the least exertion. The heat, and the consequent lack of interest on most people's part to take any action, made the thieves' job just that much easier. As they approached me, I looked around for assistance; my neighbors looked away. So this "commission" took what the thieves on the train had missed, and by the end of their tour of the cell they had collected quite a pile from the newcomers.

This day, however, they were in for a surprise. A stocky young fellow rose up, soldier-like, in the middle of the cell and called out in a commanding voice: "*Bratsi!* (Brothers!) Let's remember who we are and who we have been! I was a major of a tank division, not afraid of bombs, or enemy guns, or any danger whatsoever. I'm in here now, but I'm still a man! You, most of you, are soldiers from the front. Are you going to let yourselves be scared by these thieves, these bandits? All of you who have been robbed by these jackals and are men enough to follow, come with me! *Now!*"

In one spontaneous movement, the crowd followed him down to the thieves' corner and backed the criminals up against the wall. "Come on, now," shouted the soldier, "everyone get his stuff!" At that, the thieves jumped in to save their plunder and a fight broke out. Shouts filled the air, curses and cries of pain, and immediately the guards rushed in with drawn guns, then more guards, and finally the commandant himself.

When order was restored, the commandant ordered everybody to line up along one wall. When he asked what had happened, the major described heatedly and vehemently the treatment we newcomers had received from the thieves. The other prisoners chimed in their agreement. To his credit, the commandant immediately sorted out the thieves' ringleaders and herded them out. Under the major's charge, the belongings confiscated by the thieves were returned to their owners. Finally, the command of the room was taken over by the major and other political prisoners, instead of the thieves.

We were all the gainers. Formerly, as usually happened, the thieves had been in charge of distributing the food and had taken the lion's share. Such things went on everywhere, to judge from the prisoners' stories. The thieves, always organized, would terrorize the unorganized political prisoners in any situation, unless they were stopped.

Here at Vologda, even more so than elsewhere, conversation and the exchange of information were the order of the day. With the constant turnover of prisoners, everyone hoped that if he himself didn't meet friends at his destination, someone in the room at least would be able to pass the word of his whereabouts. One of the greatest talkers, though, was an officer named Bulatov, who had served with General Vlasov, the defender of Leningrad who went over to Hitler along with his whole army. Bulatov smoked a pipe from morning until night, and the more he puffed the more horrible his tale became. When he got started, everybody within earshot listened.

He told us one day how, after Vlasov's army had deserted to Hitler, they had appealed to the Führer for a free hand in fighting against Russia. Hitler wouldn't agree. Instead, the troops were sent into Poland, Czechoslovakia, and the Balkan states as punishment (revenge) brigades to subdue prisoner insurrections. They were also used as executioners in the penal camps, especially against the Jews.

Bulatov's tales of horror, however, were never finished. They were cut short, as was our stay at Vologda, by the announcement that we were to prepare for an *étappe*. Immediately, everybody collected all his little possessions and tied them into a bundle. There were last-minute farewells and hasty messages to other prisoners. We were off on a ride to nobody knew where, but we were certain it would be a long one. Many might never come back.

The guards led us out into the courtyard, where we mingled with prisoners from other cells, looking for familiar faces or news of friends. I searched the courtyard for news of any other priests here at Vologda, but no luck. I did meet a number of Poles, though, and I was chatting with them when I was accosted by a Russian official. He seemed quite friendly, but he was less interested in me than in my valise. He asked me outright whether I'd sell it to him. It was the one a fellow Jesuit had given me in 1934 when I left for Rome, but it was still in excellent condition.

The Poles around me began immediately to jabber away in Polish, offering advice. "It's a good valise; you ought to get a lot of bread for it on the way. Don't sell it now." The Russian waited patiently for a lull in our Polish consultations, then said, "What about it?" I appreciated the advice and I was sorely tempted to hang onto the valise for the bread it might bring on a long journey eastward, but I also thought about the train ride to Vologda and how my bag and bundle had been snatched by the thieves and ransacked. I knew the same thing could easily happen again; this time I might not be lucky enough to get it back. "But if I give you this," I asked the Russian, "what will I use?" "We'll fix that," he said. "Just wait here a minute."

He disappeared into one of the prison buildings, and came back with a canvas sack with canvas handles. "How about this?" he said eagerly. "Okay", I said. "Fine," he said, "how much do I owe you?" I knew that he could simply have taken the valise if he wanted to, so I appreciated his offer. "It's all yours", I said. "You don't owe me anything. I'd probably lose it anyhow." "You don't want any money?" he asked. "No, what would I do with money? They would just take it away from me at the labor camp, anyway." "Wait!" he said, holding up his hand, "wait right here a minute." He dashed off with the valise into the building again and came out with a full loaf of bread. He apologized for not being able to get more, then thanked me again for my generosity. And so, there at Vologda, my American Jesuit valise enlisted in the Russian Army; from that time on, I traveled light.

Instead of saving the bread for the journey, I broke it into pieces and passed it around among the group of friendly Poles. They accepted the bread gladly enough but remonstrated with me for letting my valise go so cheaply. "Ah," they said, "why did you do that? His suitcase might have been worth at least half a dozen loaves of bread on this trip." "Well," I said, "what's done is done. Now I won't have to worry about having it stolen."

As soon as we arrived at Vologda, I had applied for a pair of shoes. It was only now, when we were ready to leave, that they brought me a pair—old, and three or four sizes too large, but shoes nevertheless. As I knelt down to tie them on, I heard the guard shout "*Stanovis!*" (Line up!). The lines were already moving, and someone handed me my canvas satchel as I caught up. Off we marched, waving to those still in the prison, who stuck their heads and hands through the windows to wave and shout encouragement to us. The guards of Vologda were again our escorts, and once more we were hustled through the streets of Vologda at a trot and down to the railway station.

The siding was lined from end to end with a long string of boxcars. We could tell the cars in front were already loaded, for the guards were stationed around them and the doors were closed. Our group was lined up along the siding to wait for the officials to assign us. The sun was terrifically hot for the middle of June; even the dogs with the guards felt the heat. They stood there with their tongues out, slobbering and panting heavily, but still on the alert. If a prisoner stooped to put down his luggage, or shifted from foot to foot in the line, the dogs would immediately swing around on the leash to look at him. At last the officials came, called us out of line by name, and assigned us to our cars. One by one, we picked up our precious little bundles of spare clothing or crusts of bread and climbed into the cars.

These were strictly prison cars, used for the transfer of prisoners from Vologda into Siberia. Basically, they were boxcars with beams nailed across the car at both ends and covered with planks to serve as bunks. There were two decks, one above the other, and you had to decide quickly whether you wanted an upper bunk so you could peer out one of the four little windows at the top of the car, or a lower bunk so you'd be near the floor and able to move around more freely. There were also double-decker bunks, much narrower, along the walls on either side of the car doors. In the center of the car was a little stove with a chimney through the roof, which we definitely didn't need in the June heat. The only other furnishing in the car was a *parasha* near one of the doors. On both ends of the car, outside the prisoners' section, were small platforms for the guards who would accompany us the whole trip.

In the cars, the prisoners sorted themselves out, trying to find traveling companions or acquaintances, if possible, and picking out a place to settle down for the long road ahead. Of the thirty persons crowded into the car, ten were common criminals, the rest were political prisoners. But the orderly for our car, assigned by the guards, was a criminal named Volkov. The thieves always seemed to be a privileged class—at least in the sense they had the guards buffaloed—so they generally wound up in command of the situation.

Volkov passed on the instructions he had been given: if there were any attempts to escape, or any signs in the car of an attempted escape—loose planks, a loosening of the wire screens over the window, or any tampering with the door— the guilty parties would be punished. The punishment was not specified, but presumably it meant another prison sentence or perhaps a longer stretch in the labor camps. The rest of us listened to the instructions half-heartedly; such warnings were so common they hardly bore repeating.

All during the sweltering afternoon, the train sat on the siding. As soon as we were inside, though, the doors had been closed, and by now it was stifling hot in the car. The men were soon sitting around in various stages of undress. I chose a place on the upper berth at the opposite end of the car from where the thieves had gathered. My traveling companions were three young soldiers who had been arrested in Germany for going AWOL.

I introduced myself as an American, and they plied me endlessly with questions about America. They had been part of the Red Army units that had joined up with the Ameri-

cans in Germany; they constantly sang the praises of the
American soldiers and couldn't hear enough about life in
America, which astonished and fascinated them. Others
crowded around to hear about America, and pretty soon I was
talking to more than half the prisoners in the car.

Once more, the thieves were a law unto themselves. The
young ones stuck to Volkov like chicks to a mother hen,
cleaned his bunk, swept the floor, washed his dishes, and did
whatever else they were told. Otherwise, they were a rather
unruly lot. Their noisy card and dice games usually ended in
a fight that only Volkov could settle; his decision went un-
challenged. If the young ones didn't like it, they got battered
around a bit, so they generally accepted his decision without
a word.

Despite the fact we had been promised three meals a day,
the kitchen cars were at the end of the train, and the meals
were brought only when we stopped long enough to allow
the food to be carried from car to car. Sometimes we'd get a
double portion of bread, which we were told must last for
two days; most of the time we got our soup and *kasha* together, late in the afternoon, and we knew there'd be no supper and no stops that night. Water, too, was brought just once
a day, so everyone drank as much as he could. Some of the
soldiers still had their canteens, which they filled, and one
bucket of water was left in the car all day.

Hygiene, of course, even in the most rudimentary sense of
the word, was completely out of the question. Cleaning your
teeth was impossible, fingernails were bitten off to keep the
dirt from accumulating under them. Whenever fresh water
was brought, we'd wash out our eyes with a handful scooped
from the bucket to relieve the smarting from the dust in the
air and the salt of our own sweat. It was on journeys like this
that parasites abounded; after a few days on the road, every-

one was continually scratching absentmindedly at some part of his anatomy. We also suffered from sores on our feet, backs, and buttocks, for there was no room for exercise and no opportunity to get out of the cars.

Somehow the thieves had learned we were headed for Krasnoyarsk, a large town on the Yenisei River crossed by the Trans-Siberian Railway, about midway across the vast expanse of Siberia. It may be eighteen hundred miles as the crow flies from Moscow to Krasnoyarsk, but it's more like twenty-five hundred miles as the tracks are laid. Passenger trains make the trip from Krasnoyarsk to Moscow in less than four days, about the same time and distance as from Chicago to Los Angeles. The same trip, however, took us over two weeks. If you consider that Vologda is near Moscow, and that Krasnoyarsk is less than halfway to the Pacific border of Russia across Siberia, you begin to get some idea of the huge land mass of the U.S.S.R.

When we found out we were headed for Krasnoyarsk, we tried to figure out the towns we'd have to pass on the Trans-Siberian Railway—Kirov, Perm, Sverdlovsk, Kurgan, Petropavlosk, Omsk, Novosibirsk, Tomsk, Achinsk, and Krasnoyarsk. Those who knew anything about the towns would describe them so we could recognize them as we passed—or, really, just to have something to talk about. Much of our time was spent standing on the planks and craning our necks at the little windows near the top of the car to get a view of the countryside. The windows were never unoccupied, even at night.

For hours, there was nothing to see but open space, mainly marshlands with thick, rough hunks of grass called *taiga*, not hilly at all, but rolling away to the far-off mountains in the distance. Now and then, there would be a small shanty for the railroad crews who maintained this vital and only railroad link between the east and west. Towns were almost nonexistent. Those that did exist were practically all on the railroad line itself, or along the rivers and waterways that crisscross this part of the country everywhere. Except that it was so marshy, Siberia in 1946 reminded me of what the great American West must have looked like when the first railroad tracks were laid.

The towns usually consisted of one street, very muddy, lined with typical old Russian houses of logs or rough-hewn planks with plaster between the chinks. There were vegetable gardens around each home, and the land stretched away in all directions, but little of it was then under cultivation. We stopped only at the larger towns. It was during these stops that we received our meals, sometimes getting our complete daily ration all at once—six hundred grams of bread, a half liter of soup, and two hundred grams of *kasha*.

Volkov was in charge of distributing the meals, and he had his "boys" pass out the food. Each car was given only about ten tureens and wooden spoons and three tin cups. We used them in turn. Volkov always served the political prisoners first, leveling off each ladleful with a knife to make sure there was no excess. What was left over in the kettle after this careful measuring, of course, went to him and the "boys". The political prisoners protested. They wanted him to rotate the order of distribution, beginning with the political prisoners one day and the thieves the next. Volkov refused.

Things came to a head one day when we had stopped for dinner. The protest became so heated that a fight developed. Volkov and his "boys" got out their knives; the other prisoners tore up planks from the bunks. The doors, however, were open while the meals were served, so the guards stepped in quickly. After that, distribution of the food alternated, and we lived what might be best described as an armed truce.

For the most part, the monotony of the countryside was matched by the monotony of the trip itself. We had nothing to do, the cars were uncomfortable, and after the first few days conversation ran out. Everyone felt dirty, hot, and dusty; the doors weren't snug, and there were cracks in the boards along the wall and in the heavy planking in the floor. By the time we reached Krasnoyarsk, everyone was black from the wind-blown dirt and soot. There were white holes in our faces where our red eyes peered out.

Early in July, we reached the end of the line. The countryside became hilly, the slopes were covered with thick forests of tall pines, evergreens, and hemlock. The railroad right-of-way led through many tunnels. It was early in the morning when we reached Krasnoyarsk, and everyone jammed the four little windows for a glimpse of the city on the Yenisei. The river actually divides the town in half, and there had been no bridge across the river except the railroad trestle. Communication between the two parts of the city was achieved by boat or ferry. The city itself, an important rail juncture at the head of the Yenisei, stretches out along both banks, something like St. Louis along the Mississippi or the two Kansas Cities on the Missouri.

We sat in the station at Krasnoyarsk almost an hour. Up ahead we could hear the sounds of prisoners being unloaded, dogs barking, and soldiers shouting commands. At last our door opened, the roll was called, and we jumped down one by one. My legs were weak from lack of exercise; they seemed made of rubber as we lined up in files of four. The guards of Vologda, who had accompanied us on the whole trip, herded us off again at that familiar quick pace. We stumbled along so quickly that one of the old shoes I was wearing fell off. I tried to get it, but the guard shouted at me to keep moving, my own bundle got in my way, and I lost the shoe.

We didn't go through the town itself but took the back roads to the transit prison outside of town. This was simply a large group of barracks in the open fields, surrounded by a double row of barbed wire. We marched through the prison gates to a large open compound in the middle of the barracks, where we were told to sit down and stay in our groups and not to mingle with the other prisoners. After the fast pace of the march, on top of the more than two weeks of inactivity, we were glad enough to stretch out on the ground.

As I sat there drinking in the fresh air, another prisoner crept up to me with my shoe. He winked at me and muttered, "Tie it tighter next time", then slipped back to his own group. He had braved a reprimand from the guards for his effort, and I was touched.

Here at last we got a bath and a haircut. Then we stood around, naked, but feeling human again, while our clothes were steamed and disinfected. With so many prisoners, the process took quite a while, but as each group finished they got a kettle of soup. There were no spoons or tureens available, however, so some of the prisoners produced from their bundles old tin cans they had scavenged in the railroad yards, and we all shared those. They were rusty and leaky, but the first man shined his can with his cap or sleeve, licked it clean when he was finished, and passed it on to the next.

One of the Poles in our group, a happy-go-lucky fellow named Andre, gave me his can when he had finished. When I came back with my portion, he told me to eat it as fast as I could and follow him. He walked to the other side of the group, took off his coat, pulled a different shirt from his satchel, and went up for another portion. He gobbled it down and gave me the can again, but I was afraid to try it. I'd left my bundle with the group, so I had no change of clothing. "Go ahead," said Andre, "we're all new here and they can't tell us apart."

I was hungry enough to try it no matter what the consequences. When I stuck out my can, the orderly filled it without even looking at me. I was so surprised, I almost dropped the can on the ground. After I finished this portion, Andre went back and worked the game again. By this time, though, the kettle was getting low, and the orderly was getting suspicious. I figured I'd be crowding my luck if I tried it again.

After the meal, a series of long tables were set up in the compound. One by one, our names were called out, and we presented ourselves at the table to answer the routine questions, then get the once-over from the "board", the officials of the transit camp and representatives of the camps up north who were down here "hiring" talent. It was terribly hot in the compound, and many of the prisoners had taken their shirts off to enjoy the sunlight. As I watched the processing, I was struck by how thin and emaciated everyone looked; I could hardly tell the difference between one man and the next. The experts at the table, though, knew what they were looking for and signified their choices to the camp officials.

Suddenly, I heard the commandant call, "Lypinski!" I went to the table; they asked my name and surname. "Lypinski," I said, "Wladimir Martinovich." "What's this other name here?" said the commandant. "Ciszek", I said, and tried to explain. He asked me the year I had been arrested, when I had been sentenced, and on what charge. When I told him "58:6", he looked at the paper again. "Ah, a Vatican spy", he said. "You go over there."

I reported to a table where secretaries were filling in the various processing documents. They were prisoners, too, most of them former schoolteachers or bookkeepers. They had been kept here at Krasnoyarsk, instead of being sent on to

the labor camps, to help with the paperwork—a big problem
at this center from which prisoners were assigned to camps up
north. One of the secretaries, who had heard the commandant call me a "Vatican spy", was looking at me curiously. A
young Jew from Lvov, he began talking to me in Polish out
the side of his mouth all the while he was writing down the
data in his papers.

"You're slated for hard labor in Norilsk", he told me.
"Aren't you a priest?" I nodded. "Listen," he said, "you have
a medical exam coming up, and one of the main doctors is a
Pole from Lida (a town near Albertin). Dr. Barovski. Do you
know him?" I shook my head. "Well, remember his name and
try to get to him when you take your physical. Let him know
you're a priest. He may be able to help you get an easier job or
even stay here at Krasnoyarsk instead of going north. I'll
probably see you again around the camp, but good luck!"

By this time the next prisoner was approaching his table,
and I had to move on. The guards immediately shoved me
into line for the medical exam, which was held in a tent, a sort
of canvas extension of the prison hospital. The flaps were
open, but there was very little breeze, and the air in the tent
was pungent with the smell of alcohol and ether. Most of the
doctors, too, were prisoners who had been kept here at
Krasnoyarsk because they were needed.

Each of them took a patient in turn as the line passed
through. I kept trying to spot the Polish doctor from Lida.
Finally, I asked one of the medical attendants, "Who's Dr.
Barovski?" I looked where he pointed, then stalled around
trying to get into the doctor's line. When he finished his next
patient, the man ahead of me started toward him; I stepped
around him and slipped toward the doctor's cubicle. The man
swore at me under his breath, but I didn't even bother to turn
my head. I just kept moving toward the doctor.

Dr. Barovski looked up at me and said in heavily accented Russian, "What ails you?" Although the doctors were prisoners, they were supervised by Russian women doctors and there were guards standing nearby, so I had to watch my step. "Heart trouble", I said. Dr. Barovski began thumping my chest and listening with his stethoscope. "Does this hurt here?" he said in Russian. "Or here?" "No," I said in Polish, "right here!"

The doctor looked up at me quickly, then glanced around to see who was nearby. When he turned back, I added in Latin, "*Polonis sacerdos.*" He nodded that he understood. With that, he began a lengthy, time-consuming examination, going over me inch by inch, muttering all the time in Polish under his breath as if he was talking to himself, but loud enough so that I could hear. He asked me where I was from, and I said, "Albertin." He said he had lived not far away in the town of Lida.

"I'm going to prescribe some drugs for you," said the doctor, "so you can go into the dispensary with my secretary here." I followed the young secretary into the dispensary. First he gave me three or four glasses of cold water, because I was beginning to feel weak from the broiling sun of the courtyard and the stifling atmosphere of the medical tent. He also gave me some vitamin pills to take with the water. Talking quickly, so the guard wouldn't be suspicious if we stayed inside too long, he told me he was a priest who had been assigned at the doctor's request to help him in the camp.

"The doctor", he said, "will try to keep you, too. Good luck!"

As soon as I came out of the dispensary, a guard took me to a large temporary barrack with few windows and rows of double-decker bunks, where the transient prisoners were quartered while the groups were formed for the prison camps upriver. The few windows there were in the barrack were shut tight, the atmosphere was close and stifling, and the odor was foul. I was dismayed to find that I was one of the few political prisoners in the room. The rest were mostly young hoodlums and punks, with one or two older thieves among them whom they idolized and followed.

I hadn't been there more than a few minutes before one of the thieves managed to rob what little bread I had squirreled away, a shirt, and a pair of socks from my canvas bag. I was furious. I began to make it plain to everyone within hearing distance that I thought this continual thievery was intolerable, that the thieves were a prisoner's worst enemy. One of their leaders heard me raving and sauntered over. "What did you say?" he said with a smirk. I said, "The worst people to meet up with are these thieves."

He was in a playful mood, standing there in front of me, tapping his foot on the floor and juggling something back and forth in his hands. "Ah," he said, "you think these thieves should have their heads cut off, hey?" "No, but I just want them to know who they're stealing from!" He leered at me. "You somebody special?" His attitude infuriated me all the more. "No, I'm nobody special. I'm a prisoner just like any-one else. That's the trouble. We're all prisoners here! We're all in the same boat! If they want to steal, they can steal from the prison or steal from the Russians. Why do they want to go around stealing from prisoners? We've all got enough trouble already without stealing from each other!"

He stopped grinning and stared at me for a moment, then shrugged his shoulders and walked away. He went around among the young thieves, talking now to this one, now to that one. I was afraid some real trouble was brewing, but in a few minutes he was back, smiling, with my clothes—the bread had long since been eaten. As he handed them to me, he said with a smirk, "Here, I'd change my mind about thieves if I were you!" I said nothing, just took the clothes and stared at him, unsmiling. Finally, he shrugged again and walked away. But I was never bothered again as long as I stayed in that barrack.

That evening after supper the guard called out my name, took me to the infirmary, and put me into one of the little cubicles. He stood outside. Dr. Barovski was seated at his desk; in the cubicle with him at another table was a young nurse who looked at me rather suspiciously. The doctor motioned to me not to talk, then told me to strip to the waist. After he examined me a while, he told the nurse to prepare such-and-such a medicine. He told me to sit down while he took my blood pressure.

When the nurse went to the cabinet to prepare the medicine, Dr. Barovski whispered: "I can't get you on the list to stay here. I tried to pull some strings, but it's simply impossible. I think they're getting suspicious of me because I've been holding so many people here. I called you tonight to tell you the facts. I'm terribly sorry." By this time, the girl was back with the medicine. She gave me a few pills to take and a bottle to take along; while she watched, I swallowed the pills and left.

In the Hold of the Tug Stalin

Early the next morning, it was announced throughout the barracks that an *étappe* was being formed for Norilsk. We were told to pack our things and report outside to the prison compound. The whole area was jammed with prisoners. Many of them had been here for months, waiting for a sufficient number of trainloads to arrive in Krasnoyarsk to make the shipment of prisoners up the river "economical". Our trainload must have filled up the quota, for we left within two days of our arrival.

Once again, the long commission tables were set out in the courtyard. The officials began to call out names for the various groups. At last we set off in a rather straggling, disorderly file toward the Yenisei. At the river bank, I turned to look back. Down the road came a huge army of prisoners, more than two thousand men shuffling along with their little bundles over their shoulders or slung across their backs. Down on the river, a row of barges had been lined up along the bank with gangways reaching out from shore into the holds. As the army of prisoners reached the river, groups were stretched out along the bank, surrounded by guards, until their turn came to be loaded aboard.

The officials again called out the names, and the prisoners reported to a table where name, surname, destination (Norilsk), charge, and sentence would be checked once more against the documents on the table. Then, in groups of ten or twenty, they were led down the river bank by the guards, over the gangways, and loaded into the holds. The guards and dogs stayed with them all the way so they wouldn't jump into the river and escape—or drown.

All through the long day, I sat there watching the procedures. My name wasn't called until evening. Then I was checked through and joined a special group to one side of the table. Instead of being taken to the barges, we were taken to the tow ship *Stalin* that was to pull the barges up the river. We went onto the gangplank and up on deck, then were herded through a small hatch down into the hold of the ship.

The *Stalin* had two large holds, one in front of the engine room and one at the stern. Our group was loaded into the stern hold. It was a large, dark vault, with curving timber sides covered with iron plates on the outside. There was a false floor of rough planking raised off the keel, extending about ten feet on each side of the propeller shaft. At the wall, the planks ended, and angled wooden beams ran up three or four feet along the curvature of the hull for the bilge to spill over. Across the engine-room bulkhead at the foot of the hatch stairs was a long shelf of rough planks fixed a few feet off the floor. A similar platform ran across the stern. Down the center of the hold ran a row of thick beams to support the deck above. On either side of these pillars was another raised platform of rough planks. These were our bunks.

As we came down the hatchway, a group of us Poles stuck together near the base of the stairs along the forward bulkhead. As usual, everyone tried to stay with someone he knew; we had talked it over on the river bank and decided that the first one down into the hold would try to reserve space for the others. The thieves also hung together; they took over the bunks along the stern. The other prisoners filled up the center bunks, and some groups even decided to make camp along the slanting boards against the outside hull. The guards stayed topside. Two of them were stationed at the top of the hatchway stairs, and down at the stern end of the hold there was a trap door in the deck through which the guards could observe the prisoners. Two more guards were stationed there.

It was now the second of July. The sun was broiling hot, and the hold soon became almost intolerable. The timbers of the hull were covered with a tar or rosin of some sort, which gave off a pungent odor. The only ventilation was the hatch itself, the trap door over the stern, and the practically useless portholes high up near the deck. Practically everyone undressed, and the air in the hold was so close you could taste rather than smell the odor of sweat mixed with the tobacco smoke and the rosin from the planking.

The one good feature of being aboard the *Stalin* was that the galley was also on board. The meals were served regularly and on time. Between seven and eight o'clock in the morning we had breakfast—six hundred grams of bread plus hot water. Between 12:00 and 1:30 we had dinner, a half liter of soup. Then at six o'clock, supper. Aboard the *Stalin* this was a special kind of *kasha*, a yellow porridge popular in Russia called *pshonnaya kasha*, made with corn rather than oats or some other cereal.

There were four hundred men packed into the hold, with almost no room to move about without falling over someone else. For those four hundred men, we got fifty tureens to serve the meal; we ate in turns. And, as usual, the guards had put the thieves in charge of distributing the food. From our vantage point at the foot of the steps, we had a perfect view of the proceedings in the stern. We noticed that when the leader stirred the soup ostentatiously with the ladle, to prove he was mixing it up thoroughly, the ladle never went deeper into the kettle than a foot from the bottom. The thick soup stayed there. Of course, the political prisoners were always served first and therefore always got thin soup.

For two days, we sat in that sweltering hold and waited. The decks of the *Stalin* and the barges were being loaded with machinery, rails, hardware, cattle, and produce for the trip up the river. By the time they were fully loaded, we could see that the barge decks were nearly awash, the holds completely under water. On the third day, the engines on the *Stalin* started up. They were just the other side of our bulkhead, and the noise was terrific. Moreover, the oil and exhaust fumes were overpowering, the vibration was so bad my eyes wouldn't focus—all the images were blurred—and our speech was throaty in response to the vibration.

We soon had a headache all the time from the fumes and

the heat. The bulkhead became unbearably hot. We were forced to climb down off our bunks and lie on the floor to breathe the cooler air along the keel planks. As a result, there was very little conversation. Everyone huddled on the floor, trying to ignore the heat, the noise, the vibration—and the splitting headache.

After the ship began to move up river, it rocked constantly. The river currents would catch hold of the barges and swing them from one side of the river to the other, and the *Stalin* would heel over from side to side under the pull of the tow-lines. Some of the men got sick, which did nothing to improve the atmosphere or the air down in the hold.

By the end of the first week, the political prisoners, who outnumbered the thieves two to one, had organized. One day when the soup was brought down, a group of them went over to the thieves and told them to take a seat. "You can watch us for a change to see we don't make a mistake, but we're going to distribute the soup today." The thieves told them to get back where they belonged. The politicals didn't move. "We want the soup distributed equally and justly", they said. "That food is the only thing that keeps us alive, and you bloodsuckers are getting the best parts of it and giving us practically water. Now stand aside!"

At that, the leader of the thieves smashed the spokesman for the politicals in the face and knocked him into a heap on the planks. In almost the same motion, he reached for his knife. A full-scale riot broke out. From all over the hold, politicals began streaming toward the stern, pinning the thieves against the wall. I could see a flashing of knives among the thieves, and some of the political prisoners began to tear up planks and wade in on the run. The shouts of the rioters were mixed with the screams of the wounded. Blood began to spatter on the plankings and stream down the faces

of the rioters. Those who fell were simply trampled underfoot.

Within seconds, the guards were down the stairs, crying
out to the men to break it up or they would shoot. It was
useless. The words couldn't even be heard over the noise of
the motors and the shouts of the crowd. An officer ran down
the stairs and also shouted in vain. Then he shouted a command, the soldiers unlimbered their machine guns and fired
from the hips. Bullets slammed into the timbers above the
heads of the rioters, ricocheted off the wall, and went ringing
around the hull. Those not engaged in the fight immediately
dove for the deck and hugged the planks.

When the first burst produced no effect, the soldiers lowered their sights. The bullets stopped hammering into the
timbers and began to thud into the crowd itself. Men dropped
as if they had been poleaxed; one whole rank of rioters went
down like cornstalks before a scythe. That stopped the riot.
The soldiers came to the foot of the stairs and lined everyone
up against the wall, their backs to the guns and hands high
above their heads.

Then the first-aid crew came tumbling down the hatchway
to haul out the dead and the moaning wounded. How many
they carried out of the hold I have no way of knowing; the
rest of us were facing the hold walls with machine-gun
muzzles at our backs. After they cleared the floor of bodies,
the first-aid crew washed down the planking to get rid of the
blood and scattered disinfectant all over the floors and the
walls. At last, the guards told us to return to our places in
absolute silence. They themselves stayed on the stairway all
night with machine guns at the ready, permitting no one to
move, except to go to the toilet barrel one at a time.

In about an hour, a commission of the ship's officers and
some of the guard officers came down into the hold. They

asked very few questions. They walked up and down in front of the bunks, looking over the crowd, from time to time saying curtly to one of the prisoners, "You! Get up!" The men they singled out were taken upstairs for questioning, then transferred to one of the barges for the rest of the trip.

Actually, the affair was a black mark against the officials themselves; they would be held accountable for the prisoners they had lost. They received a certain number at Krasnoyarsk, and they were to deliver that number at Norilsk—or else have a good explanation why they were short. These prisoners had been sentenced to hard labor, they had been transported and fed all the way across Russia, and they were expected to prove useful where they were wanted; the shooting of so many would weigh heavily on the careers of guards and officers alike. They would have to prove they used guns only as a last resort.

Few of us got any sleep that night. The memory of the slaughter was too fresh, the scenes of stabbings and the sound of bullets thudding into flesh were too vivid to be driven out of mind. After that, though, the food was distributed justly. With so many gone, there was even enough food to give everyone an extra portion at least every second day. The guards remained on the stairwell for a few days, but afterward they returned topside. Life settled down again to the monotonous clanking of the motors, the pitching of the ship, and the day-long attempt to ignore the headache caused by the noise and fumes.

We reached Dudinka on the morning of July 22. At that time, the town was nothing but a river bank with houses strung along it and wharves built out into the river. Afterward, a big complex of port facilities was built there by workers from the prison camps, but then the water was so shallow the *Stalin* couldn't even pull into shore to unload us at the wharves. We couldn't even tell when we arrived, except that the motors slowed and we heard the heavy rattling of chains up on deck. The winches screamed, there was a loud thunk, the splash of anchors. The motors revved up briefly to set the anchor, then coughed into silence.

Immediately, we began to feel the cold. As the furnace died, the hold of the *Stalin* took on the chill of an icebox. We sat there waiting, putting on what extra clothes we had, listening to the shouted commands on deck and the splashing of the water against the hull. After a while, we heard the sound of oars slapping the surface of the river, and a loud hail to the *Stalin*. At last we heard the cranking sound of gangways being lowered and a final, uneven, and muffled shriek from the *Stalin's* whistle—the signal to begin unloading.

A troop of soldiers appeared at the hatch, then came halfway down the stairwell to line it on either side. An officer walked down the middle of the ranks to address us: "This is Dudinka! You will line up and leave the boat, in order, in small groups of ten. Line up, line up! Any sign of trouble or attempted escape means instant death. My men have standing orders to shoot anyone who gets out of line for any reason!"

As we came up the hatchway, blinking in the daylight, we were amazed to find that it was snowing! We had left the sweltering heat of Krasnoyarsk just two weeks earlier. On deck, in the full face of the wind, the air was so cold it took the breath right out of us. We were forced to gasp for air. Everyone immediately began to pile on anything left in his bundle of clothing. It looked like a Chinese fire drill, with everyone trying to stand on the lee side of everyone else. "My God," said a man next to me, "it's winter! What'll we do?"

The water of the Yenisei was gray and rough, the air swirling off the water was cold with a peculiar biting bitterness that cut right through as much clothing as we had. The soldiers around us were already dressed in long greatcoats reaching to their ankles, with collars turned up against the wind. The skies were cloudy, but somehow the heavens seemed far, far away, and the mottled gray vault above us looked almost infinitely high.

My first view of the famous Siberia came from the deck of the steamer *Stalin*. The land stretching away from the river bank was hilly and rolling, but the ground itself was bare, with only small patches of shrubbery or gorse. On the other side of the river, more than two miles wide at this point, I could see just a distant blue contour of rolling hills. Way off in the distance, beyond the near bank, I could see something like the camp at Krasnoyarsk, a gaggle of barracks surrounded by the black etchings of barbed wire.

Dudinka itself was just a long line of log houses looking barren in the gray-blue landscape, straggling over the hill and down along the river. The only big building in the town was on the hill overlooking the river. It was the Port Authority terminal, which commanded the wharves and the railroad yard. Out north, toward the sea, there were big steamers anchored in the river, and along the near bank to the north was a big black mountain of coal for the ships.

We stepped down the gangplank in groups of ten and into a rowboat. My legs were rubbery again from lack of exercise and numb from the cold. It was like trying to walk when your feet are asleep. We were rowed to shore, unloaded, and the boat returned immediately for another group in a continuous shuttle operation. Those who landed were taken in tow by the guards, led aside about two hundred yards up the bank, and told to sit down.

The snow was stopping, but the wind was out of the north and cold. Dudinka is well inside the Arctic Circle, the polar wind is channeled down the river by the banks and the twin rows of hills. When the wind is fully out of the north, it's like being in a polar hurricane. To unload two thousand men in rowboats, ten at a time, takes a long time. After the *Stalin* was unloaded, they began to unload the barges. And all the while, we sat huddled together on the bank in the stinging cold. And this on July 22!

Coal-Loader in Dudinka

I watched the prisoners disembarking from the rowboats, slipping clumsily up the river bank. The guards kept them in strict files, as they hugged themselves and their bundles tightly to keep warm, walking with eyes down in a forlorn silence. Then, far off down the road toward town, I noticed big columns marching toward us. I watched them approach for a while, wondering where they were from and where they were going, whether they, too, were new prisoners or had been here a while. Meanwhile the tugs were nudging the unloaded barges into the bank.

Just as we were ready to leave, the columns I had seen came abreast of us—prison brigades reporting to work. They seemed to stir into life when they saw us, and as they passed alongside they saluted and shouted, "Where you from? Is so and so there? Anyone from Moscow, or Leningrad? What kind of prisoners are you?" We began shouting back. The guards were swearing and forbidding us to talk, but the prison brigades paid no attention. "When you get to camp, look up so and so! Where are they sending you? Good luck!"

The same questions and shouts were repeated again and again by each brigade as the column passed us. They were certainly a ragtag bunch, dressed in quilted coats, with hard and rough features, faces grizzled with several days' growth of beard. It was my first glimpse of men who had spent some time in a prison camp, and I must confess I thought them a rather bizarre mixtum-gatherum. Just beyond us, they turned and headed inland. Behind them, we could see other columns coming down the road in the same direction.

Finally, we were formed up and led off along the river bank ourselves. The guards were cold, even in their greatcoats, so they set us a stiff, quick pace. It was difficult at first, but after a while it felt good, as the blood began to circulate and my body warmed to the activity. We marched about two miles to reach the camp at Dudinka, a collection of weather-beaten barracks all encircled by a double row of barbed wire.

We didn't enter the camp. Instead, we were led around it, down a little cut-off road and up a hill, to a big ramshackle barn of unpainted boards, black from the weather. This, we found out later, was the processing center at Dudinka. We entered through a zone of barbed wire, then a gate. Once inside the gate, we were told to sit down in the courtyard, despite the biting wind.

Here in the courtyard, our papers were checked, one by one, by an official of the camp. Then we were turned loose to find a place for ourselves in the blackened barn. Inside there was nothing but a dirt floor and a long row of planks along the wall, not nailed into place, but just lying loosely on some crossbars; those were the bunks. There were gaping holes in the walls and roof, and it seemed colder in the barn than it was outside. This was Dudinka; we had arrived!

The first thing to do was to look around for friends. It was impossible to be a loner in the prison camps; a man either had friends to keep him going, or he didn't survive. I found my friends the Poles, and together we picked out a place along the wall where the boards fitted more snugly and the draft was somewhat less. We left one of the men to stand guard over our belongings while the rest of us went out to look for information—or for food. Actually, food was uppermost in every mind. The last meal we'd had was the bread we got on the boat that morning, long hours ago.

We stepped out of the barn to look for the orderlies from Dudinka who worked around the processing camp. We could tell immediately they had been through a lot. Their big, watery eyes seemed to start out of the sockets; they were unshaven and their teeth were bad, almost rotting. Their clothes were ill-fitting, their shoes plopped loosely on their feet as they shuffled along. They wore no socks, but instead had rags tied with string over their shoe tops and around the ankles. Some of them were bareheaded, even in the cold, and their hair had been cut so closely by the barber they looked almost shaved.

They were glad to see us and dying to know what was happening in the outside world. "At least tell us", they said, "what was happening when you were arrested. We heard the war is over, is that true? How are the people at home? How is the food?" Eager as they were to talk, they talked very little about themselves or life at Dudinka; they were much more interested in learning the news from us.

I did find out, however, that there was at least one other priest in Dudinka: Fr. Casper, a Pole and a Roman Catholic, who had had a parish in the eastern part of Poland, where he, too, was arrested for allegedly subversive activities. He had been in the camp almost a year, one of the orderlies said, and was very popular among the men. We also learned that supper was being brought up from the main camp, so we quickly returned to the barn.

The guards brought in kettles of soup and *kasha*, with clouds of steam rolling from the pots and the smell quickening every nostril. The cook himself distributed the portions.

To make sure no one got two portions, as soon as a prisoner got his tureen he was sent outside to eat. But you can't beat the prisoners. At the other end of the barn, some of the thieves pulled out a loose plank and crawled back into the barn for a second helping.

The cook hadn't been counting, but he could tell the food was running low. He put down his ladle and began to look around suspiciously. The plank was already back in place. The cook couldn't figure it out; there was still a line to be served and the food was almost gone. When he scraped the last ladleful from the pot, there were still twenty men standing in line who hadn't gotten anything to eat. The poor cook told these last twenty that there simply wasn't any more food; he didn't even have any more in the kitchen. He had cooked all the portions he'd been given and there was nothing left. The twenty men were furious. They had waited in good faith, patiently, for their first food since morning. The cook promised to see what he could do and went out to call the commandant.

All that developed was a big inquiry that went on long into the night. Everyone was questioned in turn. The commandant even suspected there had been some skulduggery in the kitchen before the food was served. Trouble we got, but no more food. After that, everyone resolved never to be last in line. The last of the soup might be the best and the thickest, but it might also be gone before you got there.

We slept on the loose planks that night, with nothing to cover us except what extra clothes we had. Some of the men didn't sleep at all but just kept walking around the room all night to keep the blood circulating. The wind came at you underneath the planks, from above, from cracks in the wall right next to you. In the morning, the sun was out, but the wind was still from the north and keen as a knife. Those of us who had slept on the planks were so stiff and cold we could hardly roll over to stand up; the tips of our fingers were blue. Yet when breakfast was distributed, everyone managed to move outside. We were lined up and called out by name, one by one, to get our bread so there would be no repetition of last night's mixup. With the bread we got a cup of boiling *kipiatok*, which helped us to thaw out.

About noon, the orderlies brought out big tables and some benches from the guards' barracks. A group of officials arrived with stacks of documents and papers. Everyone was ordered out of the barn to line up in the courtyard. A guard stood at the door and wouldn't let anyone back in, even those who said they had forgotten this or that bag or piece of clothing. The tables were set up outside, but near the barn and out of the wind. At the table, as our names were called, the members of the commission would look us up and down, consult, point out our good and bad features like horse traders at a country auction, and then ultimately say, "Stand over there!" or "There!" In this way, different groups were formed up, each with its separate set of guards.

I ended up in a group with about thirty Chinese and ten Russians. Most of the other groups were bigger than ours, but the men in this group were all young (twenty to twenty-six) and strong, with the exception of myself and one old Chinaman. I stood there, stamping from foot to foot in the cold, trying to figure out what we had in common. When the commission finished, the guards marched us off toward the main camp. We walked five abreast, our arms behind our backs, each group separated from the group ahead and behind by two hundred yards.

I tried to talk to the young Chinese, but their Russian was poor. All of them, for instance, confused the masculine and feminine form of address. Then I turned to two of the young

Russians and found out they were from Manchuria. Their parents had fled there at the time of the Revolution; they themselves remembered nothing of Russia. From all my conversations, I could only guess that the common denominator in our group was the fact we were all accused of being spies: Chinese, Manchurian, and Vatican.

It was a short walk to the main gates of Dudinka. Like most camps, the approach to the gates was well beaten down by the marching prisoners who left and entered the camp only through the main gate, three shifts a day. The gates themselves were wooden, set in the outer row of the two rows of barbed wire that ringed the whole camp. The wire was strung on posts, higher than a man could reach. At the top of each post there were two wooden arms set at an angle, one leaning forward and the other backward. Along these arms in front and back were strung strands of loose barbed wire that would pull loose and wrap itself around anyone who tried to grab it. The space between the two rows of wire was the *zapretnaya zona* (forbidden strip). Within it, the guards would shoot on sight.

Beside the main gate was a long low building parallel to the line of barbed wire. It contained a sentry box, a guard room, and the headquarters for the officer on duty. Next to the gate, and between it and the guardhouse, was a narrow passage through which the guards could move in and out without opening the main gate. There was always a sentry on duty in the sentry box, peering out through a little slit so he could see any activity at the gate or receive pieces of paper or passes. Across the narrow passage was a little half-gate that he could raise or lower with a lever inside the box to let guards or officers pass through.

We halted at the main gate while our guards turned over their documents to the sentry in the box. He went in and used the phone in his quarters, which connected the various departments in the camp. After about twenty minutes, he came out and told us to line up in fives. Then, and only then, did he proceed to open the high wooden gates.

Still we waited. Finally, an official came out through the gates and called us one by one, by name. When we reported, he lined us up again in fives right in the gateway, between the two strands of barbed wire and abreast of the sentry box. Then he stepped back inside the camp and told the first rank of fives to move forward. They moved through the gates, marched a short distance down the main road of the camp, and were told to halt. Then the second five were called, passed through, marched up behind the first five, and halted. So it went, five men at a time, by fits and starts, until we were all lined up inside the gates of the camp.

We were marched off in groups. My group marched down the main road and took a right turn at the first intersection. The barracks were set in orderly rows along the road, and between every two or three sets of barracks, a smaller road ran at right angles from the main road to the barracks down the line. They were built of logs or planks, some two-stories high and some a single story. I guessed the one-story barracks were the older ones, because they were plastered outside and whitewashed. Most of the two-story barracks at the farther end of camp were simply of lumber, unplastered and already weather-beaten.

We "spies" were led to a large canvas tent, perhaps fourteen feet high, next to a large frame building we soon discovered was the officers' headquarters and not too far from the guards' barracks. The canvas of the tent was stretched around posts dug into the ground, from which crossbeams also arched up to support the canvas roof. There were no windows. The tent was divided in the middle by a rough plank wall, with a door at each end of the tent. Separate brigades were lodged on each side of the plank wall.

There was no floor except the ground itself. Two rows of free-standing, double-decker bunks ran the length of each section, separated by a small middle aisle. The uprights for the bunks ran to the roof and helped support the canvas top. There was no separation between the bunks, which were just rough planks laid end to end on crossbeams. They could accommodate as many men as could be squeezed into them, with one man's head right up against another's heels. There were no ladders used in boarding the bunks; just crossbeams nailed to the uprights. Immediately, everybody rushed to get a top bunk, in order to be as far as possible from the cold dirt floor. The boards of the lower bunks were only a foot off the floor at best; in some places they touched the ground. Unfortunately, I got a lower berth.

There was an old oil drum set up on bricks in the center of each section. That was our stove. Holes had been hacked in the side to stuff in the fuel, and smaller holes punctured all around it so the heat wouldn't just go straight up. The flue ran out a big hole cut in the canvas roof. Since the hole was extra large to avoid any chance of a fire, it also provided an excess of "ventilation". It was a real nuisance when it was raining or snowing outside. There were two or three washstands outside, tin tanks set up on a wooden trellis with two or three faucets and a trough below to catch the water. The dirty water simply ran off onto the ground, which was always muddy, if not frozen.

At suppertime that night, we were told to report to the office to be outfitted with working clothes. The general issue was a pair of trousers and a jacket, work shoes, and a cap. The clothes were made of a sort of synthetic fiber we called *chlopchato bumaznaya*, a blend of cotton mixed with wood-pulp fiber. We reported to the clerk individually, told him our name, then he filled out a registration card for each of us. As he did so, he told us the price of each item. We didn't pay for them, of course, but we worked off the price at prison camp wages; if we lost one of the items, we paid ten times its price.

The sizes were large, medium, and small, but nobody ever seemed to get the right size; it was a standing source of camp humor. There were a number of new brigades in camp that day, so this process of registration took until almost 9 P.M. Then we went back to the barrack and had our two hundred grams of *kasha*, while the brigadier and his helpers went to the warehouse with the cards for our brigade and brought back whatever was thrown at them across the counter—new clothes, second-hand clothes, old clothes.

About eleven o'clock, the brigadier and his boys came in with the clothes and began to hand them out by name. As usual, nothing fit anybody. Everybody began to swap with his neighbor; the haggling would have done credit to a pair of Arab merchants. If you wanted a really good pair of trousers or shoes, you had to throw in a little something extra from your personal belongings. This carnival took place until about 1 A.M., when we finally turned in for the night.

At six o'clock the next morning, we were awakened by the guards beating on the signal rails (short pieces of iron beams or railroad rails suspended from posts near the main gate, beaten with an iron pipe). We were told to be ready for work at seven o'clock. We made a quick trip to the toilet outside in the biting wind, then made a halfhearted gesture of washing up at the troughs. Breakfast was the usual six hundred grams of bread, *kipiatok*, and ten grams of sugar. We got nothing to eat again until we returned to camp in the evening, so we soon learned the trick of saving part of the morning's bread ration for our noon meal.

At 6:15, just as we were taking the first sips of hot water and beginning to feel the warmth spread to our stomachs, the first signal was given to form up outside. The second signal was given at 6:30, by which time the barracks were to be cleared. Each brigade had its assigned place in the compound to form up and its own set of guards. By seven o'clock, all the brigades had to be formed into fives. The commandant of the camp would be there with the adjutant to hand out the work assignments for the day.

Each brigadier told the adjutant the number in his brigade. This figure was checked against the adjutant's list, which also contained the names of those who were sick—or who, by hook or crook, had wangled a doctor's permit freeing them from work that day. If the brigade tally checked with the adjutant's tally sheet, we would be marched out the main gate in groups of five and formed up there. Then the guard would go through the whole checklist again and count us. But if the brigadier's tally wasn't right, we'd stand there in the freezing cold while a search was instituted for the missing man or men. The system was organized so that the brigades that worked farthest from the camp were processed and sent off first. Everyone was supposed to be at work by 8 A.M.

Our brigade marched off through Dudinka and down to the docks. Inside a fenced-off area were the huge banks of coal waiting to be loaded aboard ships. Conveyor belts led out onto the dock. We were given big coal scoops and told our quota for the day, a quota that had to be filled, no matter how long it took. Part of the brigade climbed up onto the coal pile and cascaded it down, while ten of us shoveled continually onto the belt.

All winter long, coal was brought from the mines inland to be stacked up along the river bank at Dudinka. The river was open to navigation for only a short time in the summer, so the coal piled up during the winter had to be loaded furiously onto the barges or freighters waiting to export it. Our quota for the day, therefore, was usually to load one ship; we worked until it was finished.

At noon we had a half hour to eat the bread we had brought with us. After we got used to the work, we also took that opportunity to sneak down on the docks and board the ships, looking for food. It was risky, and it meant a severe beating if you were caught, but starving men will run any risk for food. These first days, however, we were glad just to lie down on the frozen ground and straighten out our backs. Our hands and arm muscles were cramped from gripping and swinging the shovels continuously since eight o'clock that morning, with no break at all.

In the afternoon, as the ship's hold began to fill, the brigadier would send four of us down into the hold to scatter the coal around so the rest could be loaded. It was dark in the hold; there was coal dust everywhere. Still the coal kept roaring off the conveyor belts and flying down the chute. It was hard to see or to breathe, even harder to work; but our overriding anxiety was to avoid getting killed by the flying lumps of coal, some as big as a man's head.

As the hold filled up, the danger increased. There was no room to move, and there was more chance you might slip on the shifting piles of coal and fall into the path of the chunks roaring down the chute. When it finally got too bad, we would shout as loud as we could and bang on the deck with our shovels. The belt would stop for a minute, we'd scramble out, then continue distributing the coal from the hatchway. There were a lot of injuries on this job, and everyone hated it. But the work schedule had to be met; we were expendable.

Still, work in the holds had its rewards. As soon as we entered a hold, for instance, we would immediately explore every nook and cranny, looking for ears of wheat that might be stuck in the timbers or in crevices along the walls. Whatever we found was crammed into our pockets like so many pieces of gold, dirt and all. Sometimes we scavenged as many as five or six pocketfuls between us. We'd share it that night in the barracks—if we could get it past the guards.

When the ship was full, or the day's quota finished, the guards lined us up quickly and marched us off, anxious to get back to camp themselves. The whole crew would have to undress at the gate, despite the piercing wind and bitter cold, and submit to a search. It was then we might lose our precious bits of grain. Everyone was as black as the coal itself, but once past the search and the check-in nobody bothered to wash. Our first concern was food. We hadn't eaten a thing since breakfast, except for whatever part of the morning's ration we managed to save for lunch.

That first night, they brought us a half liter of soup apiece and two hundred grams of *kasha*, plus hot water. We wolfed it down. Then everyone collapsed on the plank bunks like a company of dead men. After years in prison with little exercise, this first full day of hard work had been torture. My muscles were too numb even to ache; every sinew felt like a piece of twine that had been unwound and shredded into string.

The next morning, though, when the alarm rails rang at 6 A.M., every joint had tightened up like welded iron. It was sheer torture just to get out of bed. Muscles that had hardened in the overnight cold simply refused to function. Yet, somehow, we managed to form up in fives by seven o'clock and totter painfully, our arms behind our backs as per marching orders, down through the town and back to the coal piles to begin another long day with the shovels.

Toward the end of our first week in Dudinka, Fr. Casper

came looking for me in the barracks one night. Some of his Poles had told him there was another priest in camp. He found me before I had a chance to look him up and asked me if I wanted to say Mass. I was overwhelmed! My last Mass had been said in Chusovoy more than five years ago. I made arrangements to meet him in his barrack next morning as soon as the six o'clock signal sounded.

The men in Fr. Casper's barrack were mostly Poles. They revered him as a priest, protected him, and he tried to say Mass for them at least once a week. They made the Mass wine for him out of raisins they had stolen on the docks, the altar breads from flour "appropriated" in the kitchen. My chalice that morning was a whiskey glass, the paten to hold the host was a gold disc from a pocket watch. But my joy at being able to celebrate Mass again cannot be described.

Fr. Casper had the prayers of the Mass written out on a piece of paper. Although I knew them by heart, I was so moved and so excited that morning I was glad to have them. Afterward, he made me a copy. I tore them up when I left Dudinka, for fear they would be discovered in the routine processing inspections at the next camp. I wrote them again from memory inside the camp.

The rest of the time I was in Dudinka, I said Mass frequently in Fr. Casper's barrack. I was encouraged by his example, too, to work among the men as a priest. I heard confessions regularly and, from time to time, was even able to distribute Communion secretly after I'd said Mass. The experience gave me new strength. I could function as a priest again, and I thanked God daily for the opportunity to work among this hidden flock, consoling and comforting men who had thought themselves beyond His grace.

August in Dudinka is cold, bitterly cold. We were still working in the light cotton summer clothing we had been issued when we arrived. Working at a furious pace, as we were, we could stay warm enough. But the long cold walk to work in the morning and especially the trudge home at night, when the sweat would almost freeze on our bodies, was an excruciating experience. The wind drove through the cotton clothing like a knife. Everyone tied rags around his ankles and shoe tops; an old potato sack that could be tied around the belly or the shoulders was a man's most prized possession.

Wearing extra clothing, presuming a man had any or could borrow some from one of the sick prisoners, was strictly forbidden. If the adjutant or commandant during the morning roll call detected that a man was wearing an extra shirt or a second pair of pants, he would force him to strip right there in the freezing wind of the compound. The clothing would be confiscated. And if a man got away with it in the morning, he was almost certain to be caught during the evening inspection and search after work.

After the day's work, we were issued small work tickets to be used for meals. They were given out according to the day's performance and determined the ration you got. The ordinary ticket entitled you to the minimum or "guarantee"—six hundred grams of bread, two hundred grams of *kasha*, ten grams of sugar. A "plus-one" ticket got you an extra hundred grams of bread, another five grams of sugar, and perhaps a little piece of herring. A "plus-two" ticket got you another two hundred grams of bread, ten grams of sugar, a piece of herring, and some baked goods, a roll perhaps or a piece of corn bread or a muffin. A "plus-three" ticket got you another two hundred grams of bread, twenty-five grams of sugar, a piece of herring, some bakery goods, and a handful of rough dough that could be mixed with the soup or *kasha*, or perhaps baked on the stove.

"Plus–two" and "plus–three" ticket-holders also got a different soup from that served at the ordinary mess, much thicker, with chunks of potatoes or herring or cabbage mixed into it. Prison life being what it is, of course, the brigadier and his helpers usually got the "plus–three" ration (there were never more than three or four of these rations to any brigade). The rest of us were lucky to get even the "guarantee", as our numbers were thinned out by sickness and our work quota took us longer than ever to fulfill.

Our whole aim in life, therefore, became the acquisition, somehow, of food. We thought of it constantly; men would go to any lengths to get it. After the first week in camp, when I got my second wind, I went out almost every night to work for food. After the night meal, I'd report to the kitchen and spend the next three or four hours—sometimes as long as six hours and well into the early morning—cleaning the floors or washing kettles, scrubbing pots and pans, all for an extra two hundred grams of bread or an extra liter of soup.

Next to me in the barrack slept a Pole named Gorny, a tall, thin, gaunt man built along the lines of Washington Irving's Ichabod Crane. He was one of the greatest scavengers I've ever seen, and I saw some pretty good ones in the prison camps. He regularly shared his spoils with me, for he was one of the closest friends I had here at Dudinka. A very religious man, he knew I was a priest, and he went out of his way to look after me.

Working in the kitchen, Gorny had developed an almost surefire technique for scrounging extra food. When no one was looking, he would grab a big slab of fish or fat or butter and shove it down into the coal bucket. Then he'd very dutifully carry out the bucket, empty it, fish and all, into the ash pile, refill the bucket, and ceremoniously lug in the coal. That night, about two o'clock in the morning, he would duck out of the barracks and dig into the ash pile until he found his treasure.

Gorny's greatest triumph was the night he brought home a whole pail of bean soup. It was very thick, mostly beans, and quite salty, so we stirred in just about our whole monthly ration of sugar to make it palatable. Between us, we finished the whole pail of soup. Not surprisingly, we suddenly felt thirsty. We strolled out to the yard and drank about two quarts of water each; then we returned to settle in for a good night's sleep. Even less surprisingly, we got little sleep that night. We developed severe cases of diarrhea and made regular trips to the latrine all night long. By dawn, we were so sick and weak we could talk only in whispers.

Gorny and I, of course, were not the only ones who worked for extra food or managed to steal it. Pilfering at Dudinka attained almost epidemic proportions. From time to time the guards would make surprise raids, usually about three o'clock in the morning, on different barracks. They would order everyone to line up in the middle of the room, while they went through the bunks and our few personal belongings, scrap by scrap. Sometimes they came up with enough food to feed the entire camp for one meal.

But for all our ingenuity at scrounging food, the hard work and the cold began to take their toll. Scurvy became general. Eventually, there were just too many men sick to be let off work. The camp cooks boiled big kettles of pine branches in water, and the concentrate from this boiling process became our "medicine". It was terribly bitter stuff, but if you didn't drink it, you got no supper. Some men just couldn't get it down, but I used to take a half liter a day.

Many in the camp suffered horribly from the disease; their teeth rotted away, their breath was terrible, their gums festering, their lips bloody. A man's legs might become so weak he couldn't stand for more than ten minutes at a time. But the pine-branch medicine worked for me. I managed to avoid the worst effects of the disease.

On the other hand, I developed a severe case of boils on my hands and face, my back and legs. Finally I went to the camp hospital. When the prison doctor learned I was an American, he went out of his way to give me a break. According to camp rules, the doctor (a prisoner himself) couldn't sign rest permits for more than three days at a time. After three days, if he thought the patient still needed rest, he had to send the patient to a commission of three doctors from the town. That commission rarely passed anyone for additional rest permits, unless he was absolutely moribund. So the doctor would give me three days' rest, I'd work a few more days, then he'd sign a new permit for me. With his help, and the pine-branch medicine, I gradually regained my strength.

On the days when I was permitted to rest in camp, I would go around looking for work. I'd help the orderlies clean the barracks or work in the kitchen, spending four or five hours at these chores in exchange for a half liter of soup. One day I was working in the kitchen when a barge-load of potatoes arrived in port. I went with some other prisoners under guard to haul them to the camp warehouse.

We found the potatoes dumped in huge piles on the barge decks, already frozen solid in the arctic cold. We attacked them with picks and shovels and loaded them on sleds. As we pulled and hauled the sleds through the camp, we threw some potatoes off into the snow whenever the guards weren't looking. We worked at this for half a day, then were given a full meal (i.e., a day's ration) of *kasha* and soup by the cooks.

After that, we ducked out as fast as we could and ran to rescue the potatoes from the snowbanks. We took them to the barracks, put them in a bucket of water, and boiled them on the stove. When they were more or less cooked, we ate them with salt, a bucketful at a time. Still we didn't have enough. The constant hunger of the prison camps has to be experienced to be believed, but these examples give some indication of it.

About October, when the temperature occasionally dropped to 30 degrees below zero Fahrenheit, we turned in our summer clothes and got the winter issue. We had to account for everything that had been issued to us; if anything was missing, it was charged to our account at ten times its nominal price. In return, we got a somewhat heavier undershirt, quilted jackets and trousers padded with some sort of pulp, and a pair of boots called *valenki*—a sort of high-topped, one-piece overshoe made of a mixture of clay and hair. They were more or less snow-repellent and fairly warm.

The *valenki* we put in a drying room next to the stove every night; otherwise, we slept in the same clothes we wore all day. When we got up in the morning, the padded coats and trousers would be frozen to the bed planks. Ultimately, this cold took a terrific toll. There was so much sickness in our brigade we were finally transferred from the tent to a wooden barrack.

This new barrack was made of rough lumber, plastered inside and out with a clay compound to seal up cracks and serve as insulation. It was whitewashed and it was clean. What was far more important to us, it was warm. We kept the stove going full blast all the time, and everyone in the brigade brought home coal every day from work. For every three pieces we brought, the guards took two when they searched us. It was understood, though, that unless we got to keep our share we would bring none at all; the stove in the guard room could grow cold along with ours.

One of the last ships into Dudinka that year before the river froze was an American one. It stood at the dock for two days without being unloaded; none of the officials could read the cargo manifest in English. Then, a prisoner working in the dockyard offices remembered I was an American. I jumped at the chance to help, hoping I might get a chance to talk to the crew. I even wrote down the address of my sister and a little note to pass to one of the sailors, as well as a note to my Jesuit Provincial at Fordham Road.

The next morning I went down to the dockyard. The prisoner explained to the officials and the secret service man in charge that I knew English. The officials were eager for help, but the NKGB agent didn't want me on board that ship. He questioned me closely, then apparently relented and told me to come along. I walked down the dock behind him toward the gangway with a new spring to my step and hope in my heart.

Suddenly, the NKGB agent changed his mind. He told me to return to the office and wait for him there. He came back with a copy of the cargo manifest and told me to translate it right there in the room. I worked all afternoon and on through the night to make Russian copies of the manifest; then I was sent back to camp immediately. For the next few days, the sight of that big ship at the dock almost broke my heart.

. Practically the whole camp was now formed into special brigades to get the last ships loaded and underway before the river froze. By this time, the piles of coal were frozen solid. We had to break them up with picks and chop them into manageable hunks before we shoveled them onto the conveyor belts. We were being driven at a furious pace and were on the verge of total collapse. For the first time, I really began to fear that I'd give out and never see another spring.

I went to see my friendly doctor. He told me the shiploading crisis was considered an emergency; orders had been issued that no rest permits were to be given until the work was finished. If a man wasn't ill enough for the hospital, he was to work. So the doctor told me to report in the morning for a hospital examination; he also told me what symptoms it would be best to have.

The next morning, after breakfast, I started right for the infirmary. The brigadier came charging after me. "Where are you going?" he asked. "I'm going to the infirmary", I replied. "I'm sick." "You don't look very sick to me", he said. "That's because you're not a doctor. I saw the doctor last night, and he told me to report to the infirmary this morning." The brigadier looked at me suspiciously for a moment, shrugged his shoulders, and walked away.

When I reported to the doctor, he told me that the new orders required two doctors to certify a patient for hospital admission, so he briefed me again on my symptoms. The other doctor, whose name I have forgotten, was a Jew who had been one of those accused in the Gorki case. I don't know how convincing I was in describing my symptoms, but he also certified me as a hospital case.

The camp hospital was just another barrack building, but the beds were arranged in wards, with a few private rooms for women patients. According to my symptoms, I wasn't suffering from anything that confined me to bed, so I did the work of an orderly. I scrubbed the floors, washed dishes, helped to serve the meals and clean up the other patients. I was busy from morning to night, but it was indoors, it was warm—and it wasn't shoveling coal!

My case wasn't particularly special. The prison doctors, because of their profession, were humane men. They would do anything they could to help the other prisoners as long as their own risks were not too great. My case was peculiar only in that it was a favor done to me because I was an American. That was often the case in the camps; the magic word "America" was like a charm that held listeners spell-bound for hours and made friends of total strangers.

When I got out, our brigade was working on the river, blasting lumber out of the ice. The lumber had been floated upriver during the summer for use in construction and the mines around Norilsk; now it was frozen into the river. The way we got it out was as dangerous as it was simple. Dynamite was scattered over a given area of ice, then detonated. The logs bobbed to the bottom of the river under the blast. Then we'd go out with pike poles to snake them out as they floated back to the top.

These were huge logs, two or three feet in diameter and perhaps twelve yards long. Handling them in the ice and wet was no joke. Time and again, men fell into the icy water; our padded jackets and pants were soon soaked through from handling the logs. After an hour or so, ice began to cake on the back of our hands and wrists, and our jackets and pants would be frozen. We worked out in the middle of the river, twelve hours a day, with no place to get warm. Sometimes, too, as much as two feet of snow would fall in a single day, freezing our eyelashes and making the log jams treacherous underfoot.

By the end of November, there were still logs in the river, but we had to give up lumbering because of the weather. After that, we were put to work loading trains with food for the camps around Norilsk. All summer long, the food had arrived by barge. The essential business of the short summer months, however, was the loading of coal, so the crates had simply been stacked up along the river bank in mountainous piles. There were crates of beans, flour, canned fruit, and meat, all frozen solid now and covered with as much as ten feet of snow. We had to break it loose and load it on flatcars for the trip inland.

We worked at this, twelve hours a day, until December. Then certain brigades were left in Dudinka to complete this job and unload the coal that came down from the mines all winter long to build up the fueling piles for the next summer. Most of us, however, were shipped on to Norilsk.

A Year in Arctic Mines

We were crammed into tiny boxcars on the narrow-gauge railway for the trip. We got no food except our morning bread ration, since it was only a day's ride—perhaps forty or forty-five miles—to Norilsk. The boxcars weren't heated and the plank walls, with all their cracks, weren't much protection against the polar winds and bitter cold. We stood for the whole trip, jumping from foot to foot to keep warm; even if we had wanted to, there was no room to sit down.

We reached Norilsk in late afternoon, piled out of the boxcars, then sat for three hours in the snow while the officials sorted us out for the different camps. At that time, Norilsk wasn't much. It lay at the base of a mountain range rich in coal, iron, copper, cobalt, and other mineral deposits, an area just beginning to be heavily developed. The city itself resembled a mining or frontier town. It was right at the foot of Schmidtika, one of the highest peaks in Siberia, named for the German explorer who climbed it in 1937 and whose monument is erected on its top.

There were about a dozen prison camps around the city, each assigned to two or three jobs. The idea was to build an industrial complex right there near the ore deposits. That way the raw ore would not have to be carried long distances down the river, which was only open to navigation in the summer months. Plants were built right on the site, and they could operate all year round. Some of the prison camps were at the mines, and other prisoners were building the new plants to refine the ore. Still other prisoners were building the city to house the workers, who were just beginning to arrive in ever-increasing numbers to develop the nation's resources.

I was finally assigned, the only political prisoner, to a crew of criminals and thieves about 120 strong. Under relatively light guard, we marched off toward the mountain. There were no roads to speak of; the snow was generally knee-deep, and some drifts were as high as our belt buckles. Blinded by the swirling snow in a stiff wind, we crested a saddle leading to the peak. Just over the other side was a mining camp called Zapadnaya.

It was dark by the time we entered the camp. Again we stood around in the freezing cold while the officials went through the routine of assigning us to barracks. I finally stumbled in, long after suppertime and having had nothing to eat all day, to my new home. It was a wooden barrack much like those at Dudinka, but it had one improvement: a brick stove in the center of the room. The barracks at Zapadnaya were always fairly warm.

The leader of this barrack was a fierce, wild Tartar. A mixture of Cossack and Turk, he already had eight murders to his credit and made no bones about it. He was a stocky, sturdily built, medium-sized man with black hair and stern squinting eyes. He must have once had a name, but everyone, including the guards, called him simply "Ottoman" or "Cossack". He assigned us newcomers to a work brigade, told us the order of the day, and pointed out a bunk for each of us. Luckily, I was assigned an upper berth. Even with a good stove, the corners of the room were still icy and the walls had a thick coating of ice to a point a few feet above the floor. On the top bunks, though, the air was warm and dry.

I was exhausted after the long day in the open air and the long climb up the hill. I just threw myself down on the bunk in all my clothes and was asleep before I finished my prayers. Rising time here was 5 A.M., not 6, and almost as soon as the morning's ration was distributed, we were given the signal to leave the barracks. Here at Zapadnaya, there was always a wind. Clouds of blown snow swirled so thickly that morning I couldn't see three feet across the courtyard. The older prisoners, however, led the way. Lined up near the guard house, we were counted off and formed into fives, as usual. But the commandant in this camp didn't waste much time; we were off almost immediately to the mine a mile away.

It was one of the oldest mines in the area, a horizontal shaft that ran deep into the mountain. Practically all the work was done by hand; there was little mechanization except for the scraper lines, which carried the coal to the hoppers, and the electric cars, which hauled it to the tunnel mouth. It took us almost half an hour to walk from the tunnel mouth to the work area. I was assigned to work with a gypsy named Grisha, loading the loose coal into the cars. The rest of the brigade went farther down the shaft to do the actual mining. Grisha and I worked at the top of the shaft, where there was a hopper for loading the cars.

We had to push the cars under the hopper by hand, then push the full cars down a siding until we had enough to make up a train. Then we'd signal for an engine to haul out the loaded cars and bring us another string of empties. The hopper was fed by scraper lines that pulled the coal up from below. Besides manhandling the cars into place, we also had to scoop up the loose coal that tumbled from the hopper.

Here we worked ten hours at a stretch, with no break for dinner. The pace was hectic—we couldn't hold up the work below—and the mine was constantly wet. In our section, there was enough water to flood the railroad tracks and cover the ties. It was pumped up from below as it dripped from the walls of the shaft, then pumped again from our section to the top. But the system wasn't very efficient. We generally worked in water up to our ankles; the only protection we had were our *valenki*, which were quickly soaked through every morning.

About 5 P.M., the men would begin shuffling up from the shaft below. By the time we finished the walk back to camp through the snow, our *valenki* would be frozen solid. It was lucky for us if our feet weren't frozen too. There was no running water in the camp at Zapadnaya, so we simply banged our coats against the snow to get the coal dust off, then washed our hands and face in the snow. Since we had only the one set of clothes, we slept in our work clothes, coal dust and all.

Here at Zapadnaya, I was reduced again to the straight "guarantee" ration. You had to work at least a month in any camp before you could rate a "plus-one", "plus-two", or "plus-three" ticket. Unlike other camps, the food at Zapadnaya wasn't brought to the barracks and distributed by the brigadiers; it was dished out at the kitchen. This had the advantage of keeping the food hot, but it also meant we had to shuffle through the wind and the snow to get our ration personally. Each man had his own tin can and cup, which we kept next to our bunks.

Since this meal was, in effect, both dinner and supper, we got a half liter of soup and two hundred grams of *kasha*—all at once in the same can. After we had worked in camp a month, we might occasionally get an extra ration. The theory, I guess, was that we would work harder in an effort to earn this extra ration. It never worked out that way. The brigadier got the ration tickets to distribute among his brigade according to merit and work done, but everyone knew they wouldn't be passed on no matter how hard we worked. Just as in the prisons, the thieves practically ran the camp. They were the brigadiers, they were the orderlies in charge of barracks, they were the foremen of the various crews. Whatever extra food was available, they got.

The weather at Zapadnaya was brutal. The wind never stopped; it only changed directions. If the snow got so thick we couldn't see beyond an arm's length, or the cold grew so severe no one could survive the long walk to the mines, we were excused from working for the day. The maintenance crews, however, were taken to the mines on horse-drawn sleds to prepare for the next day's blasting. Guide ropes had been set up along the route to the mine shaft, for blizzards and "white storms" were common. On days like that, the trip for the maintenance crews would take a long time; even the horses would turn their rumps to the wind and refuse to budge. But still they went.

In the barrack, I had become a favorite of the "Ottoman". He was a savage, yet in many ways he was like a child. When he found out I was an American, he immediately took a great liking to me. He told me I was to sleep next to him (considered a tremendous honor) and be his personal orderly. He let it be known that if anything happened to me, or people displeased me, they would be personally responsible to him.

On the bunks at night, he wanted to talk for hours about America. He was like a little boy, listening with wide eyes to my descriptions, asking questions, laughing, and shouting "Impossible! Impossible! Impossible!" to my answers. He couldn't imagine buildings fifty- or sixty-stories tall. He refused to believe that people had houses with five or six rooms all to themselves, only one family to a house.

That every family should have its own car, that every house had indoor plumbing, electricity, washing machines, radios, and vacuum cleaners (of which he had never heard), running water in the sinks and overstuffed chairs—all this to the "Cossack" was like a fairy tale, a vision of palaces and unbelievable people. He would ask me again and again to repeat the same facts, telling them over and over for him, for others, and then still others, never tiring of the stories. I began to feel like Hans Christian Andersen.

As the "Ottoman's" personal orderly, I took care of his bed, fetched his meals, and looked after his personal belongings. Unlike everybody else, he had a sawdust mattress and a blanket. At the kitchen, I simply handed his dish to the cook and said "for the Ottoman". He got a plateful of meat stew instead of soup, a special serving of *kasha* swimming in linseed oil and garnished with a piece of fat or bacon. I had to see that his dagger was always under his pillow when he slept and that both dagger and knife were in his coat each morning. He had special pockets in his sheepskin-lined coat to hold the dagger on one side and a long ugly knife on the other.

I also got along well with Grisha, the gypsy. He was another one who knew all the angles. He used to work every night in the kitchen to earn extra food, and he suggested that I join him. I got a job washing dishes, stoking fires, scrubbing floors. I'd report there after dinner every night and work for several hours, losing sleep but getting extra food.

Next day, every day, the gypsy and I would almost be sleepwalkers—but this was no problem for Grisha. As soon as we got down into the mine, we would load up all the cars we had. Afterward, Grisha would grab a piece of coal and jam it under the scraper lines. Then he'd phone up to the head of the shaft and tell them the scraper lines were jammed. We knew it would be at least an hour, maybe two or three, before the maintenance crews would come. Meanwhile, we could go off into a side shaft and catch an hour or two of sleep.

Grisha and I must have had the worst accident record of anyone in the mines. For a while, though, we got away with it. Either we would already have the scraper lines working again when the maintenance crew arrived, or else they would find the scraper lines actually jammed with coal, thanks to Grisha, so that it looked like a legitimate breakdown. Still, the mine superintendent must have suspected something, because it wasn't long before he transferred us to drilling.

The drillers were free men, miners and specialists, who came to Siberia to work at bonus wages. We were assigned to them as helpers. The drilling was done by compressed air drills, much like big jack hammers; our job was to help the driller manhandle the instrument and apply pressure to the face of the work. Grisha would have no part of it. As soon as we got down in the shaft in the morning, he'd take off. Where he went nobody knew.

After the holes were drilled, we'd ram the powder charges home and attach blasting caps. Then everybody scattered for shelter in one of the other shafts while the work face was blown. I remember one day we blasted, but the resulting gas wouldn't vent—which prevented us from getting ourselves killed. We waited and waited, then finally went into the shaft. The gas was so bad, however, that we halted at the entrance to the work area. As we stopped to look around, the whole ceiling caved in. It was the last blast of the day, and we were so exhausted we never even budged. We just stood there, watching the huge slabs of rock crash within feet of us, coughing in the billowing dust. We were simply too tired to care or even to be afraid.

I worked in these mines about a year. In the camp itself, there was a lot of disorder. Most of the men here were criminals and thieves, and they played rough. As usual, too, there was bad blood between the thieves and the political prisoners;

the guards found it very hard to maintain discipline. Finally, it was decided to open a new camp in the valley at the foot of Schmidtika, four or five miles away from Zapadnaya. To help camp discipline, the officials sorted out all the political prisoners and sent them to work on this new camp. The "Ottoman" was our brigadier.

At the new site there was only one barrack, built the summer before. It was full of drifted snow and ice, crammed with barrels of some kind of chemicals that had been stored there. I was assigned to a crew to clean out the barrack; the majority of the brigade was put to digging post holes. You can't have a prison camp without barbed wire, so the first order of business in constructing a new camp is to put up the posts and string the wire. It was bitter work. The ground was frozen and covered with three feet of snow. The men worked in the open, and it was the middle of the Siberian winter.

The barrels full of chemicals weighed about 250 pounds, and they were frozen together in the ice. To get them out of the barrack, we made crude sleds from old slats of wood. Two of us, working together, would dig a barrel out of the ice, half roll and half slide it onto the sled, then push and pull the sled—using wire because we had no rope—until we got it outside. To spare our hands as much as possible, we used to wrap the wire from the sleds around our chests and haul away at the heavy sled like draft horses, puffing and sliding over the frozen ground.

We worked this way from the time we got there in the morning until six, seven, or eight o'clock at night without a break. When we finally left for Zapadnaya late in the evening, many of the prisoners were so exhausted they simply couldn't make it back the steep road up the hill. So we stacked them like cordwood on a rough sled pulled by the horses. It took us almost two hours to get back up the hill to camp, and it was sometimes eleven o'clock at night when we got there. We simply ate our *kasha* and fell into the bunks.

After we had been working on this new camp only a week, the brigade was exhausted. Some men just couldn't get out of bed in the morning. Some of those who could refused to work; they had had enough. The "Ottoman", though, wouldn't leave with the brigade until everyone was present. If the men couldn't stand on their feet, he'd have us drag them out by the feet and tie them onto the sled behind the horses.

They were dragged to work that way, through snow drifts and all, down the steep, bumpy hill road. When we got to the work area, they were unhitched and left to lie in the snow. It seemed impossible they wouldn't freeze to death, but somehow, around noon, you would find them sitting by the fire in the barrack, beginning to thaw out. By afternoon, the "Ottoman" would have them at work.

By the end of a month, we had the barrack cleared, the post holes dug, the guard towers finished, and the barbed wire strung. But it was a monstrous job. The work was difficult, the food was barely enough to keep a man going, yet the weather was our worst enemy. There was always a wind howling, always snow in the air, blown by the wind into white whirling dervishes that stung.

As soon as the barbed wire was up, however, the camp was officially in operation. It was to serve as a penal camp for the worst disciplinary offenders of the old camp. Seventy-two of them came down to join our brigade of politicals; all of us were quartered in the one barrack. Our only food was bread, sent out by train from Norilsk once a day. The railroad ran some distance from the camp, so the bread was simply thrown off the train into a snowbank and later fetched by the prisoners.

On one of these bread-gathering details, I was almost killed. As we hauled the bread on sleds back to camp, I watched the thieves grab off big chunks and eat them ravenously. The guards paid no attention. Finally, I snatched a piece of bread myself.

In that same instant, I got a gun butt slammed between my shoulder blades, which staggered me; a smash in the jaw, which drove me to my knees; and a kick, which caught me off balance and sprawled me into a snowbank fifteen feet away. Immediately, I was looking down the muzzles of the guards' guns. One of them told me to get up out of the snowbank. When I staggered up, I got a kick in the face, which put me on my back again. This routine was repeated again and again. The guards threatened to shoot if I didn't get up, then kicked me squarely in the face when I did. Finally, I was shoved back into line, almost unable to walk.

Back at camp, I was put into the *bur*, the camp prison. In the *bur*, a prisoner gets just three hundred grams of bread a day, plus a cup of water. Punishment is usually for three, five, or ten days at a time, depending on the offense. When they came out, prisoners were as weak as kittens from lack of food, if they managed to survive at all. It wasn't uncommon for a man to die in the *bur* serving a ten-day sentence.

I was lucky, however. After I had been in the *bur* only half an hour, I was called by the commandant to find out what had happened. I told him. He was amused both at the story and my attempt to tell it through lips that barely functioned. At the end, he smiled, said he guessed I'd been punished enough, and told me to get out of his office.

Though we kept a fire going day and night, the barrack was always damp. The lumber never really thawed out. So every night after supper, from 8:00 to perhaps 8:30, we would have a louse hunt. Everybody was ordered to strip and kill the lice on his body, then we did the best we could with the bunks and the barrack itself. Because the camp was still so primitive, the medical aid was poor—in fact, it was practically nonexistent.

At the end of May, when the snow began to melt, everything flooded as the waters poured off the hills into our valley. The water in the camp was a foot deep in most places, sometimes deeper. One night we were all chased outside to wash up; it was the first bath we'd had since our assignment to this camp. We stood there in the open compound with the wind still howling and the snow still deep on the hillsides. We bathed as quickly as we could, but it was welcome and it felt good. All through the spring, until the work crews finally dug drainage ditches, the compound was always flooded, and sometimes the barrack, too.

Our main job at this time was to finish building the camp itself. Everything had to be done from scratch. We built our own sawmill for the lumber that was hauled in from the railroad, then set about building more barracks. After that, we built a kitchen, a storehouse for food, and finally an infirmary.

The new infirmary was always full. When the doctor, a prisoner himself, found out that I was an American, he got me to translate the prescriptions on some American drugs and medicine with which he had been supplied. In return, he would have me assigned to work with him for three days at a time. In the infirmary, I'd get tea and sugar along with the bread, plus vitamins to build up my strength. These breaks from the heavy work of the brigades were literally lifesavers.

The food in camp was still just the daily bread ration that came in on the railroad. Eventually, a spur line was built from the railroad to the storehouse we had completed. Our first delivery of food arrived when four boxcars were shoved into camp by the engine. As soon as the gates were opened and the cars rolled in, the thieves poured out of the barracks. They were halted at the boxcars by guards with rifles.

The commandant then ordered these ruffians to unload the cars and carry the food into the storehouse. They jumped aboard the cars and began unloading all right— but they took the food and ran in all directions! The guards at first shot over their heads in warning, then in earnest. As far as I could see, no one was killed, but several fell writhing on the ground. Still, the thieves carried on. Nothing would stop them.

Those in the cars threw down the boxes, smashing and scattering the contents over the ground. Others picked up the scattered food and stuffed it in their pockets. They completely ignored the fusillade of shots. Others came running at the guards with clubs. At that, the soldiers fled, fearing a riot. They came back later, and then only with reinforcements.

Immediately, the commandant ordered a search of all the barracks for the stolen food. But the thieves weren't fools; they had taken care to hide their hard-won loot in the snowbanks around the camp, where they could get it later. Those four boxcars had contained our rations for the week, so the rest of us got nothing that week except hot water, a little bit of sugar, and some very weak soup, which might just as well have been more hot water. From then on, the boxcars were stopped outside the camp. Food was carried into the storehouse by political prisoners under heavy guard, and the thieves weren't even allowed in the compound while the transfer took place.

Since this was, in effect, the penal camp for all the disciplinary problems around Norilsk, it was not surprising that trouble was the order of the day. The few political prisoners were split up among the brigades, and we did our best to stay out of the way. Even with the "Ottoman" as my protector, I used to sit on my bunk or in a corner of the barrack at night, as inconspicuous as possible.

If I ever had any doubts about how quickly I could get into trouble when the "Ottoman" wasn't around, they were cleared up one night when I went to the kitchen in the hope of scrounging a little extra food. As I walked in, I was met by a thief who was there ahead of me with the same idea. He was a one-armed fellow, ugly, carrying a club in his hand. "What are you hanging around for, you Fascist?" he growled. "What about you, you thief!" I said. Instantly, he sprang at me with the club. I ducked under the blow, caught his arm, and hung on for dear life. Other thieves came running. Instead of breaking up the fight, they ganged up on me and worked me over quite professionally. I woke up outside in the snow, badly bruised, but mercifully with no bones broken. It was a hard way to learn a lesson, but it was one I never forgot.

Among themselves, the thieves observed a rigid caste system. Sometimes in the morning, when we stepped outside the barrack, we would stumble over a body, stiff as a board and stone dead. The thieves were settling old scores among themselves; they left the burying to a work detail.

One evening, just about suppertime, a thief from another barrack came to ours on some mission or other. He fell into an argument over it with the "Ottoman", who began to curse him in no uncertain terms. In sheer bravado, the outsider ripped open his jacket and bared his chest to dramatize the fact he wasn't afraid of the "Ottoman". Before the gesture was even complete, the "Ottoman" had his knife out of his coat and plunged it full force into the bared chest. The fellow went down without a word. The "Ottoman" calmly retrieved his knife, wiped it on the fellow's jacket, and told his men to throw the fellow outside in the snow. Fortunately, he was found, taken to the infirmary, and survived the incident.

I remember, though, that I had just begun to eat my evening ration. The whole sight so sickened me I couldn't finish it; I almost vomited up what I'd already eaten. Everyone else, however, calmly went back about his business, wolfed down the evening's ration, then turned to the evening's session of talk or card games. These men were hard and cruel, and the only law they observed was their own. Even the guards were afraid of them, or at least avoided "incidents" with them whenever possible.

With the camp nearly completed, strip mining was begun. The clay under the topsoil here was of a type called *evrolit*, used especially in making fire brick. It was the first time it had been found in this part of the country, so the clay taken from our strip mines was sent as far as Krasnoyarsk. The camp itself became known as "Evrolitna". Since the ground was frozen, we would dynamite away the topsoil, then dig for the clay. After three months, there was so much demand for the clay that this process of strip mining was judged to be too slow. A big pit was blasted, and a horizontal shaft was begun at the level of the clay below the topsoil. I was back to mining.

Shortly afterward, though, I was rescued from the mines by another political prisoner named Gribunov. A former colonel in the Red Army, he was a serious, taciturn man who had few friends among the prisoners and kept strictly to himself. He never allowed himself to use slang or deviate in any way from his own standards of an officer and gentleman. He was also an ardent Communist; in fact, he said he had known Stalin personally. Consequently, he was extremely bitter about the fact that he had devoted all his talents to the service of his country and still wound up in the prison camps—because of treachery within the Party, he said.

Gribunov admired the American Army, and when he heard I was an American, he looked me up. Somehow, he managed to get me assigned to work with him at the sawmill. Camp construction was completed, but now we turned out props and supports for the mine shaft. One day, just after we had finished cutting up a log and had gone outside to fetch another, we heard the saw start up, then whine as it bit into something. We ran in to find a young fellow, one of the thieves, holding the stump of his arm. Blood was spurting everywhere, but he said quite nonchalantly, "Tie it off." We immediately threw a tourniquet about it and bandaged it as best we could. Then the fellow walked calmly to the infirmary to get it treated.

Gribunov and I were nearly put into the *bur*, though, because we had left the saw unattended and given the thief the "opportunity" to cut off his arm. Such mutilations, in order to get out of work, were quite common. Men would put their hand up against a building and whack off their fingers with one blow of an ax, almost as casually as if they were playing some sort of game. They'd make no sound, no fuss, just like the young thief at the sawmill, but simply bind up the stumps tight and go off to the doctor. Accordingly, tools were given out only to "responsible" people. It was just too bad for you if an "accident" happened with the tool you had been assigned.

There were other ways, however, less violent but just as drastic, for the thieves to get out of work. For instance, they would grind a lump of sugar into powder and inhale it like snuff. Within a week, their lungs would be badly inflamed, and they would be coughing up blood as if they had TB. So, after a while, sugar was served only in the *kasha*, already melted; it was no longer given out in lumps.

Construction Laborer in Norilsk

One morning in June 1947, I was told before work to remain in the barrack when the brigade left. I was startled. About ten o'clock, a guard came to the barrack and asked to see my register card. When I produced it, he immediately checked through my clothes to see that nothing was missing; we had just turned in our winter clothes and been given the summer issue of cotton pants, jacket, and cap. When he finished, he told me to pack up my things and come along.

I walked with the guard out the main gates of Evrolitna and managed to wig-wag to Gribunov as I went by. I never saw him again. We walked along the railroad tracks skirting the slope of the hill, down into Norilsk itself, to another camp called simply "Camp 2". Some of the prison camps around the Norilsk area had names, like "Zapadnaya" and "Evrolitna"; most of them, however, were just numbered. Once inside the camp gate, the guard turned me over to the authorities. I went through the usual routine of registration, then made a welcome trip to the bathhouse and barber. Finally, I was appointed to a brigade and assigned to a barrack.

Camp 2 was quite large. There may have been as many as fifty or sixty barracks altogether, built in rows along a series of regular streets and neatly kept, for the camp was practically in the city of Norilsk itself. The barracks were one-story buildings set on the rising ground at the foot of Schmidtika, so there was a set of wooden steps on the front of the barracks, which made them look almost like homes. They had also been freshly whitewashed. Here in Camp 2, each barrack was divided down the middle by a corridor, with two sections of bunk rooms on either side. The corridors housed the washstands as well as clothes racks and hangers.

The bunks along both walls were double-deckers, as usual, but there was a passage between every two bunks, unlike the solid rows I had seen before. On these bunks, for the first time in the camps, I saw thin mattresses and blankets. In the middle of the room was a small brick stove with a large chimney to hold the heat; behind the stove was a long table with benches. In one corner was a barrel of water for washing, as well as a tin kettle of drinking water. There was an orderly assigned to each section, whose job it was to have food on the table at the proper times, clean the room, and look after the clothing and the blankets.

Every morning, too, the orderly brought in the *valenki* from the drying shed in the center of camp where they were hung each evening. They were identified by number—my number here was zero-one-one-one—written in chalk on the *valenki* before they were hung by metal rings to dry. The chalk, however, was easily erased, so everyone added his own peculiar identifying mark to his pair in order to prevent switching. With blankets on the beds, it was no longer necessary to sleep in our work clothes, so we also hung them up to dry each night. The numbers were painted on them.

Camp 2 was also the first camp I'd been in where strict attention was paid to the cleanliness of the barracks and the men. Bath day was held once every ten days, at which time we got our hair clipped with a machine, our body shaved (as a precaution against lice), and were handed a dollar-sized piece of soap. Before we entered the bathhouse, we stripped and turned in our clothes; they were taken to be disinfected. When we came out of the bathhouse, we stood in line for fresh linen. You put on whatever you got, whether it was too big or too small; if it was too tight, you ripped it up to make it comfortable. By the next bath day, you might turn in underwear that was not much more than rags. Here, too, for the first time, they washed our wadded pants and jackets—once every three months.

The main project at Camp 2 was the construction of a huge ore-processing plant called BOF. My first evening in camp, a commission came around the barracks to question each new worker on his specialty. In my brigade was a young fellow named Mikhail, twenty years old at most, with whom I had become friendly. He knew the ropes, so he told me to classify myself as a "mechanic". There was another fellow in the brigade, a Jew named Vanya, who also signed up as a mechanic. By bedtime that night, we were all three assigned together as a technical crew—and none of us knew the first thing about machinery.

The next day we reported to work at the factory. It was only about a hundred yards from the gates of the camp to the gates of the factory area, so we were simply counted in and out, without guards, almost like punching a time clock. That morning, we three "mechanics" reported to the metalworking section. We soon discovered we were supposed to sketch out sheets of metal, sections of boilers and so forth, for welding. The foreman of the crew, a Jew named Stein, began to explain things to me. I just nodded my head at Vanya and said, "Talk to him. I'm only his helper."

Stein explained quite rapidly what he expected us to do, then gave us a simple sketch with which to begin. Vanya nodded professionally, holding his finger to his forehead and looking thoughtful, occasionally rubbing his chin with his fist. After Stein left, we hauled out our first sheet of iron and went into a huddle. We hadn't the vaguest idea how to begin or what tools to use. After a while, Stein came back. He must have seen by this time that we were bluffing, but he said nothing. Finally, Vanya took the bull by the horns and drew his first sketch—freehand, sort of estimating things with his eye.

Then, with all the assurance of a master mechanic, he called the welder over and told him to cut it out with his torch. It didn't come close to fitting specifications, of course. "Well," said Vanya, "even the experts make mistakes!"

Luckily, I soon got acquainted with a German cutter who was indeed an expert. He told us, step by step, what to do; gradually, our work became acceptable. It was a good thing, too, because it kept us off the wheelbarrow crews outside. The work was being pushed ahead fast, in hopes the buildings could at least be roofed over before the winter set in. Walls were being thrown up so hurriedly that even we "mechanical experts" had to help out from time to time on the wheelbarrows. By late summer, it was already cold enough to freeze the water in the mortar, but bricks were laid anyway. The officials claimed they had a new process for mixing the mortar and laying bricks in cold weather. It was a new process all right; after the mortar set—"froze" would be a better word— it was so loose we could scrape it out from between the bricks with our fingers.

The tempo, the weather, and the mortar combined to produce a real tragedy. A side wall of one of the factory buildings, more than two-thirds completed, collapsed without warning and buried those who were working on it. I never knew how many had been killed, because all the brigades were sent back to camp immediately, even before the rescue work had begun. The next morning, most of the construction brigades, including my own, were sent to Camp 9 on the other side of the city. But new brigades were brought in, the wall went back up, and the factory took shape.

Camp 9 was also a good camp, like Camp 2. The barracks were clean and warm, and again we had mattresses and blankets on the beds. The camp, built near a large clay quarry, was designed to provide Norilsk with the necessary building materials for all the new construction. There was a brick factory next to the camp, as well as smaller factories for producing concrete blocks, precast window frames, and glass binders for special-purpose materials. We worked in the brick factory around the clock in three shifts. There was scarcely any machinery, the mixers were primitive, and even the cutting of bricks was done by hand. The factory itself was divided into two sections: a smaller room where the clay was mixed and the bricks cut, and a large room with three kilns for firing the bricks. I was put to work in the kiln room.

The officials were everywhere, urging us to work faster, to step up the pace. Since this factory was the major source of building supplies for all the construction in and around Norilsk, the Camp 9 officials were desperate to keep up with the demand. They urged, they threatened, they promised—but for the most part they got nowhere. The prisoners in Camp 9 were predominantly thieves, and they did as little work as possible.

Finally, early in 1948, the camp title was changed to "Camp 5". The thieves were sent off to another camp, and large groups of political prisoners were brought to our camp in order to get the work done. With the reorganization of the camp, I was assigned to a construction brigade engaged in the actual building of the city of Norilsk. Brigades from Camp 2 had been working on the city in an area known as "*Gor Stroi*"; now we joined them from Camp 5. The buildings had originally been mostly two-story affairs, much like prison barracks, but by 1948 we were building four- and five-story apartment buildings.

The first stage was always to clear the site of the new building and put up barbed wire around the work area. Then we dug the foundation. For these five-story buildings, we had to go all the way down to bedrock—eighteen to twenty-six yards straight down through the permafrost, and it was all done by pick and shovel. The foundations weren't continuous, though, but simply pylons, two meters square, set on the bedrock to serve as bases for the reinforced concrete pillars that were the central supports of the whole building.

Three men worked on a pylon hole. We had to use buckets to take out the dirt, so one man worked above ground and two below—one to dig and one to load the buckets. We worked ten hours straight, with a half hour out for dinner. Although it was 40 degrees below zero above ground, down in the hole we would have to work so furiously to meet our daily quota that we'd strip to the waist to stay comfortable. As soon as a hole hit bedrock, and the pylon was ready, the concrete was poured immediately. It might take a day or two to fill the hole, since the concrete also had to be mixed by hand, and the weather was anything but ideal for the job.

Once the foundation holes were finished, the walls would be begun around these reinforced pillars. Again, all the work was done by manual labor. Bricks, cement, lumber, everything was carried up ladders or hoisted up five stories by hand. Yet, despite these primitive conditions, five-story apartment buildings were finished in the dead of winter in less than three months.

Of course, there was a lot of waste. Sometimes half a carload of bricks would be broken in unloading, or a half carload of cement would be blown away by the wind while we shoveled it. The prisoners, naturally, never bothered about it. In fact, they might chop up a beam designed to support a ceiling and use it as firewood, just to keep warm in the building. All that mattered was whether or not the building was finished on schedule or the quota of work for the day was done and passed inspection.

The work was hard and the hours were long, but life in Camp 5 was better than I had known it in a long time. The political prisoners here were an interesting lot, friendly, easy to talk to, with a good spirit of camaraderie. As we collected at the gates each night to return home, there was always a lot of joshing and fooling around. On the way back to the camp, we had to pass through the center of Norilsk. The people glanced at us with sympathy, and, though we couldn't stop and talk to them, you could see the brigade straighten their backs and walk a little taller as they marched down the streets of the city.

At Camp 5, too, I said Mass again for the first time since Dudinka. Again, Fr. Casper was my "angel". He had come here straight from Dudinka and was already saying Mass daily for a large group of Poles, Lithuanians, Latvians, and other Catholics. He looked me up the first night I arrived to ask me to help. I was overjoyed and soon took over one of his "parishes".

A Pole named Victor was the organizer of my "parish". A man of medium height, quite bald, with coal-black eyes and pale face, Victor had once been a teacher. Now he was camp bookbinder, and his office was in the headquarters building. As a matter of fact, I used to say Mass in his office. Right under the commandant's nose, as it were, I said the whole Oriental-rite Mass every evening, with rare exceptions. I had a little chalice and paten that one of the prisoners made for me out of nickel; the wine again was raisin wine, and the bread was baked especially by some Latvian Catholics who worked in the camp kitchen.

Victor himself attended Mass and went to Communion every evening. There was also a Russian named Smirnov who came often. He knew the Mass prayers by heart and answered them on behalf of the congregation. It was dangerous to have too many people in the office for fear of drawing attention to ourselves, but as word began to spread, more and more men wanted to attend Mass. After a while, Casper and I began to take chances. We would say Mass in one of the barracks where the men were mostly Lithuanians or Poles and the brigadier himself was a religious man.

Eventually, someone must have informed on me. I was taken off my job with the foundation crew and put into another brigade in a barrack on the other side of camp, under a strict brigadier who was told to watch me closely. He knew practically nothing about religion, however, and hadn't been specifically warned that religious activities were what he was to watch for. So the men would come into the barrack at night to play a game of cards or dominoes and, under the general hubbub of chatter and conversation, tell me how many confessions and Communions were arranged for that night or the next morning.

Afterward, I would go out for a walk. Strolling around the camp, I'd meet one man, then another, hearing his confession as we walked and talked. If there were a lot of confessions or Communions, I would try to have the men get up early in the morning and go to various points around the camp. I'd meet them there, ostensibly by chance, in groups of two or three and, under the guise of a morning greeting, distribute Communion. Otherwise, I tried to get all the Communions distributed after Mass at night; it was risky to keep the Blessed Sacrament overnight for fear of a barracks raid. Not that the guards would be looking for the Blessed Sacrament precisely, but in a raid of that sort they confiscated everything, and I didn't like to take chances.

The officials sometimes questioned me, and once they warned me outright not to engage in any religious work. I knew they were having me watched. Victor, however, kept his ears open for any conversation in the office next to his bookbinding shop concerning me. If he heard my name mentioned, he would try to catch a glimpse through the boards of the man who was reporting on me or watching me.

After a while, though, we moved our Mass location from barrack to barrack in order to avoid suspicion. I would say Mass in a corner of a barrack where the orderly was friendly, while he guarded the door to keep out anyone who didn't live there or who he thought didn't belong to the group. We delivered sermons and exhortations walking up and down in a group in the yard, just like any group of prisoners engaged in a discussion or a bull session. Sometimes I'd hear confessions, if there were just a few, right in the barrack over a game of dominoes or while pretending to read a pamphlet on Communism. Quite a few of the men began to make a regular monthly confession, and there were even a number of weekly ones. All in all, we had a thriving parish.

About mid-year 1948, rumors began to reach our camp of a big copper factory to be built just outside Norilsk. Some of the Camp 5 prisoners who worked in the office first heard of it from the camp officials. It was so important that construction of it was going to be directed by a general named Zveriev, a man with a reputation for getting things done on time. Then, one evening, there was a sign posted on the camp billboard: "The following are to prepare for an *étappe* . . ." My name was on the list.

Camp 4 Builds a Copper Factory

Camp 4 was two miles away. At the pace we marched, it didn't take us long to reach it. As we swung up the path toward the main gate, I admired the two-story barracks of cinder block or brick, smart and well-kept, looking like a city out here in the tundra. Yet it was still a prison camp: there were the double rows of barbed wire that formed the *zapret-naya zona*. We stopped at the gate and waited while the camp officials checked our documents with the convoy guards.

The process took well over an hour, which gave us plenty of time to look over our new home. The camp itself was flat, surrounded on all sides by tundra and thick, high grass. On the east, Schmidtika, five miles away, stood out massively, and just beyond that familiar peak was a mountain range stretching for miles, the natural-resource treasury of Siberia. On the west, the landscape again was flat, with just the barest silhouette of snow-covered hills in the far distance beyond the Yenisei. To the south and north, the land was open for miles, stretching like a valley between the two mountain ranges.

While we waited outside the gate, the prisoners inside the camp came up to the barbed wire. They welcomed us excitedly and told us conditions at Camp 4 were excellent. Everyone seemed to be in good spirits, calling out to find out who we were, asking for friends or fellow countrymen, joking a bit among the nationalities. The guards didn't seem to mind. Finally, the command was given to form up. We were called out by name, one by one, to be checked through the gates.

The checking-in process involved a whole litany of questions: name, father's name, surname; place of origin, date of birth, what was your charge? Where were you charged, where were you sentenced, and who sentenced you? In what city or town were you sentenced, on what date? What camps have you been in, how much time have you left to serve? Are there any charges outstanding against you in any previous camps? If your answers to the questions checked with the facts on your documents, you were let through the gate; if not, you were told to step aside for further interrogation when the whole group had been checked in.

Once we were inside the gates, the guards subjected us to a thorough search, then passed us on to the *naradchik* (foreman), who would assign us to brigades, and the *pompobyt* (manager), who assigned us living quarters. The foreman and manager led us to the bookkeeping department to register our belongings. We were supposed to have, and were only permitted to keep, the regular prison-camp issue: in summer, a cap, jacket, trousers, work shoes, one pair of underwear, and a long cloth to wrap around our legs like puttees, instead of socks. "Later on," the manager warned us, "when you get your assigned bunk, you must register with the bookkeeper your mattress, pillow, blanket, and any other utensils given for your personal use." When winter came, we would turn in our summer clothes and get a pair of *valenki*, wadded pants, wadded jacket, a wadded winter cap with doeskin earlaps, a heavy undershirt and heavier pair of puttees, a pair of canvas gloves, and, if we worked outside, a pair of cotton gloves. This winter issue had to last us through two winters, but the summer wear was only for a year.

After we registered, the foreman led us to the "clubhouse", a spacious one-story barrack in the center of camp. It was equipped with cards and chess sets, a few papers and pamphlets, and good workers won the privilege of reading books. Sometimes, on big holidays such as May Day and the October Feast, there might also be movies in the clubhouse for the outstanding workers. We weren't free at the moment to walk around the camp, since we had not yet been assigned to a brigade or barrack, but the men from the camp began to mill around the clubhouse, looking for old friends. They simply ignored the guards who tried to keep them away.

Here, for the first time, I met a priest I hadn't seen since

1941. He had been told I was in camp, so he came looking for me from group to group. I heard him asking for "Ciszek", but since I didn't recognize him, I kept quiet. Finally, he came over to me and greeted me warmly. The fact he recognized me didn't necessarily mean anything; I asked him who he was. "I'm Father Viktor", he said. "Don't you remember me?" "No", I said. "Remember the day you came to see Archbishop Shepticki in Lvov? I was the one who met you at the door and let you out afterward."

Fr. Viktor asked what had happened to me, what camps I'd been in, and how I was. He went on to tell me how he himself had been arrested, and how the officials in Lvov had been afraid to move against the Archbishop for fear of the people. He told me I was the ninth priest in Camp 4. Immediately, I hoped that Nestrov might be one of the others, but Viktor hadn't seen him. There were two Polish Catholic priests, three Lithuanian Catholic priests, one Latvian, and now me. I told him about Fr. Casper, who had come, too. He asked if we had said Mass; I told him about the arrangements in Camp 5. Viktor told me they all said Mass regularly in Camp 4 and assured me he would make arrangements to supply Fr. Casper and me with whatever we needed to celebrate Mass.

By this time, it was getting late, and I was still waiting to be assigned to a brigade and barrack. As a matter of fact, it was well into the early morning before I was finally called and appointed to a brigade. I followed the *pompobyt* to my barrack and was assigned to the second floor of a two-story building. The barracks were in good condition; they even had radiators and central heating, because this had originally been built as an army camp. But the rooms were crowded because so many new men had been brought in to work on this new project.

Since we had been told we were to report for work next morning, I lost no time getting to sleep. At 5 A.M. the rising signal sounded through the camp; an hour before that, the orderly was up getting our morning ration of bread and *kipiatok*. The reason for his move was obvious when the gong sounded: there was a monstrous traffic jam in the barrack. It soon became apparent that, despite the comforts of these barracks, there were just too many people in them. Not all the men could get to the washroom before we left for work; breakfast was the proverbial commuter's nightmare, eaten on the run.

The site selected for the new copper factory, the *Kombinat*, was about three miles south of the camp. There was no road to it, but we made a road by tramping, thousands at a time. It was the guards who had it rough; as always, they walked parallel to the columns, which meant that under the circumstances they were walking and jumping through gorse up to their waists.

We newcomers first saw the site as a large, open, level area more than a mile square. It was practically all cleared off by the time we were assigned to Camp 4, though not yet completely surrounded by barbed wire. When all the brigades—well over four thousand men—were present, assigned jobs, and given their tools, the place looked like a battlefield. At the signal to begin work, everything exploded.

There was the rattle and bang of jack hammers and air compressors; steam shovels growled, and the loud shriek of metal on metal rang out in the warm, clear air. Prisoners shuffled everywhere with wheelbarrows, loading trucks with earth and rock, dumping it over an embankment to the north as the foundation began to take shape. Through it all, unruffled and unhurried, walked General Zveriev and his staff. They went from job to job, inspecting, encouraging, promising prisoners good rations and extra food for completing the job on time.

As a result, the work tempo was amazing. Earth was flying in all directions, almost exploding out of the ground. By noon, there were heaps of it higher than a man's head lying all over the work site, earth that couldn't be carted away at the pace it was dug. There was no rest, no time out from the furious pace until dinnertime. But at dinnertime—wonder of wonders!—hot soup was brought out to the site in trucks. It was the first time I had seen anything like it in Siberia, and the soup was what the prisoners called "*mirovaya*" (wonderful), thick enough to stand a spoon in.

During dinner, I looked around and saw trainloads of machinery and building materials being unloaded on the sidings, even while the foundations were still being dug. Groups of trucks were roaring up from town, bringing in more machinery lashed down on trailers, unloading, then swinging off in a swirl of dust to get more. After dinner, we went until 5 P.M. without a break. If the pace slackened for a second, the brigadier or an official would be right on top of us, urging us on, promising us better rations.

By evening, everyone was bone-tired and exhausted. The brigades collected at the gate slowly, though everyone was anxious to get home. We returned to camp sometime after 7 P.M., after almost twelve hours on the job, washed up and waited for the meal. What we had been promised was true! There was more soup for everyone, *kasha*, a piece of fish, and another two hundred grams of bread for every man. It was almost a feast. That was the ordinary day at Camp 4. We also worked Sundays, if the weather was good, and in fact holidays were rare. The pace was a driving one to finish digging and pouring the foundations while the weather was reasonably good. We were told we'd get our holidays and our rest when the weather turned bad. If the work was especially hard, the brigade would get a couple ounces of whiskey per man, on the General's orders, to keep up their strength. They would also get a "plus-2" or a "plus-3" meal ticket. This was the first camp I had ever been in where we were really fed well and, as a result, the men grew perceptibly stronger. Their frames filled out, their faces were fuller. There was plenty of *makhorka* and other small comforts, and a man could easily earn an extra portion of *kasha* or soup on the job.

All these changes for the better had a good effect on most of the men, but not all. Family men, for instance, had more time to think about things other than food, so they thought of their families—some of them to point of depression. Now that the most elemental needs of clothing and food necessary just to survive were easily satisfied, some of the men began to look for ways to satisfy other appetites. If you knew the right people, you could arrange with the guards to get you a woman for about twenty-five rubles. They weren't allowed into camp, but they worked at various jobs on the construction site, so procurement wasn't exactly impossible. There was also a certain amount of homosexuality in the camp, especially among the younger men.

Here at Camp 4, most of the nationality groups stuck together. They were clannish in the sense that they took care of their own, especially the sick or emaciated workers in the group, but surprisingly enough there was very little bickering between the various groups. The Baltic peoples, the Poles, and the Ukrainians were the workhorses of the camp, the backbone of construction work. The Georgians, Armenians, and Latvians usually worked in the kitchen, though quite a few of them were brigadiers and foremen of the work crews. The Chinese and Japanese worked for the most part in the laundry, the kitchen, and the infirmary.

One of my first new friends here at Camp 4, surprisingly enough, since I always tried to avoid his kind, was a thief

named Yevgeny. He was a stocky, well-built man in his thirties, slightly taller than average, very good with his fists. The
small, restless eyes that dominated his face were an indication
of his seemingly boundless energy. Yevgeny somehow took a
liking to me and taught me many a trick for scrounging food;
he was considered a pro even by his fellow cons. Since he was
feared and respected by his fellow thieves, his friendship often
stood me in good stead. Yevgeny knew I was a priest, and,
like most thieves, he had a very primitive idea of religion,
mixed with any number of superstitions. He asked me, for
instance, to bless a little cross for him, which he wore from
then on. Yet he wore it more as a talisman or good luck
charm. He did bless himself as he put it on, but he also pulled
out a knife and warned the crowd around him, "If anyone
laughs at this cross, he'll get this knife right in the belly!"

Yevgeny had been baptized a Catholic, but he hadn't prac-
ticed his faith in so long there was little left except these superstitious externals. He was a loyal friend, though, and little
by little, over the months I knew him, I brought him back to
the point where he finally made a confession and received
Communion. After that, he went to confession and Communion almost regularly, but he still retained his own peculiar
moral code and violent ethics of fist and knife when the occasion offered—and the occasions were frequent enough.

I once saw him stand off three other thieves with his bare
hands, though I doubt if the Marquis of Queensbury would
have approved. With his back to a wall, he laid out the first
with a sickening smash to the throat, caught the second with
a kick in the groin, flattened the third with his fists. The
whole process couldn't have taken more than a minute. Afterward, Yevgeny looked around for any other takers, then
walked nonchalantly away, leaving the three men stretched
out on the ground. He was equally good with a knife, and

since in his code of self-preservation just about any use of the knife could be justified as self-defense, it was never exactly clear to him why I should make such a fuss over incidents of that sort.

Practically every day, Yevgeny would drop around and ask if I needed anything or if anyone was giving me trouble. If so, the implication was, I had merely to let him know. Every once in a while, he would come into our barrack, catch my eye, and nod for me to follow him outside. We'd go straight to the kitchen, where he would rap on the door and tell the cook to give me some *kasha*. The cook wouldn't even blink, just fill up a cup, add a slice of fat, pour in a little linseed oil, and hand it to me. Yevgeny would tell me to beat it and eat the food. That was that. He never volunteered any further information, and I knew better than to ask any questions.

Yevgeny was a brigadier, and, because of his reputation, his brigade was the roughest in the camp. He took good care of his men as to food and extra favors, but he drove them unsparingly at work. One day he bawled out two surly young Lithuanians for loafing on the job. As he turned to leave, one of them split his skull wide open with a sledge hammer. Yevgeny died without a sound. I had been working on another project that day, and I found out about Yevgeny's death only late that night. I was heartbroken. I wished I'd been able at least to give him absolution, but I had to console myself with the thought that two weeks before his death he had confessed and received Communion for the last time.

Another good friend here was a young graduate student from New York's Columbia University, a Chinese Catholic named Chung. His father had been a wealthy merchant in China, so Chung had been sent to America to study. I never learned why he was arrested, for he never talked about that.

He spoke English quite well, though, and when he found out I was an American, he looked me up and introduced himself in English. He came to Mass regularly after that, and on Sundays I sometimes gave him a short sermon in English. Because of his education, Chung was influential with the Chinese community in Camp 4. From time to time, he invited me over to converse with them; he introduced me as "a good man", so I was warmly received.

From then on, my shirt was washed, ironed, and mended every week, although normally our laundry was done (and this itself was an innovation) once every three weeks. Without fail, my shirt would be picked up Saturday night and returned to me Sunday morning, with a few pieces of bread tucked into the pockets for good measure. Eventually, Chung and most of the Chinese prisoners in Camp 4 were repatriated as a result of the Moscow–Peiping Pact. When Chung told me he was going home, I asked him to write my Provincial at Fordham Road in New York. He promised he would, and I gave him the address. That was in 1949, but I never saw or heard from him again.

Hospital Aid—Thanks to Misha

Meanwhile, the work on the factory was proceeding under forced draft. I decided the strain was beginning to tell, so one night I reported to the medical center. The place was jammed as usual. Many of the "patients" were simply playing the odds; the doctors had a special limit they could free from work each day, without consultation, simply by filling out an exemption slip on their own. Some men had friends among the doctors who would slip their name on the list if they didn't already have a quota of urgent cases. Others came just to talk to the doctors, who were prisoners themselves, on the chance of conning their way onto the exemption list.

It was like a lottery. Some of the men came back night after night with a different story or a different illness until they hit it lucky and got a day or two off. There were many, of course, who really did have a serious illness or some physical injury that needed immediate attention. But a lot of the men in the waiting room that night were simply men like myself, worn out and beginning to notice the daily strain, looking for a day off.

And the prisoners knew a lot of ways to help the "odds" along. Many of them simply drank tobacco juice or swallowed a piece of soap. But since any temperature over 100 degrees was enough to insure medical treatment, the men had all sorts of devices to induce a fever. They put hot compresses under their armpits or pepper plasters on the soles of their feet; the quickest way to get the thermometer to register, though, was to slip a piece of bitter root under the gums. Family men, especially, were not particularly eager to work themselves to death here in the camps.

As I sat in the medical center waiting my turn, the registration room door opened, and a young fellow about thirty years old came out. He was medium-sized and blond—at least what was left of his hair on an almost completely bald head. He hesitated, looked around the room, then looked at the cards in his hand and was about to go back in. I thought I recognized him; I caught his eye, then I was sure. "Misha!" I said. He looked at me without even blinking, though a bit startled, then said very softly under his breath, "*Cito!*" (the Italian equivalent of "Quiet!" or "Ssh!").

It all happened so quickly no one else in the room noticed. Then he went back into the registry office, while I sat there puzzled. Misha had been a fellow student of mine at the

Russicum. I never expected to bump into him here. I wasn't sure what his caution meant, but I had learned in prison not to push a man who doesn't want to talk or to insist on the identity of a man who denies it. After a while, the crowd thinned out, and Misha again stepped out of his office. He walked over to me with several cards in his hand and said, very officially, "Are you Ciszek?" I nodded. "Come into the office, we have to straighten out this card."

Only when all the doors of his office were closed, and he was sure no one could overhear us, did Misha drop his pose of official business and greet me warmly. "However," he said, "don't let anyone know you know me!" We talked a little then about the old days, but Misha was very cautious; he never said an extra word. "Tomorrow," he said, "you stay home and rest; I'll put your name on the sick list. If anyone asks, you have a high fever." With that we shook hands and he mumbled, "I'll see you around."

I slept like a log that night, just knowing that I didn't have to get up at 5 A.M. The next morning, when the gong rang, I just stretched in my bunk and rolled over. Other members of the brigade crowded around asking, "What's wrong with Valodga?" The brigadier came over and threatened to throw me out of the bunk onto the floor. "What do you think you're doing?" he said. "Get out of that bed!" "I'm sick", I said. "Why don't you go to a doctor, then?" "I did, last night, and I think I'm exempted for the day." "You 'think'? What do you mean, you 'think'? Get out of that bunk!" The foreman had not yet been around to the barracks with the sick list, so the brigadier made me dress, eat breakfast, and be ready to go.

Just as we were leaving the barracks, though, the foreman came in and read out my name among the list of those who were exempted from work. The brigadier was mad because I hadn't told him the night before about my visit to the doctor.

That was the standard procedure, but this was the first time I had had any time off at Camp 4, and I was so elated that I forgot to tell the brigadier. The rest of the brigade wished me good luck and a good rest and left for the morning lineup.

About ten o'clock, Misha dropped over to the barrack. We talked for a while about the old days in Rome, about life in the camps and his work at the medical center. But he said nothing about his arrest, his own prison days, or his sentence. He did promise, though, to use his influence to try and get me another job. "It will take a while," he said, "so don't tell anybody anything. Right now, let's take a walk."

We walked over to the barrack where he lived with the doctors and medical technicians. He made a few sandwiches, which we shared for lunch. Food was plentiful in this barrack, because the free doctors from the city brought all sorts of food for the staff. Misha was popular with the doctors, but I discovered he wasn't particularly liked by the other prisoners; they suspected him of working hand in glove with the authorities. In all my dealings with Misha, I never noticed any grounds for such suspicions. Perhaps a certain amount of it was jealousy, because he had such a plush job and got along so well with the officials, who allowed him many privileges.

About 11:30, he told me to come with him to the medical center. When we got there, he told me not to say anything and especially not to act familiar, then led me into one of the reception rooms. There were two young women doctors there, free doctors from the town, who gave me a thorough going-over—chest, heart, lungs, eyes, etc. Then they began to write up my history. Actually, I was strong as a bull here in Camp 4, but what they wrote was more in line with Misha's "diagnosis". From there, Misha took me to another doctor, a prisoner and a Pole from Warsaw. Misha had a short conversation with him before I entered, then ushered me in.

The doctor was a tall, heavy-set man named Gregori, big-boned, but with gentle hands and a serious, full face topped with a thatch of chestnut hair. He was a warm, congenial fellow, quite frank and outspoken. During the course of his examination, I told him I was a priest. When he had finished, he said, "Well, you're a pretty healthy specimen, but I'll take care of that." I thanked him, we shook hands, and Misha took me to a third doctor. He was also a prisoner, a lanky, jovial Ukraine from Lvov. We talked a little bit about Lvov, then he also gave me a clean bill of sickness and I left.

The next day, the foreman read out my name on the sick list again. The brigadier was a little suspicious; he told me frankly I didn't look sick. "Well," I said, "I do feel a little better today, but the doctors told me I better lay off work for another day, and they know best." That afternoon, the weather turned bitter, and the first of the season's storms swept over Norilsk. For the next two days, outside work was impossible. My vacation, therefore, lasted over four days, and I was beginning to feel pretty good.

On the evening of the fourth day, Misha sent for me. He told me he had arranged for me to work in the medical center as an orderly. "You begin tomorrow morning," Misha said, "but keep it quiet." That night I said nothing to anyone—I didn't want any slip-ups—and the next morning I walked out before the foreman came to announce any changes. I didn't want to have to explain things to the brigadier. I slipped across camp to the medical barrack, and my breakfast ration was waiting for me there, a sure sign I had been assigned to that barrack.

The place was spotless, with two sheets on every bunk, white and sparkling. I felt dirty by contrast. Misha got me a change of clothes; then, after breakfast, I reported to the medical center. What a place to work! It was clean and warm and comfortable, and, compared with life on the construction gangs, there was almost nothing to do. There were three other orderlies besides myself, a Chinese and two Estonians; one of the Estonians showed me my job. When the morning examination of prisoners started, I was in the wardrobe checking coats and giving out tickets—a far cry from jack hammers and a shovel.

When the morning examinations ended, we orderlies went to work. I was assigned two rooms, one about eight by ten feet, the other about twelve by fifteen. I swept them, washed the floors, then turned on the medical heat lamps so the floor would dry. Meanwhile, I cleaned the windows and tables, sterilized the instruments, changed the disinfecting solutions and the sheets on the examination tables, put everything back in its place, locked the door, hung up the key in the registry room, and was free for the morning! What a life!

I went over to the medical barrack for lunch and met the doctors, all prisoners. Beside Gregori and the other doctor who had examined me before, there was Leonid, a Russian who had worked in China; he was delighted to learn I was an American, and he spoke a few words to me in English, not good, but intelligible. The surgeon was a Jew from Moscow named Abrikasov. He was an extremely knowledgeable surgeon, who had even taught the subject for a while, but he was a bit weak on practice. Some even went so far as to hint he was a bit of a butcher on the operating table. He had, however, two very skilled interns, a Rumanian named Tollya and a Russian named Vashya, who performed most of the actual operations.

There was Sergei, the pharmacist, a thin and sickly Georgian who was a graduate pharmacist from Moscow. The head doctor among the prisoners was a young, silent Pole from Lvov named Pavlik. He was a highly skilled surgeon, frequently called to the city hospital in Norilsk to perform difficult heart and brain surgery. Highly esteemed by his colleagues, he operated mostly in the prison infirmary on more critical cases and left the medical center surgery to Dr. Abrikasov and his two assistants.

Counting the orderlies and Misha, there were only fourteen men in our medical barrack, including a Ukrainian dentist named Anatoly. He certainly had his work cut out for him; all the prisoners who had been in the camps for any length of time had extremely bad teeth, if not literally rotten. Anatoly, a graduate of the Lvov Medical Institute, used to work far into the night in his laboratory to help his swarms of patients here in Camp 4.

We ate a leisurely lunch and sat around talking for a long while; we weren't due back to the medical center until 5 P.M. All the men in the barrack were most gracious to me.

When the evening examinations began, I saw to it there was plenty of hot water in the doctors' cubicles, emptied the surgical trays and cleaned them, ran errands to the barracks for the doctors to check on those who were sick, and even helped carry the stretcher cases, if necessary. The doctors finished up by about 9:30 or 10:00 P.M. When they left, I began my clean-up as before, washing and scrubbing the floors, changing linen, sterilizing the instruments, etc. This might take until midnight, but the Chinese orderly would duck over to the kitchen and bring us *kasha* and soup from a friend of his who worked there.

The first night, Fr. Viktor came to see me and brought with him everything I needed to say Mass. He gave me a handwritten copy of the Oriental liturgy, a little metal chalice, paten and all, in a small portable box, and he even had real Mass wine and altar breads. When all the orderlies and doctors had finished, long after midnight, Misha stepped out of his office and beckoned me in. There I said Mass, and Misha assisted. Every night after that, with rare exceptions, I said Mass in the medical center. On holidays, as well as on Sundays, one or two of the doctors would also attend my Mass. Several of them also went to confession and Communion regularly.

Fr. Viktor was a little fellow, stocky, with chestnut hair, a pointed chin, thin nose, and glasses. He had a peculiar, mincing step to his walk, which made it easy to pick him out of a crowd, even all the way across the camp. He worked at the factory site as head of a crew that measured the temperature of the poured concrete to indicate how it was drying. Because of the weather, and the fact that construction went right through the winter, the concrete was heated by anodes connected to certain of the reinforcing rods. It was Fr. Viktor's job to walk around two or three times a day writing down the temperatures. The rest of the time he sat in a little construction shed out of the wind.

Viktor had friends galore, among both the workers and the camp officials, so he was hardly ever assigned to work at hard labor. Consequently, he had time to do a tremendous amount of spiritual work. He was always on the go, visiting the sick and hearing confessions. His little shack at the construction site was an ideal location for hearing confessions during the day or giving guidance and counseling to one or two of the prisoners.

Another priest, call him "Fr. Joe", was a tall, heavy-set, and balding Pole. He had a booming voice and punctuated everything he said with emphatic gestures. He was an extremely zealous priest but, unlike Viktor, steady and slow. A friend of his, Fr. Leonid, was also tall and almost completely bald. Like Viktor, he was high-strung, always on the go. Both he and "Fr. Joe" had great followings among the men.

Beside Fr. Casper and I, there were also two Lithuanian priests, who always went around together, and three Greek Orthodox priests, who joined us from time to time. We all said Mass regularly, thanks to Fr. Victor, who supplied everything—and never seemed to run out. Each priest was assigned his own little group or "parish", and we tried to make our work inconspicuous by keeping the groups separate and distinct. Yet Viktor saw to it that every prisoner, if he wanted to, knew at least one priest in the camp.

Working in the medical center, with a certain amount of free time and a greater amount of freedom, I was appointed by Viktor to give a three-day retreat, or spiritual exercises, to the others. I'd give one talk before they went to work, one after the day's work, and another in the evening about nine o'clock. At the same time, I was giving some retreats to individual prisoners who had asked for greater spiritual direction. On Sundays and holidays, we priests would all get together. Each would give a ten-minute sermon. We confessed to each other at least every Saturday, and we tried to hold frequent discussions of the moral problems that came up in camp and how best to handle them.

After my first month in the medical center, I began to wonder what would happen to my new job when the officials went over the list at the end of the month, as was customary. Misha admitted that there might be some difficulty, but he said he hoped to work it out. On the last day of the month, the new assignments were posted on the camp bulletin board; I was surprised to find myself still assigned to the medical center. This time, however, I was listed as an intern—thanks to Tollya and Vashya.

For the next month, I worked with them. At first I did only simple jobs, such as unbandaging and cleaning the wounds for them to treat and observing how they did it. After a few days, though, I could treat simple wounds according to their directions; I even lanced sores, cut away proud flesh, and performed minor operations of that nature. The first couple of days, I admit, I almost got sick. In fact, I got stomach cramps trying to keep myself from vomiting.

From time to time, I also assisted Tollya and Vashya at appendectomies, setting bones, treating fractures, and so forth. I even learned how to make a perfectly acceptable splint or plaster cast. All in all, I found it a fascinating month, once my stomach settled down. After office hours, in return for my "appointment" to the crew, I cleaned and disinfected all our surgical instruments and kept the surgery spotless. After that, I said Mass every night.

It was too good to last, and toward the end of the month new difficulties arose. Even Misha, this time, was worried, but the new list again assigned me to the medical center—in the pharmacy. Sergei and I were good friends by this time, and he had managed to snare me. I found the work, if anything, even more interesting than the previous month. Sergei certainly needed the help. A tremendous number of pills and powders had to be prepared every day, for very few of our medicines came already packaged. I measured out the ingredients on the scales for Sergei, who was quite literally adept at pill rolling; after a short while, I could make up most of the ordinary prescriptions by heart. I got so interested in the work, in fact, that I forgot all about the dangers of working here. I left the worrying strictly to Misha. Whenever officials came from Norilsk for an inspection tour, for instance, I was always warned to disappear. Then, just when everything seemed to be going so well, the roof fell in!

Just before the new monthly list was to be posted, I was called out one morning to the guards' quarters. When I reported, I was sent immediately to the penal brigade—no questions asked. That same evening, Misha and Fr. Viktor also arrived in the penal brigade. Misha, though, was out within three days, as soon as the director of the medical center could spring him. He was almost indispensable.

The penal brigade was engaged in building a new camp prison. We tore down the old one, cleared the site, and set to work digging foundations, again all by hand. It would have been brutal work at any time, but I was out of condition after my three months of easy living in the medical center, and I really felt it. Fr. Viktor was set to making bricks. All this was our punishment for tampering with the prison lists and removing my name from the hard-labor category my sentence required.

After a week, Misha succeeded in getting Fr. Viktor out, but it took him a while to free me from the penal brigade. Finally, when the new monthly lists were made out, Misha and Viktor succeeded in getting me reassigned to a construction crew at the factory site. The first morning I reported to work, I was amazed at how much had been done in the three months since I'd seen it. It seemed to me the buildings had sprung up overnight. I was assigned to work as an electrician, but I told the brigadier I didn't know the first thing about it. He gave me odd jobs that required little technical training.

One day, though, all the lights in the plant went out. The only "electricians" in the main shanty were myself and Aloysha, who knew less about electricity than I did. Since the foremen were demanding lights, however, we went out to have a look. We opened the fuse box—on the theory that even we could change a fuse—and discovered we were working with a three-phase system. I replaced two of the fuses and started to work on the third. I was so nervous for fear of electrocuting myself that Aloysha was convulsed with laughter. I turned around to tell him to be quiet, my finger slipped into the contacts, and—I got the full 320 volts! I was knocked flat on my back, unconscious, and was out for almost half an hour.

When I came to, Aloysha was still there laughing; when I stopped shaking, I began to laugh myself at the absurdity of it all. Later, we reported the accident to the brigadier. "Who told you to do that?" he said. "Well, they needed an electrician," I said, "and I figured anyone could change a fuse." "Yeah," he said, "well, no more of that! From now on you and Aloysha are demoted to cable carriers."

Still, Aloysha and I managed to find trouble. They told us one day to carry a high-voltage cable to the other end of the factory. As we walked into the building out of the snow, we were temporarily blinded. I stepped on a live, high-voltage line—there was a brilliant flash and a cloud of smoke. Aloysha, behind me, dropped his end of the cable and took off at a gallop. Somebody pulled the master switch; everything in the building went black. The men on the crew began to holler my name, thinking I was dead or perhaps unconscious. I answered that I was all right, but afraid to move. "The line is dead", they shouted. I scrambled out. The rubber on my shoe was a blob of jelly, and everyone in the crew "reassured" me by telling me that my survival was a miracle.

Even without such reassurances, I had had enough. I told Fr. Viktor about it that night, and he arranged for me to join his brigade; he was supposed to have only four men, but he persuaded the officials to assign me as a fifth. Two days later, I was officially transferred to his temperature-measuring crew.

By fall, the walls of the main factory were up. Work was begun on the roof. The weather turned worse, but the work went on; even in wind and snow the prisoners worked on the girders overhead. I saw men fall from the topmost girder to the concrete floor, and when a man fell from that height, he was a goner. The cause of the accidents, though, was not just the weather. It was also the prisoners' inexperience at working on high iron and the furious tempo of the work. General Zveriev was determined to finish the job on schedule. The price might be three or even four men a day, but what were these among so many?

Zveriev's determination paid off: the *Kombinat* was finished by New Year's Day 1952. The next day, the first melt of copper was to be fired up, so the brigades were kept home while the city officials and citizens of Norilsk came to witness the opening of this great new plant. The first test they made of the new furnaces, however, was accompanied by a gigantic explosion!

For the inaugural celebration, the tops of all the *Kombinat* buildings had been covered with electrified billboards bearing the names of Lenin, Stalin, Marx, Engels. After the blast, which blew the roof off the furnace section, the lights on Stalin's name were out. Some of the men in camp took it as a joke, but to others it seemed a curious omen. We were continually hearing rumors about Stalin's health, and this accident caused a lot of comment in the camp.

The Revolt

In February 1952, I was transferred back to Camp 5. Fr. Viktor stayed behind in Camp 4. Since there was very little work at that site any more, now that the *Kombinat* was finished, he came to one of the common construction sites in Norilsk, called "*Gor Stroi*", every day. He was put in charge of a warehouse that stored the gasoline and oil for the heavy machinery. Here again, he had his own little work-shack office. I used to visit him daily during the noon meal, and we would take turns saying Mass in the shanty.

Because of his job as watchman, Viktor could also be a great help to the women prisoners. There was a women's camp now, about one hundred yards from the front gates of Camp 5; the women, too, had been put to work on the construction of the city. In the women's camp, there was a group of Ukrainian nuns who had been arrested. They were a great influence on the young girls, especially, helping them and arranging for their confessions. The women couldn't cross out of their zone, but from time to time it was possible to arrange for those of them who wanted to go to confession to stand in a certain place along the barbed wire between zones, and Fr. Viktor would pass by to "hear" their confessions.

Most of the time, they wrote down their transgressions on a sheet of paper and handed it to Viktor as he passed. The notes were numbered, but no names were given, and Viktor burned them in his shanty stove immediately. The next day, the women would come back, make an Act of Contrition, signal the proper number with their fingers, and receive absolution. If it was impossible or sometimes inadvisable either to pass the notes or to absolve the women one by one, we would try at least to give them general absolution. All of us helped with this work, but Viktor, by reason of his job, had more free time at the work site, so he did most of it. Some of the notes sent this way, obviously, could have been intercepted. The women's willingness to take this risk to receive the sacrament, their openness and confidence in us, was a source of great edification to us as priests.

In general, the women had a much harder life in camp than the men. They were often considered fair game not only by the men in the camps but by the free men as well who worked on the various construction jobs, by the guards, and even the camp officials. The fact that there were two big barracks in the women's camp full of children under five years of age was obvious testimony to the way things went. Moreover, a woman who had a child was immediately put on better rations until she recovered, and she didn't have to work for the period of her recovery. If this wasn't an inducement to the women, it was at least no deterrent. This doesn't mean that all the women succumbed, by any means. The women from the Baltic states especially, as well as the Ukrainians and Poles, were often of extremely high character and most devout, despite the conditions to which they were subjected. On the other hand, like all prison camps, the women's camp, too, had its share of professional criminals.

By the summer of 1952, brigades from Camp 5 were engaged in a wide variety of activities. The main effort of the camp was still what was called "*Gor Stroi*"—or, the "building of the city"—but to accomplish it we had to man a whole host of supporting industries that had sprung up around the camp. I was working again, for instance, in the old two-story brick factory and kiln a short two-hundred-yard walk from our main gate. A railroad spur ran just to the south and west of the camp, leading to the clay pits, where the women's brigades now quarried the raw material. Along the railroad track to the west was a string of small factories that turned out cement, concrete blocks, fiberglass, resin glue, and *kepenit* (a special heat-and-cold-resistant, very strong glass). Still other brigades worked in the completed sections of town, digging drainage and sewage ditches, finishing the roads.

Conditions in the camp itself, though, were much worse. The lack of spirit among the prisoners was quite noticeable, especially after Camp 4, and the officials responded with stricter discipline. Rough handling of the prisoners, even beatings, grew common. We were aware of a general tightening up all across the board. The prisoners resented it and grew sullen. It was a vicious circle.

In January 1953, the unrest in the camp was stirred by new rumors. Free workers from the city, who supervised work at the construction sites, spread the news that Stalin was sick. Then came the startling rumors that a number of Kremlin doctors had been arrested and imprisoned. Next we heard, unbelievably, that the doctors had been released and rehabilitated. And mixed up with all of this was the stubborn rumor that Stalin himself was already dead.

Such rumors occasioned a lot of wild talk in the camps. Camp officials were as badly disturbed as the men. It wasn't long before the gathering of more than two people was prohibited; violations were punished by extra hard labor in the camp or the penal brigade. The general atmosphere, bad enough before, deteriorated even more.

More and more, now, the prisoners began to resent being called by number. They considered it degrading. More and more, the camp officials and guards began to insist on the numbers; at the morning inspection, they would check to see that the numbers were plainly visible on prisoners' clothing. The foreman would go through the ranks of fives lined up to leave camp and drag out anyone whose number was erased, illegible, or hidden. If there was any grumbling or murmuring from the other prisoners, the brigade wouldn't move until the person who had made the remark was identified and, possibly, beaten.

Several other disciplinary measures were now introduced into the camp routine. Previously the barracks had never been locked at night; now they were locked after the 9 P.M. check-up. If a man wasn't in his own barrack when the check-up was taken, he was automatically slated for the *bur*. But if he hid or was still missing when all the barracks had been checked, the alarm would be rung and a control check made of the whole camp. There were times when such control checks were made two or three times during the night, and on such nights the camp might not get to sleep until 2 or 3 A.M. Still, we were expected to be ready to get up for work at 5 A.M.

Inspections at the gate in the morning, and when the brigades returned home at night, became much more stringent. It became almost daily practice for the guards to search every prisoner thoroughly, looking for pieces of iron, knives, letters, notes. In the process, they would confiscate any extra clothes a man was wearing, and they also began to take such things as medals, holy pictures, scapulars, or homemade crucifixes. All this was done in the compound, despite the cold. The guards wouldn't hesitate to make a man strip naked if they suspected anything. Sometimes they would even insist he take off his *valenki* and the rags around his ankles, so that a man might wind up standing in the snow, barefoot, without a stitch of clothes on.

Work in *Gor Stroi* had slowed almost to a standstill. Where before the brigades from Camp 5 had put up whole buildings in two months, now they were averaging one floor of one building every six or seven months. The truck drivers who brought our supplies also brought news of similar unrest in other camps. The trainmen who ran from Norilsk to Dudinka talked of similar discontent among the prisoners at the port.

Some of the brigadiers still tried to drive their brigades hard, though. Several times after work the brigades were held at the gates of the construction site for hours while the guards went looking for a missing brigadier. He might be found immersed in the newly poured concrete, badly mutilated or even completely dismembered. Yet the officials hesitated to take drastic action for fear the prisoners might get out of hand.

"Squealers", who were always detested, were now in continual danger as a result of the growing spirit of vengeance. Many of them refused to work outside the camp; the occasions for reprisals and "accidents" were too great at the work sites. They tried to be appointed orderlies or get jobs in the office, and they tried especially to change barracks. The camp officials felt more or less obliged to help them, for the sake of the information they could supply.

I remember a young Lithuanian lad who was suspected by his fellow Lithuanians of being a "squealer". One evening, two thin, nearly emaciated Lithuanians in shabby clothes waited for him on the porch outside his barrack. When he stepped out, they jumped him and split his head open with an axe before he could say a word. They kept swinging at him over and over again. Then they didn't even bother to run. They cleaned the axe carefully, left their victim lying in a pool of blood, and went off to the camp prison, freely confessing their actions.

Another morning, just after the signal to rise, and as soon as the barracks were unlocked, three men masked and caped down to their ankles appeared at one of the barracks. Before anyone could move, they strode straight to a bunk, tore off the blankets, and grabbed at the occupant. As the poor man tried to dive for the door, he was knocked to the floor and hauled into the corridor, where he was stabbed repeatedly. No one in the barracks moved. Nobody wanted to get involved in a case that didn't concern him. It wasn't necessarily a case of "squealing"; men who had grudges and personal vendettas took advantage of the unrest to settle old scores.

The acknowledged leader of the prisoners in Camp 5 was a man of uncertain nationality known only as "Mikhail". A talented fellow, he worked in the clubhouse taking care of the library, the bulletin board, and the *Stien Gazeta* (camp newspaper), which was tacked up on the bulletin board and contained announcements of prisoner activities, outstanding performances by the camp *Stakhanovites*, or the brigade percentages for the day. Mikhail was middle-sized, tanned, and bald, sturdily built and seemingly without a nerve in his body. It was rumored that he had been a former army official before his arrest; in any event, he was the brains behind the prisoners' operations as they became more and more organized.

Something certainly was in the air, not only in Camp 5, but in the city of Norilsk itself. Even the trains coming up from Dudinka now carried slogans scrawled across the cars and engines: "We demand higher wages", "Better food and more of it", "Better conditions for work and less of it." News trickled in from the continent, and rumors spread of unrest and trouble in the camps around Karaganda, Kazakhstan, and Vorkuta to the west.

There was still much talk of Stalin's illness and of turnovers in the Kremlin, but we had few hard facts to go on. Even the free workers in town had heard only rumors and conjectures. Suddenly, one morning during the first week in March 1953, the news was broadcast over the camp loudspeakers that Josef Dzhugashvili Stalin was dead!

The immediate reaction throughout the camp was one of shock. Men met each other and whispered the news in little knots, making the sign of the cross and murmuring, "*Gospodi!*" Tension and fear were general, and the expectation that something must happen now. The camp officials were bustling about, traveling into the city and back again. Different officials, in their turn, came out to the camp from town and returned. Work was at a standstill; the foreman and his helpers seemed bewildered and pensive. The atmosphere resembled a vacuum, and I thought almost anything might happen.

The guards outside and inside the camp had been doubled. There were two men now in every tower along the barbed wire, twice as many sentries at the gates as ever before. Comments on the death of Stalin rippled like an undertow through the camp. The camp officials began to shift prisoners from one camp to another, hoping to separate leaders from their followers. Groups arrived at our camp from as far away as the continent. For the most part, these were either hard-bitten, professional criminals or else *Benderovcy*, a famous band of tough Ukrainian partisans who hated the Soviets. None of them went to work at *Gor Stroi* or elsewhere, but they walked around the camp as if they owned it. They were well dressed, not in camp clothes but civilian clothes, and they just refused to work. They dealt with the camp officials in a way that plainly indicated they didn't want to be bothered. They weren't.

The camp was soon buzzing with the tales they brought of a revolt in the camps of Karaganda. Troops had had to be called in to quell the riot there. They also told of rumors of other camps already in revolt. It seemed to me that officials at Camp 5 had just about let things get out of control now. In any event, our own revolt was not long in coming. We were already at work in the brick factory the morning it started, and as the brigades from the women's camp passed between the brick factory and Camp 5 on their way to the clay pits, they engaged in the usual morning banter with the men. As their brigades turned east around the south end of Camp 5, though, some of the newcomers were there along the barbed wire to greet them. The guards began hurrying the women along, and the newcomers hooted.

As usual, the men began to throw little notes over the wire

to the girls. Some of them were intercepted by the guards, which occasioned some curses from the prisoners. The girls threw back notes of their own; a couple of them landed in the *zapretnaya zona* between the two strands of barbed wire. For some reason, the newcomers decided to retrieve them. The young guard in the tower yelled at them to get back, but they ignored him; the guards had no permission to shoot into the camp. As they approached the fence, though, this young guard opened fire with his machine gun. Two of the *Benderovcy* were killed instantly, three others were wounded.

The prisoners hauled their wounded and dead into a nearby barrack, then threatened to assault and pull down the tower. Others ran through the camp, spreading the news of the guard's action. The women, who had watched the whole thing, were quickly pushed along the road to the clay pits. Within half an hour, the camp was in an uproar.

The camp officials themselves didn't know what had triggered the uprising. As soon as they found out, they came to the barrack where the prisoners were holed up and, in a conciliatory gesture, ordered the young guard to come down off the tower. The young fellow climbed down, amidst the threats of the prisoners, but the *Benderovcy* ordered the officials to get away from their barrack. All over the camp, men began shouting, "Murderer! Murderer! We don't want to die! You can't kill us!" The officials, growing alarmed, retreated to the north gate.

With the officials gone, a crowd of prisoners went to the bathhouse looking for two orderlies suspected of being "squealers". "Where's Marco?" they shouted as they burst through the door. Marco was taking a shower. He ran headlong out the other door, heading for the barbed wire. He gashed himself badly, but clambered over the fence and jumped into the *zapretnaya zona*, hoping to make a dash for the main gate. A guard on one of the nearby towers shouted "*Stoi!*" Marco kept running down the lane between the barbed wire, dodging stones hurled at him by other prisoners. He got about five yards; the tower guard dropped him with two shots.

While this was going on, the other "squealer" ran out and climbed over the barbed wire. The officials at the north gate finally signaled the tower guards not to shoot; the "squealer" ran along the death zone to the guard house at the gate. There he turned and shook his fist at the *Benderovcy*. Infuriated, a mob surged closer to the gate.

All work stopped. Many of the prisoners in the factory ran the two hundred yards or so across the railroad track to the barbed wire fences of the camp to find out from the prisoners inside what was happening. By this time, a committee of prisoners was already forming, with Mikhail and some of the *Benderovcy* at its head. They told the brigadiers not to return to camp, but to have their men take over control of the factories. "Did you hear that, men?" shouted the brigadiers. Nobody went back to work.

After a short lull, a number of cars came sliding down the road from Norilsk with officials from the city. They stopped at the gates, talked to the camp officials, and tried to enter the camp. The mob howled at them, and they stopped just inside the gate. Mikhail's committee went to meet them. Immediately, the prisoners accused the camp officials of cold-blooded murder. The camp commandant acknowledged that the tower guard had no right to shoot inside the camp; he promised that the man would be punished. But then the committee demanded that conditions in the camp be changed completely.

They listed some specific details: the numbers should be taken off prisoners' clothing; letters should be permitted to relatives of the prisoners once a month, not once a year; no more than eight hours of work a day; prisoners should be paid for their work; the prisoners should be given credit, in the form of a reduced sentence, for extra work; e.g., for every day of work in which a prisoner over-fulfilled his quota, three days should be taken off his sentence.

While the revolt committee was talking, prisoners surrounded the officials on all sides, everybody talking at once, shouting their gripes, relishing this sense of freedom and power, hurling shouts, accusations, and threats of all kinds. The camp officials agreed that injustices had been done; the Party officials from Norilsk wrote down the prisoners' demands. Everybody assured the prisoners that the situation would be remedied, their demands met.

The prisoners didn't believe them. As the city and camp officials left the conference, they were booed out of the gate by prisoners shouting from all sides, "Words, words, words— we want action!" After a long conference outside the gate with the camp officials, the Party officials climbed back in their cars and returned to Norilsk.

That evening, truck convoys of troops came out to reinforce the camp guards and surround the prison complex. In the camp itself, under Mikhail's leadership, the prisoners began to organize. A prisoner police force was formed to prevent rioting and looting; guards were stationed along the fences to alert the camp if any move was made by the troops. The troops began erecting spotlights all around the barbed wire to illuminate the area.

Word was passed to the factories and to *Gor Stroi* that Mikhail's committee was in charge of the camp. They asked all Camp 5 brigades to remain in *Gor Stroi* and the factories, if at all possible, instead of returning to camp. Food would be a problem, but the committee requested that we conserve what we had and stick it out. The women, too, decided to strike as long as the men did.

Early that night, under the glare of the spotlights, those in camp held a general meeting in the main compound. Over in the factory area, we strained our ears to catch what was said. First of all, Mikhail announced what everybody knew: there was to be no more work! This brought a great cheer from the crowd. "We've had enough suffering", he shouted. "We've had enough ill treatment, enough work without pay! *Vsio ravno!* (It's all the same!) We will die fighting for freedom, rather than dying at work."

All the time Mikhail and the other leaders were speaking, the guards outside were snapping pictures from all angles, trying to catch as many faces in evidence as possible. I watched them and thanked God I was in the factory area. Mikhail went on to outline the camp program. There was to be no looting, because the food had to last. The brigades would eat, each at its appointed time. The program of the day would be posted on the camp board, and everyone should observe the new camp order and obey the instructions of the committee and the camp police.

Over in the factory zone, we were cheered by the speeches as much as the other prisoners, but we didn't have any food and we hadn't had any dinner. The rest of it was all very fine, but we wanted our share. Finally, bread was thrown over the fence to us.

That night, the officials from the city came back with General Zveriev himself. They left their cars at the camp entrance, and about twenty of them, on foot, walked the two hundred yards down to the factory zone. Our brigadiers immediately passed the word to lock all the factory doors and not to talk to them, but they walked right by the brick factory and down to the smaller factories along the railroad tracks.

They had brought engineers with them and wanted to inspect the machinery to see that it wasn't damaged.

Finally, some of our brigadiers went out to meet them, but the factory doors were kept locked. The men in the camp saw the brigadiers headed for the official party and shouted across the distance: "Don't make any deals! Don't listen to them! Stick it out! We talked enough, follow us!" Little by little, the workers in the brick factory grew curious and began to slip out the doors in small groups, crowding around the brigadiers and the officials from Norilsk.

The conversation was disorganized in the extreme. Everyone was shouting at once. The workers were complaining about the strict regime, mishandling and rough treatment by the foremen and the guards, the poor food, and the long hours. The officials from the city told the men they hadn't known conditions were so bad; they agreed to all the proposed changes if only the men would go back to camp and resume work. Most of the prisoners just muttered, but others were willing to listen—especially when the officials began to talk of reprisals.

"Don't you see how you're being fooled?" said a Party official. "Your ringleaders are men with nothing to lose, but those of you who aren't to blame will have to suffer, too, if you continue acting this way." Some of the men seemed convinced. They began drifting toward the gates of the factory area. But they were threatened by those in the camp, and, as they hesitated at the gate, the troops pushed them out roughly, not toward the camp, but toward the city of Norilsk. That was the last straw. The factory workers felt betrayed; the brigadiers cursed and shouted at the officials, who hurriedly left. From our zone, they went over to *Gor Stroi*.

There the situation was much worse. The workers in *Gor Stroi* had had no supper; they were a good distance from the camp, and there was no way to get food to them. They were much more willing to listen to the officials and return to camp. They wanted to eat. But the men in the camp, who saw them lining up to march out, hurled threats and curses in their direction and told them not to come back. Finally, the workers retreated. At that, the officials gave up. The guards closed the gates, the men stayed in *Gor Stroi*, and we all settled down for the night. It was a peculiar night. Sleep came hard because of all the excitement and the continuing tension. There was no telling what the officials might do, when the troops might move.

Next morning, the camp officials came down to our area. They asked us sympathetically if we had gotten a good night's sleep and whether we had eaten, what we were going to do next, and why we were engaged in this revolt. The men said little. They just told the officials to consult with the prisoner leaders in the camp. Frankly, though, there were many in the factory area who didn't see any sense in staying here "on strike". They wondered if we were going to get anything out of the whole business at all except empty stomachs.

I chatted for a few moments with one of the officials over by the fence. He told me honestly that the revolts in the prison camps were now widespread, not only around Norilsk, but on the continent as well, and that Moscow was quite concerned. "Moscow, however, hasn't decided what to do," he said, "so no one is willing to take any action with the troops."

That morning, the prisoners in the camp held a funeral for the two men who had been shot by the tower guards. There was a great ceremony and much speech-making about these two "martyrs" of prisoner freedom, resolves to hold out until the changes these men had died for were obtained, and so forth. Then the bodies were taken to the gate and turned over to the camp officials for burial.

The people in town, by this time, were curious. We could see them peering out the windows of the taller buildings, some of them even standing on the rooftops. But no civilians were permitted close to the camp.

About 5 P.M., we noticed a commotion in the camp. The *Gor Stroi* brigades had decided to return. The guards led them back to Camp 5, but as soon as they were checked through the gates they were assaulted by those in camp for "giving in". Mikhail's committee wanted all the brigades to hold their posts and keep spread out, so that as many troops as possible would be needed to keep the area surrounded and the troop concentration in any one place would be weak. *Gor Stroi*, especially, was considered a vantage point. It was right on the edge of the completed parts of the city and, in an emergency, the leaders hoped to be able to knock down the *Gor Stroi* fences and escape into Norilsk.

Again we spent a very uneasy night. All that second day we remained at the factory, wondering what would happen; the third day passed the same way. From time to time, the city officials came out to talk to the revolt leaders, but nothing much seemed to happen. On the fourth day, around noon, we were beginning to get restless. We had had nothing but bread and water all this time, and we couldn't see that we were accomplishing much by remaining in the factories.

That afternoon, finally, word came from Camp 5 for us to return; the officials had promised better conditions. That suited us just fine. We lined up, were checked out, and practically ran the two hundred yards to the camp gate. As soon as we were checked back into camp, we made a beeline for the kitchen, where we demanded—and were served—hot soup and *kasha* for the first time in four days.

That same evening, the officials returned to take over the camp. Mikhail and his committee passed the word that no one was to work for the next three days. We would remain on strike until we saw whether the officials would keep their promises. But there were no reprisals, and the food immediately began to get better, so after three days the brigades returned to work. That night, back in camp, those who had been in *Gor Stroi* reported that the *katerzani* (long-termers) in a special camp to the south of the city had revolted and were still on strike. The free men in *Gor Stroi* had also told of other revolts. In Camp 5, though, work went on for a week or two under much improved conditions. We had gotten many of the changes we had asked for, most of the others were promised, and the only concession made on the part of the prisoners was that the *Benderovcy* had agreed to work. It seemed too good to be true, and the prisoners sensed it.

One morning, about the second week of April, the truce was broken. The brigades marched out to *Gor Stroi* and the factories as usual. My brigade went through the zone first that morning, then some others, and last of all two newly formed brigades of *Benderovcy*. I noticed there were more guards at the gates than usual that morning, almost double the number at the camp gates and the gates to the factory area, yet nothing happened until the two brigades of *Benderovcy* started to enter the gates to the factory area. Suddenly, they were surrounded by troops and pushed back, and the factory gates were closed. They were neatly trapped between the camp and factory zone, cut off from the other prisoners, subdued with gun butts if necessary.

Meanwhile, trucks roared down from the city, full of soldiers. The ringleaders were sorted out of the two trapped brigades, loaded into the trucks, and carted away. By this time, our shouts had finally alerted those left in camp. They surged toward the barbed wire with clubs, ready to break into the factory zone, but Mikhail and his staff stopped them from any premature rioting.

The camp officials again retreated to the north gate and left the camp itself to the control of the prisoners once more. Nothing much happened during the afternoon, and in the evening the brigades from *Gor Stroi* returned to camp. Mikhail told us, however, to stay in the factory area. Bread and a few fish were once more tossed over the barbed wire to us from the camp.

That evening, the city and camp officials again met with the leaders of the revolt. This time they were much more aggressive and threatened to use force. Mikhail refused to be intimidated; he told them that force would be met with force. "You promised no reprisals the last time," he said, "but God knows what happened to those men you hauled away this morning. There has got to be an end to all this, a drastic change! We gained nothing by giving in before, so this is it! This is the end, either death or life!"

At the end of the meeting, signalmen climbed to the top of the two-story building at the north end of camp and hung out a huge homemade skull-and-crossbones flag. Others stretched a big banner along the side of the barracks that faced Norilsk, with a painted slogan, "Help us get free of these murderers." The signalmen wigwagged to all the camps in the area to go on strike. They responded that they were with us to the death. From the upper windows of the factory, we could barely see the signal flags from Camp 4, two miles away. From then on, the signalmen were always at their posts on top of the building.

Even as the camp got organized, the troops were back. They stood almost shoulder to shoulder around the whole perimeter of the camp complex, including the factory zone and the women's camp. At first, the officials tried to get ev-

eryone back into camp, to reduce the size of the perimeter
and the number of troops needed, but we refused to leave the
factory zone. The city officials were worried because most of
the troops in the area were out at the prison camps, yet there
was quite a bit of unrest in the town itself. Many of the people
in Norilsk had once been prisoners, and they sympathized
with our demands.

This time we held out in the factory zone for five days. On
the morning of the fifth day, the city officials and army
officers came to the gates of our zone and gave the brigadiers
strict orders to return the men to camp that day. They meant
business and they were prepared to use force. The brigadiers
told them nothing doing; the army officials turned on their
heels and led the procession back to town. It began to look
critical, but the camp leaders told us to hold out at all costs.

That afternoon we nailed up all the doors to the factory
and began barricading the building at different points with
piles of bricks. It was a long, nervous night. We were all tense,
and nobody got much sleep. Early the next morning, trucks
full of troops armed with machine guns began rolling out
from town. They deployed around the factory, and we were
cut off in our "citadel". The women in their camp and the
prisoners in Camp 5 rushed to the barbed wire and began to
hoot in protest. But this was the regular army. They paid no
attention to the shouts; calmly and efficiently, they set about
the job they had been ordered to do.

As soon as his troops were deployed, the commanding
officer charged us to leave the factory at once and return to
camp. He got nothing but curses and shouts of defiance for
his answer from the brigadiers. There were more than seventy
of us inside the brick factory, stationed at various points behind piles of bricks, which would serve both as shelter and
weapons. Many of the men had clubs and iron bars. I was

with a group in the big kiln room at the east end of the factory.

A pistol shot was the signal for the beginning of the assault. The troops moved in from all sides at once, hammering at the doors to break them down. It was absolute bedlam. I remember the women shouting from their camp across the road, about an octave above the curses of the prisoners and the dull booming of the gun butts on the doors. The first group to penetrate the building came through the stockroom in the basement, up a ramp, and into the kiln room.

As soon as the first helmet appeared, the soldiers were showered with bricks and imprecations. They backed out and began firing bursts from their machine guns. We knelt behind our piles of bricks, petrified, but ready to shower the door again as soon as the first uniform appeared. While we were concentrating on that, though, other soldiers broke into the room behind us and took us by surprise. They didn't bother to shoot; they just used their guns as clubs. I got a whack across the back that almost broke me in two and leveled me on the floor. Somebody kicked me in the head to be sure I'd stay down, then one by one we were thrown out the windows like sacks of cement.

Some of the prisoners who were badly mangled were loaded into trucks and driven off. The rest of us were lined up outside the factory, slapped and kicked into line. Within fifteen minutes, the troops had cleared not only the brick factory but all the other factories as well. I was a little dazed, but it seemed to me the whole city was watching from windows and rooftops. The women's camp and the prisoners in Camp 5 were in an uproar. The army commandant, however, stood as immovable as a rock, grim and unyielding.

When all the prisoners had been lined up, we were marched out the factory gates. Instead of taking us back to camp, though, the soldiers marched us along the railroad tracks and down to the clay pits. There we were herded out of sight of the camp, ankle deep in water, and the soldiers stood around us with machine guns at the ready. There was a moment's pause while the commandant came up. His eyes flashed, he gave a command; the troops leveled their machine guns right at us. At that point I made an Act of Contrition as best I could, but everything inside me seemed to be both frozen and churning at the same time.

That instant of waiting for the shots seemed like an eternity. Then, in the next moment, a car roared up spitting gravel from behind its wheels, and two camp officials jumped out, yelling. The guns were lowered to the soldiers' hips. My knees went limp, and I breathed again. We were ordered to sit down on the wet ground. I collapsed.

Three officials strode around the group, calling out names from various lists they had in their hands. The prisoners went forward, one by one, and were looked over closely and checked against photographs among the papers. When my turn came, I got a good long look from one of the officials, who then consulted his papers again and whispered with the other officials. After a while, he said to me gruffly: "To the right!" By the time we were all sorted out, there were about thirty-five prisoners on the right and perhaps thirty on the left. I wasn't sure what the divisions meant.

We stood there under guard, while the officials climbed back into their car and drove off. In a few minutes, a truck roared down the road. Now that my brain was functioning again, after the extreme terror of the last few minutes, it might have been a good time to pray. But frankly, the only thought that kept running through my mind as I saw the truck coming down the road was, "Here's where we go and get ourselves dumped somewhere."

Interwoven with that refrain was a bit of self-pity and a pang of loneliness. I thought for the last time of my family at home, my friends, my fellow Jesuits, who would never know what happened to me or where I died—out here some place in a clay quarry in the wastes of Siberia. By the time the truck reached us, though, the moment had passed, and my reaction had set in: "Do you think God, too, doesn't know where you are? Do you think He has protected you thus far and has now just forgotten about you?"

I was immediately flooded with confidence in God's Providence and a strong faith. It sounds rather maudlin as I try to write it here, but it was a tremendous help to me at that moment and an experience I will never forget. My trust in God's Providence, learned during the long years of Lubianka, had been put to the ultimate test. And it had not failed.

The group on the left was loaded into the truck. They were packed in tightly together and made to sit with their heads between their knees and arms folded over their heads. The motor started and the truck drove off. One of the officials walked over to us on the right. "You men", he said, "are lucky you're still alive, thanks to us. You know what the punishment should be for open rebellion against the government. You were almost shot, remember that! Now I'm sending you back to camp with a warning: If you're ever again caught in anti-government activity, subversive work, or collaboration with the revolutionaries in camp, you'll get no mercy next time."

He went on like that for a long while. We simply stood there numb, heads hanging, licking our wounds. "What's the matter with you people?" he roared at last. "Do you want to go back to camp, or would you rather go somewhere else?" At that, there was a sort of concerted but incoherent mumbling from the crowd, which seemed to satisfy him, so we were marched off to camp, limping, bruised, and some of the men quite bloody.

The camp itself was still in the hands of the prisoners despite the fact the factory area had now been cleared. We were immediately surrounded by those in camp and a thousand questions were tossed at us. But we were in no mood to talk; we simply went to the barracks and collapsed. Even there, our friends crowded around us, chattering about the incident and how things were going in the camp. It was a long time before I was able to get to sleep. Even after the others had left, I relived the experience of the afternoon over and over again before I could fall asleep, realizing how it might have turned out, and thanking God again and again for the actual outcome.

The next morning, there was a general meeting held in the camp. Mikhail himself didn't appear, but his adjutant read us a statement by the committee: (1) Anyone caught trying to escape would be shown no mercy by the camp police; (2) the Revolutionary Committee will agree to no more talks between the city officials and the camp; we will talk only to representatives from Moscow itself; (3) we have all been branded as revolutionaries now, and we have one choice— freedom or death; therefore, we must all stick together.

Another of Mikhail's lieutenants then went on to talk about the interregnum in the Kremlin, the rumors that Beria had been accused of intrigues and arrested and that the MGB were now being blamed for most of the suffering in the prison camps.

The general who had broken the strike in the factories was still on the scene, along with the special troops that, we learned, had come all the way from Krasnoyarsk. But for a while, no further moves were made. It must have been obvious to the Party officials that there would be a great deal of bloodshed if the troops assaulted the camp the way they had assaulted the brick factory, and no one wanted to take the responsibility for such a slaughter.

On about April 27 or 28, the general made his next move. During the afternoon, while the prisoners were sitting around the barracks after dinner, smoking and chatting, the troops made a quick sortie through the main gates. It was well planned and went off with precision. They poured through the gate and quickly surrounded the three barracks at the north end of camp, nearest the main gate. Then they mounted a skirmish line of machine-gunners across the camp roads to keep the rest of us at bay. Soldiers with bayonets drove the surprised men out of those three surrounded barracks, marched them out of the camp, and herded them off toward the city.

As soon as the camp was aware of what was happening, the alarm sounded and our "army" came running pell-mell toward the machine-gunners. The troops must have been told not to shoot unless necessary, for they retreated toward the main gate. At the same time, a fire engine charged through the gate, water nozzles turned on full blast. The streams of water tumbled the leading men in the prisoners' charge and stopped the onrush just long enough to allow the troops to clear out. The prisoners regrouped to rush the fire truck. As they overturned the truck, the firemen jumped clear and ran to safety. The prisoners rushed after them in a mad charge toward the main gate, but Mikhail stopped them. If they crossed into the death zone, the troops could legally fire upon them as "escaping prisoners".

The general's strategy was now clear. He would try to strike unexpectedly and take small groups, perhaps a hundred or so at a time; in this way he might eventually clear or subdue the camp without serious incident. As a countermove, some of the prisoners tried from time to time to sneak out at night, overpower a guard, and steal some guns. But the army had spotlights everywhere; it was impossible to sneak across the death zone in the glare of the lights without being seen.

It was a week before the general tried another move. This time, he got all the city officials and camp officials together, perhaps forty all told, at the main gate. They walked into the camp after supper, stopped a few feet inside the gate, and asked to talk to Mikhail. Meanwhile, the general had massed his troops behind some boxcars on the railroad siding west of camp, unseen in the darkness behind the spotlights.

Mikhail and his assistants walked up the main road to tell the general and the officials that from now on they would speak only to a commission from Moscow. The prisoners crowded around; the officials looked uneasy. At the same time, the troops rushed in from the west, cut the barbed wire, and attempted to form a skirmish line across the southwest third of the camp, as they had done the week before at the north end.

One of the prisoners, however, suspected something. He climbed up on a barrel and shouted to the crowd surrounding Mikhail and the officials: "*Bratsi!* This is a trick, a trap! Look, you can see it in their faces! Look around, something's fishy!" No sooner had he said it, than we heard the shouts from the southwest. Immediately, most of the crowd rushed over there. The troops were just breaking through the second ring of barbed wire, and the prisoners attacked them with clubs and stones. They withdrew without firing a shot. Presumably, they had been told not to shoot.

At the gate, the rest of the crowd was furious. They began to attack the official party, and the general himself got a smash in the face. The officials broke and ran, with the crowd at their heels pummeling and kicking them. An army major ran into the barracks instead of toward the gate. He climbed to a first-floor window, tried to jump the barbed wire, missed, and hung himself by the throat on the wire.

As their next move, the officials set up a ring of loudspeakers around the camp. From then on, we were subjected to a continuous barrage of propaganda. The loudspeakers blared continually, announcing such things as a special new camp for those who broke away from the revolutionaries. It was situated somewhere east of the city, about eight or ten miles out in the tundra. The loudspeakers said over and over that it was better to be in prison, somewhere in a good camp, than to be butchered in Camp 5 if the troops had to move in. They also called out the names of the ringleaders to prove they were known and promised that those who weren't ringleaders wouldn't be punished if they came out now.

Then one day the loudspeakers announced that the commission from Moscow, which the prisoners demanded, had arrived. That same afternoon the commission, three men who had been sent to end the revolts around Norilsk, marched up to the gate. They were met by Mikhail and his staff, but only the three commission members were let in through the gate. Tables were set up opposite the dining room, and the prisoners gathered around. Groups of ten, however, were stationed all around the camp to prevent another sneak attack. The commissioners began by saying that the revolt was useless. If necessary, it could be suppressed by force; in any event, it wasn't possible to make too many changes in the camps. At that, Mikhail and the other prisoner leaders almost walked out of the conference.

Then one of the commissioners stood up and smiled. He assured us that since Stalin's death the whole question of prison camps was under review, especially as regarded political prisoners. He said Moscow was greatly concerned about the strikes in the camps around Norilsk and that he and his colleagues had been sent to make a settlement and avoid bloodshed. He was sure something could be arranged; the commission would be happy to hear any suggestions from the prisoners.

One of the prisoner leaders answered that we were ready for bloodshed if necessary, just as had happened at the camps in Karaganda and Vorkuta. Basically, he said, we wanted human treatment and certain human rights, and he went on to enumerate the prisoners' minimum demands. There was to be no more forced labor for ten hours without even a noonday meal; there should be no more calling of prisoners by numbers, like cattle.

"We have names!" he said. "We want pay and recompense for our work, and we want time off for good behavior. We want to be able to communicate with the outside world and our families—and not just a note once a year. We want to be able to receive packages from them. We want assurances that defenseless prisoners won't be shot in cold blood, as two of our men were here. We want assurances that agreements won't be broken, as were the ones after the last strike, and we want a guarantee of no reprisals. We want better living conditions, fewer men to a barrack, better food."

The commissioners dutifully wrote down all the demands. Ultimately, they assured Mikhail's committee that all demands would be met—if we would give up peaceably and return to work. At that, there was a general shout by the prisoners standing around the compound: "Not until we get what we demand!" On that note, the conference ended. For two or three days, the commissioners met in private with the leaders of the revolt, but no conclusion or agreement was reached. On the other hand, the commissioners ordered three truckloads of food brought to the camp to replenish the almost empty warehouses at Camp 5. At least they weren't thinking of starving us out.

During this period, I heard a great many confessions. The prisoners, not knowing when the shooting might begin, were like men before battle, afraid of death and putting the affairs of their soul in order. I was saying Mass every morning now for large crowds and distributing many Communions.

The end of May came. The revolution in Camp 5 had now run well over a month. For a week the loudspeakers had been calling insistently for surrender before force was necessary. With nothing to do in the camp all day, tension grew and uncertainty mounted. Some men actually broke down under the strain. The infirmary and the hospital were filled, so men lay on the grass outside. The air was warm, the weather beautiful, it was a spring such as we had seldom seen in Norilsk. And yet the atmosphere grew increasingly charged. There were constant alarms every night now. The gates were always open, and the troops had broken passages in the barbed wire on the east and west sides of the camp as well. Every so often, especially at night, they tried to sneak through the openings and cordon off sections of the camp.

Under the continual tension and lack of sleep, men grew exhausted. There was a good deal of muttering that the cause was hopeless. Nobody talked much for fear his voice would crack and betray him. Sometimes, when a man would try to joke about the situation, his laughter would suddenly become nervous, high-pitched, almost hysterical.

On the last day of May, it was obvious that the crisis was approaching. The general was at the main gates that day in full uniform, with his staff running around in all directions, saluting smartly and dispatching orders. Trucks were on the go all day long, circling behind the ranks of the besieging troops, carrying men from one place to another. Our signal towers were working overtime, telling the other camps what was happening, trying to find out, from the women's camp especially—since they had a good view behind the troops' lines—about the new troop displacements and where the concentrations were thickest.

From time to time, the troops made rapid forays to cut large sections of barbed wire, then retreated under a barrage of stones and bricks hurled by the prisoners. Still they didn't shoot. It seemed the general was deliberately trying to spread us out by opening up new possible points of attack and so thin out our defenses.

Nobody ate any supper that night. In the evening, the women signaled that a big body of troops was massing behind our camp where we couldn't see them. That night nobody even tried to sleep. Mikhail made a last tour of inspection, shaking his head as he realized that the hour had come. His "police" were everywhere, ordering men into position, exhorting them, stirring up the laggards with a blow on the back from the clubs they carried.

The tension was almost unbearable. Looking at gun barrels is not the most consoling sight in the world, especially when you have no weapons of your own except bricks and clubs. The men knew it was hopeless, and the camp police had a hard time keeping them at their posts. For the prison leaders, of course, the situation was desperate. Their necks were going to be in the noose one way or another; either they died in the battle or they would be executed, for the authorities had their names and their pictures on film.

Mikhail's committee, therefore, made it perfectly plain that anyone who deserted his post when the fighting started would be killed by the camp police before he was able to surrender. It was a case of the devil before and the devil behind, and many of the men began to feel they had only a slim chance of getting out alive if a fight really started.

Night fell, and everyone fell silent, sitting in the glare of the searchlights and waiting. Suddenly, at 1:30 in the morning, the alarm was given. The sound of the first pounding on the rail that rang out over the silent camp was like a shrill scream of doom; it sent a shiver down my back. The troops outside the barbed wire began to move, and with that move the long tension of waiting was broken. The prisoners snapped together.

Everyone grabbed bricks, stones, clubs, or whatever weapon he could find and ran into position along the barbed wire. The soldiers moved ahead slowly, deliberately, in perfect order; many of them seemed as scared as we were. My group, originally assigned to the main gate, was hurriedly sent off to the east, near the infirmary, where there seemed to be the most troops. The soldiers, seeing us rush toward the fence, halted. So did we. There was a period of awkward waiting and confrontation.

Though it was now two o'clock in the morning, the whole city seemed to be up. There were people on the roofs, and every window overlooking the camp was jammed with faces. By June, the days up here inside the Arctic Circle are extremely long; the sun never really sets at all. Most of the night is almost like daylight, and that night the brightness of the scene was heightened by the glare of army searchlights.

The main attack actually came through the north gate. The machine-gunners from Krasnoyarsk, the general's crack troops, were in the vanguard. They were into the camp with a rush before anyone really noticed them, and immediately word was flashed to our group to swing back to the center of camp and stop them.

As we rounded the barracks near the bakery and headed

along the main street of the camp, we could see that the machine-gunners had planted a line of flags across the roadway and were drawn up behind it. Their commander shouted that the line represented a neutral zone; anyone who stepped over it would be shot immediately. Yet our group was racing toward them, and we were only twenty yards away now.

Running out in front of our crowd was a Lithuanian named Yurgis, an ex-boxer, with a head that sat so solidly on his shoulders he seemed to have no neck, and big hands like hams. I had once thought he was slightly punch-drunk, too, until his friends told me his mental condition was the result of the interrogations he had undergone.

Yurgis was furious when he heard the command to halt. People tried to hold him back, but he shook them off and threw a brick into the crowd of gunners. He caught one of the soldiers on the arm just below the shoulder and knocked him to the ground. Even in the bedlam, and at that distance, I swear I could hear the bone snap. At that, the commander fired his pistol at Yurgis and told his men to open fire. They cut loose right from the hip, and the front row of prisoners went down like wheat before a scythe.

Everybody on the main road with us immediately hit the dirt; I dove to the ground. Yurgis fell dead. The man next to me dove for the ground, but his foot kicked up and a bullet smashed into his heel. Several of the men tried to duck behind the wooden fence of the latrine; the prison "police" thought they were trying to desert and stabbed them in the back.

The machine-gunners continued firing waist high to pin everyone to the ground. Anyone who tried to get up got hit. I began to crawl on my stomach around toward the cover of the kitchen building. I crouched momentarily behind a swill barrel as the bullets slammed into it right at the level of my chest. I made one last desperate dive behind the building, reached the safety of the kitchen, and hugged the wall.

I looked back over my shoulder to see rows of corpses and the wounded scattered in the roadway. I could hear the chatter of the machine guns, the curses and moans of the prisoners, shouted commands, and still, rising above it all, the high-pitched screams of the women from the direction of their camp. While I watched, troops began to pour in from other openings in the barbed wire, not shooting, but clubbing the prisoners to the ground with rifle butts.

Many of the prisoners were in the barracks, and the soldiers began to flush them out, one at a time if necessary. Some of the leaders of the revolt were found dead in the latrine, with their wrists slashed or their throats cut. They preferred to kill themselves rather than be taken alive. The troops entered the kitchen building, where I was, and began to round up the prisoners hidden there. They lined us up against the wall with their rifle barrels practically in our backs, then led us out through the barbed wire.

As we left, I saw the skull-and-crossbones flag thrown down from the roof. The wounded were being taken to the medical center; the dead were just stacked up in rows. I had no way of knowing, of course, what the actual casualties were in Camp 5; by actual count, however, I walked past thirteen corpses on my way out of camp, and I'd seen soldiers stacking others like cordwood in front of the infirmary.

We were herded into groups about 150 yards outside the camp. Mikhail was captured, taken out the front gate under heavy guard, and immediately put into a closed prison van and driven off. The women were going wild. They tore down the barbed wire around their camp to attack the soldiers but were finally driven back by fire hoses at full pressure.

Little by little, groups of prisoners were formed up and marched off.

As my group swung off, I took a last look at the whole mad scene—the city alive with spectators, the camp a wreck, the soldiers hurrying everywhere in the spotlights' glare, the shouts, the commands, the screams, the moans.

My Term Runs Out

From Camp 5, we were led off straight into the tundra. The soldiers seemed so nervous and tense, I thought sure we were to be shot. I began to pray. We walked about four miles to the west. It was almost 5 A.M. when we came to a grassy area, marshy and wet and dotted with thick shrubbery. We were told to sit down, and we sat a long time. It was so swampy, the ground sank under us, but we weren't allowed to stand up or move. Not until 4 P.M., almost twelve hours later, did we move again. By that time, the water was over my hips as I sat in the marshy ground. I was so hungry I tried to eat handfuls of grass when the guards weren't looking.

At last we were marched off again and led all the way around the city to a quarry at the foot of the mountains to the east. Just opposite the quarry, perhaps a half mile away, was Camp 3, the camp for the *katerzani*. They had formerly been assigned to work the quarry, but their revolt was still going on. The stone was needed for construction, however, so we were brought in to work the quarry. We had to live in it, too. Rations were brought to us morning and evening, but that was all. Guards were stationed around the top of the quarry, and we were told that if anyone tried to leave the pits he would be shot on sight.

We were assigned to work, two by two, and given a specific

number of carloads of stone to be quarried, loaded into small handcars, and towed to the crusher every day. It was impossible to fulfill the quota, set deliberately high, even in twelve hours of work, and it was like working in the antechambers of hell. The sun burned down into the pits, which cut off any possible breeze, and was reflected off the rocks, scorching hot. At night, we slept on the belts that carried the crushed stone to the railroad hoppers. All through the summer nights, the arctic sun stays in the sky. You have to be pretty tired to sleep outdoors, but we were exhausted.

The first week, especially, was brutal. We were out of condition, always hungry, sore to the bone from the jolting, lifting, and pushing. We spent the whole day swinging sledges, loading the big rocks into the handcar, then pushing the car up the incline to the crusher, laboring and straining under a broiling sun until I thought the veins in my neck would burst with the effort. Whenever a trainload of cars came in for gravel, we had to scramble up into the hoppers and loosen the gravel so it would flow, then go back to swinging the sledgehammer.

One night, after we had finished cleaning the hopper, I stood on top of one of them watching the locomotive haul the cars away. The rest of the men went off to get supper, but I felt so tired and depressed I couldn't face the long walk to the kitchen shack a half mile away. I just sat down on top of the hopper, completely exhausted.

The evening sun was warm and relaxing. With the work finished in the quarry for the day, everything was quiet. Tired as I was, my mind began to wander. I began to think about Camp 5 and the men who had died there, those who had confessed and those who hadn't. Then I thought of home, of my sisters and friends who had no idea where I was, and I wondered what they were doing; of my early days in school, of the time when I first served Mass—a real sentimental jag! I tried to snap myself out of it; I was beginning to get so emotionally worked up that my body was trembling. I was afraid I might have a breakdown.

I looked down from the top of the hopper and saw a bird with a nest of two young ones on a grassy hillock just across the railroad tracks. The mother was feeding them, flying off and returning, while the father stayed there and held them in the nest. I became fascinated and lost my train of thought. I even forgot how tired I was and felt a sudden surge of joy. Then, somehow, I remembered my father feeding me in the small hours of the morning when I had returned penniless, tired, and scared from a Boy Scout outing. From that thought, my mind wandered again to the men who had been killed in Camp 5, and I thought how their mothers and fathers had protected them in childhood.

I could feel the tears welling up in my eyes. I was almost ready to break down completely when I felt a slap on the back! It was another prisoner who had come looking for me. "Wladimir," he said, "go get your supper. I put it away for you." "Look down there", I said, and began to point out to him how the father and mother bird were taking care of the little ones. "Look! There's the mother bringing food now! See, look at the little ones . . ." Just then, poof! the mother collapsed in mid-air and fell dead. My companion hooted for joy. At that distance, he'd winged the bird with a stone. "What a shot!" he cried.

All at once, I began to shake all over, completely beside myself with rage. I shouted and raved at him almost irrationally until, stunned, he turned on his heel and walked away. I spat on the ground behind him in anger. That night I fell into a mood of depression that lasted for more than two days.

Fortunately, the next Sunday they excused us from work for the first time since we had come to the quarry. After breakfast, I took a walk back to an old quarry pit filled with water. I took a bath and felt somewhat better. Then I went up into the hills to look out over the city and make a meditation—a kind of spiritual as well as physical recreation. I needed it badly, because I knew I was beginning to crack under the strain. I sat for a long time, reflecting on God's Providence and how He had watched over me through all these years. In the quiet, my confidence returned. I could literally feel the tensions draining away, and after a while I lay down to sleep like a trusting child.

When I woke, it was late afternoon. I felt so relaxed that I didn't want to break the spell, so I sat for a while in the warm sunshine, looking down on Camp 3 at the foot of the hill. There were almost five thousand long-termers in the camp who had gone on strike when we did. But they were far better organized than we had been in Camp 5, and they had a lot less to lose, so they refused to give in.

Their leader was a famous underworld character called "Vladimir", known throughout Russia as a master criminal. Many of the others in Camp 3 were former army officers, and the camp defenses were well planned. The blacksmith shop worked far into the night turning out weapons: knives, swords, and axes. The known "squealers" had been put to work every day digging trenches and fortifications inside the barbed wire. The camp even had its own radio and loudspeaker to answer the propaganda from the army's loudspeakers. They refused to let anyone into camp to talk to them.

They had also devised an ingenious method of alerting the people of Norilsk to their plight. They built a number of kites, which flew over the city, and at a certain height packages of leaflets were released, urging the free citizens to help, accusing the regime of cruelty and of being "associates of Beria", petitioning the people to prevent bloodshed by stopping the siege of Camp 3. From time to time, some of the messages sent by kite fell into the quarry where we worked, but anyone caught picking them up or reading them was severely punished.

By August, everyone in the quarry was exhausted. The building of the city put a tremendous demand on the quarry for stone, rock, asphalt, and concrete, and there were only about a hundred of us to do the work that had previously been done by a thousand *katerzani*. It was the worst stretch of physical exhaustion over a prolonged period I had ever gone through.

Then, one evening after supper, we were notified that we would be leaving the next day. For the past few days, we had noticed troops arriving in large numbers and camping back in the foothills. They couldn't be seen by the men in Camp 3, but we could see them from our vantage point up on the hill. Since they were moving us out, and somebody would have to work the quarry, it was pretty obvious an attack on Camp 3 would come soon.

The next morning, we were led out of the quarry and marched away to the south. Then we circled back around the hills to the east and headed north to a big, new cement factory formerly worked by the *katerzani*. There, part of our group was sent to work in the clay pits; I was assigned to the cement factory. The men working in it already were mostly deserters from the revolution in Camp 3. They had decided to take their chances on living out a long term rather than being shot in the revolt.

From them, I learned how terrible conditions had been in Camp 3 and how the revolt had been begun by "Vladimir". They, too, expected an all-out attack any day, and they assured me the revolt was doomed. The factory itself was hot and uncomfortable. We still had no barracks and had to sleep in the factory, so I decided to stay outside at night. With a couple of others, I used to climb to the top of a water tower in the hopes of seeing the attack on the camp.

On the second night, at about 2:30 A.M., our vigil was rewarded. It was hazy under the arctic midnight sun, but we could clearly see the troops beginning to crawl up the valley. They were creeping along on their bellies, guns cradled in their elbows, sneaking toward the camp. They were still some three hundred yards away from the camp when the prisoners sounded the alarm—but not because of them. Again, the general had mounted a two-pronged attack; there were soldiers rushing the main gates of the camp, and the prisoners didn't even notice those in the valley.

The prisoners rushed to the earthworks they had built to repulse the attack from the main gate. This time, unlike Camp 5, there was no hesitation to shoot. Troops mounted on trucks roared through the gate, firing as they came, one after another. Even as they began to deploy through the camp, the troops from the valley rushed in, cut through the barbed wire, and poured across the camp in a flank attack. Our hearts were in our mouths, just watching the scene, remembering how it had been with us.

As soon as the shooting stopped, doctors, nurses, and stretcher-bearers were brought in by the truckload. Obviously, the whole operation had been expected to be bloody; no mercy or quarter was to be shown the *katerzani*. We watched some of the prisoners, as they were herded into groups, kill themselves by ripping their bellies open with knives. A man on the tower with us said one of the suicides was "Vladimir".

By the time we came down from the tower, they were

beginning to load the captured prisoners into trucks and drive them toward the cement factory. The men were doubled over in the trucks, their heads between their knees and arms folded over their heads, heavily guarded. The trucks roared through the cement factory area and turned out into the tundra. No doubt the men were taken to another camp out in the hills, although there were rumors, as always, that the men had simply been shot. We did hear later that seventy-eight had been killed and more than 150 wounded in the assault on Camp 3. We heard it, however, through the prison-camp grapevine, so it may have been exaggerated.

For a while we stayed at the factory. We still lived in the buildings themselves and slept wherever we could get comfortable for the night. But Camp 3 was being cleaned and repaired, and little by little the *katerzani* were being brought back to work. Eventually, we were formed up and marched out around the city back in the direction of Camp 5. We saw it in the distance with mixed feelings.

In a way, it was like old homecoming week. We were met by old friends, but there were now only about a thousand men in this camp that had once held over five thousand, and it seemed empty. Just out of curiosity, I made a tour of the camp, living over again the weeks of the revolt. The barracks had all been patched up and whitewashed; there was hardly a sign of the battle. No one talked much about it, either. The men had been warned that any talk of revolt, or any attempt to stir up new trouble, meant immediate transfer to a penal camp and perhaps a stiffer sentence.

On the other hand, a lot of changes had been made. There were no more numbers on the clothes, and there was a little store where we could spend the wages we now received—about one hundred rubles (ten dollars) a month—on things like sugar, bread, candy, and tobacco. There was a new provision for reduced sentences: any day a worker did more than his assigned quota, he received a reduction of three days from his sentence. Most of the conditions, in fact, that the Revolutionary Committee had demanded had been met.

The food was better, too, and the prisoners could now write letters home once a month. I decided to try and write a letter home myself. When I handed in my letter addressed to the U.S.A., the officials were astounded. They had never heard of such a thing. They called me in finally and told me the new regulations covered only letters to people living within the country.

One of the first things I did, though, when I got back to Camp 5, was to search for my Mass kit. No one had seen it. One of the men who worked on the lathes at *Gor Stroi*, however, promised to make me a little chalice and paten. He also told me Fr. Viktor was still at Camp 4 and still working at *Gor Stroi*. Unfortunately, I was assigned to a crew digging sanitation ditches in the city of Norilsk. I did arrange, though, with one of the men working in *Gor Stroi*, to contact Fr. Viktor and get me the necessary supplies for Mass—bread, wine, linen, etc.—if possible. By the end of the week I had everything I needed. Viktor sent a note with the supplies to welcome me back and say how glad he was to hear that I was all right.

I was now the only priest in Camp 5, and there were many Catholic Poles, Lithuanians, and people from the Baltic states. Moreover, with the new freedom in the camp, it was much easier to work as a priest, so I was constantly on the go. Besides hearing confessions, saying Mass, and distributing Communion, I also began giving retreats again, and I did a lot of spiritual counseling.

I was surprised, and delighted, to find that Viktor was still working in the bookbindery office. From time to time, I arranged to say Mass there again. Smirnov, too, the Russian who had served my Mass before, was still in Camp 5. He attended Mass daily, answering the prayers by heart. Misha was still here also, working in the medical center. He had actually stayed to the last, helping the sick and wounded right through the battle. As soon as the revolt had ended, his superior returned to the infirmary, and the doctors, both prisoner and free, worked around the clock with the wounded.

Moreover, Misha was in constant touch with Fr. Viktor, and he told me again that Viktor wanted to see me. Every week, Misha went to *Gor Stroi* to check the first-aid stations, so he said he would try to arrange a meeting for me with Viktor. On a day my brigade didn't work, Misha arranged for me to swap places with a member of one of the *Gor Stroi* brigades. The man was happy enough to get an unexpected day off; I was delighted at the chance to see Fr. Viktor.

It was still something of a risk, but I spent the whole day with him in his little watchman's shanty. At dinnertime, when the crews were resting, we said Mass for some of the workers. Before I left, Viktor gave me a new supply of raisins, altar breads, and other supplies for Mass.

Life in Camp 5 was almost pleasant these days. The food, for a change, was of far better quality, and it easy to obtain extra portions. I can also remember the first time I got paid; it wasn't much, but it was mine, and I felt almost free. I went into the camp store and bought a whole loaf of bread with my own money! Then I sat down and ate the entire loaf at a sitting, savoring the notion that I could go back in and buy more if I wanted to.

In October 1953, however, that life came to an abrupt end. I had been at Camp 5 little over a month when Misha told me that an *étappe* was being formed for the mines at Kayerkhan. He promised to try and keep me off the lists.

The officials were asking for only the best and healthiest workers, and Misha said he would try to doctor my medical records. For three days, men marched into camp from the other camps around Norilsk; it was obviously going to be a huge *étappe*.

On the third day, Misha told me sadly he simply couldn't swing the deal. Chances were that I'd be going to Kayerkhan. One of the problems, he said, was that nobody liked the mines; some of the criminals even resorted to self-mutilation to prevent being assigned there. As a result, the officials were checking the medical records closely and taking just about anyone they could legitimately call a good worker. As a last resort, I joined a group who claimed they knew how to fake high blood pressure. I didn't think it was worth my health to swallow soap or cut off a toe to escape the mines, but I was willing to try this.

Just before the medical examination, we went to the bath-house and took a hot shower, as hot as we could stand it. Then the trick was to hold your breath as long as possible, until your heart began pounding furiously and you felt it was liable to burst. Immediately, you made a dash for the medical center. If you were lucky, and got to see a doctor right away, your blood pressure reading would be dangerously high. Consequently, you would be exempted from work for a few days, but, more importantly, your medical record would read "high blood pressure". Some of the men got away with it, but I got a prescription from the doctor to reduce high blood pressure—and an assignment to Kayerkhan.

About four hundred of us, all told, were selected for the mines. We were issued winter clothes, with the exception of *valenki*, checked out of Camp 5, and marched off through the city to the railroad yards. It was already bitterly cold that October, and the wind tore through our padded jackets as we stood in the station yard waiting to be loaded into the small, narrow-gauge boxcars of the Dudinka-Norilsk railway. The cars weren't heated, and many of them were so old the boards were cracked and warped.

Kayerkhan is about one-third of the way from Norilsk to Dudinka. The little train crawled through the heavy snowfall that had begun, snaked its way around Zubgora, a rich mountain of ore outside Norilsk, and headed into open country. Then we stopped at a little crossroads, nothing more than two or three shacks, and waited interminably. We kept jumping from foot to foot in the cars, trying to keep the blood circulating. At last, we found out we were waiting for a crew to clean the tracks ahead of us; the snow had turned into a blizzard. It took us almost three hours to go the fifteen miles to Kayerkhan.

The town is a typical mining town. Everything centers about the mines, and the railroad station is hardly a half mile from the shafts. The station itself is tiny, but there are a dozen sidings in the big railroad yard to handle all the coal cars from the mines. Here again, as at Zapadnaya, the mine openings are cut halfway up the slopes of a long mountain that stretches for miles toward Dudinka. The shafts go back almost horizontally instead of down underground. The prison camp at Kayerkhan was between the railroad station and the mine entrance, so it couldn't have been more than four hundred feet away from the station where we were unloaded.

We were hurriedly lined up in the swirling snow, then hastily checked through the camp gates. Our convoy guards simply turned over our documents to the camp officials and boarded the train to return to Norilsk. We were split into two groups as soon as we got into camp. Half of us went to the clubhouse, and the rest went to the bathhouse to begin processing.

The processing took almost all night: registration, the classification of men according to work qualifications, the routine bath, haircut, and disinfecting procedures. What took the most time, though, was a rigid physical examination. The camp officials here didn't trust the medical records we brought with us; if anyone in the *étappe* was found to be sick, he was sent back to Norilsk. They wanted no deadwood here in the mines.

I slept that first night in the clubhouse and wasn't assigned to a barrack until sometime the next day. Here at Kayerkhan, newcomers weren't immediately assigned to work brigades. We were turned over to a special supervisor who settled us in temporary barracks, while we were instructed in the theory and practice of mining and the rules of safety. We also learned the whole layout of the mines from charts. These lectures lasted from nine to twelve in the morning, with a fifteen-minute break, and from one to three in the afternoon. The whole course took three weeks, at the end of which we had to take both an oral and written exam.

During those three weeks, too, the instructor took us into the mines three times, a different shift each time, to show us in practice what the mine was like and how each step of the operation was done. When we had passed the exam and signed a pledge to observe the mine's safety rules, we were finally assigned to a brigade. That afternoon, we moved from the beginners' barracks to a brigade barrack and started to work the next day.

Even in the mines, it was bitterly cold. The earth was frozen solid, and the huge ventilators used to prevent the formation of gas pockets created a terrific draft in the shafts. As a result, we wore winter clothes in the mines all year round: underwear, topshirt, padded jackets and pants, *valenki*, and scarfs and fur caps under our helmets. Some of the men preferred to wear boots on the job, instead of *valenki*, but if you wore boots, you had to keep moving or your feet would freeze.

Usually, there were about eight sections being worked off the main shaft at any one time. From the cars which took us into the mountain, we walked perhaps a quarter of a mile down a slope into the work shaft, which was well timbered with heavy beams. The wood was whitewashed to prevent it from rotting and also as a safety precaution. About every 150 yards, there was a bulkhead to prevent warm air from the main shaft entering the work area and thawing the still-frozen ground. From that approach shaft, we stepped immediately into the work area. Actually, there were always two shafts parallel to the working vein of coal: one for the network of belts that carried the coal up to the collecting bunkers, and one on the other side of the vein to bring in wood for shoring up the shaft.

Above each vein of coal was a layer of shale about three feet thick, and above that was sandstone. The working shafts were about ninety yards wide across the face of the vein, but no shaft could go much deeper than 120 yards at a time. Even as the shaft approached that length, we could hear the sandstone in the ceiling cracking like pistol shots and screaming as huge slabs scraped against each other. Some of the timbers shoring up the work shaft behind us would snap in two from the weight of the sandstone.

As the length of the shaft became critical, these noises increased. Sand would begin falling into the shaft from the ceiling. That was the danger signal. Immediately, the brigadiers would order us to pull the equipment out of the shaft and lie down in the side shafts. Before long, the whole ceiling would fall in with a rush, driving the air out of the chamber with such force it could hurl a man against the wall and smash his ribs if he weren't lying down. The big timbers would be snapped like matchsticks and hurled in every direction, occasionally banging into the walls over our heads as we hugged the ground.

Sometimes I'd lie awake at night, shivering, when I thought about being trapped in a shaft with the ceiling falling. Each day, as the shafts grew longer, some of the crews developed pretty bad cases of nerves. After the ceiling fell, we would bypass about fifteen yards of the vein, cut a new working face between the two service shafts, and start again. We would drill into the vein about ten or twelve yards at a time, fill the holes with powder, cap, and blast them.

After the blast, we broke up the resulting blocks of coal and shoveled them into the scraper lines, which pulled them out and dumped them onto the belts leading to the hoppers above. The shaft was immediately shored up with timbers, twenty-four inches in diameter, about a yard and a half apart. But first of all, the shale had to be knocked off the ceiling. Otherwise, water would form between the shale and the sandstone as the ground thawed, and if it fell, it could split a helmet right in two.

There was one night when I nearly got killed that way. We were making a new cut across the vein face, preparing a space for the scraper winch. I noticed the ceiling wasn't well stripped of slate; I didn't like it and told the foreman so. "Don't worry about it," he said, with a professional squint at the ceiling, "nothing will happen until tomorrow." I was shoveling out a pile of slate and coal with another man, and every time I looked at that ceiling I could swear the cracks were getting wider and grains of sand were dropping down. I got nervous and called the foreman again. He looked it over and decided it was safe enough; he told me we had to finish the cut and get the scraper winch in place because the morning crew was supposed to begin blasting. We didn't have time to spare a man for de-slating the ceiling.

We were still nervous about it, so my partner and I got long-handled shovels in order to work as far away from the faults in the ceiling as we could. We both knew what could happen if the slate fell. It was a bad night before the day shift reported to work at 7:45. I was happy to leave, but I pointed out the faulty ceiling to the new crew and the brigadier. "You better get some lumber under there fast!" I said. Before they could get to work, though, the whole ceiling collapsed. It caught one man, a Chinese, across the back and snapped his spine in two. He lived just long enough for them to get him to the mine hospital.

If the work was dangerous, conditions in the camp itself were better than in almost any other camp I'd seen. The coal from these mines was badly needed in the electric plants and furnaces around Norilsk and for export from Dudinka in exchange for farm machinery and industrial equipment from abroad. The officials, therefore, wanted the prisoners to be able to work, and work effectively, so they did what they could to make life bearable.

The barracks were well kept up, the beds were clean and comfortable, the food was good. Besides the normal rations in the dining room, there was a cafeteria out by the main gate, which we shared with the free workers and where we could always buy a meal. Such a meal would include meat(!), *kasha*, pancakes, and a dessert of custard or possibly dried apples, sometimes even prunes. The meal was expensive, but it was worth it. And here at the cafeteria, as well as in the camp store, you could also buy candy, cookies, cigarettes, and other luxuries.

The miners, both prisoners and free, received substantially the same wages: about three thousand to five thousand rubles (three hundred to five hundred dollars) per month. The government, however, deducted a certain percentage of prisoners' wages, and the camp deducted another percentage for room and board, so our actual pay was between one hundred and three hundred rubles (ten to thirty dollars) per month. With the money, we could buy meals and other luxuries, as well as onions and garlic from the farmers of *Krasnoyarski Krai*, who were allowed to sell a certain amount of their produce to the miners.

Everyone bought as much of these items as he could. They were both a source of vitamins and a protection against scurvy, which was more prevalent here than anywhere else I had been. I noticed it most in my arms and legs, which would develop blue spots and begin to feel like iron, so heavy it was really an effort just to walk. And despite the good conditions in the camp, the prisoners here in Kayerkhan were always exhausted and pale, never rested enough, and forever tired.

We could also get extra food from the free workers who worked so closely with us in the mines. Sometimes they made outright gifts to friends among the prisoners, but all of them were willing to buy whatever we wanted in town if we gave them the money. For that reason, check-ups at the camp gates after a shift were frequently stricter than usual. The guards would make everyone in the brigade strip at the gates to see if we were smuggling meat or butter or, especially, vodka.

During one of these check-ups, the guard, a young boy from Lithuania, found in my clothes a little handwritten prayer book with the whole ceremony of the Mass in Latin. He was going to confiscate it, but I talked him out of it. I admitted frankly I was a priest, since he was a Lithuanian, and told him they were the prayers of the Mass. "It means a lot to me", I said. He quietly handed the book back to me and let me pass on.

For the most part, nobody bothered about my work as a priest in this camp. Once or twice I was warned by the interrogators about "subversive activity", but I said Mass daily and distributed Communion, gave weekly talks to groups of prisoners, sermons and conferences, even some retreats. And at Kayerkhan, too, there were three other priests as well.

One was my old friend Fr. Casper, who had been with me at Dudinka and Camp 4. As soon as I arrived, he welcomed me and arranged for me to say Mass. There was a Lithuanian, Fr. Henri, tall and lanky, partly bald, with a gray mustache and goatee, who had been a monk before he was arrested. He didn't work in the mines but was an orderly in one of the barracks; his barrack, therefore, was a perfect place to say Mass while the brigade was in the mines. He also received quite a few packages from his people in Lithuania, which meant his barrack was also a good place to cadge a meal.

Finally, there was Fr. Nikolai, a tall, heavy-set Ukrainian priest with a soft voice; he, too, had been a monk, but in the Oriental rite. He was very popular among the Ukrainians here in the camp, and they would do anything for him. One of our best men, in fact, was a Ukrainian named Dmitriev, a thin, black-haired fellow with pointed nose and a goatee. He made most of the contacts among the prisoners and was an outstanding lay apostle.

The prisoners felt much freer here because of the relaxed policies. It was astonishing to note the number of men who proved religious now that there was no outward persecution, and religion was "tolerated", or at least winked at. On Christmas and Easter, we even had feast-day celebrations in the camp. The guards knew about them, though they pretended they didn't; they would make an evening check about 5 P.M., but all they did was tell the men not to be too boisterous.

Each religious group would arrange to have a barrack to

itself on these feast days: Uniates in one, Orthodox in another, Baptists in a third, and so on. Because of the spirit among the prisoners, we could even arrange that those who were believers wouldn't work on religious feasts; in return, they would work the shifts for the nonbelievers on governmental holidays. The men showed marvelous ingenuity in fixing up the barracks for such celebrations. They covered the long tables in the barracks with bed sheets, somehow managed to get dishes, silverware, and glasses from the camp cafeteria, and prepared bowls of their various national dishes. Many of them got packages from home with bologna, macaroni, meat, butter, and other delicacies at this time.

On these occasions, each of us priests celebrated Mass in a different barrack. Here in Kayerkhan, for the first time in almost fifteen years, I said a "public" Mass for a whole barrack full of men—and did they sing! No wonder the guards had warned them to keep quiet. Practically everyone went to Communion, and then I preached a long homily on the feast after Mass.

Before we ate, we blessed the food and sang a solemn prayer of thanksgiving in Russian, then blessed the barrack with holy water. After that, we settled down to feasting. Whiskey was strictly prohibited in the camp, but it was all over the table on these occasions. Even the guards would drop in for a glass and a bite of holiday food, warn the men again to keep things quiet, then walk out. They never reported any of this to the officials.

Here at Kayerkhan, many of the prisoners were coming to the end of their sentences. Almost every day, it seemed, someone was liberated from the camp. To replace those who left, new prisoners were being brought in all the time. There was a constant turnover. You could pick out the old-timers in a crowd, though, by their tired walk and the way they handled their arms and legs, heavy with scurvy. Many a man took to riding the coal belts up the shaft after work, which was strictly forbidden, rather than walking home. I fell asleep doing this one day and wound up on the coal bunker, with lumps of coal raining down on me. I was lucky I wasn't killed, and I got out of there fast. Others were not always so lucky.

The most tragic cases, now, were the men killed in the mines with only a few days left to go before they would be free. Everyone talked about it, everyone thought about it, and there were men who were close to a nervous breakdown just thinking about it. Men became reluctant to go down in the mines, terrified that they might be killed by accident, with the end in sight, after having survived all these years. This tension did nothing to decrease the number of accidents; in fact, they reached an all-time high.

Seven men were killed in a flash explosion one day during blasting. This particular crew was blasting a new cut, working in a confined space with poor ventilation. In such a situation, you can feel the coal dust in the air, tingling and sparkling. They were actually outside the work area in a supposedly safe shaft at the time, but they were simply burned to a crisp in a flash explosion following the blast.

I shuddered at the story, because something similar had happened to me one day. We had finished a new cut and were ready to blast, so I had been sent up the safety shaft to prevent anyone from entering the area. Somehow, in the dark, I got lost and stood in the shaft just opposite the opening for the new cut. When the blast came, I was blown halfway up the shaft—just picked up bodily and slammed against one of the timbers at the top of the mine. Luckily, I wasn't killed or maimed, but I was unconscious for over two hours.

By the spring of 1955, a young Lithuanian doctor named Janos, in the medical center at Kayerkhan, told me I'd have to get out of the mines if I wanted to survive. I told him my sentence only had three more months to run, so perhaps I could last it out; he told me unless I got out of the mines, I would never make it. Janos was a medium-sized fellow with chestnut hair, red cheeks, and a little mustache, a very quiet man, but he knew his business and was determined to do something about my condition.

Here, work assignments were changed every three months, rather than every month, as they had been in other camps. When the spring assignments were due, he wrote a long medical history on my card of various illnesses, not all of which I had. There was no doubt, though, that I was beginning to weaken noticeably. At Mass the next Sunday, Janos, a devout Catholic, told me he thought I'd be invalided out of the mines on the next duty roster. When the names were read out in the barracks, however, I was still slated for the mines.

I saw Janos that morning, and he was furious. He told me to go to work that day, but he would see what he could do. As we were lining up to leave the camp that morning, though, he came running after me and told me to go back to the barracks. Then he went to the infirmary and entered my name on the sick list for the day.

About 10 A.M., Janos stormed into the office of the camp doctor, who was in conference that morning with three women doctors (free) from town. Waving my medical record card, he asked the director why I hadn't been exempted from duty in the mines. "If he dies," he shouted, "I'll report you! It's not my responsibility anymore. I made out this card and recommended that he be exempted. If he drops dead in the mines, I'm filing a full report!" With that, he threw the card on the desk and walked out.

The director hurried after him into the corridor and called him back. He was terrified. With the best will in the world, doctors in the prison camps simply can't do what they should for their patients, and they know it; therefore, they don't want any investigation by the city board concerning their practice. The director accompanied Janos straight to the foreman; my name was put on the list of those to be changed.

When he was finished at the medical center that day, Janos looked me up to report that I was officially out of the mines. I was elated. Just the news made me feel stronger and more alive; I couldn't thank Janos enough.

The next day, I was officially assigned to a brigade that worked in the stables. The brigadier put me down for the night shift, by myself. I worked from six in the evening to six in the morning, because it was "light" work. All I had to do was clean and water the horses, make up their stalls, clean out the stable during the night, feed the horses at night, then again in the morning. Actually, despite the hours, it was a good job. I was my own boss, and there were long periods when I could catch a nap; and I was out of the gases and dust of the mines. My health began to improve almost immediately.

We had only eight horses in the stable and six drivers. The horses were used especially to haul supplies—dynamite, machinery, tools, lumber—to the mine on sleds during the winter or for unloading supplies and food products from the railway sidings. The horses were young and lively, but they were on the go more than twelve hours a day, and they got a good workout.

The drivers were also young, mostly farm boys. At first, I was a little afraid of the horses, but they showed me how to handle them, how to harness them, how to clean them. There was one stubby little Mongolian horse named Vashka, however, who almost proved my undoing. A compact little white stallion with grayish spots, he had the biggest stall in the line because he kicked like a mule and bit as well. The eyes glowing out of his head were always fiery red; I was convinced the horse was mad. The first two nights, I couldn't even get near him to feed him. If I so much as set foot in the entrance to his stall, he'd begin snorting and kicking viciously at the walls and the gate.

After a couple of days of this, his driver told me one evening, "There's something wrong with old Vashka these days. He doesn't seem to have his usual strength, and I can't get him to pull at all." "Well, I might as well admit it," I said, "I can't get in to feed him. Every time I try to get in, he almost kicks my brains out. I'm not going to get killed by a crazy horse with only two more months to go on my sentence."

I thought the driver would be furious, but he laughed uproariously. Then he told me he'd show me how to handle Vashka. He strode to the stall, yelling the horse's name at the top of his lungs, cursing and shouting like an old mule skinner. Vashka looked terrified. Instead of kicking or snorting, he began to back nervously into the corner of his stall with dancing little steps, his eyes flashing. "See how easy it is", said the driver. "All you have to do is make the first move and be meaner and more cussed than he is. Go ahead, try it!"

I didn't particularly like the idea, but I got a bucketful of oats in one hand and strode over to Vashka's stall. I began to bellow and holler at the top of my lungs, waving my free hand, yelling out anything that came to mind and just sticking old Vashka's name in the middle of every phrase. It worked. Vashka got that skittish look in his red eyes and minced over into one corner of the stall. Still shouting, I spilled his ration of oats into the trough, walked out of the stall, and slammed the gate behind me. I felt like a real professional after that, and I never had any more trouble with Vashka.

About the first week of April, I was called to the camp office and told I'd be liberated in ten days. Checking my records, they found that according to the new regulations I was entitled to three months off for exceptional work; I actually served only fourteen years and nine months of my fifteen-year sentence. So, in my free time, I began the round of medical exams and the red tape of paperwork preparatory to any release.

The night before I was to leave, we had a going-away party. These were almost a tradition now in Kayerkhan, because so many had left. The men took up a collection, and everyone tried to help out a little bit. Some gave three rubles or five, and somebody scrounged up a new pair of padded pants and jacket to help me along. That night we went over to the free dining room near the camp gate, took over a few tables, and talked long into the night. Everyone was full of advice, telling me where to go, whom to see, where to find old friends who had gotten out before I did. In return, I promised to see as many of their families as I could if I were anywhere in the vicinity. They gave me messages and wrote down the estimated date of their own release, so I could pass it on.

The next morning, April 22, 1955, I was wide awake. I don't think I slept a wink all that night; I just couldn't believe that after fifteen years I was really going to be free. About nine o'clock, the foreman called me and took me to the KGB office. I was there for about two hours, signing documents and filling out forms. I expected some trouble or possibly another interrogation, but this was all routine for them. They went about it quite matter-of-factly, paying no more attention to me than they would to any other prisoner being set free.

Still, I was extremely nervous and anxious. I was wearing an old pair of *valenki*, my new padded jacket and pants, and a cap with padded earpieces. All my personal belongings had disappeared years ago. In the course of the morning's processing, one of the KGB men handed over a letter and two photographs of Sonia, one of my former Albertin parishioners. She had sent them to me in 1949; I got them now. I stuffed them into my pocket alongside the fifty rubles (five dollars) that were all I had in the world. They represented my pay, what was left of it, and the gifts from the party the night before.

I kept waiting for some sort of instructions from the KGB, but they simply explained at great length the details of my new status. When you leave the prison camp, you don't get a passport. You get a "document of liberation", so-called, which is a certificate stating that you have completed your sentence, and a statement of your citizenship status. A man may either be fully liberated and rehabilitated or only partially, as in my case. As a convicted spy, I got what is known as a restricted certificate, or *polozenie pasporta*.

With the *polozenie pasporta*, you're restricted as to where you can live and, in a sense, how much you can earn. For instance, at that time there was a very generous polar bonus, called the *zapolarie*, for those who worked in the Siberian Arctic. It was a government inducement to get workers for this fierce frontier. The longer a man worked here, the greater was the bonus; if a man worked in Siberia for five years, he could earn double his salary as a result of this *zapolarie*.

With my restricted citizenship status, I wasn't eligible for this polar bonus. Neither could I live wherever I wanted. I wasn't allowed to live in any "regime city", i.e., the big cities like Leningrad, Moscow, Kiev, Vladivostok, Tashkent, or in any of the border cities from which, presumably, I might be able to leave the country. I could visit such places for a period not to exceed three days, with the express permission of the government. And, with a *polozenie pasporta*, one of the first things I had to do in any city was report to the police and register my presence there.

After the officials had explained all this to me and checked out my camp documents for what seemed the one hundredth time, they told me to report to the police in Norilsk with my documents of liberation. There I would be given a formal set of identity papers. By 11:30, it was all over, and I walked out the main gate of the camp for the last time. Automatically, after I had gone about fifteen paces, I stopped and waited for the guard. The prisoners and the guards were watching me, laughing—nine out of ten liberated prisoners made the same mistake.

I was so self-conscious, I didn't know how to walk like a free man. My arms, dangling at my sides rather than folded behind my back, felt strange. I took a long look at the camp, almost as if I'd have to tear myself away, then put my hands in my pockets and walked toward Kayerkhan. There was a train at the station. I boarded it, and no one paid the slightest attention to me. I couldn't believe it. It seemed like a movie, as if everything were just a series of pictures unrolling before my eyes, or as if I were in a dream and might wake up at any moment.

The conductor, a woman, collected my fare. I was expecting her to ask me questions or to raise a difficulty of some sort. She just smiled politely. I sat down in the seat looking out the window, almost in tears—a free man, treated like a free man. I kept waiting for something to happen, for somebody to shout or something to stop the train or someone to point at me. Nothing happened. I sat back and looked at the mountains, the mines, the coal pouring out of the hoppers, the camp—then the train began to move, and I was on my way to Norilsk.

Chapter Four

A FREE MAN, RESTRICTED

Union Member in Norilsk

Even in the two years since I'd seen it last, Norilsk had changed. It had assumed less the aspect of a frontier town and more that of a city, thanks to the buildings and the industries put up by the prisoners. By 1955, its population was more than 120,000, and those who were lucky enough to have houses were living for the most part in the former prisoners' barracks and the five-story apartment buildings I'd helped to build while at Camp 5.

The industries, like the big BOF plant we'd built at Camp 2 and the huge *Kombinat* we'd built at Camp 4, were right at the foot of Schmidtika, Norilsk's most striking geographical landmark. From there, the main road, Oktobrskaya Street, ran west through the old city to Lenin Platz, a traffic circle, beyond which the new city began. West of Lenin Platz was Sebastobolskaya Street, with the police station, the new hospitals, schools, theaters, and department stores. All along the streets that paralleled Sebastobolskaya were the five-story brick apartment houses I remembered building.

Two years earlier, I had left Norilsk on a narrow-gauge railway. Now I arrived in town on a wide, standard-gauge railroad that had been completed in the interim. Big Stalin-type locomotives were standing in the yards, coal-burning monsters used on the continental runs, now transferred for use in the north.

As I stepped out of the train on arrival, the air somehow felt warmer than in Kayerkhan. Everywhere, however, there was a coat of heavy snow, dirty with factory smoke. Having known the city as a prisoner, I felt strange walking through it now as a free man. It was a peculiar feeling of mingled pride and nervousness, a sense of mastery and of loss, for I felt somehow out of place.

I did carry with me two addresses. One was Fr. Viktor's; he'd been released from Camp 4 two months earlier and was living just off the main boulevard, Oktobrskaya. The other address was that of another former prisoner, a young Pole named Ladislas, who had invited me to look him up in Norilsk. Since I was closest to Oktobrskaya, I walked that way, past the stadium and theater, along the main street of the old city, just looking at the shops and the buildings, and feeling somewhat shabby in my padded prison clothes. Yet most of the people I saw were dressed as I was; many of them, no doubt, were former prisoners, too.

Out beyond the stadium, I could see a random conglomeration of shanties, huts, and shacks (called *boloks*) that had once housed a large Chinese population and was called "Shanghai Town" by the people of Norilsk. When I came to where the tracks of the spur line to Tecz, the electric power plant, crossed Oktobrskaya, I turned left as per Viktor's instructions.

About two hundred yards in from the boulevard was another jumble of shacks and shanties made of old boards and packing crates, built one onto the other like a series of dominoes. The walls were usually double, made of the thin scrap lumber, then filled with ashes for insulation. The better ones were covered with tar paper or clay or plaster on the outside.

There was no discernible order, so I stopped at the first shack and asked for Viktor. The family inside directed me to one of the jumbles nearby, and eventually I found Fr. Viktor's *bolok*, a tumble-down shack in the middle of one of these rabbit warrens. He was living with another priest, Fr. Neron, who had been in Kayerkhan and liberated before I worked there. They had two beds in the room, separated by an altar; this little room, ten by ten feet, served as their chapel as well.

They were delighted to see me, as I them. They cooked me a dinner on the little electric stove that served both for cooking and for heating the hut. Then we talked for hours. They wouldn't hear of my going anywhere else, so that night we put three chairs in the little space between the two beds, and I used my padded coat and pants for a mattress. As soon as we got up in the morning, we cleared out the beds and prepared to celebrate Mass.

By 6:30, there were ten or twelve people in that little room for Mass. On Sundays, the people jammed not only this room but the corridor beyond the open door as well. To accommodate the growing crowds, Viktor and Neron said two Masses every Sunday and preached a sermon at each, and there might be sixty or more people at every Mass. For this, in effect, was a parish church.

That first morning, after Mass, I went with Viktor to the police station to register, as I'd been instructed. I handed in my documents and the police registered me, then gave me a set of identification papers. They explained again the restrictions I was under because of the *polozenie pasporta*, my "limited rehabilitation" status. They also added a new twist. Since my political charge, 58:6, had been for espionage, I was subject to further limitations. I had to live where I was told, in this case Norilsk; if I wanted to move to another city, I could do it only with permission and for a good reason, such as health. I was not so free, in short, as I had thought on walking out of Kayerkhan!

They asked me where I was living, and I told them I didn't yet have a place of my own. But they insisted I had to have some address for the MVD[1] register, which contains the address of every citizen in the city. I told them I was living with Viktor. My name was accordingly entered in the police book at that address, then in Viktor's "house book", a registration certificate that every householder must have (something like a driver's license), containing the names of all the residents in his house. Now I was officially registered.

I lived with Viktor for more than a week while I looked for a job and a place of my own to live. Meanwhile, I met Viktor's parishioners and neighbors. Ludwig, the choirmaster, lived in the *bolok* next door to Viktor's with his wife and teenaged son. He was a short, dark man with Mongol features, extremely dedicated to the church, who sang Mass every morning before going to his job as a boiler repairman. His wife, Niura, was also small and dark, with glowing cheeks and a warm personality. Unlike most of the women in Norilsk, she didn't work during the day, for Ludwig's skill was much in demand, and he was highly paid. So Niura was happy to spend her time as housekeeper for the priests and sacristan for our little chapel.

In the *bolok* immediately behind Viktor's, and built onto it, lived two Lithuanian women, Nina and Ludmilla, who cared for an old and infirm Greek Orthodox priest, Fr. Foma. He used to say Mass for them early in the morning, after which they would come over to attend our Masses. They worked in the surgical hospital on Oktobrskaya, and they used to help

---

[1] The police, also called "militia". In 1954, after Beria's downfall, the police ministry was split into the MVD and the KGB, the internal security or "secret" police.

mend our clothes, wash the floors, and bring us food from the hospital kitchen.

After a week, I still hadn't found either a place to live or a job. Finally, I looked up five young Poles whom I'd known in the mines, former prisoners, who were living in a sort of bachelor's barrack near the *Kombinat.* They worked as an emergency rescue squad for the mines in the area—as far away as Kayerkhan and up in the mountains to old Zapadnaya—wherever and whenever they were needed. They had a room about ten by twelve feet in which the five of them lived, but they invited me to bunk with them.

One of them was always on duty, so we arranged that I'd sleep in the duty man's bed. Moreover, there was a dining room in the barrack, which served good meals, so I wouldn't have to continue scrounging from Fr. Viktor—without a job, I couldn't afford a restaurant. It wasn't the best arrangement, but I thought it was better than overcrowding poor, generous Viktor, so I decided to move in with them.

Meanwhile, I had gone to see the young Pole, Ladislas. He was working at BOF in the laboratory, and he told me there would be a job opening at the plant in a couple of weeks. He had spoken to his supervisor about me, and he felt sure he could get me the job.

I still went to Viktor's every morning to say Mass, but on Sundays, with a valise full of Mass equipment provided by Viktor, I'd go out to one of the old barracks that had been part of Camp 5. Now it was part of the city housing, and I said Mass there, at 9 A.M., for another "parish" of Poles. Before Mass, I'd hear confessions, then after Mass I'd have baptisms and weddings, in ever-increasing numbers as the people found out I was available every Sunday.

I always refused to take any money or stipend for this work, but the people wanted to do something to show their appreciation. Since I wouldn't take money, they asked me at least to accept some clothes to replace the prison camp clothing I was still wearing. They took me down to the new part of the city beyond Lenin Platz, where there was an avenue of new stores: a big food store called the *Gastronom*, something like a super-market; the *Promtovarni Magazin* for manufactured goods, much like a department store; and a row of shops for specialty items.

I was amazed at how full and well-stocked these stores looked, even out here in Siberia. It was only when I began to shop for clothes that I realized how difficult it was to get the quality or the size I really wanted. In fact, it was taken for granted by the people that the clerks made extra money by seeing to it that you got what you wanted. I had to take an overcoat that was a size too small, because it was as close to a fit as I could get. I couldn't get shirts with collars, or a pair of low-cut shoes. For that matter, there weren't any shoes in my size, so I had to be satisfied with a very uncomfortable pair a size smaller. The few galoshes they had were much too big— until I paid the clerk to look again. Then he found my size.

One morning, when I came to say Mass, Viktor told me there was a possibility I could get another apartment, at least for several months. One of the families in his "parish" had told him their neighbors were going away for a few months, and they could arrange for me to have the *bolok* if they could have an answer that same day. I jumped at the chance. Imme-diately after Mass, Viktor and I went to make the arrange-ments.

I went home with Viktor that evening and helped him celebrate a *Panikhida*, or Requiem, a very beautiful Russian memorial service for the dead. The ceremony is sung and takes perhaps forty minutes; all the people know the chants by heart, so everyone sings. During the ceremony a *kutia*—a small bowl of rice mixed with raisins—is placed on the altar, and after the ceremony everyone partakes of it, along with cookies and cakes provided by the family. After the ceremony, I stayed the night with Fr. Viktor and the next morning, after Mass, I went to my new apartment. It was a small *bolok*, but it had three rooms. There was a little kitchen, perhaps three by five feet, a bedroom just big enough for two beds, and a small sitting room. But it was a good base of operations for me, since it was private, and I said Mass here daily for a constantly growing number of people. I continued to say Mass on Sunday, however, at the Polish barrack out at the old Camp 5.

A few days after I'd settled into my new *bolok*, Ladislas came to tell me that the supervisor of the laboratory at BOF wanted to see me. BOF—*Bolshaya* (Major) *Obogatitelnaya* (Refining) *Fabrika* (Factory)—is a massive building that sits almost halfway up the hill overlooking the city. Ladislas was waiting when I arrived the next morning and took me up to the second floor, which housed the laboratory. We went first to his office, where I waited while he checked with the supervisor. He was back in a moment and led me down a corridor to the supervisor's office. The supervisor was a thin woman in her late thirties, with black hair, dark eyes, delicate features, and a beautiful face. "Anastasia Nikolayevna," said Ladislas, "this is Wladimir Martinovich." She got up, came around her desk, and shook hands. She asked me to sit down for an interview, and I narrated my background; I admitted frankly that I had no experience. "But I need a job," I said, "and I'm willing to work."

Anastasia smiled. She said she would be happy to have me. I would work in the laboratory as Ladislas' assistant until I acquired some experience, and she asked if I would be satisfied with a starting salary of 1100 rubles ($110) a month, with a two-hundred-ruble bonus for good work. I was almost overcome, and I thanked her profusely. She told me she would like me to start the following day.

The next day I reported to work before 8 A.M., wearing my good clothes because I had no others except for the padded suit I had worn in the prison camp. It was possible to take a bus practically to the door of BOF, but that morning I walked to work; it was my first job as a free man, and it was a strange feeling to return to BOF, the plant I had built as a prisoner, in a new position of responsibility at a good salary.

Ladislas was already waiting to show me around the lab. It consisted of four big rooms, each of them outfitted with two work benches, two electric stoves, sinks, and all the necessary chemistry equipment. Three girls worked in each room, running tests on the ore samples for copper and nickel content. These test samples were then bagged, tagged, and filed for later reference. There were forty girls in the lab all told, twelve or thirteen for each shift, but besides Ladislas and me there were only three men in the whole department.

One was the head chemist and instructor, whom I barely knew. The other two, Maxim and Basil, were office managers like Ladislas, in charge of the other shifts. I worked with Ladislas on the day shift, which was the heaviest; Maxim, a nervous, high-strung Russian, had the four-to-twelve shift. Basil, a Ukrainian, managed the twelve-to-eight shift, but unlike Maxim, he was so easy-going he never worried about anything.

My job was simply to keep the girls supplied with the necessary chemicals and materials, then to file the completed test results. Ladislas said these packets had to be kept at least a month in case further tests were required on that batch of ore, or in case the refined ore didn't show the same percentages of copper and nickel as our tests had indicated.

Now that I was settled in Norilsk, and things seemed to be

going well, I decided to try again to write home to my family—my first letter in more than fifteen years. At Viktor's suggestion, I went first to the KGB offices in Gorily and asked if it was all right; I explained that I hadn't written home since 1940. The KGB agent in charge said it was no affair of theirs; it was a militia (i.e., police) matter. He told me to take it up with the chief of the MVD.

I waited in the MVD office one day for almost four hours and finally got to see the chief sometime in the afternoon. He listened sympathetically as I explained my case again. I told him it had been so long since I'd written that I didn't know whether anyone at home was alive or not. He was most kind and said he had no objections; he even showed me how to address the envelope so it would be certain of delivery, then gave me a special envelope to use for overseas mail.

I had to address it just the opposite to what I would have considered normal—writing first the name of the country, then the state, the street number and the name, using both languages, Russian and English, in alternate lines. Then, at the very bottom of the envelope, I added my return address in Russian. I wrote to Sister Evangeline, my sister, because I still remembered the address of her convent—if she was still there.

I wasn't sure anyone would get the letter, so I kept it short and to the point. Prisoners had told me that long letters never got through; most of them simply wrote "Alive and well" to their families when letters were allowed. In any event, there was little sense in my writing a lot of news until I knew if the letters were reaching America. The militia chief had assured me there wouldn't be any problem, but I kept the letter short anyway. I signed it very simply, "Your brother, Walter."

On my way home that afternoon, I bumped into Petro, a young lad from the Urals who worked in the iron-stripping mines. He invited me in for a drink, since it was payday.

During our conversation, I told him I had written home. That was all the occasion he needed. He told his wife, Katcha, to make some *pilmeni* (little dough-covered meatballs), and he brought out the whiskey for a real celebration. "Ah, it's a big day, Valodga," he said, "you have to let us celebrate!"

Since I had missed the noon meal and Petro's wife insisted on cooking the *pilmeni*, I couldn't refuse their offer. While Katcha worked in the kitchen, I sat down with Petro. First of all, we had to toast America. So Petro filled up two water glasses with vodka. We raised the glasses, clinked them together for America and chanted, "*za vashie zdorovie!*" (To your health!). The only way to drink vodka, at least the vodka that was common in Siberia, is to turn the glass bottoms up and drain it in two gulps—then hold a piece of rye bread tight under your nose, sniffing deep to clear your head of the fumes. We drained the glasses.

After we toasted America, we toasted my family, the good news, and payday. Then Katcha came in with a delicious meal of *pilmeni*. She and Petro talked of their plans to work for five years here in the polar regions, collecting the big *zapolarie* in order to build a nest egg, then return to the Urals to buy a house and farm. "And you know what, Valodga?" said Petro. "Pretty soon you're going to baptize my first son!" I congratulated them, and we drank to that; then the celebration went on into the evening.

Petro's idea of a little celebration pretty well knocked me flat, but that Saturday night I had to face another one. I had promised to marry Ladislas and his fiancée, Raya; they swore they had waited for me to get out of the prison camps just so I could perform the ceremony. At seven o'clock on Saturday evening, I arrived at Ladislas' apartment for the wedding.

It was a beautiful place in the new part of the city on Komsomolskaya Street, on the fourth floor of one of the new five-story apartment buildings. There were two large rooms, tastefully furnished, with all the modern appliances. He was lucky to have it, and in fact it wasn't really his; he was occupying it while one of the directors of BOF was away on another assignment. No one in Norilsk ever wanted to leave his apartment empty or unoccupied; with everything in such short supply in the town, robberies were common. The director, therefore, had asked Ladislas to take over his apartment while he was gone.

Ladislas and his bride-to-be were delighted, of course. Now that they had a place of their own, they could get married. Since they were Polish, the marriage ceremony was in the Roman rite, and I celebrated a Nuptial Mass. Everyone had brought something for the party, and Ladislas and Raya had been visiting the stores and shopping for a month to prepare for the celebration, so it was a long, wonderful evening.

Meanwhile, at BOF, I was learning more and more. I found the work interesting and the people quite friendly. Most of the girls at BOF knew I was a priest before I had been working there very long. They didn't necessarily show me any special signs of respect, but they were willing to cover for me if I came in late or had to leave early because of a wedding, baptism, and so on. The supervisor herself, Anastasia, was especially friendly. Before a month was out, she asked if I would take charge of the night shift. I was happy to do it, because it left me free most of the day and evening for apostolic activities.

Occasionally, though, the girls in the lab would drop into my office to talk religion. One night, Tashya, a tiny and lively Russian with chestnut hair combed straight back, like the majority of Russian women, came in hesitantly. She had heard I was a priest, and she wanted to know if I was Russian.

I told her no, I was an American. That stumped her; the only priests she had known were Russians, and she had no idea, for instance, that Mass could be said in the Latin rite as well as in the Oriental rite.

Whenever Tashya talked to me about this, she would leave the room if anyone else came in, then catch me again when I was alone. This began to pique my curiosity, and I thought she must be leading up to something. Finally, one night she came out with it. "I want you" she said, "to sing a *Panikhida* (Requiem) for my husband." It was my turn to be surprised. "You were married?" I said. "Yes," she said, "my husband died almost exactly a year ago, and I want you to sing a *Panikhida* on the anniversary of his death." Then she told me the whole story.

Her husband had worked in the factory at BOF, grinding ore. One day his machine had developed some trouble; he tried to save time by repairing it while it was running. He slipped and fell into the jaws of the machine. He was ground up and mashed into the ore and had to be buried that way. It was a gruesome story and rather sad, for he and Tashya had been married only three months. I agreed to sing the *Panikhida*, then Tashya asked me to baptize her little boy, too. That evening I walked home with her, sang the *Panikhida* with her father and mother present, and made arrangements to baptize the boy on Sunday.

This is a big occasion for a Russian family, so the house was full of guests. In the Oriental rite, baptism is by triple immersion; the whole ceremony takes almost forty minutes, and at the end of the baptismal ceremony, confirmation is given. After the ceremony, many of the guests came up to ask me to baptize their children. That was the way my work grew, and the process was unending.

Another evening, while I was filing some batches of test

results, Ninja came quietly into the office and waited for me to look up. She was a pretty young girl, a member of the *Komsomol* and married to a Party man. "Can I ask you a few questions?" she said. "Of course", I said. She hesitated. "Are you a priest?" "Yes", I said. "No fooling?" she pleaded. I laughed.

Ninja fell silent for a moment, then she said, "I've been reading a Bible that I borrow now and then from an old woman I visit, and there are a lot of things in it I don't understand. But it says that everybody, in order to be saved, must be baptized. Do you know how to do it?" I smiled. "Of course", I said. "Could you baptize me?" I was a little startled at that. "Now who's fooling?" I said. "It's not quite so easy; we'll have to see."

Just then someone came down the corridor, and Ninja ducked out. As a *Komsomol*, she didn't want to be caught talking to a priest about religion. She came back later and began immediately by asking, "When can I be baptized?" I had to smile at her anxiety, but I said, "Well, when I find out what you know about God, about baptism, about salvation, and a lot of other things. Also, I have to make sure how sincere you are." She was so eager, however, that I told her to read several passages in the Bible and made arrangements to meet her regularly so she could begin instructions.

Working with Ninja, night after night, I could actually sense the grace of God at work—in her sincerity, in her enthusiasm, and in the change that had come over her. Now she not only wanted to be baptized herself, but she wanted her three children baptized as well. Her husband, however, would be against it, she knew; he was a sincere Party man. But she begged me to do it anyway and promised that she would bring up the children in the faith.

Finally, when her husband was called away to Moscow for

a meeting of the Party, Ninja pleaded with me not to put it off any longer. I couldn't refuse. Her mother was there and the old woman who had been the cause of it all by lending Ninja her Bible. In fact, she was the sponsor for the whole family. I never in my life experienced such devotion. I could almost feel the Holy Spirit flowing in the waters as I baptized Ninja; her reaction moved me deeply. Then I baptized the children and gave them all little aluminum crucifixes I'd gotten from Viktor. After that, we had a party.

A week later, when Ninja's husband returned, the little boy let the cat out of the bag. He told his father all about the party and showed him the "present" I'd given him—the little crucifix. The father was no fool; he suspected immediately what had happened, and he was furious. He threatened to have the priest who had done it arrested. Eventually, though, the storm blew over; he even allowed Ninja to bring up the children in the faith.

He wasn't the only one. I remember another Party man in Norilsk who told his wife, as he boarded a train for a Party meeting in Moscow, that when he returned he had better find his baby baptized, or there would be trouble in the house. Another high-ranking official in the city, who used to give thunderous public speeches denouncing religion, considered it a distinct honor to be the godfather of his sister's child the day I baptized the boy.

On the occasions of the great October and May holidays, the government used to give out acknowledgments, premiums, and certificates for outstanding work. The first October I was at BOF, I got a bonus certificate for one hundred rubles. Every premium period after that, I got something—a seventy-five-ruble bonus, or a certificate, or a premium. More important than the actual cash or the certificates, though, was the fact that, every time I won an award, the notation "*Blagodarnos*" (Exceptional Worker) was entered in my personal file and working papers. That meant I'd always have excellent references if I tried to get a job somewhere else; it also meant that when the KGB checked up on me, as they still did from time to time, they wouldn't find anything but good reports in my record. If they weren't impressed, at least they would find no ammunition to use against me in the interrogations.

About this time, too, I was received into the *Provsoiouz*—the Union of Soviet Workers. At the meetings in the plant, which we had almost every Monday morning, they insisted that everyone should belong to the union. They kept pointing out the benefits and privileges we missed by not joining. After much persuasion, I finally agreed to join.

The procedure was simple. You wrote out a standard petition, which was read at the local union meeting, and the chairman asked the members if it should be considered. In my case, they agreed to consider my petition; I was then asked to rise, give a short autobiography, and answer any questions that might be raised from the floor (there were none). Then a motion was made and passed—and I became a member of *Provsoiouz*.

For small monthly dues, one ruble per hundred rubles of salary, I received the following privileges: sick benefits, including free medical treatment, and 60 percent of my salary while I was laid off; the first choice of sanatoriums and rest homes if I needed extended treatment, and for these items I paid only one-third the normal cost; first consideration given to any application for a new job, or for transfer to a better-paying job when it became available.

On the other hand, the union becomes all-encompassing. Not only are questions of work and working conditions raised at the meetings, but the members' private lives and their shortcomings are also freely discussed. At one of the union meetings, for instance, a young couple was called up to explain their marital problems. Both of them were *Komsomol* leaders and, therefore, supposedly outstanding Party members. They seemed an ideal and happy couple, but the husband wanted to divorce his wife because they had no children.

Since most of the workers at BOF were women, the poor husband didn't stand a chance. He was shelled from all sides: "Is this any example for a *Komsomol* leader to be showing the youth?" "She was good enough for you when you married her, but now you're getting tired of her, is that it?" "What about the new Soviet code for family life, even if there are no children?" The situation was almost laughable, but the fact that the union had such a control over its members wasn't funny at all.

Norilsk Is My Parish

One morning, when I came home from work, I found a telegram from the family who owned my *bolok* saying they were on the way home. I talked to Viktor and Ladislas, and the latter insisted I move in with him for as long as he had his new apartment. I hated to inconvenience the newlyweds, but I had nowhere else to go, so I agreed to take over one room of their two-room apartment.

Viktor warned me not to be too active at Ladislas'. Most of the government apartment houses were strictly controlled by the building superintendent, who reported any "suspicious activity" to the police. As a result, I usually went to Viktor's in the evening to sing the *Panikhida*, or to the people's homes to perform baptisms and other ceremonies. I did, however, do some baptizing at Ladislas' apartment—and promptly got called out by the KGB. They asked me to report, not to KGB headquarters, but to the City Center.

When I was ushered in, there were four men seated around the table. They asked me to have a seat. The session began with the routine questions: How was I finding life now that I was liberated? How was I getting along with people? Did I like my job? and so forth. Suddenly, they zeroed in. "Who gave you permission to do missionary work?" said one of the men. "You know that requires Moscow's approval." I was startled by the suddenness of the question; then I told him frankly that I was doing what my conscience told me to do and what the people needed.

"I have a right to say Mass at home or to pray if I want to", I told them. "The Soviet Constitution guarantees freedom of religion and freedom of conscience. And if anybody comes in while I'm saying Mass, I'm not going to chase him out. I'm not agitating, not advertising, but if somebody wants to come, I won't send him away. And if someone asks me to do him a favor, as long as it isn't against the law, I'll do it—like a good Soviet comrade."

They reminded me that it was against the law for a priest to take money from the people. All "authorized" priests had their salaries paid by the government. "You just prove one case where I so much as asked for money", I answered. "You just try! You know you can't, because if you could prove that I ever took money from people or asked people for money, you would have had me in here long before this!"

We went on that way for over an hour, arguing, while they began to drop broad hints that I should stop my "subversive activities". I told them simply that as long as people came to me freely, I would continue to help them. Legally, there wasn't much the KGB could say to that, but at the end of our little "chat" they warned me to "watch out". That night I went to see Viktor and Fr. Neron to tell them I'd been called out. It wasn't particularly news to them; they had also been called recently.

Viktor was in the weakest position of the three of us, because he didn't work. He spent all his time looking after the needs of his people, and in return his "parishioners" took care of his needs. The KGB wanted to know where he was getting his money, since he had no job. Neron and I, on the other hand, did have jobs, I at BOF, and Neron as a night watchman on a construction job. Viktor, for one of the few times since I'd known him, was worried. I told him what I had told the KGB, however, and he thought we could probably get away with it a little while longer.

Actually, by this time, my work as a priest had doubled. A group of Lithuanians, who lived in another shanty town behind the *Kombinat*, had asked me to say Mass for them on Sunday. So every Sunday, I still said my first Mass for the Poles in the barracks down at the old Camp 5, then walked across town to say another for the Lithuanians. I was beginning to have so many requests for baptisms I couldn't keep up with the number. Depending on what shift I worked, I used to ask Anastasia, the supervisor, for a day off occasionally so I could catch up. She never asked me why I wanted the day off, although I think she knew, but she was usually glad to help me out.

After a while, I became so busy that I had to rotate the places for Sunday Mass. I went to different quarters of town on the different weekends to keep up with the requests, sometimes even taking a taxi up the hill to Medvierskaya to say a second or third Mass. I knew the KGB was watching me, but I didn't care. As long as I didn't ask for money, I knew I had at least an arguable case. Certainly they had no grounds for complaints on other scores, especially with my record of citations and certificates at BOF.

It was about this time that I got an answer from my sisters, Helen and Sister Evangeline. They wrote how glad they were to hear from me and told me I'd been presumed dead. Masses had been said for the repose of my soul in the Society, at my old seminary in Orchard Lake, and elsewhere. They enclosed their addresses and told me that if I needed anything, I had only to ask for it. I read the letter to Viktor and talked it over with him and some others; they encouraged me to write.

Ultimately, I wrote a short note asking for clothes—shoes, socks, shirts, gloves, a whole outfit. I could always use the clothes, of course, but I really wanted to find out if the package would come through. Viktor was rather sanguine, because he used to get packages regularly from Poland. However, as I had learned by experience in Camp 5, it was one thing to write to Poland and another to write to the United States.

These days there was only one prison camp left around Norilsk. The others had been closed down, and the prisoners who had not been liberated had been sent elsewhere. The one remaining camp was solely for political prisoners, and they, in a sense, were quite free. They lived in barracks in the camp, but they came to work in town without guards and mingled freely on the job with others. By 1958, this camp, too, was liquidated, and those who hadn't completed their sentences were transferred somewhere else. So, one by one, the old prison camps had been dissolved, and the barracks remodeled and turned into homes for workers.

As the camps were closed, though, a lot of the thieves and criminal elements drifted into Norilsk, as they would to any boom town. Many of the crafty ones became speculators, and a rather brisk black market developed in food products and housing. More dangerous, however, were the groups who turned to crimes of violence; robberies and thefts became commonplace, murders almost a daily occurrence. In certain areas of the city, the streets were not only dangerous after dark, they were deadly.

The former camp where many of our Ukrainian "parishioners" lived, for example, was more than half a mile from the nearest bus stop. Their children, especially those in the second shift at school—from 2:00 until 7:00 in the evening—were always in danger along the unlighted streets. Complaints were made to the police, but the way things were going in Norilsk at the moment, the police already had their hands full.

So the Ukrainians formed their own "militia". Every night, three or four men patrolled the worst places and trouble spots around the old camp. If they caught anyone hanging around whom they didn't know, they killed him on the spot—no questions asked. Then they threw him out in the middle of the road with a sign pinned on his chest, as a warning to other thieves and criminals. It was brutal, but it was effective.

The Ukrainians were organized in other ways, too. They were almost militantly religious. In fact, they clung to religion tenaciously, as a part of their national heritage and tradition. Out in their camp, they held huge weddings and christenings, openly religious. And when one of their leaders died, they organized a mammoth funeral—with a choir of more than two hundred and a big cross with flowers and crepe to lead the funeral procession.

From the camp, they walked right through the main streets of town on the way to the cemetery, singing "*Sviati Bozie*" (Holy God) at the top of their lungs. The cortege walked straight down Oktobrskaya, stopping traffic, with the cross and choir leading the procession, then the men bearing the coffin on their shoulders, followed by huge crowds of mourners. The people on the sidewalks of Oktobrskaya, the main boulevard, were astounded at such a big religious demonstration. Some of them crossed themselves as the coffin passed.

At the cemetery, the Ukrainians chanted the full burial ceremony; then they returned in procession to the dead man's home to eat a ceremonial meal and pay their traditional respects. Afterward, there was quite an investigation by the KGB to find out who had organized the whole thing. Fr. Viktor was called out several times, since he was known to work among the Ukrainians. He was severely cross-examined and threatened by the KGB for what they considered his "subversive activities" and "agitating".

Viktor, in fact, was worried. He was beginning to wonder if it might not be better for him to leave Norilsk. I asked him to wait just a while longer, since there was still so much good he could do in Norilsk, and the risk was worth it.

In the spring of 1956, Ladislas got a telegram from the director whose apartment we were occupying. He said he was about to return home, so I had to start looking for another home. This time, I found a place almost immediately in another little shack-town across Oktobrskaya, thanks to a good friend of Fr. Viktor, a German mechanic named Hans. Hans had just moved into his superintendent's apartment on Sebastobolskaya in the new part of town, a modern two-story apartment house. The superintendent was going to Moscow for a while and on his return would have an option, because of his position, on a newly built house. Accordingly, Hans and his wife, Margarita, offered to let me have their little *bolok* in shanty town, furnished as it was.

I was delighted to get it. It meant that for the first time in almost a year I would be alone. I moved in the next morning. When I had finished moving, I had a few hours to catch a nap before reporting to BOF, so I just stretched out on the bed, clothes and all. It was cold in the room, since Hans had moved out a few days earlier, but I didn't bother lighting a fire. A few days later, Hans came around to see how I was doing. He found me stretched out on the bed; when he tried to rouse me, it was obvious I had a fever.

Hans immediately notified Fr. Viktor, who hurried over to help. When he saw how sick I was, Viktor made arrangements with the two Lithuanian sisters who lived next door to him to take care of me. They were the ones who had taken care of the old Greek priest, Fr. Foma, but his health had become so bad he had finally gone back to live with relatives in the Ukraine. Viktor and Hans helped me to walk the four or five blocks to the cluster of huts where Viktor and the sisters lived. They gave me some aspirin and hot tea, and the next morning I felt much better.

The two sisters, Nina, who was fifty-three, and Ludmilla, who was thirty-eight, were not married. Their house, though very small, was immaculate; everything was white-washed, the wall between the kitchen and the main room was freshly painted. Between them, they saw to it that I ate regularly and well, that my clothes were always clean, and that I took decent care of my health. I soon felt better than I had in years.

About this time, I received my first package from the United States. It was a big box from my sisters containing two suits, two topcoats, two pair of shoes, shirts, socks, and just about everything else in the line of clothing—including a cassock. I already had a complete set of vestments, in all the liturgical colors, made by my parishioners, as well as the other linens needed for Mass. I split up the clothes with Fr. Viktor, who needed them even more badly than I did. He was delighted to get them, but I was overjoyed; it was proof that packages sent from the U.S.A. would reach me in good condition.

All through that summer and fall, we three priests worked even harder, if possible. The more work we did, the more work there seemed to be. At the beginning of 1957, however, I was called out again by the KGB. They told me point blank this time to stop priestly activities; this was the "last" warning. Viktor and Neron were also warned to stop their "unwarranted activities" among the people. They felt that this was, indeed, the final warning for them. When they came home, they were talking seriously about leaving Norilsk. For a long time that night, we sat around and discussed our future.

At length, quite reluctantly, I agreed that it might be better for Neron and Viktor to leave Norilsk and go to the Ukraine. Many of our Ukrainian "parishioners" had already gone home, and it was obvious from their letters the need was almost equally great there as it was here in Siberia. Viktor and Neron felt it would make more sense for them to return and be of service to the faithful in the Ukraine than to be hampered or even arrested here out of sheer bravado.

Fr. Neron, accordingly, left shortly afterward. He was to notify Fr. Viktor upon his arrival in the Ukraine what conditions were like and where to join him. Viktor stayed on to help with the Lenten and Easter observances, which were growing larger every year as more and more people heard about them from friends. After Easter 1957, however, Viktor decided not to wait for a message from Neron but left immediately for the Ukraine. It was probably the best thing for him, for his health was getting worse and he was developing a bad case of nerves under the constant threat of surveillance.

I was continually on the go now. I had inherited not only Viktor's chapel but his congregation as well. On Sundays, I said Mass in the little chapel at eight o'clock in the Oriental rite, then again at ten o'clock in the Latin rite. There were always confessions to be heard before each Mass, baptisms and weddings to be performed after Mass. Whenever I could, I tried to say one of my Sunday Masses at the old Camp 5 or for the Ukrainians in the old camp out behind the *Kombinat*.

Sunday, as a matter of fact, I was on the go all day after Mass—blessing homes, baptizing infants who were too small to be brought to the chapel, performing weddings, distributing Communion to the sick, and so forth. On weekdays, I said Mass every morning at six o'clock, then, if my shift at BOF permitted it, sang a *Panikhida* or *Molebien* (the little office of the Blessed Virgin, a popular devotion) almost every evening.

That summer, Ludmilla and Nina received a letter from relatives begging them to come home to Lithuania. They had been a tremendous help to me in the past three months, keeping the chapel clean, doing the linens, and looking after my personal wants in a way I was much too busy to do. Still, I told them I'd buy the *bolok* if they wanted to go. They had already received one offer, and it wouldn't have been fair to ask them simply to donate the *bolok* to me. On the other hand, I didn't want to have to move back into Viktor's *bolok* and take up space that was now so badly needed in the chapel.

So I went with the two sisters to ZKU, the housing authority, filled out the documents, and had the deed for the *bolok* made out in my name. Then I helped them pack and saw them off for Lithuania, although I was sorry to see them go. The choirmaster, Ludwig, and his wife invited me to have my meals with them. I was happy to accept their invitation, because it left me just that much more time free to work with the people.

Not long after that, I was approached one day by a small group who asked me, quite hesitantly, what kind of priest I was. I told them I was a Catholic priest, but of the Oriental rite. They themselves were Orthodox, but they had seen me working among the people, and they had come to me with a proposal to build an Orthodox church. They were ready to write to Moscow for permission, but they needed a pastor and they wanted me to help. I was almost positive Moscow would never give permission for such a thing, so I told them to write and I would tentatively agree.

Within a few days, the KGB had me on the carpet to ask why I was "agitating the people" after I'd been severely warned. I replied boldly that I wasn't agitating anybody; the people themselves had come to me and asked me to be their priest. "As long as it's not against the law," I said, "I won't refuse to help anybody. These people knew the law. They were writing to Moscow for permission, so why should I refuse them?"

Then we had a little talk about the difference between the Catholic Church and the Orthodox Church. The KGB suggested that I might write an article for the local newspaper about religion, giving specific information about the Church and Church practices. I didn't know exactly what they were up to. Perhaps they were trying to make it look as if I had somehow separated myself from Rome and was now an independent authority on religious matters; or perhaps they would use the article in some way to make fun of religion and show the young *komsomols* how strange and superstitious Church practices were. In any event, I knew they weren't up to much good.

So I gave them the titles of a few books they could consult about the Church and Church practices, but I said, "I'm not writing any articles." They ended our little chat with a strong warning to me to cease and desist my religious activities. "We're not going to warn you any more," they said, "but you keep it up, and we'll take whatever measures we feel we must."

The people, of course, didn't know anything about all this. Even as I returned from KGB headquarters, I found four or five people waiting patiently for me in front of my *bolok*—all of them to arrange baptisms. I simply hadn't the heart to tell them I couldn't help, by order of the government, so I took their names and addresses down in a notebook. I was working the day shift at BOF that week, so I arranged to visit them next evening, which was a Saturday.

Of the five appointments, three were in different parts of Norilsk, but two were far up into the mountains at Medvierskaya. After work on Saturday, therefore, I immediately finished two of the baptisms in Norilsk, then caught a taxi for the appointment at Medvierskaya. It was starting to snow rather heavily, but I made it on time. After the baptisms there, another family asked me to baptize their child. I apologized to them but said I still had an appointment in Norilsk. They pleaded with me to come back that night, told me they would pay the taxi fare both ways, and begged until I finally agreed.

On the way down from Medvierskaya, however, the taxi got stuck in the snowstorm, and I was two hours late for my appointment in Norilsk. Afterward I started back to Medvierskaya. The taxi driver thought I was crazy and would take me only part way up the mountain. I had to climb the rest of the way on foot. I arrived at the house at 2 A.M., but the family was still waiting up for me. The worst of it all was that this was a Saturday night. It was 5 A.M. before I made it back to Norilsk on foot, just in time to begin hearing confessions for the Sunday Masses.

I was so busy that winter, in fact, that I never lit the stove in my *bolok*. When I was home at all, I simply plugged in the electric burner and used it both for heating and for what little cooking I did. During this winter, too, my sisters wrote to tell me they had contacted the State Department and that the American Embassy in Moscow would make efforts to get me out of Russia. The idea excited me momentarily, but I hardly gave it much thought. I felt I was destined to spend my life doing what I could for my "flock" here in Russia who, as our Lord had said, were like sheep without a shepherd. Let the KGB do what they "must". The Lord was my shepherd. He had proven that.

Moreover, just looking at the human side of it, KGB officials had told me more than once, by way of threat or as a tactic of persuasion, that I would never see America again. I was quite ready to believe them. After a previous letter from my sister Helen, for instance, in which she wrote that she was trying to contact the State Department, I had decided to check on my own citizenship status and apply for an international passport. There were some Chinese and others in Norilsk with such a passport, so I wrote to Krasnoyarsk, the *oblast* (county) seat.

I didn't consider myself a Russian citizen, I wrote, but I felt that I was entitled to something more than just the status of a released prisoner deprived of any civil rights. A few days later, the MVD had called me and asked whether I'd written to Krasnoyarsk concerning a passport. I said I had. "Krasnoyarsk informs us", the agent said, "that you don't need an international passport because you're considered a Russian citizen."

"On what basis?" I said. "I have no passport, I can't move freely from one place to another . . ." "Well," he said, "we can give you a Russian passport." "I'm not interested in a Russian passport", I retorted. "If I took a Russian passport, it would be like admitting I was a Russian citizen, and I'd lose my American citizenship." "What difference does that make?" he snapped. "You're not going back to America anyway!"

I had well believed him then, and I could still believe it. Since then, though, some things had changed. Khrushchev had made a speech denouncing Stalin before the twentieth Party Congress; a semi-secret letter had been read behind closed doors to all the workers' organizations and unions in big plants like BOF and others in Norilsk. This had also contained, in part, a denunciation of the "personal cult of Stalin", and the whole tone of the letter was bright with promises of reforms and better conditions in the future.

Everyone at the meeting knew what was meant by the Stalin regime—the hidden terror, the knock on the door after midnight, police action without trial, etc. By and large, the workers were much encouraged by that letter; even I, hearing it, felt as if a great weight had been lifted. You could sense the change of attitude in the room. In little groups after the meeting, people talked hopefully of a new era, new policies, a new mood. So now, when my sister wrote about the American Embassy's efforts to get me out of Russia, I felt a momentary excitement. But I had my work and my people to care for, and I soon forgot all about the idea.

A few days after my sister's letter had come, however, a militiaman came to my *bolok* and asked to see my passport. "I have none," I told him, "all I have is this police I.D." "Ah, you really ought to have a passport", he said, "maybe you had better drop down to headquarters and see about it."

When I went to MVD headquarters, a day or so later, they began asking a lot of questions and filling out blanks. I suspected immediately that something was up; our meeting was becoming more of an interrogation session than a routine application for a passport. "Why do you insist on being an American?" asked the interrogator. He went on to praise the glories of Communism. "All right," I said, "look at Norilsk! Is that an example of Communism? The people don't have any houses, they live in shanties, they have to stand in line for hours to buy food. What sort of life is that?"

He got angry at that. He accused me of being bitter and of being an agitator. I answered that I wasn't bitter, just objective; anybody who walked down the street outside could see what I was talking about. The argument became rather vehement, and he became quite frank. He told me they knew all about me in Norilsk; they knew my background and my history—they knew I was a spy for the Vatican! "So let's not have any talk about being objective", he shouted.

Eventually, we returned to the matter of the passport. He told me I wouldn't be able to do anything or go anywhere without a passport, but, of course, the final decision on that would have to be made in Krasnoyarsk. "Now," he said, "we can give you a temporary document, which won't affect the outcome of your case or your later status; it will, however, permit you to travel and so forth."

I didn't want it. I was afraid that, somehow or other, it would be interpreted as a Russian passport, implying Russian citizenship. And even if the document itself were only for a short term, the very fact that I'd agreed to become a Russian citizen would mean I was no longer an American citizen. Again and again, the militiaman assured me that this document wouldn't affect my final status. It would simply allow me to travel freely like any Russian citizen, and therefore I would be able to take my case personally to Krasnoyarsk. Finally I agreed, filled out the blanks, and signed the necessary papers. He issued me what is called a *Kratkosraczni Pasport* (Short-Term Passport).

When I got home, though, and showed the passport to friends, they laughed. "Well, Wladimir Martinovich," said one, "they finally got you! That's a Russian passport, and it makes you a Russian citizen. You'll never get out now!"

"That's not the way they explained it", I answered and joined in the laughter. Anyway, I wasn't particularly worried; I had no plans for going anywhere. There was too much to do in Norilsk, and Lent and Easter were approaching again.

That Lent of 1958 saw some of the busiest weeks I've ever spent as a priest. In previous years, there had been three of us priests, and every year the congregation had grown steadily. In 1957, after Neron left, there had still been Viktor and I; now I was all alone, and there was more work than ever. For Easter is the biggest feast in the Oriental liturgy, and even today the people celebrate it at home with as much pomp and ceremony as they can. On this feast, they say, even nature itself takes on a festive air.

During Lent, according to the custom, there were no marriages, but I was asked to make frequent visits to the cemetery to chant the *Panikhida* over the graves, and I spent all my free time hearing confessions and baptizing. On Palm Sunday, I said three Masses, with a sermon at each, and announced that the full Holy Week services would be held, beginning Thursday, in the chapel. After the Masses on Palm Sunday, the people crowded around to make arrangements for the blessing of the Easter food.

This is a wonderful tradition in Russia and the Slavic countries. On Holy Saturday and Easter itself, the people bring baskets of food to the church to be blessed, and the blessing prayers in the Oriental liturgy are beautiful. The baskets are filled with colored eggs, butter, *salo* (fatback, like bacon), different kinds of stuffed rolls, candies, and cakes. But above all there is the *pascha*, a specially baked cake, rich in eggs, topped with icing, and decorated with candy crosses or Easter figures. It's the first thing the family eats after the Easter services. The Easter basket is an integral part of the tradition, for in order to observe the feast properly, the people fast very strictly all during Holy Week and abstain from all meat.

Because I was alone this year and there was so much to do, we had formed a committee of men to organize the blessings of the Easter baskets. In a special notebook, we sketched a map of the city of Norilsk and picked out certain assembly points and set specific times, so that anyone who couldn't make it to the chapel could meet me there for the blessing of food. When the arrangements were more or less completed, I calculated that I would have to begin at 5 P.M. on Friday, work around the clock, and hope to finish, with luck, in time for the Easter Mass.

I made arrangements at BOF to be excused from Thursday until the following Wednesday. A friendly doctor signed a certificate stating that I should "rest", and Anastasia, who knew what was going on, was happy to accept it. Thursday, immediately after the services in chapel, I left for Kayerkhan and again said Mass there. Afterward, I blessed the food, which had been gathered in one room of the big barrack (there must have been a carload!), heard confessions for hours, and then visited as many homes as I could, blessing the rooms—another traditional Easter custom.

All day Friday, back at the chapel, I heard a tremendous number of Easter confessions, as I had every night that week after work. On Friday evening, together with Ludwig, I set out after the Good Friday services to begin my tour of the city. We had to do it all on foot, for the most part, crossing and recrossing the city to the many little shack-town settlements in out-of-the-way places. Every place I went, there were people waiting—and this even in the middle of the night or the long cold hours of early morning. It was a lot of walking, and the weather was still bitterly cold.

Ludwig and I got back to the chapel Saturday morning in

time for services at 6 A.M. Many of the people had been there overnight in order to get a place before the altar for this long Easter Vigil service. Many of them, too, stayed in the chapel after the Saturday services until it was time for the Easter midnight Mass, with nothing to eat all day, so that they could be close to the altar. After the services I started making the rounds again, doubling back to the chapel every few hours to bless the baskets of food that filled my little *bolok* from wall to wall, a new batch every time.

None of this could be kept very secret, of course. The crowds were too obvious. The people told me the militia had been to the chapel several times asking for me, but they didn't interfere with the people or say anything about the baskets of food. Fortunately, I didn't see the militia that day; our paths never crossed.

By 11:30 P.M. Saturday, I was back home, but I couldn't get anywhere near the chapel. Even the corridors and my own *bolok* were jammed; crowds of people were swarming around outside in the midnight cold. The militia were there, too, but I ignored them. There was barely room to move anywhere, but by twelve o'clock I was vested—I couldn't lift my arms, so someone had to pull the vestments over my head—and ready for Mass. The altar was covered with flowers and candles, and Ludwig had contacted a famous old choirmaster named Anatoly for the occasion and rounded up a choir of trained voices for him to work with.

As I began the solemn intonation of the Easter Mass, I thought the chapel would explode with sound. The Easter Mass is a joyous one to begin with, but the enthusiasm of the people that night I shall never forget. Tired as I was after more than forty-eight hours without sleep, hurrying from place to place, I felt suddenly elated and swept along. I forgot about everything but the Mass and the joy of Easter.

The MVD stayed for the whole service. Anatoly, the old choirmaster, told me later how tense he had been at first, for fear we would all be arrested. "But you didn't look nervous at all", he said. I wasn't. Once the Mass started, I paid no attention to the police at all; I was practically carried out of myself with joy. I gave a little sermon on the joy of Easter, but it was impossible to distribute Communion because no one could move. Communion had to be distributed after Mass.

The services ended at 3 A.M., but at nine o'clock the next morning I was still distributing Communion to a constant stream of people. I could hear the crowds outside, going home through the Easter dawn, shouting the traditional Easter greeting, "*Khristos voskres!*" (Christ is risen!), and the joyous answer, "*Voistinu voskres!*" (Indeed, He is risen!).

After it was all over, I came back to my room alone and sat down at the little table in my *bolok*, completely exhausted. Yet I was deeply satisfied; I knew a joy that day I have rarely known. I felt that at last, in God's own good Providence, I was beginning to live my dream of serving His flock in Russia. "And all this," was the thought that kept flashing through my mind, "all this took place in Russia, in Norilsk!"

The next thing I knew, Ludwig was shaking me awake. The room was full of people, happy people, repeating over and over, "*Khristos voskres! Voistinu voskres!*" Everyone was shouting and laughing at once, and they told me to dress up and come along for the celebration. So, late that afternoon, I went to Ludwig's home for the traditional Easter dinner—the *pascha* in the center of the table and the blessed food all around it. There were about eight of us, including Anatoly and his wife. We began the meal by singing the traditional Easter "*Tropar!*" and then sat down to partake of the *pascha*, everyone talking at once about the joy of the day.

The next day, according to the Russian custom, is also a

feast day, and so is Easter Tuesday. On those days, I said High Masses for large crowds and sang solemn Vespers every evening for crowds just as large. On Wednesday, I went back to work at BOF. The girls in my shift were all smiles; some of them had even been to the Easter Mass. Every time there was a break in the work, we talked about Easter.

During one of these breaks, around 10 A.M., one of the girls came hurrying over and said, "Wladimir, you're wanted in the office." Her look tipped me off; I knew right away there was trouble. As I entered the supervisor's office, I was met by two MVD men. One of them, short and stocky, with a small mustache and a badly colored left eye, spoke to me quite abruptly: "Wladimir Martinovich?" "Da", I said. "You will please change clothes and come with us." I didn't have to ask where.

The agent with the mustache waited for me while I dressed. We drove straight to the new KGB headquarters in the modern part of the city on Sebastobolskaya. There I waited in one of the antechambers for almost half an hour, then the same agent came out again and led me through several rooms into a large office. A big black desk outlined against four windows dominated the room. Standing behind the desk, leaning on his hands and looking at me severely, was a tall handsome official with dark hair and dark eyes, deeply tanned.

I walked up to the desk, saying nothing. He kept staring at me coldly, then finally said abruptly, "Wladimir Martinovich, your missionary work here in Norilsk is not needed. Do you understand?" "Da." "You have ten days to leave Norilsk," he said, "and never think of coming back." He paused, then began to tap his finger on the desk to underline his next words. "If you attempt to come back, you will be arrested and put into prison. I am in charge of the KGB here, and those are orders." I said nothing, just looked at him. After another long pause, he said again, quite coldly, "You may leave."

I walked out, and the MVD agent who had escorted me from BOF drove me to the government building on *Komsomolskaya Ploschad* (Komsomol Square) that houses the police headquarters, city hall—and also the jail. But he took me up to his office on the fourth floor and asked me to sit down. "Look," he said, "you have to be out of the city within ten days. If you have any trouble getting plane tickets, phone me here at this number." With that he handed me a little slip of paper with a phone number on it. "In two or three days," he continued, "collect your severance pay and quit your job at BOF."

"What about my *bolok*?" I asked. "I need time to sell it." "No, you won't sell it"; he said bluntly, "that belongs to the government. Now, we will check from time to time to see that all this is being done." He waited for me to object. I said nothing. "Moreover," he continued, "you are to go to Krasnoyarsk and report to the MVD there. You will live at the Hotel Syever, and you are to do nothing in the way of religious work among the people. In ten days I will personally escort you to the airport." Again, he waited for me to comment or object. Again, I said nothing. It was afternoon when I left his office, so I went home rather than back to BOF.

That night, I told Ludwig and some close friends among the parishioners about the "interviews". They were downcast. Word spread quickly among the faithful that the chapel would soon be closed. At work the next morning, I went immediately to Anastasia Nikolayevna, my supervisor. She was careful not to say anything about the KGB, but she said she was sorry to see me go and would do what she could to help me. She didn't write "MVD" in my severance record, as she was supposed to, but simply noted that I'd been laid off. It meant I would be able to get a good job at the next place I applied.

That evening, Ludwig and the other parishioners came over to discuss what to do with the chapel. I wanted to dismantle it and send the vestments and sacred vessels to Fr. Viktor, since this chapel *bolok* was still in Viktor's name. But the people pleaded with me to leave the chapel as it was; at least there would be a place for devotions and meetings of the faithful. I finally agreed. Whatever furniture I had in my own *bolok*, I gave away to parishioners; I got rid of everything and moved in with Ludwig and his wife.

All the while, people were dropping in to visit and say goodbye. Many of them were bitter that the government would "take our last priest away from us". Despite the warning I'd been given at MVD headquarters, I said Mass every day until I left and preached a little sermon to encourage the people. I heard confessions, baptized, visited the sick, and did everything they asked of me in those last few days.

I tried to purchase an airplane ticket to Krasnoyarsk, but none was available. All the flights, as usual, were sold out. I didn't make any extra effort to get the ticket; I figured that if they wanted me to leave, they could worry about it. Sure enough, on the eighth day, the MVD agent came looking for me.

"What about the plane ticket?" he said. "There were none available", I answered. He frowned and said with a small edge on his voice, "Why didn't you phone me?" "Oh, you know all about it," I replied, "and besides, nobody can get tickets on such short notice." "Look," he said, "give me the 460 rubles and you stay put. I'll bring you the ticket." Late that afternoon, he was back—with the ticket. There's no such thing as a full airplane as far as the MVD is concerned. If room has to be made for their purposes, they make room.

On my last afternoon in Norilsk, I stopped in the post office to tell them to forward my mail. The girl behind the counter suddenly asked, "Is your name Lypinski?" I hesitated. "Why?" I said. "Is it your name?" she insisted. "Yes," I said, "I have a double name." "Well," she said quickly, "then I have some mail for you." She searched for and finally found two big envelopes from the American Embassy, marked "Special Delivery" and sealed with Embassy stamps.

They were unopened, but by the date on the postmark they must have been in the Norilsk post office for ten days at least. The girl was extremely apologetic about that, since the envelopes were marked "Special Delivery", but she asked if I'd sign for them without a formal complaint. I did. When I opened the envelopes outside, I found a document authorizing me to come to the Embassy in Moscow and a letter asking me to attempt to get an exit visa ("Impossible now", I thought). They asked me to notify them of the receipt of the letter and where I would apply for the visa.

I wrote a letter that night from Norilsk to the Embassy, notifying them that I had received the letter and saying that I would apply for my exit visa in Krasnoyarsk. I thought I at least owed it to my sisters to go through the motions, even though I knew it was futile. And just to be safe, that same evening I went to the offices of the MVD to show the Embassy letter to my friend with the mustache who'd been haunting me.

He wasn't impressed. "That's not our business", he said. "Take it up with Krasnoyarsk." He had only one thing on his mind, and he put it quite succinctly: "We'll be there tomorrow morning to pick you up at ten sharp; you be ready to go!" I left the offices of the MVD and returned to Ludwig's for a little farewell party, but no one was much in the mood for a party that night.

The next morning, for the last time in Norilsk, I said Mass at 6 A.M. The little chapel was crowded, and after Mass I distributed Communion and officially said farewell to my parishioners. I went home with Ludwig and his wife for breakfast. It was April 13, 1958, and still bitterly cold. At 10:00 on the dot, a jeep drove up to the entrance of the building. I saw the MVD man get out, and before he could reach the apartment, I went to meet him, luggage in hand. We drove to Lenin Square, then turned left down Oktobrskaya; I looked around sadly for the last time as the city dropped behind.

This had been "my country" since 1946, as both prisoner and priest, and I was tremendously sorry to be leaving. I thought again of the people I was leaving behind, saddened by the thought that I could do nothing for them any longer but commend them to God. For myself, I had no fear. I put all my trust and my confidence in His divine will. As we headed out into the snow-covered countryside, I repeated over and over again: "Thy will be done."

Hounded in Krasnoyarsk

Nadiezda (Hope) Airport, which also serves Dudinka, is almost twenty-five miles from Norilsk, and the jeep trip took us over an hour. The airport itself is nothing fancy, just an oblong two-story terminal, whitewashed, like so many of the barracks I had built as a prisoner. We could hardly see it against the snow. I took a seat in the waiting room while the MVD agent went into the airline office, because the ticket he'd "purchased" for me wasn't even for this date. He came back in twenty minutes with a ticket for the next flight to Krasnoyarsk.

When I boarded the plane, I was lucky to get a window seat. As the motors turned over, I watched the MVD agent walk back into the terminal now that I was "safely" on my way. This was the first time I had ever flown, and as we hurtled down the runway I felt a pounding in my heart, then a ripple of cold knots down my spine as the plane rose from the ground. I leaned back hard in the seat and shut my eyes, trying not to move a muscle; I could feel the drumming of the motors in my head until my ears popped.

When the motors slacked off somewhat, and the plane seemed to level out, I looked out the window—a magnificent sight! Stretching away below us was the severe North, with snow everywhere and mountain peaks standing out in harsh, sharp silhouettes against the brilliant white. There was no shrubbery to be seen, nothing but the vast, unchanging white and the raw similarity. I gazed in true awe at the scene, then closed my eyes again and leaned back in the seat, hoping the uneasiness at the base of my stomach would disappear.

As we flew on, I could actually feel the change in climate, and at Krasnoyarsk, for the first time in twelve years, I experienced the warm softness of a spring day. It was almost like moving in a dream. The trip from Krasnoyarsk to Dudinka had taken over two weeks in the hold of the *Stalin* twelve years ago; it had taken only four hours to fly back.

The terminal here, unlike the little whitewashed barrack at Nadiezda Airport, was an imposing structure of brick and glass, with gleaming stairways and huge counters. I was carrying two suitcases—my Mass kit and vestments were in one—and the day was so warm that I was soon perspiring in my winter clothes. In front of the airport terminal I hailed a taxi. According to my instructions, I was to stay at the Hotel Syever until I reported to MVD headquarters, so to the Hotel Syever I went.

South from the airport, past the hill called *Pokrovka* (Our Lady's Veil), Stalin Boulevard, the main street of Krasnoyarsk, goes all the way to the railroad station of the Trans-Siberian Railroad at the south end of town, then curves around Nikolayevka, a residential suburb on a hill overlooking the Yenisei to the west. Across the river, on the *Pravi Biereg* (Right Bark) is the industrial section of the city. Paralleling Stalin Boulevard is another broad avenue, called Lenin Avenue, and the Hotel Syever is on this, just about midtown. It is a six-story building of dark yellow—almost orange—stucco, lined to resemble stone blocks. Two blocks away from the Syever is the city hall, on Stalin Boulevard, as are most of the main buildings of Krasnoyarsk.

When I asked the girl at the desk of the Syever for a room, she immediately wanted to know where I was from. "From the north (*syever*)", I said. "Let me see your certificate", was her answer. I gave her my documents, plus the stub of my plane ticket—and a letter from the police in Norilsk. She asked all sorts of questions before she finally filed my passport in the desk, as is the custom, and gave me the key to room 213. The price was fifteen rubles ($1.50) per day if the room was single, or twelve rubles per day if I shared it with someone else.

It was about 6 P.M., and I hadn't had anything to eat since breakfast. The hotel restaurant, however, was closed for remodeling, so I went outside, looked around for the street with the heaviest traffic, and headed in that direction. The weather was extremely mild, almost balmy; I took my time looking for a good restaurant, just enjoying the stroll. A few blocks past the post office, near the corner of Stalin Boulevard, I found a fashionable place called the "Yenisei". The menu was impressive in its variety, and I picked out a salad, some chicken soup instead of the usual *schi* (cabbage soup), beef stroganov with french fries for the main course, served with a *garnitura* of vegetables (beans) and dressing, plus dessert. The whole thing cost me fifteen rubles. I ate leisurely, watching the crowd around me, for I had nowhere to go and knew no one in the city.

After dinner, I strolled toward the post office, looking at the shop windows along Stalin Boulevard. On the spur of the moment, I stepped into the post office and wrote a letter to my sisters in the United States, telling them of my move—unexpected, but perhaps not final—and of receiving their last letters. Afterward, I asked for MVD headquarters and learned it was only a block away. I walked over there, but it was closed, so I walked back at last to the Hotel Syever.

When I returned to my room, I found the lights on and another guest already there, a young buyer from Kalinin, near Moscow. We sat and chatted for a while, then about ten o'clock we went down to the lobby to watch TV. The picture wasn't very clear, and the evening movie was on. For the most part, Soviet television runs only during the evening hours. Here in Krasnoyarsk, for instance, it ran every day from 5 P.M. until 11 P.M. The first programs were for children, the next was generally on science or industry, then a program of news and talks on politics or the economy, followed by a program of dances or music, and, finally, a movie or play. There were no commercials. When the movie ended at 11:00, we went into the bar and had a beer, then finally walked upstairs to bed.

At nine o'clock the next morning, I walked leisurely over to MVD headquarters. I asked for the chief; he wasn't there. Finally, I cornered one of the agents as he came out of an office, told him why I was here, and showed him my documents from the American Embassy. He looked them over, then told me to go to a building that he pointed out across the courtyard. That turned out to be OVIR (Office for Foreign Visas).

Inside, there was quite a crowd. I stood in line, reading all the signs, beginning to feel just a bit anxious to know what the answer would be to my request to go to Moscow. Then a secretary came out to tell us the official in charge was busy; he wouldn't be able to see anyone for the next three hours. The line dissolved in disgust. I was a little disgusted myself, so I told the girl I had some very important matters to settle and had been directed here by the MVD. She asked me what it was all about; I showed her my documents, plus the letter from the Embassy in Moscow. She looked startled, then told me to wait. She came back in a few minutes to tell me the official in charge would see me the first thing next morning.

As I turned to go, though, the secretary asked me to step into her office for a minute. She was a small young woman, with chestnut hair and finely chiseled features. In her office, she began to speak almost in whispers. "Are you really from America?" she asked. I told her I was. She asked me then how I had gotten here, what of my family in America, and so forth. Finally, she said softly and a little sadly, "They won't let you go." "It's not my idea", I said. "I'm here because the Embassy sent me. It's the Embassy they have to deal with, not me." "No matter," she said, "they won't let you go."

The next morning, I arrived at OVIR before 8 A.M. There were already people in line ahead of me. At 9 A.M., business began for the day, and the young secretary called my name first. As I entered the office, she sat at a desk beside the official, a balding, gloomy man with rimless glasses and a chunky face, somewhere in his fifties. The secretary gave me a knowing look. I greeted the official and got a grunt in return. He glanced through my documents, but he couldn't read the English letter from the Embassy and went into the next room with it. When he came out, he said nothing to me but mumbled a few words to the secretary. She came over to me with a handful of blanks and official forms; the official kept my papers. The girl asked me to fill out the blanks at one of the tables in the waiting room; if I had any trouble, she added, she would be glad to help.

By this time, the waiting room was crowded with people of all nationalities—Mongolians, Chinese, Japanese, Lithuanians, Poles—all trying to get exit visas. At the table next to me sat an old man, perhaps in his seventies, almost completely bald, his skin all wrinkled. With him at the table was a young woman in her forties whom I took to be his daughter. I didn't pay much attention, though, but went to work filling out the forms. I finished one and put it aside. The old man unabashedly leaned over and read it. When I looked up, he asked me if I was Polish. I said yes. He told me rather proudly that he could speak Polish, although he was a Lithuanian; then he began to chat on about his life and his hopes of returning to Lithuania. He introduced the young woman as his second wife and told me about his children, now married, and especially about his youngest son, of whom he was exceptionally proud because he was studying in the Medical Institute at Krasnoyarsk. I was beginning to get a little annoyed.

He told me, finally, that he was a Catholic, then asked if I were. I admitted I was. He asked me if I knew any priests. I tried to find out what he had in mind, but finally I told him I was a priest. At that he became quite animated: "That's what we need, a priest! We have a parish here, a fine one, but two weeks ago our priest, Fr. Janos, a Lithuanian priest of the Latin rite, died suddenly. The people came in for Mass one morning and found him dead on the floor of his room next to the sacristy." The old man was excited. He invited me to his home to meet the parishioners; I told him I couldn't promise anything until I knew what Moscow would say to my request for an exit visa. He was downcast at that. Then he asked me to come and see him if I decided to stay in Krasnoyarsk. I promised I would.

With all this conversation, it took me more than two hours to fill out my forms. When I had finished, I took them back to the official, who told me it would be three months at the earliest before an answer to my application came from Moscow. As he was putting the papers in order and handing back my documents, he said suddenly: "I want to tell you outright that you'll never see America! And there'll be no life for you here in Russia, either—just like the old White Russians who still survive around here!"

I was startled by his openly antagonistic attitude, but I said nothing. I took my documents from him, slipped them in my coat pocket, and walked over to the post office. There, just for formality's sake, I wrote an account of the whole proceedings to the American Embassy, notifying them that I had applied here in Krasnoyarsk for an exit visa as they requested.

It was late in the afternoon when I got back to the hotel. The young buyer was there and told me he'd finished his job. He was leaving for Moscow the next day, so he invited me out for a "farewell dinner". During the meal, he waxed eloquent over his deals, and I told him my progress—or, rather, lack of progress—with OVIR. Finally, I told him I thought I'd buy a ticket to Moscow, too. I had been thinking about it all afternoon, and I couldn't see any reason why I shouldn't go to the Embassy in Moscow while I still had my passport, my documents, and the opportunity. He lifted his glass and laughed: "That's the way! Strike while the iron is hot—while you've got the documents!"

After breakfast next morning, still determined, I went to the airline office and bought a ticket for Moscow. It cost me

780 rubles (seventy-eight dollars) and there was no trouble, but the earliest reservation I could get was for a flight two days later. Then, since I had nothing to do and was in no particular hurry, I went to a little garden behind the hotel and sat on a bench in the warm air, just soaking up sunshine and watching the children at play.

The next day, too, I simply relaxed. I went from store to store for a little leisurely shopping but, as in Norilsk, although the stores looked full, the things I really wanted they didn't have, or at least they didn't have it in the size or quality I wanted. So I spent a few more hours that afternoon in the hotel garden, feeling more relaxed and lazy than I had in a long time. My work in Norilsk had been more of a drain on me than I had been willing to admit, especially the last two weeks, and I was glad of this opportunity to get some rest.

The next morning, I went to the airline office to check on my ticket. Everything was confirmed for that afternoon. When I returned to the hotel, though, the girl at the desk said, "Go to the manager's office right away." The manager told me to report immediately to the militia; they had been phoning all morning. I suspected some trouble, so I didn't hurry. At MVD headquarters, however, no one seemed to know much about it; I was bounced from office to office until I finally ended up with the chief.

He knew what it was all about. As soon as he heard my name, he said, "You're going to Moscow, huh?" "Yes," I said, "I have a ticket, and I confirmed it this morning." "Well, you go right back to the airline and cancel that ticket. After that, you come back and see me!"

The chief was emphatic, so there was nothing to do but go back to the airline and cancel the ticket. They didn't want to do it: the flight was all arranged, and it was too late to cancel.

"Look," I said, "I'm not doing this of my own accord. This is an order from the MVD." The clerk looked startled, then asked me to step into the director's office. The director was a woman of about forty, solid and severe. I told her the story, but she still didn't want to cancel the ticket. Finally, I suggested she call the MVD. She did. When she hung up, she very quietly wrote out an order for cancellation and refund— minus 10 percent for the cancellation.

When I reported back to the MVD office, the chief told me flatly I was going to stay in Krasnoyarsk. We didn't discuss it; he wasn't interested in any discussion. He suggested that I find a place to live quickly, then come back to register with his office. He also suggested that I try to stay out of "trouble" from now on.

As I walked out of his office, I kept wondering how they could have found out about the plane ticket so quickly. I even began to suspect that the young buyer from Kalinin might have told them of my decision to go to Moscow. Then I remembered that there is an MVD agent at the airports and train stations, whose job it is to check the registers and ticket sales daily, and I realized there wasn't much chance of my going anywhere unless the MVD permitted it.

When I got back to the hotel, I wrote a postal card to Pranas, the old Lithuanian I had met in the offices of OVIR. He came to my hotel the next day, and, after we talked for a while, he invited me to come with him and meet some of the other parishioners. I went to his apartment for supper, in a little suburb across the Yenisei. While we were still eating, members of the old parish began dropping in, one by one, overjoyed to have a priest among them again. There was one other priest in town, they said, a Ukrainian named Fr. Honofri, who lived just up the street. They had asked him to take over the parish, but he was under close surveillance and refused to risk a public Mass. I told them I'd be happy to take over the parish and that I would say Mass next morning here in Pranas' house.

Many of them came the next morning for Mass, and after breakfast I set out with them to see what the parish was like. It was in Nikolayevka, back across the river, so we caught a local train to Krasnoyarsk, then took a bus up the hill to Nikolayevka. We went first to a little house on the crest of the hill, built so close to the edge of the road that the buses caused every furnishing in the house to rattle as they swept by. Here I met Rosa, a tall, stately, and gracious lady in her forties, one of the parish leaders. In a few moments, her house was full of parishioners who crowded around to tell me how God had answered their prayers in sending a priest, and how much work there was to be done.

The church itself was about five blocks from Rosa's. It was a big, one-story, barracklike building, and the whole inside was the chapel, a long, high-ceilinged room, which could accommodate more than two hundred people. It had a beautifully carved altar, stations of the cross along the walls, and a confessional to one side, for all the world like a parish church anywhere. There was a sacristy behind the altar, and beyond the sacristy a room for the priest to live in. I was delighted with the place and wanted to move in right away. The parishioners, however, didn't want me to live there; they were afraid something might happen to me, too, as had happened to Fr. Janos—although no one could say specifically just what had "happened" to Fr. Janos. Finally, though, they dissuaded me. We made arrangements for Sunday Mass then, and I agreed to live at Rosa's.

The next morning, Pranas and I took my things to Rosa's place. I wasn't there an hour before the people of the parish were bringing gifts: eggs, homemade jam, cheese, butter, meat—enough food to last us for a month. That evening, Rosa, her mother, and I entertained callers far into the night. Sunday morning, I was at church by seven o'clock. Mass wasn't scheduled until nine, but already the church was nearly full. Most of the people wanted to go to confession. By nine o'clock, the lines in front of my confessional just kept growing. I was still hearing confessions at ten o'clock and finally, around 10:30, I said Mass.

Most of the people here at Nikolayevka were Lithuanians, so I said Mass in the Latin rite, but it was a High Mass, and the people sang beautifully. There were many, many Communions at the Mass, and following it we had Benediction. Then, after that, even on that first Sunday, I had eight or ten baptisms and made arrangements for more during the week, as well as for visiting the sick and instructing some of the children for First Communion. Before I finished and returned to Rosa's, it was late afternoon.

Thus began a busy week of priestly duties, and I kept adding "extras" as I went around the "parish". But Thursday afternoon, when Rosa was at work and I was at home with her mother, I heard the dog begin to bark suddenly. I went out to see what was the trouble—and there was a young militiaman. "Here we go again", I thought. He asked first of all to see my passport. After that, he asked if I didn't know I was supposed to register with the MVD within three days of my arrival in the city. According to their records, I wasn't registered for this house. Actually, he was a friendly lad, this young militiaman, and he told me to register soon or "they'll be after you."

The next day, Rosa went to the passport office to register me as a boarder in her house. They wouldn't accept her word; they told her I'd have to register myself. Rosa was angry and so was I when she told me. "Where is this place?" I said. Rosa gave me her "house book", and I went down to the office. I filled out the necessary forms and took them over to the two girls at the counter.

I handed my passport and papers, and Rosa's "house book", to the younger of the two girls. When she opened my passport and saw that I was from the United States, she couldn't do enough for me. The other girl kept glancing suspiciously at us, looking up from her work, but she said nothing. The young girl stamped Rosa's "house book", wrote down my name, stamped all the papers and registry blanks, chattering and asking questions about America the whole time. I paid the three-ruble registration fee and thanked her. "Oh, no," she said, "thank *you!*"

Now that I was registered, I felt more secure and I spent more time than ever working openly with my "parish". I even posted the Mass schedule inside the church, along with a list of weddings and baptismal appointments. I didn't bother to get a job, for the people themselves took care of my needs, and there was too much work to do. It had been a thriving parish under Janos, and now it was back in full swing. Within a month, though, rumors began circulating that the authorities had never "approved" this church. Nothing was said officially, but the word seemed to get around.

One Sunday, just after I'd turned back to the altar following the sermon, I sensed a stirring among the congregation, but I didn't pay much attention to it. During the quiet when I bent over for the Consecration, I heard someone trying the outside door. Again, I paid no attention. But when Mass was finished, the landlady waited more than twenty minutes before she opened the doors; the congregation sat silently and somewhat frightened. At last, the landlady opened the doors and said the militia had been here during Mass, demanding to get in. She had told them the doors were locked and only the priest had a key. They had tried the doors, walked around the building, then finally left.

The parishioners were determined to keep the parish open. Accordingly, they held a meeting in the church and drew up a signed petition, addressed to the City Council, requesting that a parish be opened for themselves and other Catholics of the Latin rite in and around Krasnoyarsk. I was skeptical; in fact, I doubted the prudence of such a move. The people, however, were sure they would receive a favorable answer, for a previous petition had been turned down just after Fr. Janos' death on the grounds that no priests were available.

When it was completed, a committee of parishioners took the petition to the City Council. After much insistence, they obtained an appointment with the head of the Council himself. He wouldn't give them a direct answer, however, or sign the necessary document; he insisted it was a matter for Moscow, and they would either have to send the documents there or take them personally.

By this time the people were not to be put off. They called another meeting in the church and decided to send a committee to Moscow with the petition, along with another petition to have a former Catholic church, now used by the government as a radio station, reopened. This second petition was addressed to Khrushchev himself, and to it was added an additional list of names, which had been collected since the first petition went to the City Council.

Rosa, as one of the leaders of the parish, was chosen to go to Moscow along with the choirmaster. Unfortunately, the man's wife got sick at the last moment, so Rosa left for Moscow alone. Still, hopes were high among the parishioners for a favorable answer to at least one of their petitions. In Moscow, Rosa tried for three days at the Kremlin to see

Khrushchev personally, but to no avail. At last, she was received by the Minister of Religious Cult, who heard her story, took the papers and documents, and told her to come back again the next morning for an answer. That answer was that such matters were to be settled and approved on the local level, in this case, Krasnoyarsk. Rosa argued that Krasnoyarsk had referred us to Moscow; the Minister insisted it was a local matter.

When Rosa returned with the news, the parishioners refused to be discouraged. They became more convinced than ever that the City Council would have to approve the petition now. They even continued the work of remodeling the chapel, which they had begun—e.g., adding a baptismal font and another confessional—so it could function as a real church.

By my second month in Krasnoyarsk, I had thriving "mission" parishes on the *Pravi Biereg* and in the outskirts and suburbs of the city. One German settlement, out beyond the Yenisei Station, took over a whole barrack when I said Mass. More than eight hundred people attended, and there were baptisms and marriages before and after Mass, sometimes for hours. I also served another German community in a *kolkhoz* farther out, and, since I still had my regular parish and the "missions" on the Right Bank, I had to hold these suburban services on Saturday.

By now, the parishioners were becoming impatient with the City Council. The committee had been making what amounted to an official merry-go-round, from office to office, to the individual ministers, and back again to the City Council. Yet things still dragged on without any ultimate decision, so after Mass one Sunday in July they held another consultation in the chapel. They had abandoned hope for the reopening of the big church on Stalin Boulevard; the government would never evacuate the radio station, that was clear. But they decided to draw up another petition, emphasizing the fact that they now had a priest, which eliminated the only reason why a previous petition had been denied. They asked again, therefore, for official "approval".

That night, Rosa and I sat up at home, talking it over. Suddenly the dog began barking furiously, pulling on his chain so hard we could actually feel it in the house. I went to the window. It was about 1 A.M., and a jeep was parked outside. Finally, someone knocked on a side window—they couldn't get to the door with the dog in the yard. Rosa went out and called the dog; up walked three officials.

They barged right into the house as if they owned it and looked all around without saying a word. A couple of them seemed a little drunk to me. Finally, they came into my room. Then, at last, one of them demanded: "Who's the owner here?" He was a tall man of about forty, well-built, but with a hard, meaty face, dark complexion, and dark hair. "I am", Rosa answered. He never took his eyes off me.

"And who are you?" he barked at me. "A boarder here," I answered, "legally registered in Krasnoyarsk and, in fact, sent here to live by the MVD." "Uh-huh," he sneered, "if this woman wasn't here, I'd tell you a thing or two! You be in my office tomorrow at 3 P.M., do you hear?" "What office?" I said. "The Passport Bureau," he said, "I'm the chief there." "What for?" I said. "I'm legally registered there." He glared at me. "Yes," he said, "but the girl who registered you had no business doing it, and she's no longer working there either!"

With that he turned on his heel and walked out. The other two, who hadn't said a word the whole time, followed. Rosa was terribly disturbed, and we sat talking on and on. She was convinced it meant the end of the parish, just when everything looked so bright, and she became despondent. I didn't say much; I'd been through it all so often before that I felt there really wasn't much to say.

At three o'clock the next afternoon, I was at the Passport Bureau. The director was seated at his desk, and as soon as I came in he began glaring again. He didn't bother to greet me, just said very severely, "Give me your passport!" I gave it to him. He opened it, crossed out my registration, stamped it heavily "CANCELED", and threw it back across the desk. As he did so, he said coldly: "Forty-eight hours! You be out of town, or we'll get you out!"

"What's going on?" I said at last. "I'm registered here!" "That girl had no right to register you," he shouted, "and she got what was coming to her." "Who do you think I am?" I shouted back. "I know who you are," he said, "and I told you as plainly as I know how to be out of town in forty-eight hours. And don't forget to check with the police!" I grabbed the passport off his desk, too angry to reply, and walked out, slamming the door.

Back at Rosa's, many of the people of the parish had already gathered, and I told them the story. They decided to go immediately to the City Council and protest. I told them it was useless; I had to see the MVD in the morning. They still weren't satisfied, and early the next day a group of them appealed to the Council. It was no use. The councilmen told them the matter was police business; the Council would not interfere.

By the time I arrived at the offices of the MVD, I was furious again. I told them they had no right to take such action, that I was sent here explicitly from Norilsk and legally registered. "Furthermore," I said, "I wanted to go to Moscow and you interfered. Now you insist I leave the city. You refuse to give me any reason! When is all this going to end?" The agent didn't bother to interrupt me; when I finished, he completely ignored my remarks. "Wladimir Martinovich," he said, "you have been warned repeatedly, and this is your last chance. You can go either to Abakan or Yeniseisk, that's all— and you will leave today!"

I told him it was physically impossible for me to leave that day. I couldn't get a ticket on such short notice, and he knew it. His eyes flashed at me for a moment, then he shouted: "All right, but no later than tomorrow! Abakan or Yeniseisk?" I had never heard of either place, so I asked him where they were. When I found out Yeniseisk was to the north and Abakan to the south, I chose Abakan. "Very well," he said, "now let me make one thing clear: In Abakan you will do no more of the work you've been doing here and in Norilsk—or else you will wind up where you started. Do I make myself clear?" It was a bit cryptic, but it was clear to me. I just asked him to give me a written note authorizing my stay overnight, so that I wouldn't be picked up by the militia when my original forty-eight hours ended. He refused to give me the note but promised to see that I wasn't bothered.

I came home to Rosa's to find the house crowded with parishioners. I told them I had no choice, that I was going to Abakan. But I promised to come back and visit them if I could, and I asked them to keep me informed about the chapel, especially if they ever got a decision from the City Council or Moscow. Many of them were despondent and some bitter at the thought that now the City Council would use the fact that I had left as an excuse to turn down their petition again—on the grounds that they had no priest.

They helped me pack that night, and the next day many of them came with me, openly and unashamed, to the station. It was a hot July day as we waited for the evening train to Abakan. When I entered the car, they handed me gifts; many of the women had tears in their eyes. As the train moved off,

I sat staring out the window long and silently—and deeply lonely. I began to brood about the months at Krasnoyarsk: how much I had done in so short a time, how hungry the people had been for my help, how well things had seemed to be going, and now. . . . It was like Norilsk all over again. I sat listening to the regular clicking of the train wheels, growing sadder as the light faded. I fell asleep praying for the people of Krasnoyarsk.

A New Start in Abakan

I could have flown from Krasnoyarsk to Abakan in fifty-five minutes, if I had been able to get a plane ticket. The train trip lasted almost twenty-four hours. For the train goes first to Achinsk, waits there as long as necessary to meet the Trans-Siberian and connecting passengers, then winds interminably along the Yenisei, up and down hill, through tunnel after tunnel, stopping at every small town to load and unload produce and make deliveries. We didn't arrive in Abakan until almost six o'clock the following evening.

On the station platform, I looked around trying to decide where to go. A total stranger, I watched the crowds going off in different directions and felt lost. I spotted a taxi on the other side of the street and hurried over. The driver, however, already had a call, but he said he'd come back after delivering that fare and get me. He warned me, though, that it might take an hour.

I sat in the waiting room of the station, watching the crowds. The people here, at least the majority of them, were Khakassians, a Mongol type, descendants of the original settlers of Abakan, with narrow eyes and straight, jet-black hair. The women, especially the older ones, were dressed in the national costume: long skirts down to the ankles, long-sleeved, embroidered blouses of different colors, with beads and ornaments about the neck, big earrings, and braided hair twisted high into a coil. The young people, on the other hand, were dressed mostly in Russian or Western clothes, but they, too, spoke their native language.

They were a reticent and shy people, a pastoral people, who had once herded enormous herds of cattle in the hilly and mountainous raised plains of Khakassia, a formerly independent territory in the *Krasnoyarski Krai* (Krasnoyarsk Territory). Now the pasture lands were gone, most of them plowed up in the *tselina* (virgin lands) campaign, which had turned the area into a dust bowl. The plaza in front of the station was unpaved, and dust hung in the air as trucks, cars, and taxis moved about in the wake of the train's arrival. It was the second week of July and exceedingly warm, so everyone was dressed very lightly.

A little after seven, the taxi returned. After all that waiting, it turned out to be only a five-minute drive to the hotel, a four-story building on the corner of Oktobrskaya, the main street, and Roza Luxemburg Street. In the lobby, the girl told me there were no rooms to be had; the hotel was reserved for guests who were coming to celebrate the 250th anniversary of the union of Khakassia to Russia. I told her then that I was a stranger from Krasnoyarsk who didn't know a soul in the city and asked if she could help me find something. She suggested a street that ran parallel to Oktobrskaya, called Chertegasova, where many of the families were willing to take boarders, at least overnight.

It was almost eight o'clock now, and Chertegasova Street, only one block removed from the main thoroughfare, proved to be unpaved, hot, and dusty. I was sweating profusely. I felt dirty and grimy, psychologically lost and depressed. I came to the *Narodny* (Peoples') Courthouse, so I decided to ask there for help. The courthouse was deserted, but I met a scrub-woman in the hall and asked her if I might sleep there overnight. "Not allowed", she said. "I'll sleep on a bench or the floor," I said, "just any place at all where I can be off the streets until morning." She told me she simply couldn't permit it, but there was a judge, working late in his offices, and she'd ask him.

The judge came out and I explained my problem. He told me he didn't know anyplace I could get a room and suggested I had better go to the MVD offices on Schetinkina Street. I left my baggage at the courthouse, found Schetinkina Street, and managed to locate MVD headquarters. I told the officer at the door I had come to see the chief. He looked at me suspiciously, then asked who I was. I told him I'd been sent by the MVD in Krasnoyarsk to live in Abakan and that I expected them to get me a room here. Suddenly, he laughed. "It's useless", he said. "Many of us don't even have apartments. We have to rent rooms from private families."

As a help, though, the young militiaman gave me the addresses of some old women who lived alone and might be willing to take me in. But this might be considered a rather odd hour to approach them, he added; perhaps it would be better if I waited until morning. I thanked him for his help and retraced my steps toward the courthouse. I walked slowly now, feeling tired, dusty, and very much alone. From time to time, I stopped on the spur of the moment at one of the houses along the street to inquire if I might rent a room. No one had an empty room. By 11 P.M., I was back in the courthouse. The scrubwoman was waiting anxiously for me to retrieve my baggage so she could close up for the night.

I walked a half block up Chertegasova Street, then decided to call it quits. I just resigned myself to sleeping in the street and taking my chances with the dogs, thieves, and the police. I arranged my bags in a heap on the sidewalk alongside someone's wooden fence, then curled up as comfortably as I could. I was exhausted, but I couldn't sleep; I prayed to the only Friend I knew I had in Abakan.

About midnight, I heard someone talking in the yard beyond the fence. "It wouldn't hurt to ask", I thought. I stood up, dusted myself off, and walked along the fence until I came to the gate. Remembering Rosa's dog, I stepped in cautiously and found myself in a little yard and garden. I stood in the dark for a moment, listening to locate the voices, and saw a light around the corner of the house. Between the houses was a well, and the two men were working on an electric pump.

"Can I come in?" I called. The men looked up, and one of them, dressed in pajamas, asked me to come over. I told him I'd just arrived in the city that afternoon, and recounted my trip to the hotel, to the courthouse, and to MVD headquarters, my fruitless search up and down the streets at private houses for any place at all to sleep. I ended by asking if he had a spare bed for the night. "Of course," he said, "we can always make room for one night."

I could hardly believe my ears. I went out to the street and retrieved my luggage, then followed him into the house. It was a typical four-room family house, with two rooms in the front—a living room and a bedroom—and two small rooms at the back, the kitchen on one side and a bedroom on the other. The man, who introduced himself as Stepan, took me into the room opposite the kitchen and signaled me to be quiet. There were a pair of beds in the room, on either side of a single window, and a little boy was asleep in one of them.

As Stepan whispered to me to put my baggage in the corner, the lad woke up. Startled, he ran crying to his father; his mother came in from the other room. Stepan explained the situation to her and introduced me. I could see immediately she didn't like the idea, but she said nothing. The next morning, I tried the addresses given me by the guard at MVD headquarters, but with no luck. Stepan was waiting for me when I came back, and he and I had a quiet talk. He told me his wife was disturbed about my presence, especially since I'd told them I was sent to Abakan by the MVD. She wanted me out of the house, Stepan said, but he insisted I should stay until I found a room.

The next morning I had no better luck. At noon, though, Stepan came home with a notice that had been posted on the public billboard in the marketplace near the station. A room was for rent at 44 *Tarassa Schevichenko* (Schevichenko Street), it said, and anyone interested should apply to Svetlov. I skipped lunch and left immediately, hurrying in the hopes that no one else had yet applied for the room.

I couldn't find the place and had to inquire at the market for further directions. It was after three o'clock before I found number 44, the first house on the left beyond the railroad crossing on Schevichenko Street. I rapped and rapped on the gate in the yard, which was locked from the inside. Nobody answered. I didn't want to leave for fear of losing my chance at the room, so I waited around. After what must have been twenty minutes, I heard someone timidly approach the gate from inside. A woman's voice asked, "Who's there?" I asked for Svetlov, and the woman replied, "He's not home." "Would you open the gate?" I asked. "What for?" was the answer. "I have a notice here," I replied, "and I'm looking for a room to rent."

There was a pause, then finally she opened the gate. A very pleasant old woman of seventy-two, with gray hair and a wrinkled face, she told me the landlord was out and wouldn't be back for a while. But she invited me in to the kitchen of her own house. At 5 P.M., we were still waiting and chatting. There seemed no end to the number of questions she could ask.

Shortly after five, the old woman jumped up from the table and looked out the window. "Here they come," she said. Through the window I saw a big, tall man of perhaps fifty, with chunky features and gray hair, crossing the yard with two women. The old lady and I hurried to meet them. She told them I'd come to rent a room, and I pulled out the notice that had been posted on the board in the marketplace. The man's name was Iosip. His wife, the older of the two women, dark-haired and with a full face and regular features, was named Valya. The younger woman was her sister, Maria. They invited me into the house to tell them something about myself.

I told them the whole story, rather sketchily. When I had finished, they seemed cautious but agreed to show me the house. It was also four rooms: a small bedroom next to the kitchen in back, a large dining room–living room, and a bedroom in the front. The flooring was of wide planks, and the walls were plastered with a clay, sand, and binder combination, then simply whitewashed. The stove in the kitchen was built of brick, in such a way that its corners jutted into each of the rooms to heat the house.

We talked for almost an hour. I was satisfied with the house, but they didn't seem too eager to give me a definite answer. Iosip was an invalid, living on a pension, and Valya herself was sick—in fact, they had just come from the polyclinic—so they admitted they could use the money that a boarder would pay. At last, they asked if I could pay one hundred rubles (ten dollars) a month for lodging and another fifty rubles for meals, laundry, and so forth. It was pretty steep, but I agreed. The next morning I moved into the little room next to the kitchen. It was such a tiny room that if I sat on the bed my knees would touch the kitchen stove. But at least I had a room of my own in Abakan.

Iosip was a great conversationalist. He was a farm boy, who had gone only as far as the third grade in school, but he was a Party man, a staunch Communist, and before his illness had been the secretary of the City Council. He and his wife, Valya, were very good to me—but also quite reserved at first. It was only after nearly a month had gone by and we had become good friends that they told me they had at first suspected I was a thief who was hiding out in Abakan. We laughed at the notion then, but Iosip explained that my story had seemed so sketchy, and my willingness to pay whatever price they asked, as if money were no object, had really frightened them.

By this time, they knew I was an American, and I had also told them about the years I had spent in the prison camps, but they didn't know I was a priest. For that matter, knowing who Iosip was, I didn't think it would be particularly prudent to mention it. I used to say Mass daily after everyone else went to bed, and I sometimes stayed up into the night making my spiritual reading and other spiritual exercises.

I had decided, when I came to Abakan, to take a year's vacation. I'd worked in the prison camps for almost ten years, and I had worked practically ever since my release from prison. Moreover, both in Norilsk and Krasnoyarsk, I had worked long hours as a priest, sometimes going around the clock and getting no sleep at all for more than seventy-two hours. Now that the government had forbidden me to work as a priest, I decided I'd get a good rest. I had saved most of my salary at BOF, so I felt I could manage it.

When the weather was good, I spent most of my time in the garden behind the house, getting a good suntan and doing exercises. I was worried especially about my knees, which had been frozen in the camps and still occasionally bothered me. I

read a lot, and two or three times a week Iosip and Valya
would take a walk with me about town. I came to know
Abakan pretty well.

The town itself isn't large—its population while I was
there was only about fifty-six thousand—but it is still growing. Since it's the terminus of the branch railroad from
Achinsk and the capital of the Khakass Autonomous Oblast
within the *Krasnoyarski Krai*, it assumes an importance much
beyond its size. With the completion in 1962 of a modern
bridge across the Yenisei and the completion of the Abakan-
Taishet railroad line, Abakan became more and more a railroad center for the region. Before the new bridge, though, all
traffic across the river was by pontoon bridge, and the railroad
ended at Abakan.

Since Abakan is the *oblast* center, all the governmental
offices are located in the town, as well as the major educa-
tional and medical facilities. The Teachers College for the
area is located on Pushkina Street at the corner of Schetinkina
Street, not more than a block from the MVD headquarters I'd
visited the first night. The big hospital is also on Pushkina
Street near the corner of Karl Marx Street, while the surgical
hospital and TB clinic is only a few blocks down *Tarassa
Schevichenko*, near Chertegasova.

Warehouses to supply the regions around Abakan are also
located in the city, so it's a busy place. The streets are full of
ZIS trucks carrying food, produce, and manufactured goods
to the surrounding countryside. Because the area is so hilly,
trucks are the only practical method of transport and supply
for the other towns in the area. Consequently, there is also a
big government garage, ATK-50, to service the taxis, trucks,
and buses that provide the transportation in the city itself and
to the outlying areas.

Fortunately, the new bridge across the river has also affected transportation for the better. In the old days it was possible to wait in traffic over half a day just to cross the Abakan River by pontoon bridge. And crossing the river, somewhere, sometime, is essential in Abakan; the city lies in a deep bend of the Yenisei, which almost surrounds it on three sides, very much like New Orleans. The city is like New Orleans, too, in that it lies below the river level and is protected by levees fifteen to twenty feet high all around the bend to prevent the city from flooding.

As a man of leisure during that winter of 1958, I got to know not only the city but a great number of people as well. I was home most of the time, and Iosip's house was always full of company. Because of his former position, he knew just about everyone in Abakan—and everybody was always welcome. Since most of them wound up talking to me in my little room, while Iosip discoursed at length in the living room, I made many friends.

In a way, the constant going and coming was a big help to me. Despite the fact that I had been warned by the MVD not to do any priestly work, or even let it be known that I was a priest, by the end of my first month in Abakan there were people coming to me in secret. They were hardly noticed at Iosip's. Not only did people feel free to drop in there, but they might wind up staying overnight or as long as a week. Iosip never seemed to mind and was always a genial host; the guests would sleep right on the living room floor in blankets or bearskins for as long as they cared to stay.

By spring of 1959, though, the militia was beginning to wonder why I had no job. Possibly they had hesitated to make a move because of Iosip's reputation, but now they began to pester me. For the first time in years, I felt well rested and in excellent condition, so I decided the time had come to look for a job.

On one of the first warm days of spring, however, I received a letter asking me to come to Krasnoyarsk for a few days. It might be my last chance to go before I became tied down to a job, so I told Iosip I thought I'd make a visit there for a few days. Nothing was done to prevent my making the trip, but I was no sooner off the train in Krasnoyarsk than I was followed by the militia.

I spent the night at Rosa's, where a crowd of my old parishioners was waiting to welcome me. We talked far into the night. The next morning, I said Mass, baptized the children, began hearing confessions, and kept it up steadily for the next three days. I finished up those rather hectic but happy days of spiritual labor with a missionary swing across the river to the Right Bank, where I planned to spend the night with Pranas.

I got to his house early in the evening. It was a warm spring dusk, so I told him I thought I'd visit Fr. Honofri, the Ukrainian priest who lived a few blocks away. When I asked for Fr. Honofri at his apartment house, though, his neighbors looked at me strangely. I rapped on the door. There was no answer. I rapped again several times before I heard someone approach the door very softly. Then the door opened slowly and quietly, just enough for someone to peer out.

"Who do you want?" said a voice from behind the door. "Does Fr. Honofri live here?" I asked. The door closed, leaving me without an answer. Suddenly, it was opened again and the voice said, "Yes, come in." I stepped in, the door was locked quickly behind me, and I found myself face to face with two young KGB men.

One of them asked to see my passport. I told him I had left it in my room about four blocks away; I would be happy to get it. I made a move to go but was abruptly grabbed. They told me to sit down at a table on the other side of the room, away from the door. Two other men, whom I hadn't noticed, were sitting by the door. They were people who lived here in the apartment building and had been dragooned into "witnessing" the search.

The agents were going through everything, examining things thoroughly, then replacing them carefully. The search dragged on until almost 1 A.M., with one very curious incident: among the bookshelves, they found a missal and a prayer book; one of the young agents was afraid even to touch them.

When they had finished their search, they wrote down an inventory of everything in the room, which they asked us to sign. I refused, unless they added a clause to the paper specifying I wasn't a "witness", but had simply happened into the room during the search. When they agreed to that, I felt they weren't interested in me, and I relaxed somewhat. Then they dismissed the two elderly men from the building who had served as official "witnesses"—but told me to come along.

As we passed through the darkened courtyard of the apartment, I remembered I had a note in my pocket from a friend of Honofri's. I slipped my hand in my pocket, crumpled the note into a ball, and in one quick motion flipped it away into the blackness. They noticed the movement, though; immediately, they ordered me to stop. They looked at my hands and in my pocket, then asked me what I had done. "Well, it's late," I said, "and I was checking to see if I had my key." They said nothing but began to probe the ground around us with their flashlight beams. Luckily, they didn't find the paper.

We walked down to the Yenisei Station, where one of them made a phone call while the other stayed with me on the platform. The man on the phone didn't seem to be having much luck; he was still phoning when the train for Krasnoyarsk came in. They were in a hurry to catch the train, so they told me to report to the MVD office the next morning in Krasnoyarsk at eleven o'clock and left me standing there on the platform.

When the train left, I retraced my steps to Pranas' apartment. It was now almost 3 A.M., but he was still waiting up for me. He knew I must have been in some sort of trouble, so he was worried. I told him the whole story, and neither of us got much sleep that night. After Mass the next morning, I deliberately stayed at Pranas' and caught the eleven o'clock train. Consequently, I arrived at MVD headquarters about 11:30.

I asked the girl at the switchboard for the two men with whom I had my "appointment". She said they had been called out about 11:15 but had left a number for me to call. I called, but I couldn't reach them. I decided to settle the matter once and for all, so I told the girl I wanted to speak to the chief. I told him the story of the previous evening and asked if there was any report on me. I added that I was due to catch a train back to Abakan that day. "Go ahead," he said when he had heard me out, "and if anything does come up, I'll know you were here to see them about it. It's not your fault." I was glad to get on the train for Abakan that night without further incident.

Back in Abakan, I said nothing to Iosip about my experiences. I told him, though, that I thought it was time I found a job, so he got in touch with a friend named Pavel, who was the main dispatcher at ATK-50, the city garage out on Schetinkina Street, along the road to the airport. About a week later, Pavel came to tell me he had made arrangements for me to have an interview the next morning with his supervisor. I was there ahead of time the next day, waiting for Pavel. He took me to meet the superintendent, a man named Kruglov, tall, well-built, affable, and quite handsome. He seemed happy to meet me, looked over my passport, then suggested that I work temporarily as a mechanic repairing the cabs until a better job was available.

Once I agreed to the job, however, I had to go to the head of maintenance to find out if he needed men. The head of maintenance was a medium-sized, stout, red-faced man named Petruchin, perhaps fifty years old and growing bald, with a deep voice and a rolling walk—very talkative. Pavel explained things to him, including Kruglov's decision. He agreed to try me, so I wrote out an application for the job, he signed it, the superintendent okayed it, and at last I was told to report for work the next day.

That was June 13, 1959. Sedov, the head mechanic, a heavy-set man of about fifty, with a fair complexion and a miniature Roman nose, assigned me to help the driver of Car 69, a little four-cylinder Pobieda, which was far from new. The driver asked me how much I knew about the job; I told him frankly I was just a novice. "Well," he said, "the first thing you have to learn here is to take only the tools you need and keep the others locked up. Never leave a tool in the car or under the car. If you do, you're sure to lose it. They vanish like smoke!"

The car was standing over a pit. He told me we had to take off the fenders and the radiator in order to get the motor out of the car. He went to work on the transmission and wiring under the hood, then noticed me struggling with the bolts that connected the engine to the frame. "Here," he said, "you can't waste time on that." He came over and knocked off the bolts with a chisel! Then we attached a U-shaped yoke to the motor block, shoved a long pipe through the collar of the yoke, and whistled for two other mechanics, who came over and gave us a hand lifting the motor out of the car.

At ATK-50, everything was done by hand that way. If welding or patching was needed on the bottom of the car, six mechanics simply turned it over on its side ("Who cares about fenders?") and propped it up with a beam while the welder dove in to do a crude—but fast—job. At that time, everything was paid for by piecework, so no one had time to bother with the niceties; the idea was to get the job done as fast as possible.

The first month, under this system, I earned only 150 rubles (fifteen dollars). Others were earning 1,200 or even as much as 5,000 rubles. Petruchin was surprised when he saw my pay envelope. "Wladimir Martinovich," he said to me, "what happened?" "I don't know," I said, "I even worked overtime a couple of days to finish a job." The second month, I earned 253 rubles. Finally, the accountant called me into his office and showed me how to make out a job slip. "Put down everything you do," he said, "and that means everything! Write 'I took off the wheel, cleaned the axle, greased the axle, put the wheel back on, tightened the nuts, pumped the tire'—every move you make. Don't just say 'I greased the axle', because every phase of the operation counts as a piece of the work." Gradually, I had to learn from the people in the shop to work the way they did, knocking things apart and slapping them together again.

As a result, the garage never managed to fulfill its "quota" according to the "monthly plan". City Council members used to come to the regular Monday morning workers' meetings to exhort us, but they never made much of an impression. Spare parts, taxis, buses, fares—everything was government-owned; the men were interested only in making money. It was obvious the city authorities weren't satisfied with the management of the garage. Investigations were made, meetings were held. Eventually, we began to hear rumors that changes would be made and a new staff brought in to help the garage "make its quota".

My Sister Proposes a Visit

During this summer of 1959, I received another letter from the American Embassy. They enclosed a verification of an agreement between the Embassy and the Soviet Foreign Office with regard to my release, if I requested it. The Embassy told me, if I wished to go to the United States, to write a petition to the Soviet Foreign Office, and they supplied me with the name of the official in charge and the exact address.

I was curious to see what would happen, so I decided to write to the Foreign Office, asking them to grant me a visa for a return to the United States. I listed as reasons for the request: my age, a consideration of my family at home and their constant efforts to have me returned, and the fact that, because of my limited rehabilitation after the prison camps, I would get only a small pension when I reached the age of retirement in a few years.

I sent the letter off, along with another letter to the Embassy acknowledging receipt of their letter and a notice that I had written to the Foreign Office requesting a visa. For a while I heard nothing. Then the Soviet Foreign Office wrote to say they had received my letter, but since they were not authorized to deal with the question directly, they had sent the letter under file number such-and-such to the Office of the Interior (KGB). So I wrote in turn to the KGB, saying I had heard from the Foreign Office that my petition had been forwarded to them and asking them to consider it and give me an answer.

I heard nothing definite about my petition for three months. Then one day I was called to MVD headquarters in Abakan and read an answer from Moscow to my petition; it was negative. I asked for a reason; the agent said none had been given. So I signed the slip indicating I had received an answer, and that was that—except that I wrote to the American Embassy telling them of the answer to my application.

During the three months I had waited for that answer, though, I made a visit to the Passport Bureau for my semi-annual renewal. In the midst of all the routine proceedings, the agent suddenly suggested I ought to change my "short-term" passport for a permanent one, instead of coming every six months and going through all this.

"All you have to do", he said, "is choose one of the two names in your passport here (Lypinski–Ciszek), add an explanation of how this happened and a short biography, and send it along with a petition to the Central Passport Bureau in Moscow. In a year or so, you'll get a permanent passport." I stared at him for a moment, then thanked him for his "suggestion". I didn't bother to ask why he suddenly brought it up now, after two years "of all this". Nor did I bother to take his suggestion; I told him I didn't want a Russian passport.

At the garage, things went on about as usual. We fell steadily behind our monthly quotas, but nobody seemed to care much. Then, one day, a meeting was announced for 5:15 in the garage hall; everyone was expected to attend. It was announced that the City Council would meet with us on a matter of the highest importance. There was a lot of talk in the shop that day about the announcement and much speculation about what it meant. Just out of curiosity, attendance that night was excellent.

One of the first speakers was a member of the City Council. His opening statement electrified the crowd. He announced he was here to change things and added that in the U.S.S.R. there was no such thing as an indispensable man. "Everyone", he said, "can be replaced, no matter what position he holds." He paused for effect; the tension mounted.

"Therefore," he went on, "since it is necessary to change conditions here at the garage, and since Superintendent Kruglov, though a Party man and a very responsible administrator, has not done the job we expected of him, it has been decided to replace him."

The councilman then went on to enumerate Kruglov's failings in detail. Poor Kruglov just sat there, head down, through the cataloguing of his faults—which seemed to go on forever. When the councilman had finished, there was an embarrassed pause. "And now," resumed the speaker, "I want you to meet your new director." His name was Sofronov, and he strode to the platform and stood alongside the councilman while his qualifications were explained and his virtues extolled. Then the "prompters" began to clap.

Sofronov was a man of about fifty-five, of medium height, heavy-set and strong. His black hair had receded somewhat, but he was tanned and broad-shouldered, with a firm jaw and tight mouth, a Roman nose, and darting eyes. He was also, of course, a Party man. When the "applause" died down, Sofronov acknowledged his introduction. He had a strong voice and spoke decisively. He began by repeating again all the troubles of ATK-50—he had obviously been well briefed—then he began to outline his plans to change the picture radically. After that, the councilman went to work on Petruchin.

Petruchin, too, was called up to the front and sat there with his head hanging while his faults were chronicled, chapter and verse. He was red as a beet, so red, in fact, I began to think he might burst a blood vessel. After his faults had been read out at length, and he had been told he was fired, Petruchin was asked to get up and reply. He admitted his faults and the problems in the garage in a voice so weak and thin he could hardly be heard. The wags in the audience, who were used to hearing Petruchin bark orders in the garage, began to cry out: "Louder! Louder!"

When Petruchin had finally crept from the platform, the councilman asked the workers themselves to get up and speak. Some of the Party men, obviously prompted, got up to criticize Kruglov, made a few passing remarks about Petruchin (he was popular among the workers), but said very little about the violations of which we had been hearing so much. After a while, Sofronov broke in to suggest that perhaps everyone was defending his fellow workers. At the end of the meeting, Pavel, the old dispatcher and the man who had gotten me the job at ATK-50, was also asked to turn in his resignation.

As a result of Sofronov's shake-up, I was given another job. I was assigned to a small wooden shed outside the garage proper, along with another mechanic named Vassily. He was a specialist in transmissions and rear axles; I was made responsible for the shock absorbers and steering gears. The shock absorbers were of the latest telescoping, hydraulic type; the only problem was, we had almost no spare parts.

Since necessity is the mother of invention, I soon grew adept at making replacements out of scrap. I was under terrific pressure, though, because no car could be out of service more than twenty-four hours. Moreover, I knew these same cars would be back out on country roads where the best shocks in the world wouldn't last two weeks. To make a hectic situation even worse, officials from the city government, the army, and the airport used to bring their shock-absorber troubles to ATK-50, and it all piled up on me. It was just too much for one man, and I told Sofronov so.

In an attempt to lick the problem, I even made dies by hand to stamp out the replacement parts. For this I got an award, a governmental *grammota* (diploma) signed by the garage and city officials for "outstanding service". I also got the *Zvanie Udarnika Kommunisticheskogo Truda* (Shock Troop of Communist Labor) Award, one of the highest worker awards in the country. That was presented to me at a solemn meeting of all the workers, with the head of the union on hand to present it personally, then my name was added to the framed list of *Udarniki* on the wall of the workers' hall. Naturally, I took quite a ribbing about it all.

More importantly, I also got a pair of handsome bonuses—and a helper at last! Friends in the garage told me that the helper had been picked out by the Party as much to watch me as to help me, but he did the job. The union also brought students out from town to learn from me, and an apprentice was sent from the garage at Chernogorka to learn the technique. The crowning irony of the whole episode, however, was when the MVD sent a mechanic to learn from me. Afterward, Sofronov called me out one day and began to ask me in a friendly way about the job and whether I was satisfied with the pay. From there he went on to ask all sorts of questions, including a seemingly innocent one about whether I, as an American, listened to the Voice of America. I told him I had no radio at all where I lived. "Oh, good," he said, somewhat taken aback, "yes, that's better. Don't listen to it."

After an awkward pause, Sofronov asked whether there was anything at all he could do for me. He seemed to be taking such an interest in my life that I felt something was up. I told him, though, that if he could get me an apartment somewhere I would certainly appreciate it. He looked momentarily startled, then explained that the garage barracks were full and he couldn't do much for me at present. He suggested that perhaps the City Council could help. "I've been going there for over a year", I said. That stopped him.

"But," he ended magnanimously, "if there is anything else you need, don't hesitate to ask me."

I was concerned about another apartment because all during the winter Iosip had been asking me to try to find another room. He was ashamed to tell me the reason, but finally he admitted it: the City Council had "suggested" that it looked bad for him, as a leading Party member, to have me—a foreigner and a possible spy—in his house. At the beginning of spring, Iosip had again begun to talk seriously of my getting another place to live; they were pressuring him at the City Council. He told me as far as he was concerned I could stay forever, but "perhaps it might be better if you could find a room elsewhere".

Finally, our next-door neighbor, Dmitri, offered me a room in his house. His mother, the old *babushka* who had met me the day I first came to Iosip's, lived with them and slept in a room similar to the one I had at Iosip's, next to the kitchen. The *babushka* wanted me to have her room; she would sleep in the kitchen. I accepted eagerly, for in many ways it was an ideal solution. I knew Dmitri and Ilyena, his wife—and the old *babushka*—quite well, for they were always dropping over to Iosip's. Moreover, I would still be close to Iosip, Valya, and all the friends I had made there.

The move had other advantages, too. For one thing, it would give me a chance to say Mass every day without waiting until everyone had gone to bed. Dmitri and Ilyena never got home from work before 6:30; I was generally home by 4:30, and I could say Mass then. There would be fewer visitors and a quieter house in general—a place to read and relax, or even to watch television if I wished, for Dmitri and Ilyena had one of the few sets in the neighborhood.

I paid the *babushka* about three rubles a month, and in return she would have hot soup or *kasha* for me, plus three or four slices of rye bread, when I came home at night. That was my daily fare. I used to make a big pot of soup, or borscht, a couple times a week, which would last me for three or even four days. The soup was made of potatoes, cabbage, beets, onions, and lamb bones—or anything else I could get to thicken the pot—then enough lard so the grease on top would be as thick as my little finger. I'd have a bowl of soup in the morning before I went to work, and the *babushka* would have another ready when I came home at night.

For lunch at the factory, I took a piece of fatback as big as my hand, or a herring, or perhaps an onion or pickled tomatoes, with a thick chunk of rye bread. That, too, was standard. It was normal to see a man at the garage pull an onion and a piece of bread from his pocket for lunch; nothing else. I still drank hot water (*kipiatok*) rather than tea or coffee, and if I had meat once or twice a week, it was all to the good.

Sunday was our weekly holiday, but of course it has lost much of its religious significance in the U.S.S.R. Sunday today is the main shopping day, and the streets are crowded with people hurrying, not to church, but to the stores to stand in line. For me, though, Sunday was an opportunity to be alone with God. Dmitri and his wife used to leave early in the morning to go shopping or visiting, and the *babushka* would spend the day with neighbors. I had the house to myself, so I could say my Mass without fear of interruption and read the Bible for as long as I wanted. And besides the spiritual satisfaction of Sunday, I enjoyed a complete rest.

The strain of work, frankly, was again beginning to tell on me. My legs and knees, especially, were getting tired from standing seven hours each day on the cold concrete; my hands were stiff and tired from the constant pulling and pushing required in repairing the shock absorbers, the immersion in gasoline. I was honestly beginning to feel old age catching up with me. I tired easily; at the end of a day, my arms and legs felt heavy, and my breath was short. Perhaps it was as much the steady diet of fat and rye bread, with no fruit or fresh vegetables or milk, but it was becoming increasingly notice-able. Every morning, except Sunday, I did a half hour of gymnastics in the courtyard before breakfast to keep my muscles toned.

More than my physical condition was bothering me, though. I was increasingly annoyed at the way the MVD kept checking up on me. Iosip's frank admission of his reason for asking me to move was just one indication. Shortly after I moved in with Dmitri, I got an anonymous letter warning me not to go to certain houses or visit certain people—"or you will land in the same place you came from". I also received a letter from a former prisoner with whom I'd been corre-sponding for a long time, asking me to please stop writing "because I've been warned".

Then, at work one day, another mechanic came to me and told me he had been questioned not long ago by the MVD about his association with me. Not only that, he said, but he had been asked to collaborate with them and watch me. He told me quite frankly about the incident, because he liked me, and warned me to be on my guard. Ironically, shortly after he walked away, someone who had seen us talking sidled up to warn me that he thought the fellow was spying on me.

There was no doubt but that, for some reason or other, the surveillance was being tightened on me again. Perhaps my letters to the Embassy or the regular letters I was now getting from my sisters at home had something to do with it. No doubt, though, the MVD just couldn't believe I was simply one of the "Shock Troops of Soviet Labor"; they had warned me not to work as a priest, and they were watching me closely.

One morning, as I entered the garage, I was stopped by an old man in his seventies. He was of medium height, with a military bearing and stride, a wind-burnt face, broad forehead, and wavy white hair. He asked me for a mechanic; I referred him to the chief. As I spoke he noticed an accent and asked if I would mind if he asked me a few questions. I shrugged my shoulders.

"Aren't you a Pole?" he asked, first of all. I hesitated, then nodded my head. "My parents were Polish," he said, "but I've forgotten the language. In any event, I'm very glad to meet you. My name is Dutov." I introduced myself in return. "Do you work here?" he continued. I said I did. "Well, then, perhaps you can help me out. You see, I work at the Abakan Museum, and I lost the key to one of the display cases. I wonder if someone here could make me another?"

I told him that I could do it, but not at the moment. (If I was caught doing outside work, I'd have been docked the rest of the day's pay under Sofronov's new rules.) We talked for a while longer, and before he left he told me that he would like to meet me again, so I gave him my address. From that chance meeting, we became good friends.

As I got to know him, I found out he was an archeologist who had been working here in the Far East for more than fifty years, excavating the burial grounds of the primitive inhabitants. In Abakan, he told me, he had found interesting relics of the people, the Khakassians, which went back as far as three thousand years. I also learned he was considered *the* leading authority on archeological questions concerning Siberia; every year he gave a series of lectures in Moscow, Leningrad, or the other big university cities about his most recent findings.

Some of those findings, he said, bore striking resemblances to findings in China and Japan. Occasionally, then, I was able to help him by translating his Russian articles into English for publication in various international journals. He was also in frequent correspondence with a Chinese professor of archeology at Cambridge. The Chinese knew English, but not Russian, so I used to write Professor Dutov's letters for him and translate the English answers that came from Cambridge.

I was also able to do him one very special favor, thanks to the Jesuits at Gonzaga High School in Washington, D.C. The professor often came across references in his work to Müller's *Handbuch der Archaologie*, but he told me there were only a few copies of the book in all Russia, at the big university libraries. I wrote to the Jesuits at Gonzaga, who had already sent me other packages, and they were able to get a copy of the book. Professor Dutov thought it was almost a miracle, and he never forgot it.

In the months I knew him, we became quite close. He knew I was a priest, but he couldn't understand why I wouldn't get married. He had even picked out the ideal wife for me, a lady friend of his, about forty-five, who had her own apartment and a nice job. "You should have someone to come home to," he used to say, "someone to take care of you now, as well as when you get old. You may be all right now; you're strong, you have a good job. But in ten or fifteen years what are you going to do?"

I just used to laugh at him. "Oh," I'd say, "I'll take care of myself." "But what if you can't?" "Then God will have to do His share." "Ah! You and your God!" (The professor always claimed he was an atheist.) Then he would forget about the question of marriage and launch into an argument about religion; he loved a good argument. We had many good times together, including the arguments, and he told me I was the one really true friend he had ever made. He even invited me along on some of his archeological trips around Abakan, but I was never able to make it.

Sometime in April 1963, I came home from work one evening to find a letter from my sister Helen telling me she had at last received a visa to make a tour of Russia—Leningrad, Moscow, Kiev, Odessa, Lvov. The tour would begin in Moscow on June 19, and she asked if I could meet her there on that date. Since it was suppertime, I read the letter to the *babushka*, then to Dmitri and his wife when they came home. The *babushka* was overjoyed. She alternated between asking a lot of questions (most of which I couldn't answer) and exclamations like "Oh, the Lord is good to let you see your sister before you die!"

I was continually distracted at Mass that night, thinking about the news. I went to bed much later than usual, but I couldn't sleep. The more I thought about it, the more it seemed a problem—this getting to Moscow. The idea of walking into a hotel in broad daylight and joining a group of American tourists—how would I ever get permission for that, and from whom? I tossed and turned all night, and got up the next morning more tired than when I had gone to bed.

The next day at work, I went to see Sofronov. "Ah, Wladimir Martinovich," he said when I walked into his office, "what's the matter? You don't look well." "I'm all right, *Tovarisch Nachzalnik* (Superintendent)," I answered, "but I have a problem." "Nu, nu, what is it?" "I got a letter yesterday from Washington . . ." "Where?" "From my sister in America. She has a visa to visit me here in Russia, in Moscow. But you know that my vacation time, according to the schedule, is already finished. Can I get a second period of leave?"

Tovarisch Sofronov, as a matter of fact, was badly disturbed by the whole situation. He hardly knew what to do. We discussed the problem a little, and he finally told me he couldn't make the decision. He promised, though, to take it up with the "committee" and let me have a definite answer soon. For the next month, I asked him almost every morning about the decision. He kept putting me off. There was nothing to do but wait; I couldn't answer Helen until I knew definitely.

I made up my mind, though, that if worse came to worst, I would quit my job at the garage on June 1 and go to Moscow for a month. After that, if the militia weren't already looking for me, I would return and try to find another job. It was a risky step, I knew. If I quit, my passport would be stamped: "Not holding a job." That would make the officials in Moscow even more suspicious and less likely to let me see my sister freely. But the longer I waited for Sofronov's answer, the more determined I grew that I was going to see Helen, even if just for a day. (The idea that I might go back to America with her, or ever, didn't so much as cross my mind.)

In the middle of May, I still hadn't heard definitely from Sofronov. I knew my sister must be getting anxious for an answer, so I decided to act. I walked over to Sofronov as he was standing near the driveway checking out cars. "*Tovarisch* Sofronov," I said, "my people in America have been waiting a whole month now for an answer. What must they think? I have decided to take the case somewhere else and see if I can get a definite answer about going to Moscow." "No, no", he said. "Look, today I can't tell you; tomorrow, I will call you out and tell you definitely."

That day never seemed to end. I had all sorts of difficulty doing even the simplest things; I sometimes put a shock absorber together two or three times before I got all the parts in correctly. At home that night, I could think of nothing but what Sofronov's "final answer" would be.

The next morning, I went straight to Sofronov as soon as I reported for work. He told me to come back at 9 A.M. I went to the shop, but I didn't even bother to put on my work clothes. Precisely at nine, I headed for Sofronov's office. "*Tovarisch* Ciszek," he said, "I can't get the whole committee together yet; you'll have to wait until eleven o'clock." I went back to the workshop and found a crowd had gathered. By this time, practically everyone at ATK-50 knew of my sister's proposed visit. When I told them what Sofronov had said, they roared with laughter. Some of them snorted "delaying tactics", and others predicted I would never get a definite answer—at least not until my sister had come to Moscow and gone.

I put on my work clothes and tried to work, but again I couldn't concentrate. About 10:45, I washed up, changed clothes again, and went back to the office. I was surprised to see four men sitting there with Sofronov: the president of the union, the head of bus maintenance, the head of taxi maintenance, and the head of the labor department.

Sofronov began very solemnly: "*Tovarisch* Ciszek, it is not customary for us to give second vacations to any worker. Considering your case, however, how long it has been since you have seen your family, and how fine a worker you are, the committee has decided to give you twelve days leave of absence from ATK-50. If you fly to Moscow, you will have ten full days there. If you take a train, you will have only five days in Moscow. But, of course, we must leave that up to you."

He paused and looked at me. I mumbled my thanks to him and the committee. "Now," he said, "you must understand that this is a serious matter. By giving you this permission, we are putting ourselves in a dangerous position. We have no one to replace you in this job; that can be handled. But your sister is from America, and you know the Americans, what tales they tell, so you have to be very careful what you tell her. Otherwise, the American papers will exaggerate as they always do, and you—and we, too—will suffer, eh?" All five of them looked at me.

I glanced at the others, but I spoke to Sofronov. "You must also understand *my* situation. You all know me, and you know my record; I will do my best, but now you have to trust me." They seemed satisfied. Sofronov asked the others if they had anything to say, but they all shrugged. I thanked them again for their permission and left. I could hardly work all that afternoon, talking happily to friends and receiving their congratulations. That evening, I told *babushka*, Dmitri and Ilyena, Iosip and Valya the news they were all waiting to hear. I couldn't wait to finish supper (*babushka* wouldn't stop talking) so I could write the good news to Helen.

Before I wrote, however, I said Mass. Starting that evening I began to say Mass specifically that God's will be done. I deliberately didn't pray that I would see my sister but only that I would do what was His will and what was for the best. In all my excitement and enthusiasm, I didn't want to begin interfering now with His Providence after all these years of protection . . .

The fifteenth of June came and went, but I heard nothing further from Helen. I looked for a letter every day, but none came. Of course, there was always the possibility that my letter or her answer had been delayed somewhere, so I prepared to leave for Moscow. I decided to take the train to Moscow, then perhaps fly back to Abakan. The train took three days, but it would give me a chance to see some of the country I'd never seen. Moreover, and perhaps more importantly, it would give me a chance to rest and collect my thoughts as I could not do on a plane.

I bought a train ticket for Sunday, June 16. At nine that morning, I walked out into the street and was just closing the gate into our courtyard when a young girl came hurrying up the street and called, "Does Ciszek live here?" I was so startled that for a moment I hesitated. "Yes." "I have a telegram for him." "I'm Ciszek." "Well, this is the strangest telegram I ever had to deliver. Will you sign for it?" I told her I'd like to see it first to be sure it was for me. I opened it—it was all numbers! The only thing in plain text was the point of origination, "Washington"; I knew it must be from Helen. "Well, this is no good to me", I said to the girl. "I can't read this code and it's very important. I was supposed to catch a train today."

The poor girl told me she was just a messenger. She could only give me the name of her supervisor at the local post office. I hurried down there, but the supervisor couldn't read the telegram either. "Well," I said, "it's very important. Can't you do something about it?" The supervisor went to the phone, made several calls, then finally gave me the name of a woman to contact in the main post office downtown.

I took the bus down to the main post office, growing increasingly anxious and irritated. I showed the telegram to the woman there and said, "Look at that! What's that supposed to mean?" She called upstairs to the telegraph office; a young girl came down, looked at the numbers and smiled. "Just wait," she said, "wait here for half an hour and I'll get you the translation." In less than a half hour she was back, but this time she was puzzled. She asked me if I understood the telegram.

It was in English: "Encountering delays. Will keep you informed. Helen." The telegram had been sent on June 13; it had taken three days to reach me. I told the girl I understood, signed for it, and went out. I was puzzled, but all I could do was wait for more information from Helen. So I waited anxiously for a letter, without writing myself; I was afraid our letters might cross in the mail and just make things more complicated by containing alternate suggestions.

June 19 came. There was no letter from Helen. I figured something was wrong. As a matter of fact, it was almost a month before I got a letter, and then it was from Sister Evangeline. She said she had decided to come to Moscow with Helen, but because she was having trouble getting a visa, they had had to postpone the trip. She added that she would let me know when they were coming.

That evening, while we were all watching television— Iosip and Valya, Dmitri and Ilyena, the *babushka*—I mentioned that two of my sisters were coming and that their trip had been delayed because my other sister couldn't get a visa. Iosip blamed the American government; he said they didn't want my two sisters to come to Russia. I tried to convince him the delay was in Moscow, that it was the Soviet Embassy in Washington that refused to grant them a visa. We started to argue, and the group told us to be quiet and watch the television set.

There was a pause, then Iosip began to muse that my sisters must be coming for a reason. "Both of them insist on coming," he said, "so it can't be just a trip. They must be going to try and get you out." Dmitri was skeptical. He rarely got into any conversation concerning politics or the government, but he said there was no chance for my sisters to get me out. "Perhaps," he said flatly, "sometime later, if our government has to make an exchange for one of our own men, they *might* just possibly give you up." Iosip laughed, and the conversation drifted off after that. But I remember it, because it was so rare for Dmitri to talk at all on such matters.

Chapter Five

MY RETURN HOME

The KGB Baffles Me

One sunny September day, when the air had already turned cold, though the sun was warm, I was at work at ATK-50, not even thinking about my sisters. With the summer gone, the possibility of their coming seemed remote. I was listening to Vassily tell some stories of his escapades and waiting for the end of the shift, for I was tired. Shortly after three o'clock, Sofronov's secretary came in. Vassily, who had an excellent nose for trouble, muttered to me, "Something's up!" The secretary smiled. "Wladimir Martinovich," she said, "*Tovarisch* Sofronov wants you to come immediately to his office. Please put your tools away, change clothes, and come quickly." I was surprised, but as I hesitated Vassily said knowingly, "News from Moscow about your sisters."

When I got to Sofronov's office, there were three workers standing in front of the desk. Alongside Sofronov, behind the desk, was a man in civilian clothes who looked directly at me as I opened the door. I took one long look and immediately I knew him—a member of the KGB. He was in civilian clothes, but I couldn't miss the mark of the breed, not after all these years. Sofronov looked up and asked me to wait a few moments until he had finished with the three men. When they came out, Sofronov said, "Wladimir Martinovich, this

401

man has come to see you. I have some other work to do, so if
you don't mind I'll leave you with him." With that, he said
goodbye to the KGB agent and left.

The agent was a young man of about thirty, of medium
height and so bland of manner he seemed almost simple. He
stuck out his hand and said directly: "I'm from the KGB. If
you'll sit down for a minute, I'll tell you why I'm here. Our
chief, General (I didn't catch the name), is here from Krasnoyarsk and would like to see you right away. Perhaps at 4 P.M.,
at the hotel on Oktobrskaya Street? He'd prefer to see you
there in order to make it more pleasant for you. If you came
to KGB headquarters, you might be seen, but at the hotel no
one will pay any attention to you. I'll be waiting outside the
hotel at four o'clock and take you to him."

Despite all his politeness, his last words sounded like an
order of sorts. It was already 3:30, and the next bus for our
neighborhood left at 4:00. I caught a bus downtown instead,
then, and walked home from there. *Babushka* was surprised to
see me so early. I asked her if a letter had come for me (I
thought that might be what the KGB were anxious about);
she said no. Then I told her I had to meet someone and that
I would eat dinner later that night. I dressed, shaved, and
walked to the market square, where I took a bus to the post
office. As I got off, it was nearly five o'clock.

I walked back the block toward the hotel from the post
office and saw the KGB man pacing nervously on the sidewalk. He didn't see me coming, because he was expecting
me to arrive from the other direction. "*Zdravstvuite*," I said.
He looked startled, recognized me, then looked relieved.
"They're here already", he said. "Let's go right up."

As we went through the lobby, people turned to stare.
Most of them can tell a KGB officer in or out of uniform, just
as I could. We walked up to the second floor and entered a

two-room suite. Two men were already there, and one of them called out heartily: "Wladimir Martinovich, come right in, come right in." He was an older man in a dark suit, almost completely bald, but tanned and solidly built. He shook hands with me and said, "I'm General (again I didn't catch the name), and this is Viktor Pavlovich." I shook hands with Pavlovich, a young man in a white suit, with a fair thin face, long nose, and blue eyes.

The General did most of the talking, and he was exceedingly cordial. "Well, how are you?" "All right." "How do you feel? Is your health all right?" "Yes," I said, "I'm fine." "Where are you living now?" I was sure he knew, but I played the game and told him. Then in short order we went down the rest of the routine: my salary, my fellow workers, whether the supervisor was kind to me, the union, etc. I told him everything was just fine.

"Yes," he said at length, "we get excellent reports of your work. Your fellow workers think highly of you; I understand you have won some certificates and bonuses. Now, taking all this into consideration, we would like to do you a favor. Do you remember the petition you sent us about an exit visa to the United States?" Once he said that, I became cautious. This wasn't the first time I had been called out about those petitions.

"I wrote about four or five", I said. "Yes, well, now, we've been looking through the file, and we happened to see them. Up to this time, there hasn't been much possibility of our granting such a request—but things are different now. Let's forget the past. Today is today." "Yes," I said, "very unpleasant." "Wladimir Martinovich, let's not talk about that now. You're different; we're different people. We know you'd like to see your family, and in these new times it might be possible for us to do something for you." "That's nice", I said.

Then the General began to go on a little fishing expedition. He asked my opinions of life here, of Communism, the system, the technical progress, current developments, and the social life, etc. "I've lived here twenty-three years," I said, "and you've never heard me complain. Moreover, you can ask anybody I've lived with. Rules are rules, and I live by them wherever I happen to be."

Something was bothering me, but I couldn't quite put my finger on it. He was fishing for something; I'd been through too much of this sort of thing to miss that point. Yet I couldn't quite make out just what he was after. We talked for about three hours, getting nowhere as far as I could see. The General seemed to want to review everything and yet talk about nothing. In a sense, he was like a boxer sparring for an opening—yet he was always most cordial, most pleasant, and most understanding, no matter how short and abrupt my answers became.

Finally, however, the General said he must be going. "I would like to see you again tomorrow," he said, "but if I can't make it, Viktor Pavlovich will be here. Shall we say 4:30, here at the hotel? Why not come as you are from work, there's no need to change clothes. No one at the hotel will pay much attention to you." We stood up, shook hands again, and I walked out.

The next day at work, everyone wanted to know what had happened and why I had been called out. Some of the girls from the office told me they hadn't slept all night; they knew the man in Sofronov's office had been from the KGB. "We were afraid they would send you off", said one of the girls. "We were afraid you would never come back." "Well," I laughed, "you can see that I'm here!" "Yes, but what happened? What did they say?" "It seems to be a question of my petition about going back to the United States; they think I might be able to go home. I don't believe it, of course. I think it has something to do with my sisters."

All day long, in the shop, on the way to the warehouses, wherever I went, I talked to workers and officials alike, and everyone was interested in the case. "Wladimir Martinovich," said one of the mechanics, "the whole trouble is with our government." "I don't doubt it", I said. "You'll have a hard time getting anywhere without compromise," said another, "but don't give in!" By noon, the story was all over the garage via the grapevine, and everyone wished me luck.

After work, I washed up quickly and walked to the bus stop with Vassily. We talked about the previous day's interview, but I didn't tell him I was on my way to another one. "Well, here's luck to you!" said Vassily as he boarded the bus. "The same to you", I answered. I took a bus past the hotel and saw Viktor Pavlovich walking up and down near the door. A block beyond the hotel I got off and walked back. He was reading a sign when I came up behind him.

"Oh, you're here!" he said, startled. "Good!"

He hurried into the hotel, and I followed him. I felt dirty and out of place in my work clothes as we went up the stairs to the second floor and back again to the same suite. "Well, how are you today, Wladimir Martinovich?" he said as we sat down. "I'm all right", I said without much enthusiasm. Viktor told me the General was not able to make it that afternoon; he hoped I wouldn't mind. I shrugged. Then he went on to say how highly I was thought of by the General, and how they wanted to help me—and that I should return the favor. (That did it. I could feel the skin crawl on my spine; I didn't even answer.)

Viktor began to talk of many things. He spoke of Communism and of how much good it had done, how much progress had been made. The more he talked, the less I said;

With God in Russia

our conversation soon assumed the aspect of a monologue. He must have realized it, for he abruptly shifted gears. "You know, Wladimir Martinovich, we will more than likely send you to Moscow. You will be able to see the good of Communism, travel wherever you like, see what you want."

"Yes, well, I'd like that. I think I would like to see European Russia."

"Well, you know, when you get to Moscow you'll be able to see all the famous places, the historical landmarks. It's quite a city. There is even a Catholic Church there, which you can visit if you like, or go to confession. You needn't be afraid that we would have anything against it." When he said that, my nerves twitched. I knew then where he was heading with that particular line: the same old pressure. They wouldn't exactly want me to spy on the Catholic priest in Moscow, but it would "be nice" if I reported my "impressions".

From that point on I was tense and depressed. I began to build up a full head of steam, and soon I was almost physically sick. Viktor didn't seem to notice but went on chatting pleasantly about other priests. "You know who they are," he remarked almost offhand, "you probably have their addresses. You ought to have a wonderful time visiting them."

"Addresses?" I broke in. "I'm not sure . . ." I did have an address book in a drawer back at Dmitri's. If they had already seen it, I couldn't deny that I had it; if they hadn't seen it, I didn't want them looking.

Then, somehow, he was on Norilsk: "Whom do you know there?" It was like a knife at my heart. I was sure he knew whom I'd been corresponding with there, and whom I had known when I worked there. I rattled off a few names that I was certain he must know. "Yes, yes, I remember them," he said, and then went on to chronicle other people, activities, times and places and dates, even the money I'd got-

ten. "We don't mind, you see. We know you call them sti-
pends and that you didn't ask for that money. You can see
how understanding we are." (I saw all right. I saw how closely
I had been under surveillance all the time!)

I could feel the muscles under my jaws beginning to work,
I was so furious. Then back he went to chatting about the trip
to Moscow, Leningrad, and so forth. He told me there was no
need to take all my things, that I could travel light. He didn't
see any reason why I couldn't leave most of my possessions
here in Abakan. (Uh-huh!) At length, he seemed to notice
that I was angry.

"What's the matter, Wladimir Martinovich," he said, "are
you sick?" "No, I'm tired." "Well, I'm sorry, I really am terribly sorry. I see that it is getting late; I had no idea I'd kept
you so long. We really ought to talk more about this, I think,
but not tonight. Perhaps I should see you again some other
time, and we can talk this over more definitely. I'll give you a
call."

In order to "make things easy on me", Pavlovich arranged
that for our next little chat he would simply send me a postcard from headquarters in Krasnoyarsk. That would be an
indication that he would be in Abakan the next day at the
hotel and would like to see me there. I nodded, and left the
room. The more I thought about the interview, the angrier I
became. It wasn't only my own troubles; I thought of all the
people he had mentioned who were obviously under surveillance because of me. After all these years, it was starting again!

When I reached home, there was no one in the house. The
stove was burning in the kitchen, but *babushka* wasn't there.
Remembering Pavlovich's remark about the addresses, I
seized my chance. I went to my room immediately and gathered up all my letters and addresses—anything and everything
that would connect me with anyone else—and burned them

in the stove. If anything happened to me, at least no one else would be involved.

Babushka came in then, along with Iosip and Valya. When I hadn't come home from work, *babushka* had become worried and hurried over to consult Iosip. They knew something must be wrong, and as soon as they saw me at home they came over immediately. They were so excited and I was so depressed that I couldn't tell them what had happened. "Well," I said, "they called me out . . ." "Who?" "The KGB, I guess; I don't really know. Anyhow, they told me they were going to help me, to do me a favor, perhaps even send me to Moscow—but I could leave my things here!"

Immediately, that opened the flood gates of speculation. My sisters were already in Moscow; they had been to the Kremlin; they had seen Khrushchev. Perhaps I was going home—no, otherwise I wouldn't be told to leave my things here. Maybe I was just going to visit with my sisters—then why hadn't they told me where they were or when I could meet them? I hardly paid any attention, and I barely touched my dinner. I excused myself early and went to bed.

But I didn't sleep. That night was one of the worst I spent in Abakan, or even in prison. I couldn't sleep; I couldn't breathe. No matter what I tried to do, I kept thinking of Viktor Pavlovich cataloguing again the names of all the people I had helped or worked with. It was like a nightmare, except that I stayed awake.

At last I made up my mind that the next time I was called out I would make it short and sweet: "Please don't ask me anything else! I don't want any favors of you, so don't ask anything of me. Just don't bother me!" I didn't trust them at all. I no more believed that they were out to "help" me than that I was Khrushchev himself. I didn't want any more meetings, any more names mentioned, any more people spied on.

I was sick of the whole business. I decided once and for all to tell them so.

I went back to work the next day, expecting to be called out at any time. Sofronov, for once, didn't seem to know what was happening. When he met me at work, he would ask in a general way how things were going and when I was going to meet my sisters. He assured me I still had permission to take twelve days off. On the other hand, he never mentioned the KGB or my being called out by them. The people at work, for the most part, seemed to connect it all with the visit of my sisters.

A week went by. I kept waiting for another call. It wasn't that I worried so much about the KGB, but I was hoping for word of my sisters. I had begun to think that my "interviews" might possibly be a preliminary (to see how I was disposed?) to the visit of my sisters. Still, I hesitated to write to them now, especially if there was still a chance of their visit this fall. I didn't want to take any chances at all.

About the middle of the month, I received a postcard from Krasnoyarsk asking me to report the next day for some routine matters concerning my passport. I knew it meant I was to meet Pavlovich the next day at the hotel. Going to the hotel that afternoon, I kept thinking about my decision. I was determined to listen just once more to what they had to say, then tell them bluntly and finally that I wasn't interested.

When I reached the hotel, I saw Pavlovich outside again, reading a sign in one of the windows. He greeted me cordially and we went in. Again I was only in work clothes, and I felt a little shabby walking through the lobby of the hotel. When we entered the suite, there was another KGB man standing in the center of the room. Pavlovich introduced him as Aleksandr Mihailovich. I greeted him warmly; now that I had made up my mind, I felt almost in control of the situation. Pavlovich, in fact, commented on my good spirits. I answered that I was feeling fine today.

When we sat down, Pavlovich again began explaining the whole proposition, including the hazy hints about our doing "favors" for each other. Aleksandr said nothing, I said little. When Viktor finally ran down, he asked me quite cheerfully, "Well, what do you think, Wladimir Martinovich?" I said bluntly: "I don't believe a word you say!"

Pavlovich looked like he had been stabbed. "What? Why?" "Because," I said, "I know you people too well to believe you. You've called me out just too many times, made just too many promises. Nothing has ever happened and it won't happen now." "But Wladimir Martinovich, you can see how different things are now! We're not what people think we are anymore, we're different people altogether."

"I'll tell you the problem", I said. "I was in Lubianka five years with the NKVD; they made all kinds of promises. And what did it all mean? Fifteen years in prison and the prison camps! Now, no matter what you say, I can't shake that feeling. It's part of me. I just can't believe you."

"No, but times have changed!" Viktor insisted. We sat there in that hotel room for the next three hours, while they tried to tell me that they had changed, and I kept trying to convince them that, even if they had, it was psychologically impossible for me to trust them anymore. At last I stood up. "You can talk all you want about changes. I came in here not trusting you, and I don't believe you now. There's nothing you can do to change my feelings, no matter what else you change. Words won't do it. I'm sorry, but that's the way it is."

With that, I left. They didn't stop me. Neither did they say anything about another meeting. So, I felt that, for good or ill, this was the end. At home and at work, whenever anyone asked me about my sisters or the visit to Moscow, I said the same thing: I had finished talking; I had refused to make any deals. After that, I didn't know what to expect.

September turned to October and I heard nothing, either from the KGB or from my sisters. I began to get caught up again in the daily routine. Gradually, I stopped thinking about the whole business. After work one Thursday, I went to the store to stock up my larder and prepare for the winter. As I unpacked all the supplies, I jokingly told the *babushka* that I had enough for three weeks. "Why?" she said. "Maybe you won't need all this." I laughed. "It won't spoil," I said, "but I think it's about time to stop wishful thinking."

After supper that evening, I sat in the kitchen with the *babushka*, talking, listening again to stories I had heard fifty times, feeling almost carefree again. Ilyena was resting in the front room, and Dmitri was at work. After a while, I took the papers and went to my room. It was about 8 P.M., so I read a little while to relax, then did my spiritual reading and said Mass. After that, I sat down to read again. Suddenly, there was a sharp, loud knock on the kitchen window!

It was so loud that it startled me. Ilyena jumped up from the couch where she had been resting. Since the house had no door in the front, and the gate to the courtyard was locked after dark, it wasn't unusual for people to knock on the front window to attract our attention. But there was something so sudden, so commanding—so imperious—about this knock that I was certain it meant trouble.

It was about 9:30 P.M. I put on my hat and coat and went out into the courtyard. "Who's there?" I asked. A man's voice answered: "Is this where Wladimir Martinovich lives?" For some reason, I hesitated to answer that question, so I asked again instead, "Who is there?" Again he didn't give a name but simply asked, "Is Wladimir Martinovich home?" I suspected it was the KGB, and I wanted to say, "No, he's not home, come back some other time." But I knew that was just postponing the inevitable, so I said, "Yes, I'm home." "Oh, is that you, Wladimir Martinovich?" "Yes." "Well, I've come to get you."

The gate to the courtyard was still locked, and I didn't offer to open it. "I'm tired and I've had a hard day at work", I said. "I don't want to see anybody." "Would you please open the gate?" I walked down to the gate and opened it; he began to argue with me. "I have a car right here," he said, "you won't have to walk at all. Just come down to the hotel for a talk—I promise you it won't take long—and I'll drive you there and back."

I wasn't enthusiastic about the idea, but there was really little I could do. As I left, I called to Ilyena not to lock the gate because I wouldn't be long. She said nothing. I didn't tell her where I was going, but I think she guessed. It was a five-minute ride to the hotel, and nothing was said. We again went up to the second floor but to an entirely new apartment.

This time there was only one man in the room, Aleksandr Mihailovich. He was quite cordial as he asked me to sit down, and he promised, "I won't keep you long, because I know it's late." I took a seat by the window. "This won't take long, Wladimir Martinovich, because I just have a few things to tell you. Tomorrow morning, I want you to go to the superintendent at ATK-50 and tell him you want to leave work for good. If he has any objections, have him call this number (he handed me a slip of paper) and ask for Aleksandr Mihailovich. I think you should pay off all your debts, too, because you'll be going to Moscow. However, I would suggest you take only what you think you'll need and leave the rest here. Do you understand?"

Things were beginning to happen fast. I was a little surprised, but I managed to nod. "Now, Monday," he continued, "buy a plane ticket for Krasnoyarsk and I'll meet you there. That gives you three days to make whatever arrangements you need, and that should be enough. If you have any questions, however, call this number (he gave me another slip of paper) or this other number in Krasnoyarsk (he pointed out the second number on the slip)." With that he stood up. "I think that's all I have to say. Do you have any questions?"

Before I could reply, he went to the sitting room of the suite and came back with a bottle of five-star cognac, two pieces of *torte* cake, and some chocolate candy. He opened the bottle and filled two water glasses. As he handed me a glass, he said: "An old Russian custom, a drink to seal the bargain." Then he lifted the glass as if in a toast and said, "Here's luck to you!" I didn't ask him why I needed luck; we drank down the cognac, and I took a little nibble of the cake.

He began to refill the glasses as he talked again about "wrapping everything up in three days". We drank again. I said, "Here's luck to you!" He filled up the glasses again, we saluted each other without bothering with "luck", and drained them again. "Well," he said, "I'm certainly glad things are developing the way they are. I wish you the best of luck." With that he started to fill the glasses again, but I stopped him. "No, no more for me."

I got up and put on my hat and coat. He followed me outside, without a hat or coat. I told him I'd walk home, but he said, "The car is here." As I got in, he stood on the sidewalk; I noticed, however, that the driver looked at him, and he nodded solemnly. My heart sank—the glance and the action looked so familiar—and I only hoped I was wrong. We drove off, while Aleksandr stood on the curb looking after us. Yet we drove right to Dmitri's and not a word was said. When I was safely outside the car, I thanked the driver for the ride, stepped in quickly, and locked the gate.

It was almost 11 P.M. As soon as I came into the house, Ilyena sprang up with a frightened look on her face. "You don't know what I've been going through here", she said. "I thought they had taken you to prison. After that knock, I just knew there was going to be trouble." Then, to reassure her, I told her the whole story: I was going to Moscow; I was to quit work, pay my debts, pack only the necessary clothes, and be in Krasnoyarsk on Monday.

This was Thursday night. Ilyena was excited, and I was a bit excited myself. I couldn't figure out what it all meant or what I would be doing in Moscow. Aleksandr had told me nothing about that, only that I was going there and that I should be in Krasnoyarsk by Monday.

The next morning at ATK-50, I had no difficulty with Sofronov about leaving work. Perhaps he had already been informed. People crowded around to congratulate me and wish me luck. "Whatever happens, don't give in," said Vassily, "and good luck!" Everybody echoed his sentiments. I finally collected my pay about 3 P.M., took a last look around the garage where I'd been awarded an *Udarnika* citation and made so many friends, and went home.

Sunday we arranged a little going-away party. There were about fifteen in the party at Dmitri's house: Iosip and Valya, Dmitri and Ilyena, Professor Dutov, several other close friends, myself as the guest of honor. There were a lot of good wishes and a lot of toasts to good luck; even the professor, who never drank, took a glass of whiskey in my honor. The *babushka*, too, drank to my farewell, and she soon began to cry; before dinner was over, she was lying on the couch. When the party was over, I had to help carry her to bed.

That Sunday evening, for the last time in my room in Dmitri's house, I said Mass. Despite the fact that I was leaving most of my things here, I couldn't be sure I'd be back. I said

the Mass with a special thanksgiving for my friends here—
especially those in the next room watching television—and
commended the future to God. After the Mass, I went back
in and joined the group around the television set, but there
was more talking than TV-watching that night.

The next morning, Monday, October 2, everyone at
Dmitri's was up early. I promised that I would write at least a
postcard wherever I went, and they promised to forward my
belongings wherever I ended up—if it wasn't Abakan. I intended to catch the bus for the airport about nine, in order to
give myself plenty of time, but shortly before that a jeep drove
up: the KGB again. Ilyena and the *babushka* immediately became anxious; they got panicky when the KGB man told me
to come along, without any preliminaries or the usual formalities.

Aleksandr Mihailovich was in the jeep, checking to see if
everything was all right and if I had enough money. "Can I
see the ticket?" he said. I handed it to him, and he looked it
over carefully. "Well, we'll have to make a change. You won't
leave for Moscow at 5:00 tonight, but on the Tuesday morning flight at 7:15, so it won't be dark in Moscow when you
arrive." "Fine," I said, "then I'll take the last plane from Abakan tonight, instead of the morning flight."

"No, you won't", said Aleksandr. "You get the eleven
o'clock plane, and I'll meet you in Krasnoyarsk at noon and
show you around." With that he got back in the car and
drove off. Ilyena and the *babushka* were relieved when I came
back to the house; I explained to them what the interview
was all about. By now it was almost 9 A.M., so I told them
we'd better go.

I looked around at everything, wondering if I was seeing it
for the last time or would be back. The *babushka* was crying
again. She wouldn't come with us to the bus stop but went

into the house in tears. Dmitri and Ilyena, Iosip and Valya, walked to the marketplace with me, where there was a bus for the airport every hour. Nobody said much. Professor Dutov was at the bus stop, waiting. When the bus came, I said goodbye to the two families quickly; most of them had tears in their eyes. And so did I. The professor had taken a half day off to see me safely on the beginning of my journey, so he boarded the airport bus with me.

He came with me, in fact, all the way to the airport ramp, somber and almost in tears. "I wish you the best of luck, Wladimir Martinovich," he said, "but I'm very sorry to lose you." I promised again to write, then turned quickly and walked up the ramp into the plane. A few minutes before eleven, the motors started; by eleven, we were taxiing. I caught one last glimpse of the professor through the plane window and waved. As the plane took off, we passed over ATK-50 and the city of Abakan. I swallowed a lump in my throat that had nothing to do with the takeoff, then I sat back filled with memories.

VIP Treatment

In fifty-five minutes, which seemed like five, we were in Krasnoyarsk. As soon as I got off the plane, Aleksandr was waiting for me. He had already made arrangements for a room at the nearby airport hotel, so I checked the bags in the airport and we walked the short distance to the hotel. I signed the register; they gave me my key in exchange for the passport; I pocketed the key quickly lest Aleksandr ask for it.

"I have things to do," he said, "so I hope you can keep busy. I know I promised to show you the town, but something has come up. But come back to the airport with me now, and I'll show you how to get your ticket squared away for tomorrow morning. At least that will be out of the way. Then I'll see you tonight . . ." "I think I may go to a movie", I broke in. "I'll try to catch you after work," he went on, "but if not, I'll be back tomorrow morning to see you off."

At the airport he took my ticket to the counter and soon had it processed. Then we shook hands and he walked away; I watched him to see if he was really going. He got in the car, his chauffeur drove off, and I breathed a sigh of relief. I crossed the street and took a bus down old Stalin Boulevard (now renamed Mira Boulevard) to Gorki Street. There I caught another bus and went up the hill to Nikolayevka and my old parish.

No one was home at Rosa's, but I decided to wait. The first one I met was Rosa's brother on his way home from work, then Rosa herself came. They were amazed and delighted to see me and wanted to know why I hadn't written to say I was coming. I told them I was on my way to Moscow, where I guessed—and hoped—I would meet my two sisters. We talked about that for a while, then the old days and the parish. It was very late when Rosa suddenly remembered to prepare supper, and I didn't get back on the bus until 11:00 P.M. Aleksandr was not at my hotel, nor had he left any message.

The next morning I was up early so I wouldn't be late for my seven o'clock flight. The terminal was jammed even at that hour. At the last moment, I decided to send a quick card to everyone in Abakan, telling them I was on my way. There was still no sign of Aleksandr, but he arrived ten minutes before flight time, greeted me, walked to the ramp of the plane with me, and wished me a pleasant goodbye and a good trip. I got on board and watched Aleksandr through the window; he stayed until the plane took off.

The takeoff seemed awfully swift. By the time I looked out the window, all I could see were clouds far down below. I was a little disappointed, for I had hoped to see some of the country. I closed my eyes and began to pray for a while, then said a rosary; but thoughts kept crowding in upon me, and I tried to sort them out. Who would meet me in Moscow, the KGB or my sisters? Perhaps because he was late, Aleksandr hadn't said a word about Moscow—where I would land, who would meet me, or where I should go. If nobody meets me, I thought, what should I do? Should I try to go to the American Embassy or would that be too risky? Suddenly, I laughed at myself. After all these years of God's loving protection, what a time to be worried!

Just before noon, they served us a meal—in mid-air! There were two small rolls, butter, meat, sauce, fried potatoes, green peas, a small square of some sort of gelatine for dessert, lumps of sugar, a choice of coffee or tea, plus two small mint candies to top off the meal. For more than three years, I had eaten borscht twice a day and was happy to have a piece of bologna with my bread for lunch. Now the young girl put this feast before me while we were racing high over the earth toward Moscow!

I had hardly finished the meal when the loudspeaker announced we were approaching Vnukova Airport in Moscow. It was about 1:00 P.M. They were remodeling and resurfacing the field when we landed; everything was so torn up that the field didn't seem particularly impressive, except for the number of airplanes. I walked down the ramp, following the crowd, looking anxiously around. The terminal was very modern, with glass everywhere, but I hardly noticed it, because I kept looking to see if there was someone to meet me. I saw no one, and I didn't ask.

I waited for a while, but after fifteen minutes I figured I

was on my own. I picked up my baggage and started for the exit. Just then I noticed two men rushing through the waiting room of the terminal, dressed in topcoats, but one of them was without a hat—Viktor Pavlovich! They hurried over to the ramp of the plane from Krasnoyarsk, looked around, saw no one, and began arguing. I couldn't help smiling. They started to leave then, so I walked over to say hello.

Viktor wasn't in the mood for pleasantries, but he introduced me to the other fellow, a Mr. Kuznetsov, who seemed most pleasant. "You go with him, Wladimir Martinovich," said Viktor, "he'll take care of you." ("No doubt!" I thought to myself. "But in what sense?") Kuznetsov offered to carry my bag; I grabbed it myself. I followed him down the line of taxis until we came to a Volga, standing there with the driver inside and the motor running. "Here we are", said Kuznetsov.

Kuznetsov made himself agreeable. He told me that Vnukova Airport was about twenty-five miles from Moscow and suggested we see a little bit of the city on our way. Wherever we were going—and Kuznetsov said nothing about that—there wasn't much I could do about it by worrying, so I tried to relax and enjoy the drive.

We passed by tall apartment buildings, "skyscrapers" in the Soviet style. I was impressed because it had been a long time since I had seen anything like that; there was certainly nothing to rival them in Abakan or Krasnoyarsk. We saw Lenin University, a massive place with a whole complex of towering buildings, and Kuznetsov had the driver stop so we could walk around the grounds for a few minutes.

We drove for a while along the Moscow River, on a broad and beautiful boulevard, then along other streets not quite so wide and broad. Still, there were no roads anywhere in Siberia like those we drove over that morning. For two hours or more, we seemed just to roam around the town. Somehow I began to feel strange as I reflected that I had seen more already in two hours than in my previous five years' stay in the city of Moscow. Then, I had seen only its prisons and its railroad yards and, just once, its streets lined with bomb rubble. I saw places now I'd heard prisoners in Lubianka talk about but which had been only names to me then. Lubianka itself I didn't see, though it still wouldn't have surprised me. Despite my resolutions to enjoy the ride, I couldn't help thinking about where I was going.

Eventually we pulled up at the side entrance of the Moscow Hotel. We walked in, and Kuznetsov went right to the registration desk, where he soon wound up arguing about a room. I gathered they didn't have quite what he wanted. "You go and inquire", he said to the girl at last. "You find a room!" She came back a little later and said, "This is the best we can do—a room with a shower." Kuznetsov turned to me and asked rather apologetically, "Will this do?" I laughed. "Well, I wanted to get you a bath and a sitting room, too," said Kuznetsov, "but there doesn't seem to be any available."

I signed the register, turned over my passport, and got my key. We went up in the elevator to the fifth floor; everything was clean and spacious, with wall-to-wall carpeting. When we got to the room, Kuznetsov opened the door like a trained bell-hop and said, "Here you are." Then he proceeded to show me around the room. He showed me the shower—it was leaking. There was a big bed, easy chairs, a sofa, a radio, and even a TV set. Across the street from my window was a ministry building of some sort and a big boulevard down below.

Finally, Kuznetsov gave me his phone number and said, "Why don't you get a nap or a shower and a meal, and I'll be back to see you about 5 P.M." He still said nothing, however, about why I was here or where we might go when he came back at five. When he had gone, I loosened up a little.

I decided not to go to bed—frankly, I was too excited—but instead to take a walk and find something to eat.

I walked out the front door and directly opposite me were the walls of the Kremlin, Red Square, and GUM across from it, and the big basilica and towering cupolas of St. Basil's. I found it chilly, for I was wearing only a raincoat; but I began to walk along with the crowd. Everywhere I went, though, people seemed to be standing in line, so eventually I went back to the hotel to eat.

It was 4:30 by the time I finished the meal, so I hurried back upstairs to my room. I was no sooner in the door than the phone rang. "Where have you been?" said Kuznetsov when I answered. "I've been calling you over and over again." "I was eating." "Fine," he said, "meet me in the lobby at five o'clock exactly." I put down the phone and went in to wash up, with the tingling feeling of anticipation that now, at last, something was about to happen.

When I met Kuznetsov in the lobby, however, he said, "I bought tickets for the Moscow Dramatic Theater. I thought you would like to go." "Fine," I said, after a pause, "let's go." Kuznetsov had called for me early so we could walk and see the city, taking our time. We walked along the broad avenues like tourists, and I was surprised at the traffic. At most of the busy intersections there were underpasses for pedestrians, so the traffic flowed steadily.

Suddenly Kuznetsov said, "Here we are." I looked around. It seemed to me we were standing in front of an apartment building. There was a playbill, however, that said "Moscow Dramatic Theater. Now Showing: Mary Stuart." Kuznetsov took me into a little supper club on one of the upper floors, where we had a bottle of beer and caviar, then another.

The buzzer sounded for the curtain, and we went downstairs to the theater on the second floor. I thought the acting was excellent—especially the girl playing Mary Stuart—and the production good. I had a most enjoyable evening, and as we walked back to the hotel I told Kuznetsov so. He seemed genuinely happy to hear it. He didn't come into the hotel with me but told me he would call for me at nine o'clock the next morning.

I went up to my hotel room and sat down to watch television for a while, but my mind wasn't on it. I kept thinking, "What are they up to? What's going on? This is all very fine, but why? What is it all about?" All day long, every time I had entered the lobby of the hotel, I'd spent a few moments looking around, hoping to see my sisters. "Perhaps," I thought, "it was too late for them to arrange anything today; maybe tomorrow, at nine o'clock, I'll be going to see them." I took a shower then and went to bed. After wrestling with the same questions all over again, I finally fell asleep.

Kuznetsov was at my room at nine on the dot and asked me how I felt. "I think we ought to go to the Bolshoi tonight," he said, "I think you'll enjoy that. Now, let's go for a walk." I put on my coat and prepared to follow him, convinced he had something in mind besides a walk and the Bolshoi Theater and was heading somewhere special. Then, as we walked out the hotel doors, Kuznetsov said, "Let's go over to the Kremlin." We walked in through the Spasski Gate, then past Lenin's Mausoleum with its long lines of people.

Kuznetsov began to point out all the buildings, the Palace of Congresses, the Palace of Armaments, etc., telling me the history and function of each—but I was listening with only half an ear. The square was crowded with tourists, and I kept looking for some Americans, especially my sisters. No such luck. At last, I told Kuznetsov I'd like to see some of the beautiful old Orthodox Churches in the Kremlin; he didn't want to go in, but he told me to go ahead.

I walked through them, hurrying from one to another so Kuznetsov wouldn't get nervous, but I was delighted to see how well they had been kept up. Only, from time to time, I felt a twinge when I thought that God had been so thoroughly removed from these buildings that they were now just tourist attractions, like some peculiar kind of art museums. Kuznetsov was waiting patiently when I came out. He was a most pleasant companion, intelligent, quiet, and soft-spoken.

The sun was warm, so we walked around the Kremlin gardens. There weren't many flowers left in October, but the grounds were well kept and still attractive. "How about lunch?" said Kuznetsov, just after the bells of the Kremlin chimed twelve o'clock. (Those Kremlin bells were an echo to me; I had listened to them for five years. Now I was standing in the sunshine of Red Square, listening to them again.) "Fine," I said, "I'm hungry."

"Well," said Kuznetsov, "you go where you like, and I'll see you this afternoon about three o'clock. All right?" I nodded and he left me standing in Red Square. I was really beginning to wonder if anything was ever going to happen. I was tempted to try to avoid Kuznetsov for the afternoon, but I didn't want to miss any appointments that might turn out to be the "purpose" of the trip. If only he would give me some idea of what it was all about!

When I finished my meal at the hotel, Kuznetsov was waiting in the lobby. "Where have you been?" "In the restaurant; it took me over an hour to get a table for lunch." "Well, let's go. The car is here." Immediately, I thought something was up. Yet we simply drove around the city for a while, while Kuznetsov showed me the sights. My mind was elsewhere. When it became obvious we weren't going anywhere, I turned again to the riddle. I was living in the best hotel and nothing seemed to be too good for me; yet, pleasant as Kuznetsov was, he was still a chaperon. Why?

Were they just trying to keep me occupied until my sisters arrived? Had they been delayed? It must have something to do with my sisters; otherwise, why the delay? If we weren't waiting for something or somebody, why didn't we just go to the KGB headquarters and get it over with? Eventually, we drove back to the hotel. "I'll see you at seven", Kuznetsov said as he let me out of the car.

I met him in the lobby at seven. He was full of apologies because he hadn't been able to get tickets to the Bolshoi; we went instead to the Palace of Congresses, the "Glass Palace" as they call it. Everything about it is huge and shiny; there is marble on all the walls, the escalators, everywhere—a real showpiece, including the washrooms. When it's not being used for Party congresses, the "Glass Palace" is used for entertainments and exhibitions. Tonight there was a concert of folk music.

We went first of all to the top floor, where there is a huge ballroom. At the moment, the floor was covered with tables of sandwiches, cookies, candies, hot dishes, and drinks of all the various nationalities in the U.S.S.R. Kuznetsov offered to treat me to a real Russian dish: a round, cylindrical bowl full of mushrooms, onions, and peppers in cream sauce *à la mode Russe*, served with rye bread and a cup of steaming coffee. It was delicious. Afterward, we went into the convention hall itself, a massive place with plush leather seats and an earphone at every place for simultaneous translations.

The auditorium wasn't filled, which was not surprising because it's a monstrous place, and the stage, too, is enormous. There were many in the audience in native dress—Asians and Africans—and behind us, to my surprise, was a group of Americans. My surprise became chagrin, though, as they continued to laugh and talk through the whole performance. I wanted to turn around and tell them to behave, but with Kuznetsov beside me I didn't even talk to them.

The program of folk songs and dances in Russian and Georgian I found somewhat monotonous. Kuznetsov himself became bored, and we left the auditorium before the end of the program. Kuznetsov didn't seem to be in any hurry to get me back to the hotel, but eventually we strolled over there, and as he left me at the door he said, "Tomorrow, you wait for me. I'll get here sometime before noon. There are a few things I have to attend to in the morning." I walked up to my room more puzzled than ever.

The next morning I felt cooped up. I looked out the window, paced my room, and went down to walk around the lobby. At last, I wrote some cards to Abakan and Krasnoyarsk. I went back to my room about ten—and the phone was ringing. "Where have you been?" said Kuznetsov. "I've been ringing you up constantly." "I've been down in the lobby", I answered. "I just got tired of sitting around." "I'm coming right over", he said. "I'll give you a call from the lobby."

He didn't call from the lobby, though. The next thing I knew he was at the door of my room. He walked over and sat down on the bed. "I have something to tell you, Wladimir Martinovich", he said. ("Here it comes," I thought, "at last!") "By noon tomorrow, I want you to get rid of all your money except for ninety rubles. I don't care what you do with it, what you buy, how you spend it, but get rid of everything except ninety rubles. Tomorrow, at one o'clock, I will meet you right here, so wait for me."

He didn't say why, or what the money had to do with the reason for my visit to Moscow. Since he wasn't volunteering any information, I didn't ask; it's safer that way. I agreed to get rid of the money and meet him the next day at one o'clock. On that note, he left. I figured I had about twenty-four hours to myself.

Remembering the signs I had seen in Red Square saying that Lenin's Mausoleum was only open from 11 A.M. to 2 P.M., I skipped lunch and made a dash for the Kremlin. It was about 11:30, but the line was coiled around for blocks when I got to the end of it. While we walked slowly along the Kremlin wall, I noticed the graves of the famous old Communists buried there—including several Americans—many of them with marble busts and ornaments on top their tombstones. Joseph Stalin is there, under a plain, unadorned, straight slab, which carries only his name and the dates of his birth and death. Someone, though, had put a wreath of fresh flowers on his grave.

As we approached the doors of the mausoleum, I could hear the soldiers softly chanting instructions: "Please bare your heads, no talking, absolutely no picture-taking allowed. Please move quickly, and watch your step." Once through the doors, we went down a stairway about two flights, turned left along a hallway, then turned right again to enter the round mausoleum. It was dark inside. Everything seemed to be built of black, grayish marble, and the scent of flowers or incense was everywhere.

The glass coffin of Vladimir Ilyitch Lenin is above your head as you enter the room. You mount about fourteen or fifteen steps, then walk slowly, but continuously, around a semicircular platform, looking slightly down at the body. Lenin is dressed in dark, if not black, clothes and is illuminated from the waist up by a special spotlight, which bathes his face in weak, but very distinct, lighting. His color is marvelous; even his sandy mustache and beard seem alive with a bristling reddish quality, and there is enough light so that colored reflections play in the highly polished marble of the walls.

The people were all hushed as they circled around the coffin to the steps on the other end of the platform and the door leading out of the mausoleum. I said a prayer. "He was a man, after all," I thought, "and he may be in need of more prayers than he's getting here." As I stepped out of the mausoleum, there were photographers and tourists everywhere. There was also a fellow who specialized in pictures of "You at Lenin's Tomb", so I had my picture taken in front of the mausoleum. Unfortunately, I later forgot to pick it up.

It was now almost 1:30, and I had four hundred rubles with me that I had to get rid of somehow. I headed across Red Square for GUM (*Gosudarstvenni Universalni Magazin*), Moscow's famous department store, which is open all day until midnight. The GUM building takes up a whole block, and it was jammed. There are three open courtyards, each under a skylight in the roof, surrounded on all sides by balconies (arcades). All the shops open off these arcades—something like a three-story, twelve-sided Rialto. Each section carries a label advertising the goods sold in that department—theoretically, you can get anything at GUM.

I went through the whole store, floor by floor, arcade by arcade, looking at everything. I was shopping for shirts, for one thing. Even here in Moscow, though, I couldn't get the size I wanted in the quality and color I wanted. Since I had to get rid of all my money, price was no object. Still, I couldn't get what I wanted. The first thing I bought was a little valise, the best that money could buy. The "best" was a 24-by-36-by-10-inch fiberboard case, covered in brown imitation leather and with bright, shiny steel plates on the four corners for protection. It looked as if it might have come from a 1920 American bargain counter.

I also bought some razor blades, the first new blades I was ever able to buy in Russia. Then I bought a pair of brown oxfords; a reversible Czechoslovakian overcoat, checked on the inside and a green pea sort of color on the outside; a watch, *Moskva*, sixteen jewels; a camera, also *Moskva*, made in East Germany. I bought some gifts for friends back in Abakan, then a lot of little things like fingernail files, nail clippers, etc., just to get rid of the money. Four times I went through GUM from top to bottom until I was exhausted.

I came out of GUM and saw people going into another store, standing in line. On the Russian principle that wherever you see a line something is for sale, I walked over and got into line. When I got to the store, though, it turned out to be a sale of women's nylon hosiery. "Oh," I said, "if I had known that . . ." I started to go but the woman behind me stopped me. "Don't go", she said. "Please wait, it isn't long now, and the limit is two pairs to a customer. Please, stay in line and buy two pairs for me." I told her that I didn't have much time, but she pleaded until I finally agreed to wait and buy her two pairs at five rubles apiece.

I dashed back to GUM. I still had money to get rid of, so I went from top to bottom through the store. Practically everything I wanted was "*Nyet*" in my size or in the quality I wanted. I asked, for instance, for cod-liver oil: "*Nyet*." I asked the salesgirl where I might get it; she sent me to the Central Drugstore just down the block. I went there: "*Nyet*." (And this was in Moscow!) Finally, I returned to the hotel.

Now that I had stopped running, I had time to think. But the more I thought, the more puzzled I became. What was going to happen tomorrow at one o'clock? Where were my sisters? And what did the money have to do with it? If I was going into exile of some sort, why should I buy all these things? Every answer I came up with seemed to have something wrong with it. I finally dropped off to sleep, as puzzled as ever.

A Blessing for Russia

The next morning, by nine o'clock, I was beginning to feel tense. I still had some money, so I went to the hotel restaurant and ordered the best of everything. But I was getting so nervous I couldn't eat. I went back to my room and began to pack the suitcases. I'd bought so many things that I couldn't close them. The phone rang; it was Kuznetsov asking if I was in my room. "I'll be right up", he said. Kuznetsov asked me how things were going, and I told him I'd done just about everything but I couldn't close my suitcases. He smiled.

"Before you lock them, do you have any Russian documents?" I told him my passport was downstairs at the registration desk. "Yes, but besides your passport?" We went through the luggage, and I dug out my work book, my union card, my identity card, even some of my "certificates" and "diplomas" for outstanding work, including my *Udarnika* award. He took them all (I didn't ask why), then helped me close the suitcase and the valise. "Ready?" he said. He looked around the room and said, "Be sure you're not leaving anything." I looked around after him and said, "I'm ready." "Then let's go", he said.

He took the valise and I took the suitcase; we caught the elevator to the lobby. I paid my bill and turned in the key in exchange for my passport. Kuznetsov took that. As we walked out on the sidewalk, the Volga pulled up. Kuznetsov put my suitcase and valise in the trunk while I got in. Then he gave the driver some instructions, and we started off.

I recognized certain parts of the city as we drove, but I couldn't figure out where we were going. At length, we pulled into Mezdunarodni Airport—not Vnukova—and drove right up to the terminal. Kuznetsov went in and told us to wait; he was back in a few minutes and asked the driver to pull over to the side. He didn't get into the car but walked nervously up and down beside it. Several times, he went into the terminal and came out again. I began to suspect that my sisters were here or would soon be here.

With that idea, I started to watch the planes arrive, marked with the flags of various nations, looking especially for an American jet. There was a certain amount of commotion when an Italian football team arrived, but I was hardly even distracted from my American flag vigil. The longer we waited, the more nervous Kuznetsov got. "Let's go into the cafeteria", he said, "and get some coffee." The driver and I got out and went in with him; they had no hot water in the cafeteria, so we came back out.

We stood around the Volga again for a while—the more nervous Kuznetsov got, the more nervous he made me—then he noticed a car racing up the drive to the terminal. Kuznetsov told us to get in the car. He himself got into the driver's seat and backed our car alongside the other as it slid to a stop. The man in the back seat of the other car didn't look Russian (he turned out to be Marvin Makinen), but I really didn't pay much attention at the time. I was looking only for my sisters.

Kuznetsov and I got out of the car. As we did so, he said softly, "Wladimir Martinovich, if you want to stay, you can stay with us. You might have a hard time there." I was startled, as much by his sympathetic tone (he sounded like a man who was about to lose a friend) as by the words themselves. It struck me as peculiar. I thought for just one minute he might be talking about my going home—but I dismissed the thought.

"If you want to," Kuznetsov continued when I didn't answer, "just say so; we can call the whole thing off. And, if you go, any time you want to come back, just let me know." Again I looked at him, unsure what to answer because I wasn't sure what he meant. So I said nothing. Meanwhile, the KGB man was getting my suitcases out of the back of the car. Kuznetsov and I walked into the terminal then and down the corridor to a little office.

There were a group of KGB men already there, smiling among themselves, but they said little to me. One of them, however, told me he had brought in my suitcases. I nodded. Makinen came in and sat down on the bench next to me. I had no idea who he was, and we didn't talk to each other at all. Besides, I was badly confused; I was just beginning to ask myself if it was possible they might be sending me home. My head was spinning, but I refused to accept the answer.

Suddenly, Kuznetsov said "Let's go." I reached for my suitcases, but he told me not to bother. We walked down a corridor to another room; it was almost 4 P.M. by that time. There were two KGB men there already, smiling, and they asked us to sit down. Makinen sat on a couch, and I sat on a chair. Then two more men entered, not Russians by their looks. One of them immediately shook hands with Makinen, then turned to me. "Father Ciszek", he said, "I'm glad to meet you."

I was startled, then I smiled and thanked him for the greeting. It was the first time in years anyone had addressed me as "Father". Even in Siberia, those who had known I was a priest never used the term; they called me only "Wladimir Martinovich" or "Djadja Valodga" (Uncle Wally). The man introduced himself as Mr. Kirk, from the American Consulate in Moscow; he asked me how I was, then turned to talk briefly again to Makinen. He lit a cigarette, and he seemed nervous.

I couldn't figure anything out. Kuznetsov was nervous, Kirk was nervous—but about what? Everybody stood around for a moment in silence, as if they were at a wake. Finally, Kuznetsov said, "Well, shall we get it over with?" "Good," said Kirk, "let's get it over with." The two of them shook hands, then Mr. Kirk turned to me. "Father Ciszek, would you come over here?" I went over to the table as Mr. Kirk pulled a paper from his inside coat pocket. "Would you sign this?" He handed me a pen, and I signed; I was so badly confused I hadn't even the sense to notice what I was signing.

"Now, Father Ciszek," said Mr. Kirk, "you're an American citizen." "Really?" I asked, momentarily stunned. "Yes," he answered, "you are an American citizen again." "It's all a fairy tale", I mumbled. "Yes, it's a fairy tale, but a fine fairy tale," smiled Mr. Kirk, "and it's true." It was too sudden. All at once I felt free and loose; it was as if a great weight had suddenly been lifted and the bones in my spine had sprung into shape like elastic. I felt as if I ought to sing. Mr. Kirk turned to Makinen; the other American from the Consulate changed my ninety rubles for a hundred dollars while Makinen was signing some papers.

Actually, I had ninety-three rubles in my pocket, so the young American gave me back three rubles along with my hundred dollars. I met Makinen then and found out who he was. Both of us began talking and congratulating each other, and suddenly everyone in the room was talking and smiling. Waving my three rubles, I invited everyone in the room to the airport cafeteria. Kuznetsov and my KGB driver laughed.

We walked down to the cafeteria, talking and laughing and saying the same things over and over again. Everyone ordered tea, and I put the three rubles on the table with a flourish. They were the last I had, and I wasn't sorry to see them go. We had hardly begun to drink the tea, though, when a KGB man came running over to the table. "Hurry up," he said, "don't miss the plane after all this!" He opened a side door from the cafeteria, and we walked out of the terminal onto the airplane ramp.

The plane was a big BOAC jet. The British captain met us at the foot of the steps. "Father Ciszek? Mr. Makinen? Could I see your tickets, please?" My ticket was for first class, Makinen's for tourist, but the captain led us in through another door and sat us down in a seat together. I looked at Makinen, he looked at me—and we both turned to look out the window.

Mr. Kirk was there, along with Kuznetsov and a group of KGB men. Makinen and I waved to them as the plane taxied, but they didn't wave back. Suddenly, the plane gathered speed. I blessed myself, then turned to the window as we took off. The plane swung up in a big circle; there were the spires of the Kremlin in the distance! Slowly, carefully, I made the sign of the cross over the land I was leaving.